QC 10, QTP 10 and Automation Framework

Automating Automation

QC 10, QTP 10 and Automation Framework

Automating Automation

Saurabh Chandra
Head, Automation and Performance, Clarity R&D Unit
Computer Associates, India Technology Center

Tata McGraw Hill Education Private Limited
NEW DELHI

McGraw-Hill Offices
New Delhi New York St Louis San Franscisco Auckland Bogotá Caracas
Kuala Lumpur Lisbon London Madrid Mexico City Milan Montreal
San Juan Santiago Singapore Sydney Tokyo Toronto

Tata McGraw Hill

Published by Tata McGraw Hill Education Private Limited,
7 West Patel Nagar, New Delhi 110 008.

ISBN (13): 978-1-25-902781-9
ISBN (10): 1-25-902781-3

Vice President and Managing Director—Asia Pacific Region: *Ajay Shukla*
Publishing Manager—Professional: *Vibhor Kataria*
Editorial Researcher—Computing: *Saswata Mishra*
Sr. Copy editor: *Neha Sharma*
Sr. Production Executive: *Rita Sarkar*
Asst. General Manager—Sales and Business Development: *S Girish*
Deputy Marketing Manager—Science, Technology & Computing: *Rekha Dhyani*
General Manager—Production: *Rajender P Ghansela*
Manager—Production: *Reji Kumar*

Typeset at DigiConv Technologies, C-240, Flat No. 103, First Floor, Pandav Nagar, Delhi 110 092, and printed at Rajkamal Electric Press, Plot No. 2, Phase IV, HSIIDC, Kundli, Sonepat, Haryana 131 028

Cover Design: Mukul Khattar

Cover Printer: Rajkamal Electric Press

RZZYCRLHRBBQX

The McGraw·Hill Companies

To

The testing and automation community of the world

and

my parents Kiran Roy and Ram Krishna Roy

Advance Praise for the Book

"This second gem from Saurabh should help readers of his first book move up and look at HP Quality Center deployment, customisation and also its integration with QTP. Furthermore readers are likely to gain better understanding of automation framework and rolling it out in complex, high demand deployment scenarios. Availability of a large number of functions that one should use when going for automation should be added bonus for readers. I hope that this book will prove to be even more useful than the first one."

–Vipul Kocher, *President, Indian Testing Board*

"This is a complete practitioner's guide. The real life examples used make the book easy to understand — how to make most out of automation technology in testing."

–S.Y. Shenoy, *Vice President, Oracle Applications Development, Oracle Corporation*

"A good read for every automation professional in software industry. The in-depth discussion on the framework and the concrete examples will help both the beginners and experts to design a robust and reliable framework."

–Narayana Kala, *Sr. Director, Software Engineering, Computer Associates (CA)*

"This book is a great gift for the entire QA community. If you were looking out for tips on enriching yourself on automating the automation techniques, then you have it now. This is 'The book' for it."

–Murali Krishnan, *Director, IT, Intuit Technology Services Pvt. Ltd.*

"Key to success today for any entity is to maximise efficiency and reduce cycle time — something that can only be achieved by 'automating automation'. Thoroughly researched and must read for all the leaders of testing, automation and performance domain."

–G. Sahoo, *Professor and HOD, IT Department, BIT Mesra, Ranchi*

"Those who would like to excel in automation world can grab the proven, time-tested and most powerful strategies, framework, and techniques from this book."

–Subhakara Maguluri, *Senior Manager — R&D, Informatica Corporation*

"Saurabh, having vast experience in automated testing world, brings up this need of the hour topic 'Automating Automation'. He has explained the underlying principles with commonly used tools — QC, QTP and Selenium, that would ensure its reach to masses of tester world. He further discloses some intricate aspects of automation framework that cements individual elements together and proposes methodology for automation infrastructure, these are must refer ready-made tips for all those in-charge of designing automation infrastructure/framework for their organisation/team."

–Amit Trivedi, *QA Group Manager, Financials, Oracle Corporation*

"An insightful guide which clearly identifies the key aspects of automation. Saurabh narrates them in simple and practical terms which make it easy for any reader to comprehend and add value to their automation efforts. A very timely read with great content."

–Manoj Jain, *Manager — Quality Assurance, Computer Associates (CA)*

Foreword

Most QA organisations within software companies today have renewed focus on automation. This focus is not without a good reason — automation has helped streamline the SDLC by discovering bugs sooner, sped up time-to-market, increased the overall quality of software being delivered thus enhancing overall customer experience. The benefits of repeatability and predictable reproducibility are at the core of this drive towards automation.

The degree to which this has now been embedded into the culture of an organisation differs from company to company, however, there is no argument that a well-articulated strategy complemented by a good architecture and tooling are necessary to take the organisation to the next level in delivering quality software.

However, most companies stop there. While a good tool and quality coverage form the essential basis, an organisation can enhance its strategy further by not only automating the tests but also its infrastructure.

There are several steps in the entire automation infrastructure that need to be considered, all of which can be automated. These typically include the test repository, the build process, code deployment, the test execution engine, triage and analysis of the results, and finally, the reporting. Many companies have automated some of these tasks to varying degrees but its usually done to meet specific needs rather than as a specific strategy to automate the automation process.

In his first book, *Automation Testing*, Saurabh Chandra talked about the many benefits of automation and outlined a strategy that involved automation using the QTP tool. In this book, Saurabh takes the necessary next step of talking about "Automating Automation" and guides us to consider the underlying infrastructure and the benefits of automating the entire process.

In the first section Saurabh guides the reader through the deployment, customisation and usage of HP Quality Center 10. In the second section, he discusses the methodology of integrating Quality Center with conventional and open source tools such as QTP and Selenium. In third section he provides for some plug and play by identifying methods and functions that should be considered during automation and finally, he discusses pulling it all together as part of the overall automation framework.

Saurabh Chandra is one of the leading authorities on automation and guides the user through practical implementation details. This new book is a must read for all software developers and QA practitioners alike.

Robin Sahai
Senior Director of Engineering
Oracle Corp.

Preface

This book primarily talks about making automation more robust and intuitive by having sound technical strategy. It also talks about availability and usage of few tools which would help narrow the cycle time and will give more ROI to the project and business per se. This book will unveil new framework on automation layout which has been proven successful and is running live in Oracle, my ex-employer and Computer Associates, my current employer. Nonetheless, this also houses in-depth strategy, framework and technique using which Sr. Staff / Leadership team can initiate automation roll out organisation-wide. Framework talks about technical architecture, which would integrate builds to automatic kick-off of scripts to publish results. To summarise, this book would throw light upon utilising automation in the most efficient way to make technical infrastructure more intuitive and predictable and thus having lesser cycle time to market and therefore, giving the optimum ROI to the business and organisation.

Brief about *QC10, QTP 10 and Automation Framework: Automating Automation* book:

- The audience for this book would be automation experts/enthusiasts, ranging from IT engineers to IT managers to IT Sr. Staff. It also has the potential to be a reference book in engineering schools.
- First section of the book talks about deployment, customisation and usage of HP Quality Center 10.0.
- Second section of the book talks about discussing methodology on integrating QC with QTP and Selenium.
- Third section of the book houses 24+ methods/functions that one should use when going for automation – will be plug and play solution.
- Fourth section of the book talks about in-depth understanding about pulling up automation framework, which will be compatible with QTP, Selenium, LoadRunner, SilkPerformer and Jmeter.
- Fifth section houses the methodology to roll out automation infrastructure in Global MNC.

Saurabh Chandra

Acknowledgements

This book is a product of more than seven years of questioning, researching, training and consulting in the field of software testing, both automation and manual. During this period, I realised that very few ideas are original but rather are inspired by one source, which we call "a walk of life". When we disassociate ourselves and question the source then ideas that originate are termed as "Original" and hence mark the beginning of true learning. I can't thank Tata McGraw Hill enough, which gave me an opportunity to share and bring those learning onboard via this book.

While writing this book, one thing that I realised is that though the cover page of the book gives credit to one individual, it is never the outcome of author's effort alone. Therefore, I express a deep sense of gratitude towards entire Tata McGraw Hill team, who worked on this, in addition to extending special mention to:

Saswata Mishra, Editorial Researcher, who kept the project and process rolling inspite of hurdles. Additionally, he continually instilled the inspiration and motivation in me, to stand through every rough wave and then working it out in the most conducive and efficient manner so that this project becomes a reality.

It will be a miss if I do not mention my colleagues and friends, without whose support, I would not have got the strength and freedom to learn, think big and hence chase to realise my dream — Balaji Babuji, Mrinmoy Kar, Manish Ralekar, Sreevani Kakarala, Aakash Jain, Rangarajan Lavanya, Amit Trivedi, Robin Sahai, Arlene Nichols, Amy Murakami, Mindy Chan, Rajesh Bella, Srikanth Krishnan, Joyjeet Banerjee, Nischal Mahajan, Ekta Mahajan, Dr. Rahul Lath, Dr. Madhavi Singh, Dev Lath and Deepali Lath, Ashok Suyal, Vipul Kocher, Manoj Jain, Sanket Atal, Ponniah Rajagopal, Kala Satyanarayana, Varun Velamuri Srinivasa, Chakradhar Jillellamudi, Sameera Shaik, Anil Kumar Dugganaboyina, Vinod Kumar Palla, Sandeep Aulakh, Badal Burathoki, Aravind Selvan, Deepti Ahlawat, Pooja.

Special thanks to Mridula Kanwar, who gave me strength to question on existing philosophy and come up with new ideas to complete this book.

I would also like to extend my thanks to my dearest friend and brother Vishal Ranjan, who kept my confidence intact throughout this journey of writing the book and hence substantiated my strength to think big and achieve big.

I extend my heartfelt thanks to all these people who hold their utmost faith in the discussed subject matter and hence have endorsed my work — S.Y. Shenoy, Vipul Kocher, Manoj Jain, G. Sahoo, Subhakara Maguluri, Narayana Kala and Amit Trivedi.

Special thanks to Robin Sahai, Sr. Director Engineering Dept., Oracle Corporation, USA — who graced the book, by penning his invaluable thoughts in the "Foreword" of the book.

At this moment of sheer learning and selfless knowledge sharing, I would like to hold special mention of my alma-mater, BITS Ranchi and IIM Lucknow, which taught me to be competitive enough to cater with any technical and business related challenge and at the same time embedded value which says, "You get what you give". I am indebted to all my teachers and mentors who helped me posess the ability to think about such a valuable project and groomed me enough to achieve the same.

I have had delightful opportunities to lecture several of Engineering graduates and MBA graduates at conferences and various executive programs. It will be worth mentioning and extending my heartiest thanks to all of them as they have often taught me as much as I have offered them.

Additionally, I would also like to extend my thanks and gratitude to all those people and entities, whom I might have missed mentioning here but can't forget their contribution in helping me learning things continuously.

Nonetheless, my greatest debt is to my family including Mithi, who gave me unflinching support and smilingly bear my erratic time and schedules. Finally, at this moment of jubilation and pride, I would like to take a pause and thank my parents, Kiran Roy and Ram Krishna Roy, who taught me all good values and lessons of life because of which I'm in a position to contribute whatever little I can share with the world today. And of course, to my younger brother Shikhar Chandra, who keeps me on toes to match up to his caliber and helped me learn dynamics and complexities of competition, of his generation.

SAURABH CHANDRA

Contents

List of Abbreviations

Action: Individual script in QTP is denoted as action

AIX: Advanced Interactive Executive by IBM

API: Application Programming Interface

CPU: Central Processing Unit

Data table: Data table in all the discussions mean Microsoft .xls sheet.

DBA: Database Administrator

Dev: Development

ETA: Expected Time of Arrival

Ex, e.g.: Example

FDD: Functional Design Documents

g_rerun: Global Rerun Parameter

HA Cluster: High Availability Cluster

HP QC: Hewlett Packard Quality Center

HP QTP: Hewlett Packard—QuickTest Professional

HP: Hewlett-Packard

HTTP: Hyper Text Transfer Protocol

HTTPS: Hyper Text Transfer Protocol Secured

IBM: International Business Machine

IE: Internet Explorer

IIS server: Internet Information Server

JVM: Java Virtual Machine

LOR: Local Object Repository

N/A: Not Applicable

No.: Number

O/S: Operating System

OR: Object Repository

QA: Quality Assurance

SDLC: Software Development Life Cycle

SPARC: Scalable Processor Architecture

SQL: Structured Query Language

TC: Test Case

TDD: Technical Design Documents

TSL: Test Scripting Language

UI: User Interface

URL: Uniform Resource Locator

VB: Visual Basic

1

HP Quality Center 10: Introduction, Technology, and Architecture

Chapter Objectives: This chapter will give an overview of

- ☐ *Introduction — HP Quality Center*
- ☐ *HP QC 10 testing process*
- ☐ *Technology layout behind HP QC 10*
- ☐ *HP QC deployment architecture*
- ☐ *HP QC 10 — New supported environments*
- ☐ *HP QC 10 — New features*

1.1 Introduction — HP Quality Center

For any organisation, data holds the key to success. As time progresses, business grows by and the data grows by. Therefore, one of the most important tasks for any department in any organisation is to keep data pertaining to past, present and future planning intact.

Even in the software industry, it is the same. In any department of a software organisation, be it development, release, project management, finance and administration — ensuring structured methodology to keep technical data intact is very important. This further helps in fostering improvements, key decision making, and future planning. However, when work is carried out on one platform and data collection becomes an independent and segregated activity, data loss can't be avoided. Therefore, many organisations are putting in continuous efforts to build new tools and processes, with a motive to bind work and data collection, in tandem and automatically, and hence minimizing the chances of data loss.

In one such department of software wing, i.e., testing, collection of data at such segregated events becomes very difficult. If an organisation doesn't have a methodology to capture data alongside work, the cost that company may have to bear due to incorrect data or loss of data is immensely huge. At times this can lead to losing customer and business.

Let us see how the scenario unfolds and hence complexity increases.

A software vendor gets work order from some customer, which is to test the mail client. The software vendor asks for the requirements from the customer. Customer ships the requirement, but after 10 days, and then asks to review the requirements and give a plan on priority. The vendor takes 5 days to review and shares the plan, with an agreement that they themselves would be breaking the requirements into smaller modules and hence tests case. After review, the review comments are sent back to the customer and this process goes on for a couple of times until requirements are frozen. After that, the software vendor breaks the requirement into cases, and hence testing starts. During the course of testing, several issues surface in the application for which bugs are logged. They get fixed; but as and when testing progresses few regressions are caught. Again for such regressions, bugs are logged, and accordingly, patches are applied. But, then to test stability of application, the tester has to start testing from initial condition and hence work packet size gets increased.

Take a pause here. You would see so many activities happening here. Requirements, requirements review, designing of cases, testing, bug logging and re-testing. Think about this: if during the progress of the project, the customer asks the vendor to provide the following details:

- Areas which get revamped in requirements documents?
- The number of test cases per module?
- Such modules, where maximum bugs are found?
- The number of regression bugs per module per requirement?
- All the bug numbers and description of issue and current status?
- Number of areas impacted due to open issues?
- Pass history of all such cases where regressions are found?
- Further risk analysis and detail?
- Current quality of product or project?

These are just few of the areas for which I have enlisted the questions. There may be several more. Just think that, if for such a small case study these questions baffle you, how big an impact it can have to the business, if there are many more such data-centric questions for the repository of thousands of test cases.

In fact, it will not be surprising if you say, it's not possible!!

However, to counter argument your answer, I would say — it's not impossible. It is possible if we have properly structured tool, processes, and definition, which can help capturing the data set alongside the occurrence of real-time events. It is not too burdensome an affair to manage and maintain both concurrently. To cater to all such requirements, especially to manage the test management activities, HP provides a test management tool, famously known as "Quality Center".

1.1.1 History — Quality Center

Quality center was one of the latest testing tools in the offering by legacy Mercury Interactive Corporation. On July 25, 2006, Palo Alto, California, as per the news release by HP, the world witnessed an important consolidation, where HP announced the acquisition of Mercury Interactive Corporation. Therefore, from that day onwards, the tool was rechristened as "HP QC". Throughout this book, we would be denoting this tool as HP QC. Furthermore, wherever it is mentioned as "QC" in the book, implicit meaning is "HP QC".

Because of this strategic acquisition, HP got positioned as a market leader in "IT Management Software" space.

HP QC tool is also known as "Test management tool". In fact, this is one of the most famously used tools across medium and large-size corporations.

This tool provides a definitive and ascientific approach towards mapping and tracking requirements from inception to end, and hence integrates testing business process to much greater extent. Going into further details, to name a few advantages, HP QC also provides the facility to design test cases, execute test cases, record history of each execution, record events at all actions and facility to pull reports. To add up to the powers of this tool, this also facilitates integration with third-party tools. The most brownie aspect of the tool is that this has seamless integration with almost all HP testing automation tools.

1.1.2 Quality Center — Versioning

Now the other question that might be baffling you would be, what does the suffix "10" in HP QC 10 mean?

Any organisation, which releases a product, also tries to enhance it as and when market or technology demands. On a similar ground, HP has done the same by giving a version number to its latest HP QC tool released. This is "10".

The higher the version number the later is the product. Currently, at this phase of book writing, HP QC 10 is the latest version of the tool available in the market. It may be worth noting that even though the newer versions are released with few enhancements, the basic mechanism of the tool usage does not change. Generally, a newer version always comes with additional features retaining all the older ones. In my opinion, if anyone is familiar with this version of the tool, it should not be a problem to understand the knowhow either in the upgraded version or the earlier version of the tool.

Additionally, I'm taking benchmark of version 10, which is the latest offering of HP QC, however all the principles discussed in this book hold good for HP QC 9.2 as well.

Another important point to be noted here is that since HP QC has integration facility with HP automation tools, if an organisation plans to buy licenses for both such tools then version compatibility should always be kept in mind. For example HP QC 7.0 may not be compatible with HP QTP 9.5.

1.2 HP QC 10 Testing Process

To understand as how in unison, HP QC may prove to be helpful in aligning testing business process, let us first try understanding how organisations plan their product testing strategy for few initial phases.

First, of course, is zeroing upon product, product utility, and its market.

Second is to understand several activities involved in evolving the product, such as testing, development, operations, release, etc.

Third, put a strategy for testing. While doing it, organisations ensure:

- Testing schedule
- Availability of requirements for testing
- Test case design schedule
- Test case execution schedule
- Automating test cases
- Defect tracking and management

The relevance of HP QC comes into picture for aligning and tracking testing business process. HP QC integrates the start to end testing procedures, which otherwise are always exercised in seclusion. HP QC testing process can be summarized as:

- *Define release schedule*
  HP QC provides a feature to define release plan of the product or project. In this phase, business unit head, along with its strategy team, defines "Release schedule" milestones. This release schedule, in turn, is tied up with smaller milestones that help in tracking progress and risks.

- *Define "cycle" for the release*
  Each release, for better traceability, is divided into smaller milestones and is known as "cycle". Therefore, both release schedules and cycle are tightly coupled within HP QC 10. Through cycle, one can keep a closer watch on smaller work packet progress, defects and progress over fixing defects. For ease of understanding, a graphical representation of all such traceability matrix can also be viewed via "cycle" section of HP QC 10.

- *Specify and define requirements*
  To make project a success, various kinds of requirement documentation are studied and consolidated in order to frame a testing plan. This testing plan when put in a consolidated fashion, is known as "Testing Requirements". Requirements are then tied up with cycle and release. Furthermore, these packaged requirements are segregated in smaller units known as tests. All of them are tightly coupled with each other for ease of traceability.

- *Planning and designing tests*
  In this phase, the scoped features are further segregated into smaller modules known as "Test scripts or tests". Test script is a collection of various test cases. Once test scripts are identified,

then test case designing and drafting happens via HP QC 10. There is a definitive template, in which test case drafting should take place. This definitive template for test case planning and execution helps in having a standard approach followed organisation wide and weeding out any possibility of confusion .All these test cases and in turn test scripts are tightly coupled with their respective requirements, cycle and release.

- *Test execution and analysis*
  Once all the test cases are in place, the cyclewise testing task kicks off. Testing task consists primarily of execution of all functional and non-functional test cases. As and when test cases are executed, their outcome is captured, i.e., either passed, or failed, or blocked, or pending. All such activities and results are captured into a lab area, known as "test lab". Not only test execution results but the execution history also gets captured, which in turn helps in analyzing the pass rate or the fail rate of the test case or test script. Since these tests are closely coupled with requirement, cycle, and release, there is a traceability matrix which keeps on developing and helps senior staff view the current progress and risks, if there are any. These kinds of statistics in turn help in taking proactive measures keeping project deliverables and commitment to mind.

- *Defect logging and tracking*
  The functional and non-functional defects found during test execution exercise get captured in HP QC 10 in the test lab area. These defects are managed and maintained in a specific area which categorically caters to storing defects, its description, status and details. All such defects are in turn correlated with test case, test script, feature, requirement, cycle and hence release. This is one such repository which in turn also reflects the health of the product and becomes one of the most important data set for the management to track progress of the product or project well being.

- *Reports*
  You would have noticed as how specific release, cycle, requirement, feature, test scripts, test cases, and defects are tightly coupled in HP QC 10. Therefore, adding further to the usefulness for customer delight, HP QC 10 provides powers to generate reports as well as customize reports.

Figure 1.1 and the above-mentioned details provide a broader view of things that HP QC 10 does. Lets go ahead with further sections and chapters to get finer details of HP QC 10.

The integrated process of HP QC 10 not only helps in bundling all testing events into one packet, derives meaningful result as per organisational needs and keeps all history intact, but also, to top it all, all such HP QC 10 details and features are accessible through single UI rather than several segregated pages or files.

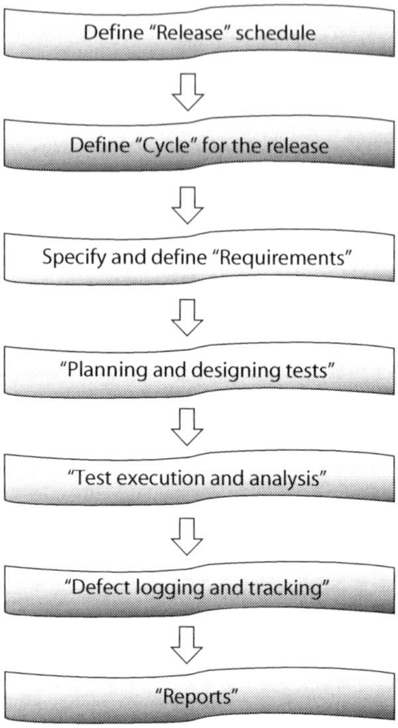

Figure 1.1 *QC Testing Business Process.*

Additionally, to keep security intact, all these phases are tightly coupled with defined users. Non-admin users do not have privilege to change or delete any such sensitive details.

1.3 Technology Layout Behind HP QC 10

Unlike several testing related software installations, HP QC installation is highly scientific. There are several checks that need to be in place either related to machine configuration or database set up or middleware set up. Before I explain those, let us understand definitions of few of the technologies and configurations:

- *J2EE Technology*

  This technology provides flexibility to design, develop, assemble, and deploy application in component based approach.

  - *Cluster*

  This is a group of application servers.

  - *Node or cluster node*

  Each application server in a cluster is known as "node" or "cluster node".

1.3.1 More About Cluster Mechanics

As the name suggests, cluster means grouping of servers. In this space the most important configuration of clustering is "HA Cluster" or "Failover Clusters", where HA stands for High Availability. HA Cluster is the one where if any of the server fails then node configuration automatically detects the other server and hence mounts the services of the application on the running one, ensuring that services do not stop. Due to this property, such configuration of servers is known as "Failover Cluster" or HA Clusters.

HA Clusters are typically used for managing mission critical databases. Some of the applications that primarily use such services are electronic commerce applications, stock broking entities, etc.

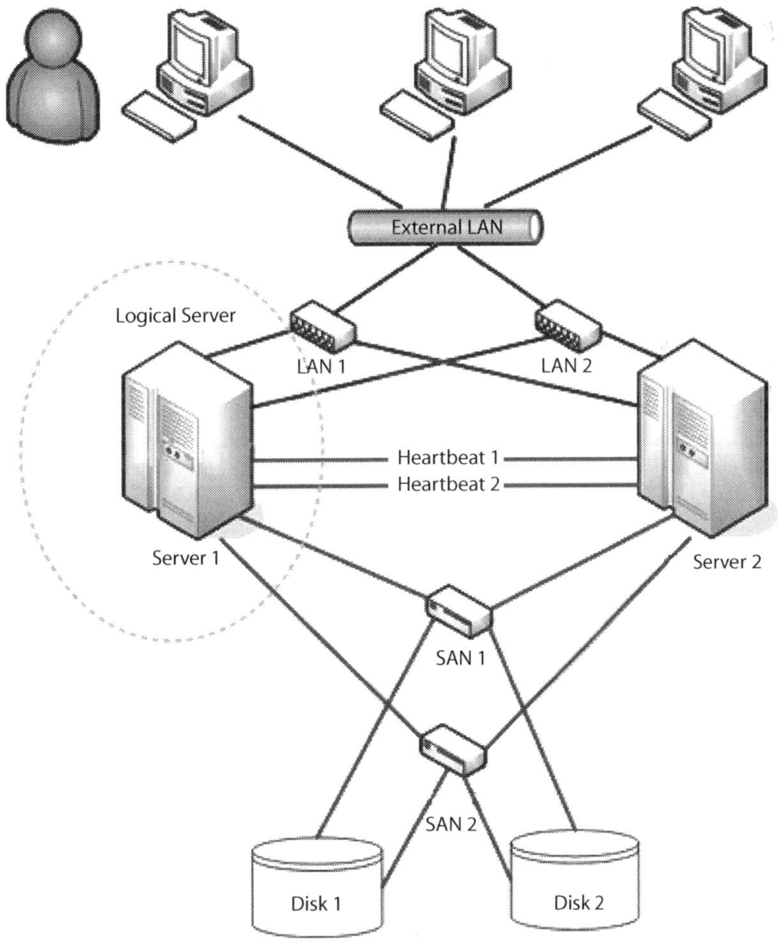

Figure 1.2 *Two-Node High Availability Cluster Network Diagram.*

1.3.2 Node Configurations

The most common size for HA Cluster is two-node configuration. A two-node configuration is shown in Fig. 1.2.

It can be seen from Fig 1.2, the end user is connected to the client, where application is under access. Application services are mounted over servers and they are tied up in a cluster fashion. In case any of the servers crashes, automatically other server starts functioning ensuring that services do not stop for end users.

1.4 HP QC Deployment Architecture

Now that you are aware of the basic definition of J2EE, clustering and node configurations, let me explain how QC utilizes these technologies for its configuration purpose.

As Fig. 1.3 represents, quality center is an enterprise-wide application that is based on J2EE technology. QC software is deployed on application server; internet is accessed on users' desktop, i.e., client. Several clients can be tied up to QC software. Each application server is tied up with two such databases, one HP QC database and another site administrator database. Two-way communication takes place between database and server.

Application server can be laid out in a cluster format also. Cluster format would provide mission critical services ensuring high availability and maximum scalability. Load balancer is used in order to ensure that client requests are routed in the most optimal fashion across servers and hence allowing infinite number of users to access QC database without response time issue. The cluster of servers can run on Windows, Linux, Solaris and AIX platforms.

1.5 HP QC 10 — New Supported Environments

HP QC 10, unlike its earlier version, extends support to the below mentioned new environments:

- *Database*
  - Microsoft SQL server 2005 standard/enterprise edition with service pack 1
  - Web or Application server
  - JBoss 4.0.2
  - WebSphere 6.1
  - Operating Systems
  - Suse Linux Enterprsie 10
  - Solaris 10 OE
  - AIX 5.3
  - Windows 2003 server with service pack 1 standard / enterprise edition
- *Browser*
  - Microsoft Internet Explorer 7.0

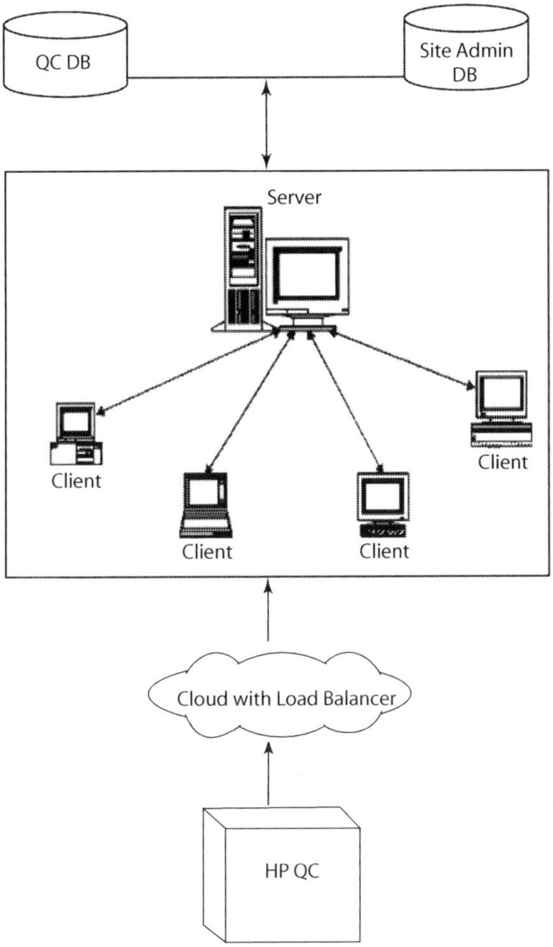

Figure 1.3 *HP QC Deployment Architecture.*

- *Java Virtual Machine*
  - JVM 1.5

1.6 HP QC 10 — New Features

HP QC 10 boasts of the below mentioned new features:

- *Better release management*
  Newer release management gives flexibility to integrate multiple cycles and tightly couple the requirements. Additionally, for ease of understanding, this module provides graphs and analysis of all the occurrences within that release and cycle. Additionally, better traceability of defects across cycles and release can be ascertained with this new feature.

- *Requirement traceability*
  Better and much powerful requirement traceability can be achieved through this newer version. HP QC 10 gives much better integration with all required entities and hence traces it through and through the requirements channel. Additionally, there can be traceability matrix that can be developed across requirements as well. With this, the additional advantage is that one can understand the impact of issues in one requirement but found in another requirement.
- *Risk based quality management*
  This newer version helps in better planning the future risks that may not be known in the beginning. Therefore, accordingly, it helps in risk based quality management across cycles, and empowers users to make it quantifiable from the beginning.
- *Excel reports integration and export feature*
  Newer version provides better integration of HP QC 10 with Microsoft Excel. HP QC 10 provides more flexibility to pull Excel based reports by integrating HP QC projects DB with external VB codeline or by defining SQL queries. Additionally, with this feature analysis becomes easier and can be ported in graphical pattern also.

2

HP Quality Center 10:
Pre-Install Procedure and Configurations

Chapter Objectives: This chapter will give an overview of

- *HP QC 10 installation stages*
- *HP QC installation stages — until Stage 13*

2.1 HP QC 10 Installation Stages

To install HP QC 10, there are several pre-install checks, access permissions and machine configurations that need to be in place. The relevance of such pre-install configurations and permissions is pretty high, because if due care of those is not taken well, they may make QC installation unstable.

HP QC 10 installation is a fifteen-steps process. Till stage thirteen, these are pre-install checks, and fourteen and fifteen are installation phases.

All such stages will be discussed in detail. This chapter will throw light upon the pre-install stage and the next chapter will take you through the last two stages.

In all thirteen stages as discussed in this chapter, I will take you through all such checks and balances that should be accounted for, before going for HP QC 10 installation. Point to note here is that if the stated checklists are not abided by religiously, then HP QC 10 installation can be unstable, hence costing data worth trillions.

Various Stages for HP QC 10 Installation.

- *Stage 1*: Verify system configuration (Server side)
- *Stage 2*: Verify system configuration (Client side)
- *Stage 3*: Know about installation checklist at server side
- *Stage 4*: Know about permissions required on various folders and registry at client side
- *Stage 5*: Know about permissions required on various folders and registry at server side
- *Stage 6:* Clustering details

- *Stage 7:* Application server details
- *Stage 8:* Web server details
- *Stage 9:* Mail server details
- *Stage 10:* HP QC demo project configuration
- *Stage 11:* DB configuration and permissions
- *Stage 12:* HP QC repository path configuration
- *Stage 13:* Text search component installation
- *Stage 14:* Install HP QC 10
- *Stage 15:* Install add-ins

2.2 Stage 1: Verify System Configuration (Server Side)

HP QC 10, as discussed in chapter 1, is based on the client-server architecture. Therefore, it becomes mandatory to validate both server and client machines before HP QC installation. Hence, the very first step is to validate whether both the machines have required configurations. Additionally, if you are working with Citrix or VMware, then both the systems configuration also needs to be made compatible with what HP QC 10 demands.

Let us see the system configuration required for server system configuration.

2.2.1 Step 1: Verify System Configuration (Server System Configuration)

QC can be installed on any of these operating systems:

- Windows
- Solaris
- Linux
- AIX

Let us see the specifications that server system configuration should have:

- CPU
  - *Windows:* Pentium IV or equivalent x86 compatible processor
  - *Linux:* Pentium IV or equivalent x86 compatible processors
  - *Solaris:* Ultra SPARC-III+ / 900 MHz
- Minimum 1 GB memory RAM and 3 GB free disk space. More RAM would be required if application server being used is Jboss and default heap size of application server is increased.
- Database
  - Oracle 9.2.0.6 Standard/Enterprise Edition
  - Oracle 10.0g Release 2 Standard/Enterprise Edition
  - Microsoft SQL Server 2000 Standard/Enterprise Edition with Service Pack 4

- Microsoft SQL Server 2005 Standard/Enterprise Edition with Service Pack 1
- MSDE 2000 Release A (Limited up to 2 GB of memory; supports up to 5 concurrent users.)

□ Web Server

- IIS 6.0
- Apache
- JBoss, WebLogic, or WebSphere HTTP server included with the application server

2.2.2 Compatibility of O/S, Application Server and JVM

After you have ensured the above-said configuration, the next question that should tickle your mind is *"which operating system to be deployed and how?"*. Therefore, you need to keep a note that each operating system is compatible with specific application server and each application server has compatibility with specific JVM (Java virtual machine). Given below is the compatibility matrix for each configuration.

□ **O/S:** Windows 2000 Server with Service Pack 4

OR

Windows 2003 Server with Service Pack 1 Standard/Enterprise Edition

Table 2.1

Application Server	*JVM*
JBoss 4.0.2	JVM 1.5
WebLogic 8.1.5	- BEA JRockit 1.4.2_04-8130 - Sun SDK 1.4.2_04
WebSphere 5.1.1	IBM Java 1.4.2.04
WebSphere 6.1	IBM Java 1.4.2.05

□ **O/S:** Red Hat Enterprise Linux AS/ES, version 3

OR

Red Hat Enterprise Linux AS/ES, version 4.

You must take into account that HP QC 10 supports Red Hat Enterprise Linux on Intel based systems only.

Table 2.2

Application Server	*JVM*
JBoss 4.0.2	JVM 1.5
WebLogic 8.1.5	- BEA JRockit 1.4.2_04-8130 - Sun SDK 1.4.2_04
WebSphere 5.1.1	IBM Java 1.4.2.04
WebSphere 6.1	IBM Java 1.4.2.05

- **O/S:** SUSE Linux Enterprise Server 10

Table 2.3

Application Server	*JVM*
JBoss 4.0.2	JVM 1.5
WebLogic 8.1.5	- BEA JRockit 1.4.2_04-8130 - Sun SDK 1.4.2_04
WebSphere 5.1.1	IBM Java 1.4.2.04
WebSphere 6.1	IBM Java 1.4.2.05

- **O/S:** Solaris 9 OE OR Solaris 10 OE
  You must take into account that HP Quality Center 10 supports Solaris on SPARC-based systems only.

Table 2.4

Application Server	*JVM*
JBoss 4.0.2	JVM 1.5
WebLogic 8.1.5	- BEA JRockit 1.4.2_04-8130 - Sun SDK 1.4.2_04
WebSphere 5.1.1	IBM Java 1.4.2.04
WebSphere 6.1	IBM Java 1.4.2.05

- **O/S:** AIX 5.3 – AIX is a series of proprietary UNIX operating systems developed and sold by IBM.

Table 2.5

Application Server	*JVM*
WebSphere 5.1.1	IBM Java 1.4.2.04
WebSphere 6.1	IBM Java 1.4.2.05

2.2.3 Citrix Server Requirements

In order to run HP QC 10 on Citrix server, following configuration needs to be in place.

- Citrix presentation server 4, on:
  - Windows 2000 Server with Service Pack 4
  - Windows Server 2003 Standard/Enterprise Edition

2.2.4 VMWare Server

If you have a question whether QC can be deployed on VMWare or not, then the answer is "yes". This can be one of the most important insights with respect to (w.r.t.) HP QC 10 installation because VM-

Ware is one of the most sought after servers in today's competitive scenario, and if HP QC 10 installation is compatible with the same then it's a delight to organisations.

2.2.5 Key Points — During Server Side Verification

Few other important key points that you should be aware of:

- HP QC 10 should be installed only on such operating systems that have supported service pack installed.
- JBoss and WebLogic application servers can also be configured to work with HTTPS protocol.
- In Linux, Solaris and AIX environments, before installing HP QC 10, you should ensure that these environments have supported kernel. Command "*uname –a*" can be used to verify the same.

2.3 Stage 2: Verify System Configuration (Client Side)

At client side, before HP QC 10 installation, the system needs to be checked for all the configurations and settings as mentioned below. If the client machines are not configured as stated, there is a possibility of instability during or post HP QC installation.

- CPU
  - Pentium III (or higher) or equivalent x86 compatible processor
- Memory RAM
  - Minimum 512 MB
  - Free disk space
  - Minimum 300MB
- Operating System
  - Windows 2000 Server/Professional with Service Pack 4
  - Windows 2003 Server with Service Pack 1 Standard/Enterprise Edition
  - Windows XP 32-bit Professional/Home Edition with Service Pack 2
- Client software
  - Microsoft .NET Framework 2.0 or later
- Display
  - Color palette setting of 256 colors or higher (65536 colors or higher recommended)
  - Resolution 1024x768 minimum
- Browser
  - Microsoft Internet Explorer 6.0 with Service Pack 1
  - Microsoft Internet Explorer 7.0 or 7.0+
  - Quality Center Explorer

- Microsoft Word
  - If you need to use rich text-based editor then risk-based quality management reports are only available using MS Word 2000, XP or 2003
- Microsoft Excel
  - Excel-based or risk-based quality management reports are only available if one uses MS excel 2000, XP or 2003

2.3.1 Citrix — Client Side Configuration

To verify Citrix client side configurations, before HP QC 10 installation, you should ensure that:

- Citrix client should have program neighborhood, version 8, on:
  - Windows 2000 Server/Professional with Service Pack 4
  - Windows XP Professional/Home Edition with Service Pack 2

2.4 Stage 3: Installation Checklist (Server Side)

Once you have verified about the machine configuration, the next step for any engineer or architect is to understand that before they start deploying the software, what all details should be kept handy across areas; for example, w.r.t database server, w.r.t login credentials of site administrator, etc. Therefore, I will take you through all such checklists that you should keep handy with before starting the deployment of HP QC 10.

- License key and Maintenance key
  - Once you buy the software from HP, then they will provide you with both the keys based on which software can be unlocked and hence used.
- Cluster description – You need to answer these.
  - Are you going to use clustering or not?
  - What all are the cluster host names?
- Application server – You should be handy with the answers for the below-mentioned questions.
  - What is the server type that you have chosen to use (JBoss, Weblogic or WebSphere)?
  - Version number of the server?
  - If you are using JBoss then "Port" to be used?
  - To run JBoss as a service to windows machine, you need to find out username, password, and domain. All these information can either be plugged out by you or you can accordingly ask the required operations point of contact or system administrator for the same.
- Web Server
  - Which web server have you planned to use, Jboss or IIS?
  - Which version will it be?

- Mail Server
  - Which mail server are you planning to use?
  - What is the host to which this server will be plugged in?
- Demo project
  - In HP QC, each user has access to its relevant project and domain. Therefore, you need to decide, if you require a default demo project or you would want to create new one specifically.
- Database server
  - You need to know:
    - DB Type
    - DB Version
    - DB server name
    - DB administrator username
    - DB administrator password
    - DB port
  - If you are planning to use Oracle DB, then in addition, you need to know:
    - DB SID
    - Default tablespace
    - Temp tablespace
- You need to know - site administrator access detail, such as username and password
- You need to know - Path for HP QC repository folder
- Nonetheless, I'm sure you would be thinking what if I already have existing QC installation and have existing schema. In that case, what all are the things that should be taken into account so that the same can be ported to new installation. Therefore, to answer your question, below mentioned are the details that you need to be handy with:
  - QC version of old and new installation
  - QC host
  - DB server name
  - DB admin username and password
  - Site admin DB schema username
  - Site admin DB schema password

With this, now you are ready with the details that are required during QC installation at server side and hence would be asked to punch in for during the installation process.

2.5 Stage 4: Permissions Required to Install HP QC (Client side)

2.5.1 .Net Framework Installation

In order to install HP QC 10 on the client, there is a mandatory requirement to have *"Microsoft .Net Framework 2.0"* installed. In fact, if by any chance you forget to install the same then during HP QC installation, set up wizard detects for the same and if not available then prompts to get *"Microsoft .Net Framework 2.0"* installed. You can install it then as well.

At the following location, *"Microsoft .Net Framework 2.0"*, i.e., **dotnetfx.exe** should get stored: **C:\Program Files\Common Files\Mercury Interactive\Quality Center**

2.5.2 Permissions Required at Client Machine

Generally, in organisations, a user accessing the machine does not get "Admin" related access but get local user related access. As a result, few of the important registry settings can't be altered. Therefore, before you start installing HP QC, you need to ascertain that you have all required privileges on that machine. Let us see the list of such areas and privileges that you must have access permissions.

- You must be logged on to the machine with administrative privileges.
- You must have full read-write permissions on the folder where HP QC files and executables are stored.
- If you have a plan to execute HP QC executables on windows O/S, then you need to ensure that you have full read-write permissions on **\C:WINNT** . This is where your **.ini** file would be stored unless you have opted for another folder.
- You should have full read-write permissions to the **temp** directory. On windows operating system, it is generally at the location:
  C:\Documents and Settings\<username>\Local Settings\Temp
- You should have full read-write permissions on the following registry:
  - HKEY_CLASSES_ROOT\AppID
  - HKEY_CLASSES_ROOT\CLSID
  - HKEY_CLASSES_ROOT
  - HKEY_CLASSES_ROOT\Interface
  - HKEY_CLASSES_ROOT\TypeLib
  - HKEY_CURRENT_USER\Software
  - HKEY_LOCAL_MACHINE\SOFTWARE
  - HKEY_LOCAL_MACHINE\SOFTWARE\Microsoft\Cryptography\RNG

2.5.3 IE Configuration

Before HP QC 10 is installed, it is very critical that correct IE custom level security settings are configured. Let us see what those settings are:

- Open IE browser
- Go to **Tools -> Internet Options**

Under **"Security"** tab, **"Internet or Local intranet"** should be automatically selected. If not, select one.

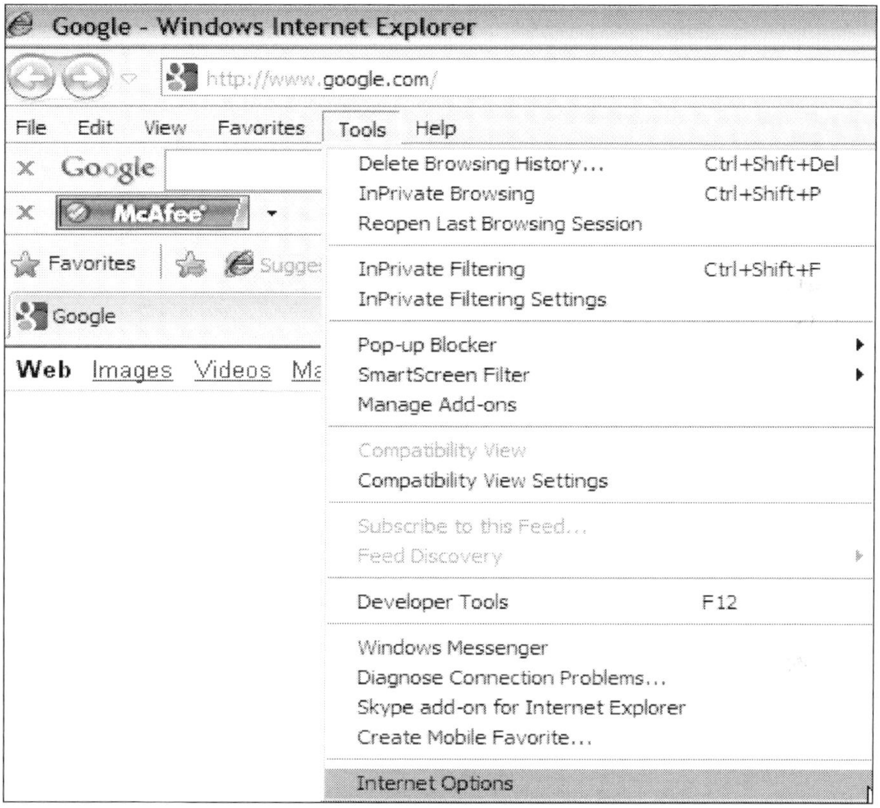

Figure 2.1 *Internet Options.*

2.5.4 IE Configuration Verification — Post HP QC Installation

There are few noteworthy IE settings that should be taken care of post HP QC installation. They are:

- In the *".Net Framework-reliant components"*
  - Enable – *"Run components not signed with Authenticode"*
  - Enable – *"Run components signed with Authenticode"*
- In the ActiveX controls and plug in section
  - Enable – *"Run ActiveX controls and plug-in"*
  - Enable or prompt – *"Download signed ActiveX controls"*

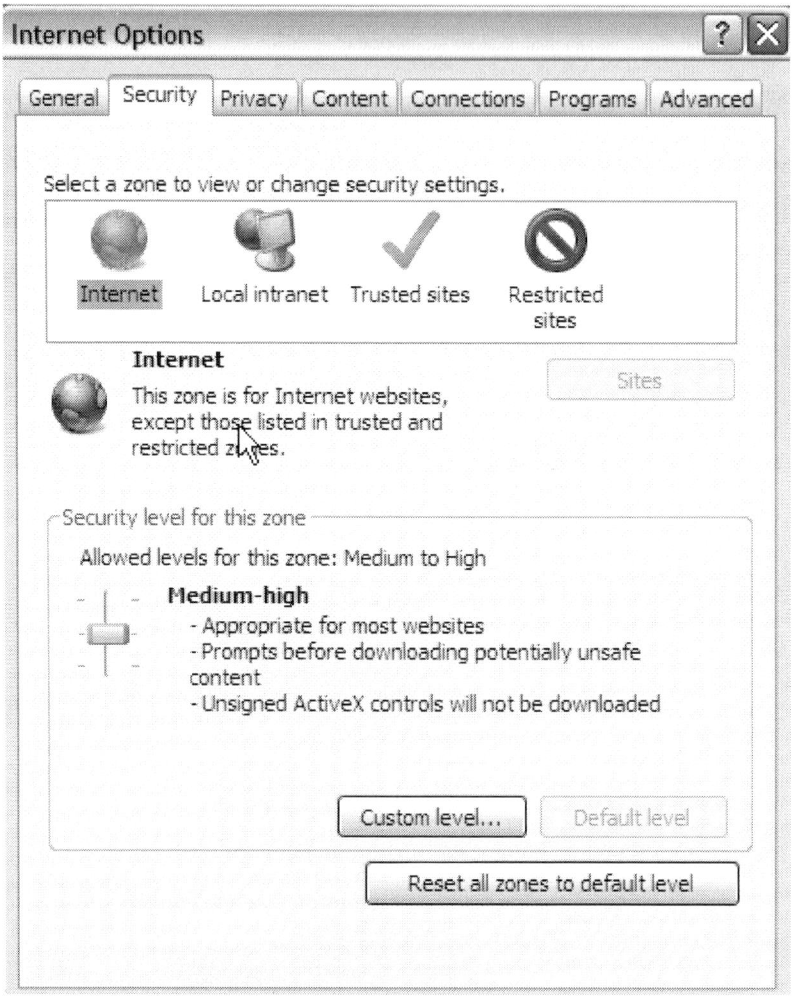

Figure 2.2 *Security Tab, Internet.*

2.6 Stage 5: Permissions Required to Install HP QC (Server Side)

One should ensure that, based on the flavor of the server being used for HP QC 10 installation, required permissions and privileges are obtained by the user.

2.6.1 On Windows Server

- One must be logged on to the windows server having administrative privileges.
- One must have full read-write permissions in the directory where HP QC 10 executables are stored.

- One must have full read-write permissions to the **"Repository"** directory where *"Site administration"* and QC directories are stored.
- One must have full read-write permissions to system root directories **(%systemroot%).** You should keep in mind that even if one does not have full read-write permissions to system root directory, then also HP QC installation can happen but patches can't be installed.
- One should have full read-write permissions to **"temp"** directory.
- One should have full read-write permissions to the following registry.

  HKEY_LOCAL_MACHINE\software\Mercury Interactive

2.6.2 On Solaris, Linux or AIX Servers

- One must have full read-write permissions to the directory where HP QC 10 executables are stored. By default they get stored in "**/opt**" directory but user has the flexibility to choose other directory as well.
- One must have full read-write permissions to the **"Repository"** directory where "Site administration" and QC directories are stored.
- One must have full read-write permissions to **"home"** directory.
- One must have full read-write permissions to **"temp"** folder.

2.7 Stage 6: Clustering Details

As discussed in the previous chapter and sections, HP QC 10 can be deployed either on a single server or a cluster. Therefore, if one deploys HP QC 10 on clusters then the additional areas to keep under check are:

- Verify and shortlist the number of machines you would use. This would depend on number of users both standalone and concurrent, who would be accessing HP QC server.
- Verify and identify the machine, which you would use as a first node.
- Ensure that the same version of HP QC is installed on all the nodes.
- As per the one used in the first node, ensure that the same repository and DB details are inserted throughout the node.

2.8 Stage 7: Application Server Details

At this stage, one needs to first shortlist an application server that should be used during HP QC 10 installation. HP QC 10 supports all these three application servers, i.e., JBoss, WebSphere and WebLogic.

Important point to note is that JBoss application server is included with HP QC 10 installation package. If you extract HP QC 10 installable, JBoss would get deployed and installed automatically on the machine. However, for others, one will have to deploy it manually.

Let us see the checks that one should ensure during JBoss installation:

- One should ensure that JBoss application server heap memory size is sufficient. Default is 1024 MB.
- Ensure that maximum JBoss application server heap value does not exceed RAM size. JBoss memory heap size can be changed during installation through "**JBoss advanced options dialog box**".
- Ensure that JBoss port (8080) is not reserved or already in use. Additionally, in case, you want the port to be changed, JBoss gives the facility to configure new port number through "**JBoss advanced options dialog box**".
- For JBoss on windows, ensure that user account for JBoss is the same as user account used to install HP QC 10.
- If you already had HP QC older version installed on one machine and if you are upgrading HP QC version on the same machine then ensure that you have the same window username, password and domain that you used to enable JBoss to run as a service using your local network. If you are upgrading or installing HP QC 10 afresh, then the user account can be created afresh.

Note: For Webshpere and Weblogic application servers, the requirements remain the same. It is just that they need to be installed separately and are not part of HP QC 10 installable DVD.

2.9 Stage 8: Web Server Details

Below mentioned are the suggested configuration for application server and web server, recommended for HP QC 10 installation.

- If you are using JBoss application server then you can integrate the same with IIS or JBoss web server.
- If you are using application server other than JBoss or JBoss with Apache web server then do keep in mind that you must deploy web server after installation of application server.

2.10 Stage 9: Mail Server Details

HP QC 10 supports sending of mails at the occurrence of few specific events. Therefore, in order to enable this feature, one must have mail server configured with application server.

2.11 Stage 10: HP QC Demo Project Configuration

HP QC demo project installation is one of the options that you get while installing HP QC 10. The relevance of this option is that it gives the flexibility to install HP QC 10 components. You don't have to configure or deploy any additional software to have this option enabled. The components that get installed by selecting this option are:

- *HP QC Demo project:* This helps you in traversing HP QC tutorial, in sequence, if HP QC demo project is installed.

- *Mercury tours:* This is sample web-based travel reservation application. You must install this in order to work with HP QC tutorial.

Note: In spite of the fact that this option is not something that you would be able to exercise before HP QC 10 installation process, knowing about the same will not confuse you during installation process. Therefore, I am citing these details in pre-install checks and this should be part of your checklist too.

2.12 Stage 11: DB Configuration and Permissions

When all the above configurations are done, you must sync with the administrator of the network and database and hence integrate all the layers of QC, application server, web server with the database where all data interactions to and fro QC would happen.

To install HP QC 10, the DB related tasks that need to be conducted are:

- Creating the quality center project user schema.
- Copying data between projects.
- Checking that there's sufficient storage in a specific tablespace.
  If you are working with Oracle DB, then you need to have the further stated privileges, before installing HP QC 10.
- CREATE SESSION: Required to connect to HP QC 10 DB.
- CREATE USER: Required to create new project user schema when you are creating HP QC 10 project.
- DROP USER: Required to delete the schema for defined quality center project.
- CREATE TABLE WITH ADMIN OPTION: Required for granting the permission to a newly created HP QC 10 project user schema.
- CREATE VIEW WITH ADMIN OPTION: Required to create views for HP QC 10 project.
- CREATE TRIGGER WITHADMIN OPTION: Required to create triggers for HP QC 10. Triggers are primarily used to collect change history for specific tables.
- CREATE SEQUENCE WITHADMIN OPTION: Required to create sequences for HP QC 10 project.
- CREATE PROCEDURE WITHADMIN OPTION: Required to create stored packages for HP QC 10 projects.
- CTXAPP ROLE WITH ADMIN OPTION: This privilege enables HP QC 10 to use the Oracle text searching feature. For this feature to be active, it is mandatory to have Oracle text search component installed.
- SELECT ON DBA_FREE_SPACE: Required to check free space on DB server.
- SELECT ON SYS.DBA_TABLESPACES: Required to collect list of tablespaces that exist on DB server.
- SELECT ON SYS.DBA_USERS: Required to verify the existence of HP QC 10 project users..

- SELECT ON SYS.DBA_REGISTRY: Required to validate whether text search component is installed on the database server.
- SELECT ON SYS.DBA ROLES: Required to validate whether text search role (CTXAPP) is installed on the database server.
- SELECT ANYTABLE WITH ADMIN OPTION: Required for various administrative operations.
- INSERT ANY TABLE: This is also required for various administrative operations that may be called for during porting the existing QC DB.

HP QC 10 creates a project user schema, when creating a new project or using the existing one. This schema holds all the tables used by the project. The privileges that are required for a QC project user schema are:

- QUOTA UNLIMITED ON: <default tablespace>
- CREATE SESSION:
- CREATE TABLE:
- CREATE VIEW:
- CREATE TRIGGER:
- CREATE SEQUENCE:
- CREATE PROCEDURE:
- CTXAPP ROLE:

Point to not here is that even for other databases, similar kind of permissions would be required, as what has been discussed for Oracle DB.

2.13 Stage 12: HP QC Repository Path Configuration

During HP QC 10 installation, you will get an option to give location for deploying repository directory. By default, this would be kept under **C:\Program Files\Mercury\Quality Center\repository** and by default storage location should be opted for during installation process.

2.14 Stage 13: Text Search Component Installation

Text search configuration option is available only if the text search component is installed and configured on Oracle DB server or Sql DB server. For Microsoft SQL 2005 and Oracle 10g, the text search feature is installed by default and no additional configuration is required. But for Oracle 9i, you must install this component additionally. For Microsoft SQL 2000 server, this component is not supported.

You have now understood about all the pre-requisite that one needs to have before HP QC 10 installation starts. Indeed, this is one of the most important aspects of HP QC 10, which is not so exposed yet.

Primary purpose of this chapter was to equip readers with HP QC 10 pre-install and permissions requirement. In next chapter we will discuss upon "stage 14" and "stage 15" i.e., HP QC 10 and add-in installation process.

HP Quality Center 10: Add-In — Installation

3

Chapter Objectives: This chapter will give an overview of

- *HP QC 10 installation procedure*
- *HP QC 10 add-ins*

3.1 HP QC 10 Installation Procedure

In this chapter, we will discuss about stages 14 and 15 (as per Chapter 2), i.e., the procedure behind HP QC 10 and its respective add-in, installation.

The very first question that would tickle your mind is from where to get the installable of HP QC 10. The answer to this is that HP QC 10 is licensed software. In order to buy license, you need to get in touch with HP. Once you purchase license, HP provides you with installation DVD, license key and maintenance number.

Before, we take you through the installation steps, the important point to re-iterate here is that all pre-install areas, as discussed in Chapter 2, should be taken care of beforehand, i.e.,

- All required configurations and permissions should be obtained, as referenced in Chapter 2.
- Take a back up of your existing QC projects, if you are trying to upgrade QC version.

Let us now assume that you have all the pre-installation configuration and permission in place and also the HP QC installable DVD with you. It's time to go through the journey of fresh HP QC 10 installation.

Step 1) Be sure, on which particular O/S are you installing HP QC 10. If you are installing it on:

- Windows
  - Then run **setup.exe** that will be there in installation DVD
- Solaris – Console mode
  - Then type: **./setupSolaris.bin-console**
- Linux – Console mode
  - Then type: **./setupLinux.bin-console**

- AIX – Console mode
  - Then type: **./setupAix.bin-console**
- Solaris – UI Mode
  - Then type: : **./setupSolaris.bin**
- Linux – UI mode
  - Then type: **./setupLinux.bin**
- AIX – UI mode
  - Then type: **./setupAix.bin**

Note: *We will primarily see the installation steps on windows 2003 server, throughout the discussion.*

Step 2) Insert DVD to the CD ROM of your machine. The "Welcome" screen comes up.

Additionally, you can also store the dump at some location on your machine and then click on **"setup.exe"**

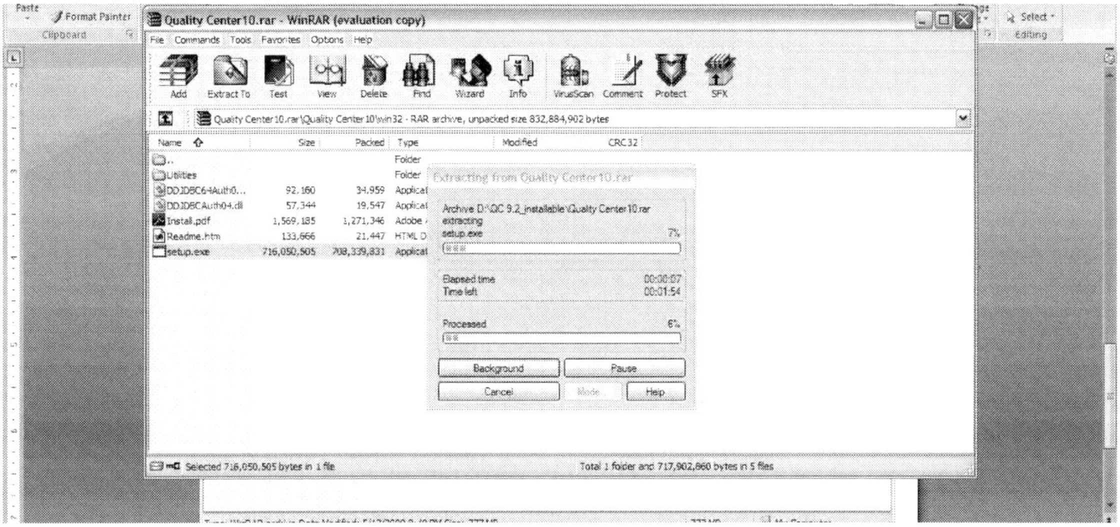

Figure 3.1 *setup.exe Stored at D:\ Drive.*

Click "setup.exe", file extraction starts.

Once file is extracted, the "Welcome" screen comes up. Click "Next" on "Welcome" screen. License agreement window pops up. You need to accept the license agreement and hence click "Next"**.**

In the screen shot, there's an error message that states all the platforms against which QC can be deployed. If you try to deploy the same elsewhere besides what is stated, then "Next" button gets disabled and does not allow you to proceed further.

Step 3) Let us say that we are deploying it on Windows 2003 server and "Next" button is enabled. Therefore, click "Next" and "License Key" dialogue box opens.

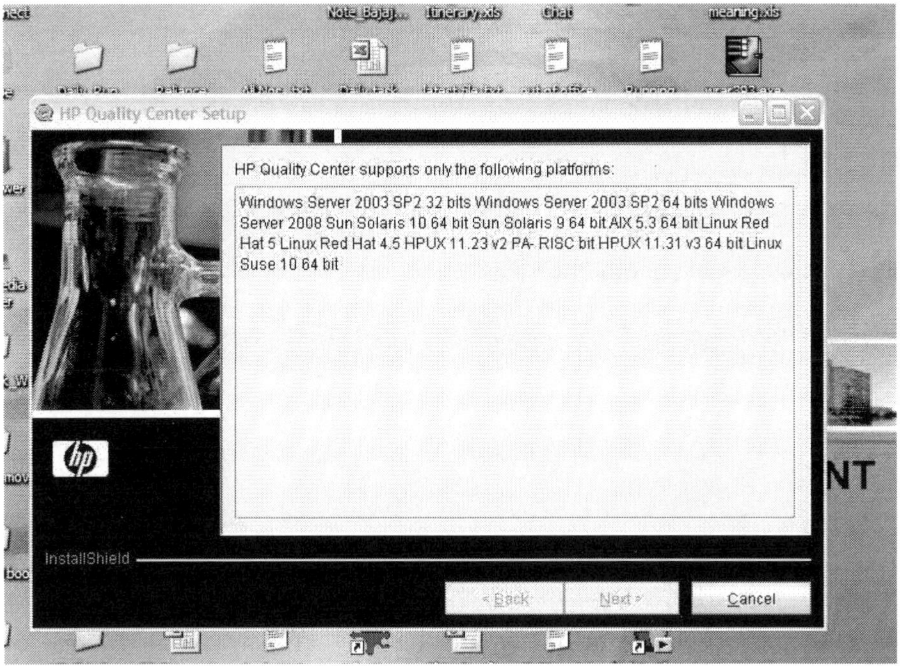

Figure 3.2 *"HP QC 10 Platform Support" Screen.*

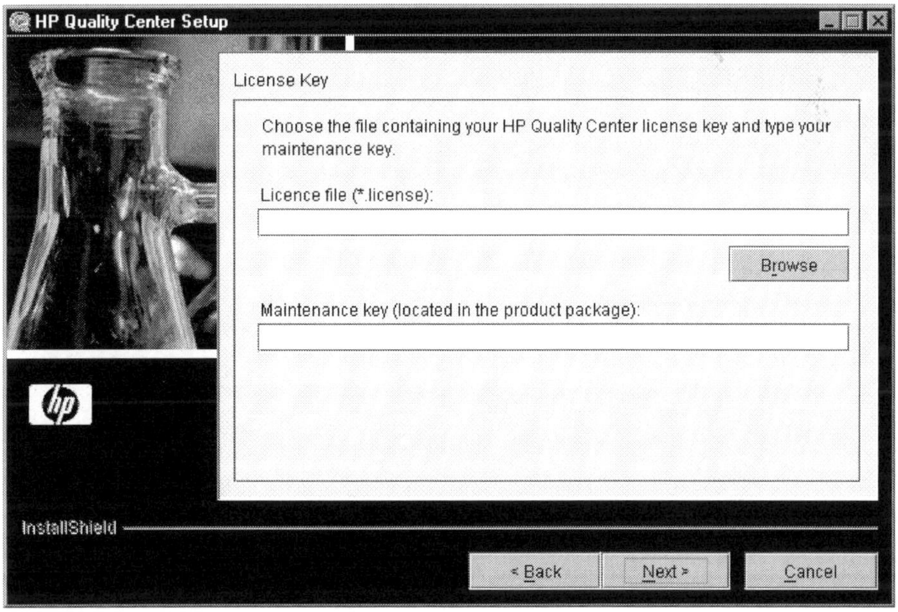

Figure 3.3 *"License Key" Window.*

- *License File* – You get this license when you purchase the tool from HP. Give the location of the license file path in the "License file" field.
- *Maintenance Key* – This key you will obtain when you would purchase the software. You can choose to enter or skip this field as this is not mandatory. Though, this is non-mandatory, I would advice to fill this up with required key.

Click "Next".

Step 4) "Cluster Configuration" window opens.

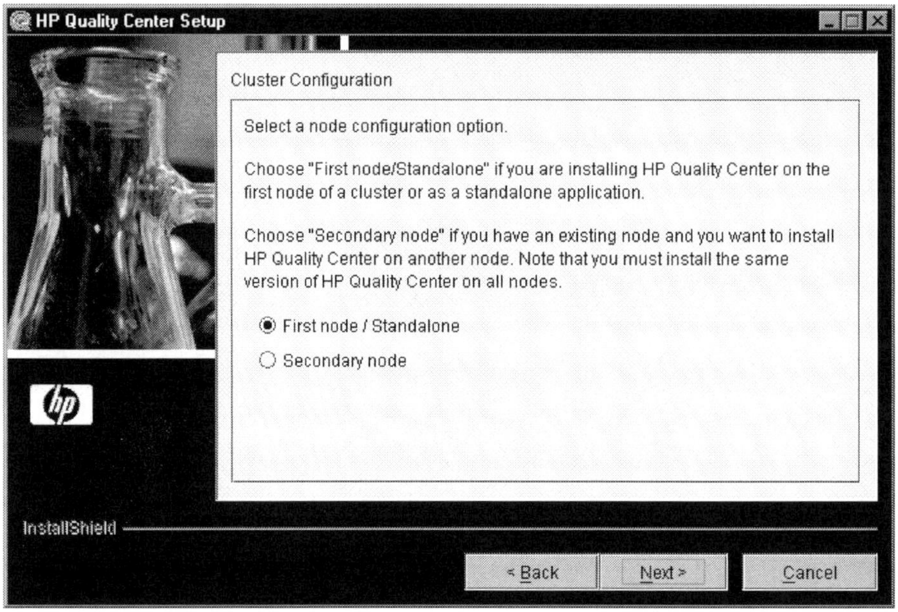

Figure 3.4 *"Cluster Configuration" Window.*

As the message box suggests, either you can go for "First Node/Standalone" installation, or if you have existing QC base installed, then you can go for "Secondary node" installation.

We will consider the installation to be fresh installation here; hence we will select "First node/Standalone" installation.

Click "Next".

Step 5) "Directory Name and location" window comes up. Specify the path where you want to store or install the HP QC 10.

Click "Next".

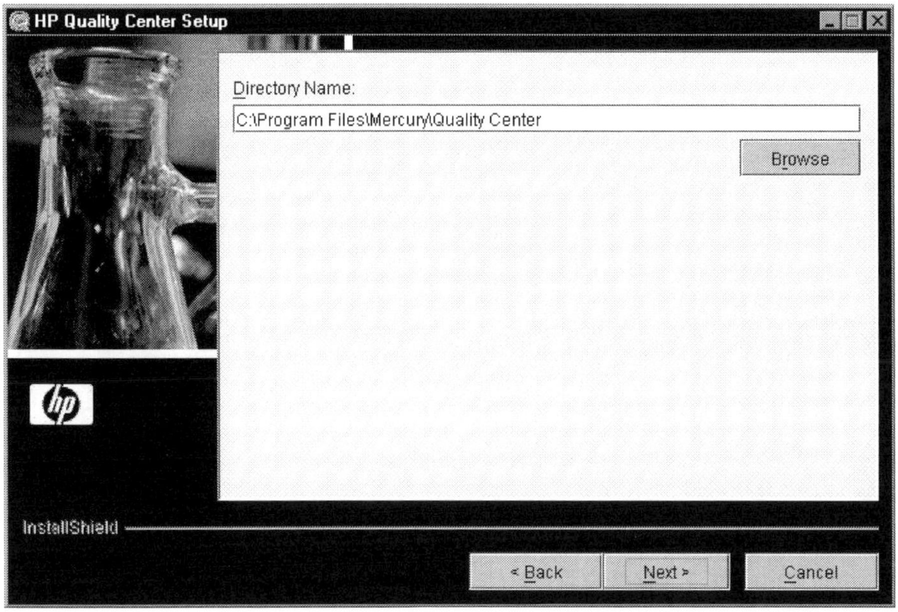

Figure 3.5 *"Directory Name" Window.*

Step 6) "Application Server Configuration" window comes up. By default, JBoss is the application server that is selected. However, as discussed in Chapter 2, to install other application servers, one can choose the "other application server" option.

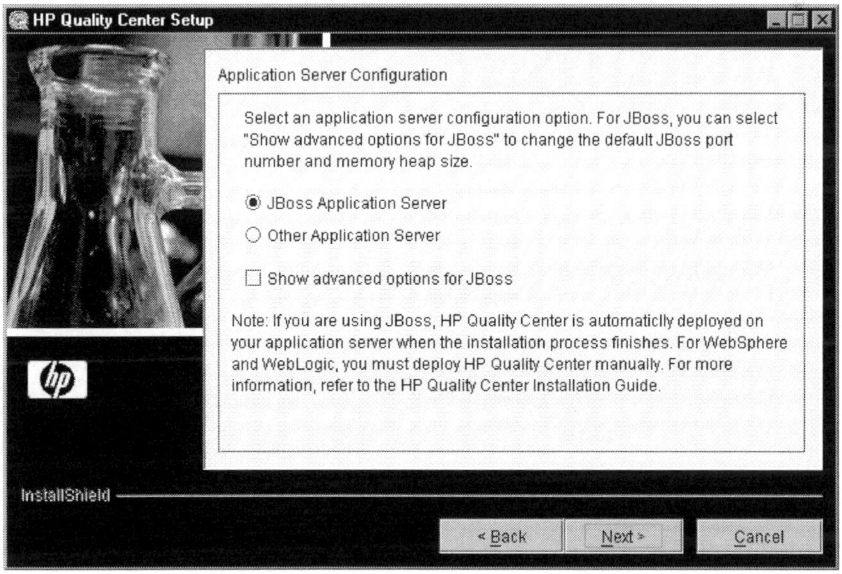

Figure 3.6 *"Application Server Configuration and Selection" Window.*

To continue with our discussion, we will go ahead with JBoss application server.

Now, you will observe there's a check box named, "Show advanced options for JBoss". Let us select that and see what comes up.

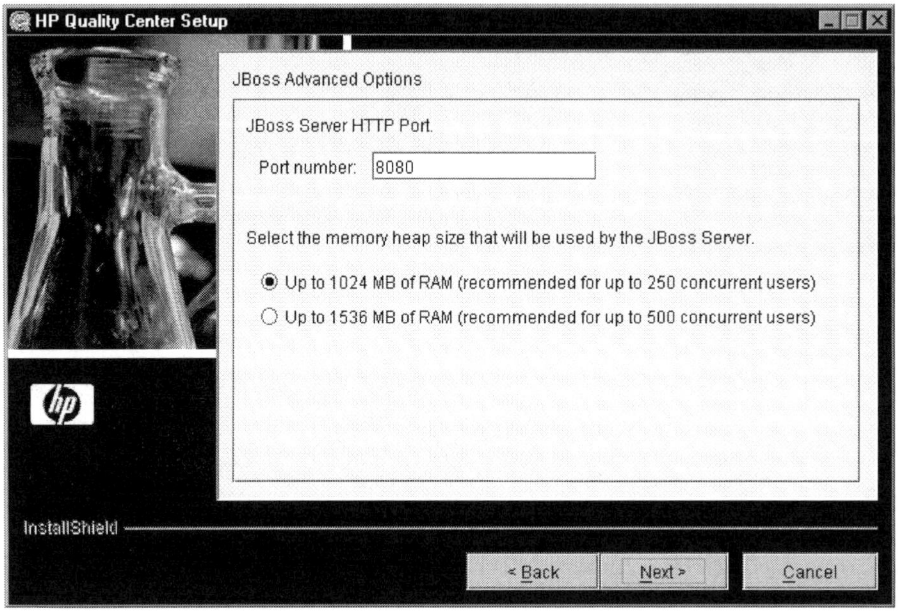

Figure 3.7 *"JBoss Advanced Options" Window.*

In this advanced options window, you need to configure port no. As discussed in previous chapter, now you can appreciate more as why 8080 port was meant to be freed up during pre-installation and configuration procedures.

Additionally, based on the number of concurrent planned to use HP QC 10, you need to select the other choice, i.e., either "Up to 1024 MB of RAM (recommended for up to 250 concurrent users)" or "Up to 1536 MB of RAM (recommended for up to 500 concurrent users)".

I reiterate that in case you plan to select heap size to be 1536, then you need to ensure that it does not exceed your server RAM Size.

Click "Next".

Step 7) "JBoss service and login credentials" window will come up. Here you need to set the login credentials for JBoss server.

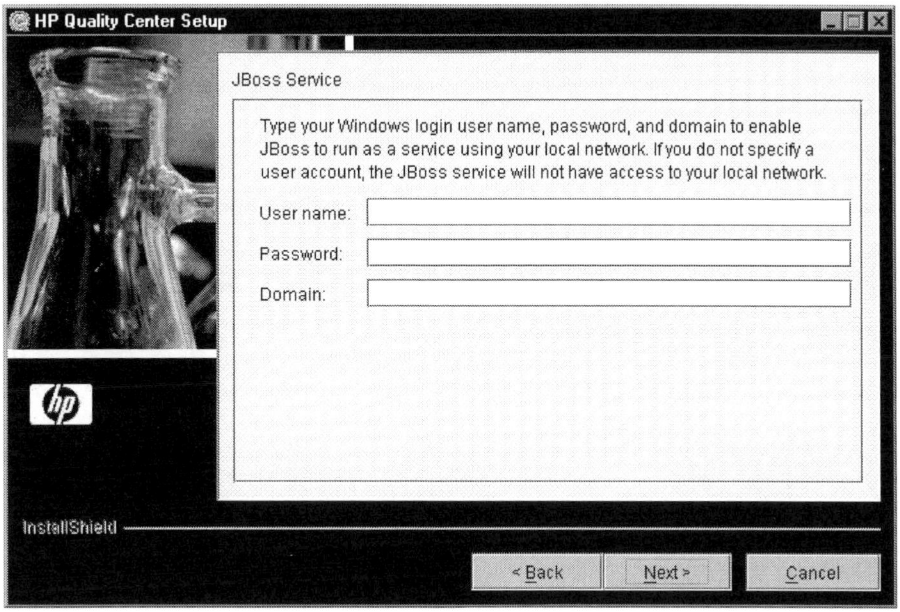

Figure 3.8 *"JBoss Service" Window.*

Click "Next".

Step 8) Post step 6, HP QC looks for web server. If JBoss or IIS web-server is installed on the machine by default, then the installation would proceed further without any botheration. Otherwise, the below window pops up where it asks to deploy and configure web server.

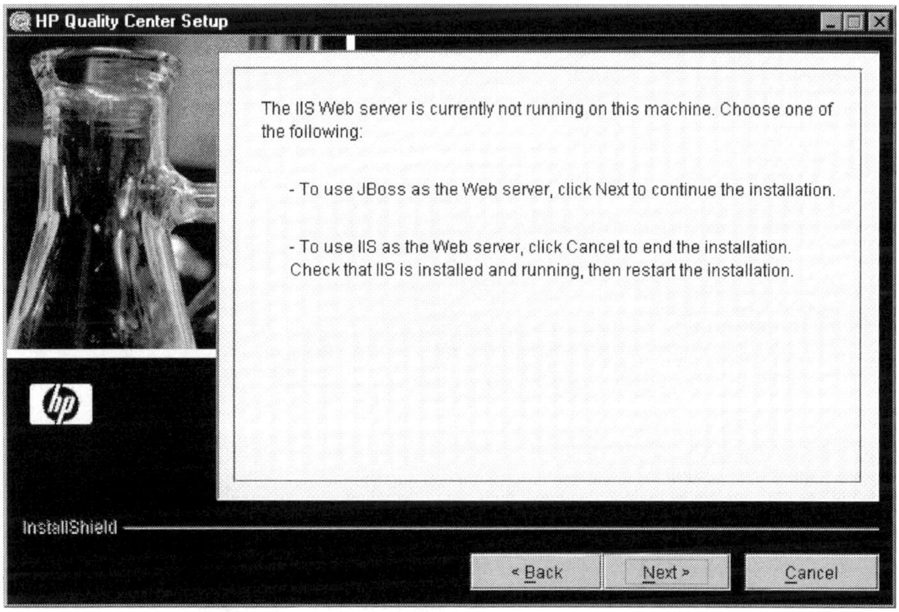

Figure 3.9 *Web Server Deployment Check Window.*

In case, you have a requirement to go with IIS webserver, you will have to check the pre-installation instructions for IIS server as discussed in Chapter 2. Additionally, if you have reached this configuration stage, without having IIS web server installed, then you will have to cancel the installation process and install IIS web server first and then again traverse these six steps, what we had seen till now.

For our discussion, we would assume that IIS web server was already installed. Therefore, by clicking "Next", below displayed window pops up, where you need to select option "IIS".

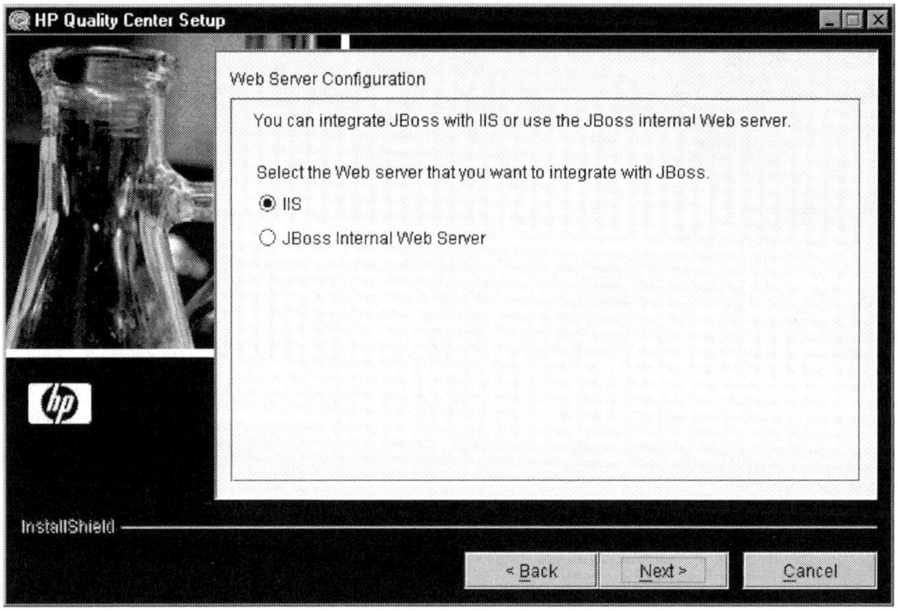

Figure 3.10 *Web Server Selection Window.*

Again, at this stage, assume that you have both JBoss web server and JBoss server installed and you want to change server to be used from IIS to JBoss. You get an option to change web server in this window. Let's change the server to be JBoss and proceed further with the discussion and hence click "Next".

Step 9) After JBoss server has got installed, you need to ensure whether HP Quality Center 10 components have got installed or not. Therefore, the next window that you would see is:

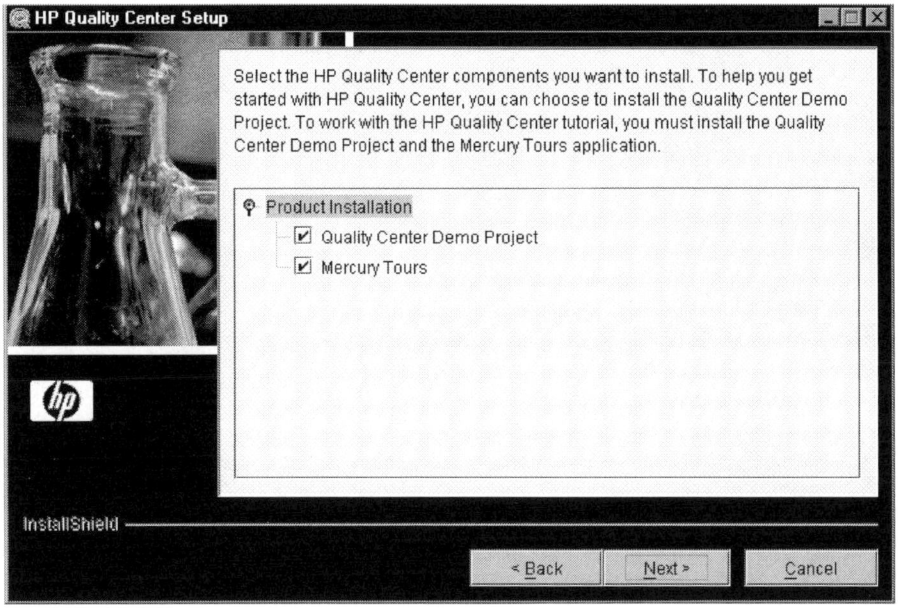

Figure 3.11 *HP QC 10 Components.*

Select both the options, i.e., "Quality Center Demo project" and "Mercury Tours".

- *HP QC Demo project:* This helps you in traversing HP QC tutorial, in sequence, if HP QC demo project is installed.
- *Mercury tours:* This is sample web-based travel reservation application. You must install this in order to work with HP QC tutorial.

Click "Next".

Step 10) Email server configuration window pops up.

Figure 3.12 Mail Server Properties.

There are several options that you see in the displayed window. One is about selecting an option to configure e-mail SMTP services option for Microsoft IIS configuration. Another one is "SMTP server", which is the most famous options in any organisation as almost all their mail servers are configured with SMTP server option and the last one is "none", which by virtue of its meaning says that one need not configure mail server with this installation. Therefore, my recommendation would be to opt for existing SMTP server. Provide the "SMTP server" name in the displayed text. Configuring this option would ensure that required HP QC 10 users, receive mail, when set for specific conditions.

Step 11) In the displayed window, you need to select the DB type that you need to configure. We will take Oracle DB option to take our discussion further.

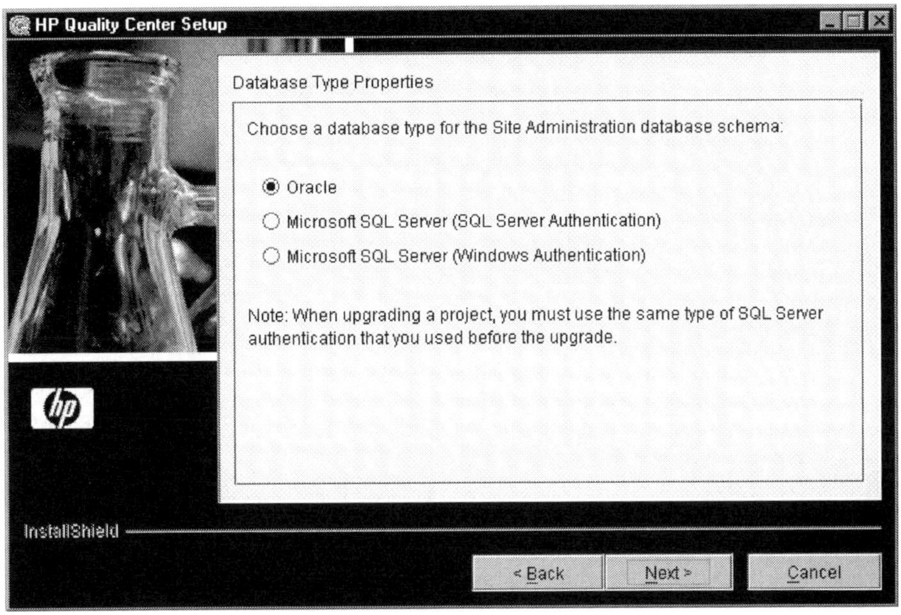

Figure 3.13 *DB Selection Window.*

And yes, I'm sure you remember that now pre-install permissions, as discussed in Chapter 2, need to be handy at this juncture.

Step 12) Provide the DB details.

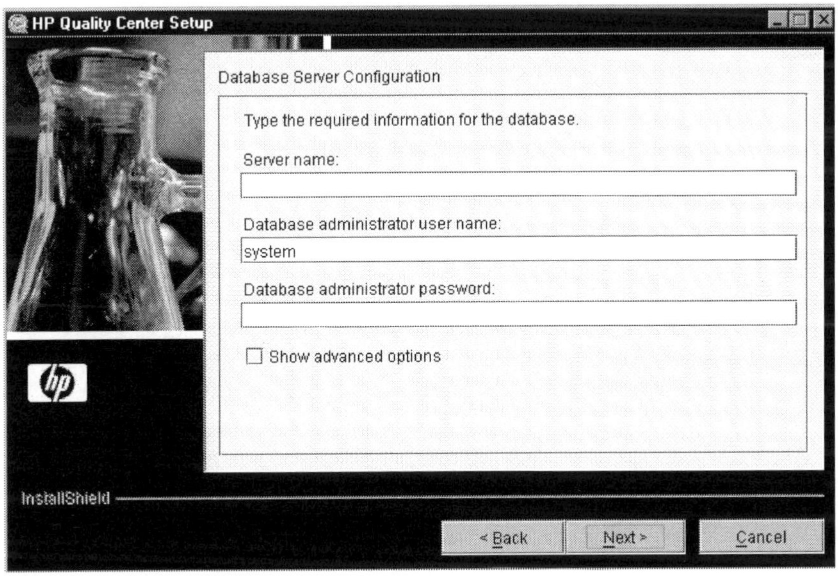

Figure 3.14 *DB Server Configuration Details.*

In case, you select advanced options, then the below displayed window comes up.

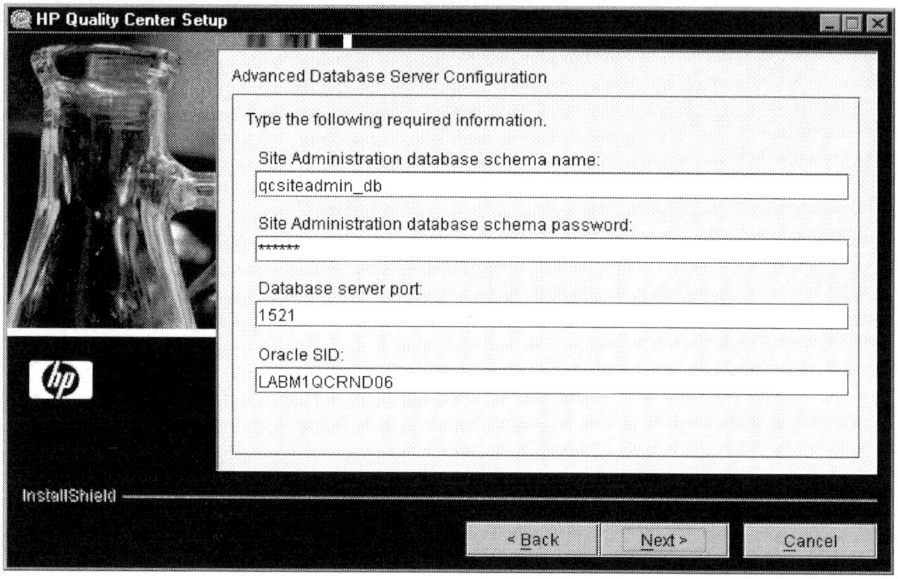

Figure 3.15 *DB Advanced Options Window.*

In the options displayed in Fig. 3.15, you need to provide the site administrator DB schema login credentials, DB server port and Oracle SID (Oracle System identifier). Oracle SID is used to connect and identify the specific oracle instance on the host machine, on which Oracle server is installed.

Click "Next".

Step 13) "Database schema found" window comes up. Here you need to either choose an option i.e., to upgrade existing schema or to upgrade a copy of existing schema.

"Upgrade a copy of existing schema" is used when you are upgrading QC version from one to another and you would want to use both the schema.

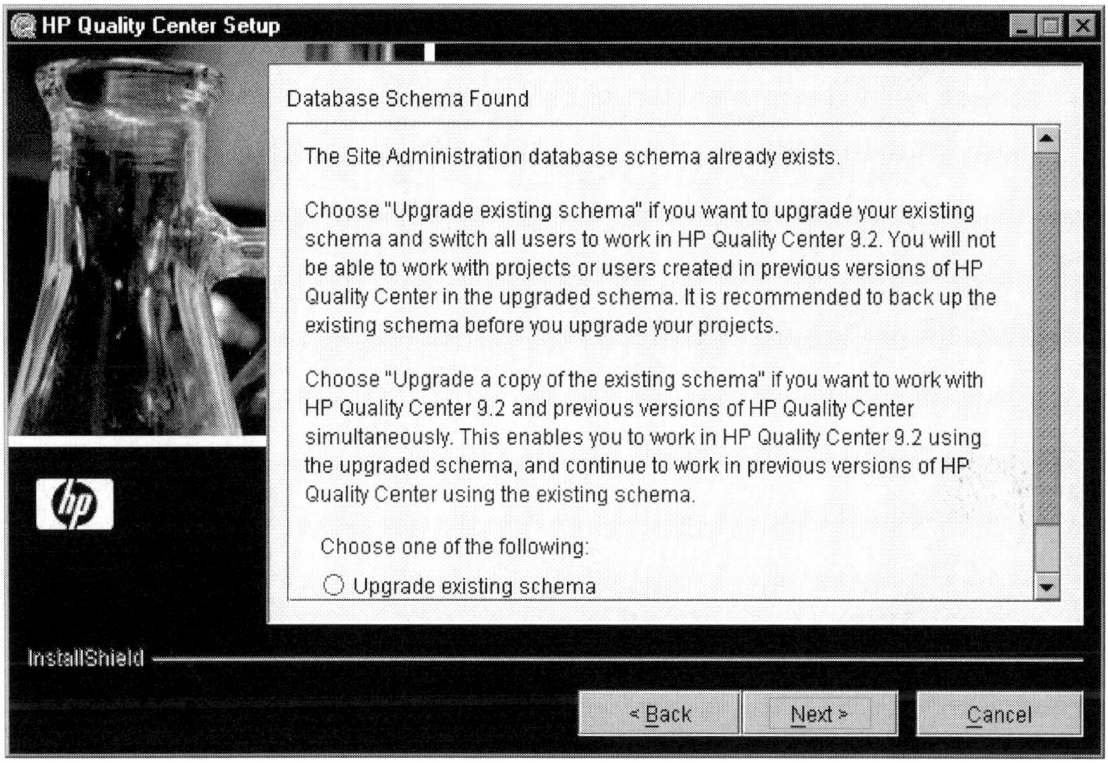

Figure 3.16 *"DB Schema" Window.*

Choosing "Upgrade existing schema" and on clicking "Next", below displayed window comes up.

Step 14) In this window, site administrator details need to be provided. This needs to be the same one as what you would have defined in the beginning phase of this installation process.

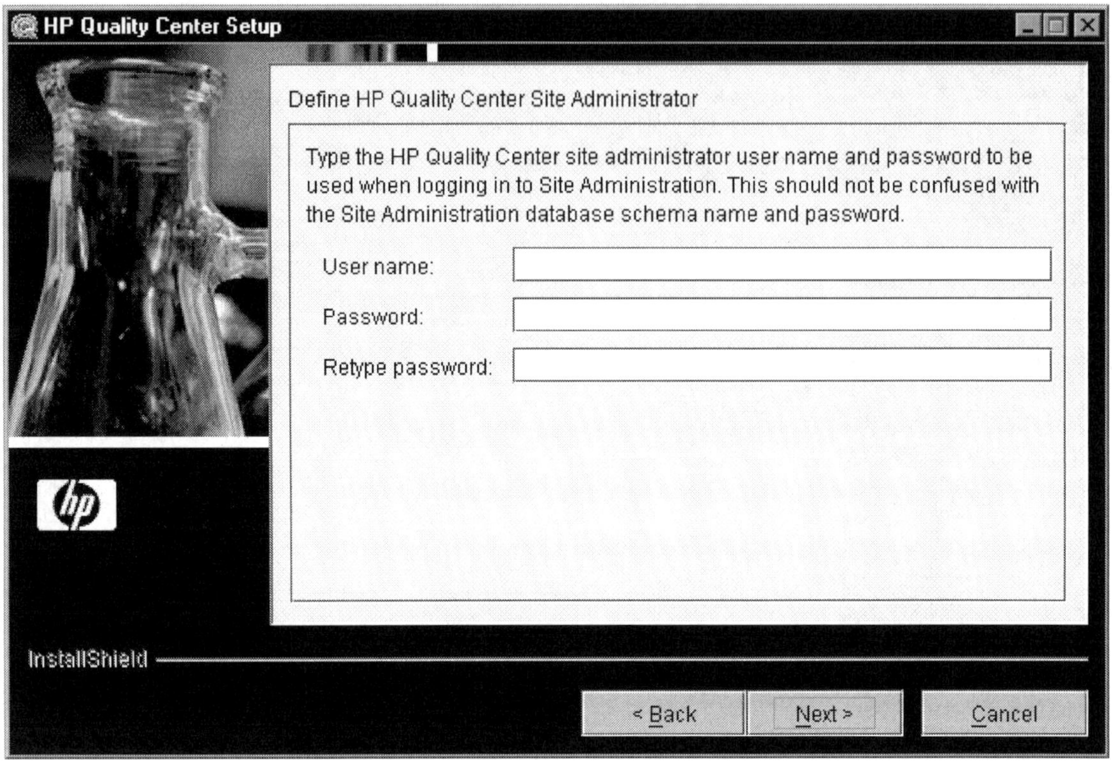

Figure 3.17 *HP QC 10 Site Administrator Window.*

After inputting the required credentials, click "Next".

Step 15) Here you need to define the path of the "Repository", where you would want to store the "Repository" details.

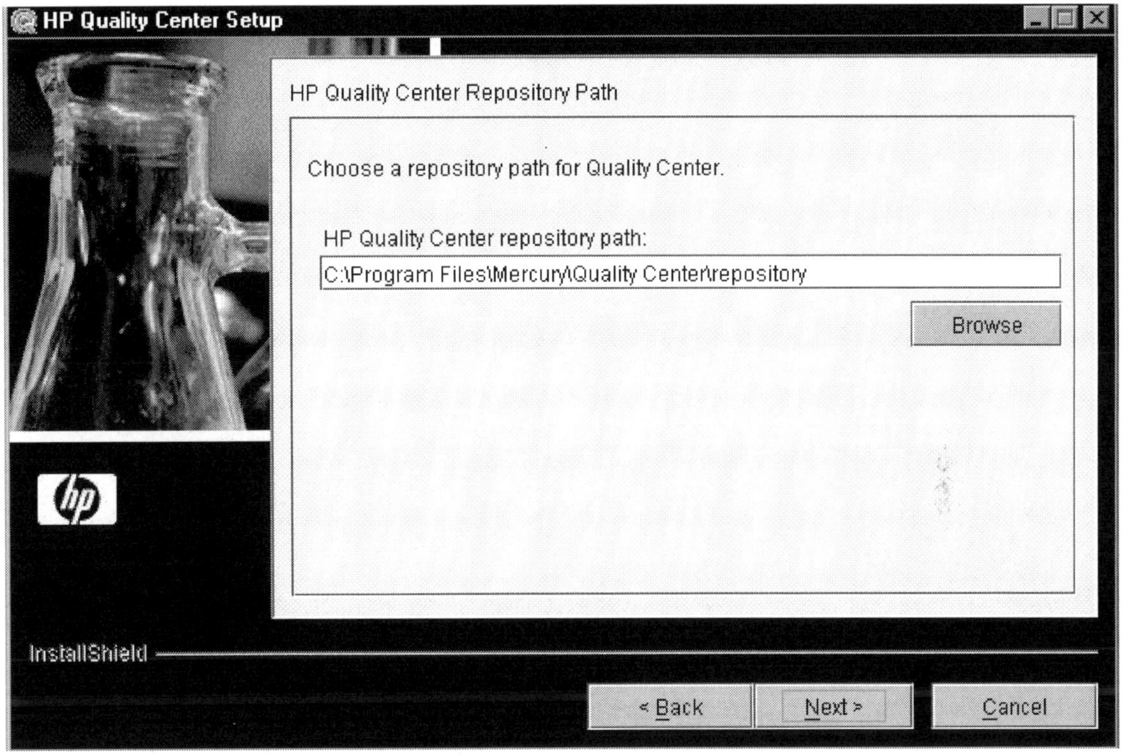

Figure 3.18 *HP QC Repository Path Definition Window.*

Click "Next". Clicking "Next" here would pop up installation summary window. And again clicking "Next" on that window, before installation completes, a window would come up, which would ask you "Whether you want JBoss server to start".

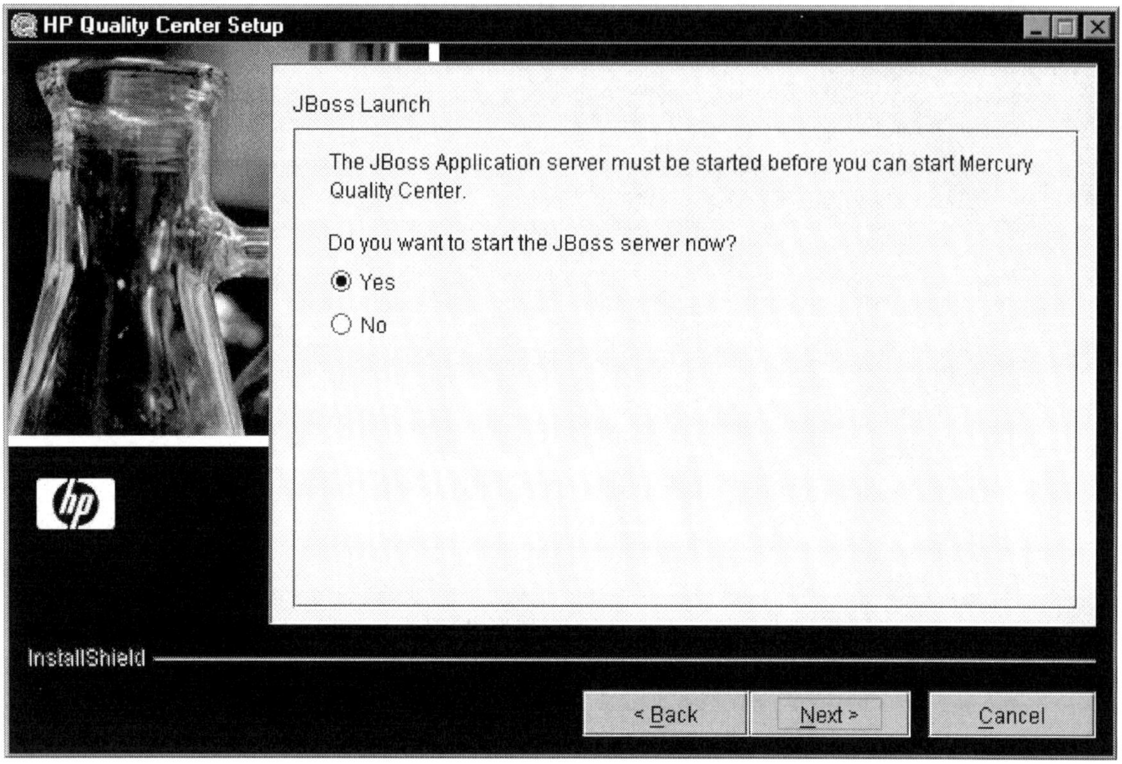

Figure 3.19 *JBoss Launch Window.*

I would recommend going with "Yes". This ensures that after installation is complete, you don't need to start JBoss server manually and at that stage you are ready to use HP QC 10.

Click "Next"

Step 16) Installation completed window will come up and it would prompt you to restart the machine. You may choose to restart it later but the recommendation here would be to restart it on priority, before HP QC 10 comes under use.

This brings you to a point where you have unfolded the mystery behind HP QC 10 installation. My recommendation for readers would be to keep this information handy whenever they are going for HP QC installation.

3.2 HP QC 10 Add-Ins

Add-ins literally mean are the components which empower software to do something extra than what they actually were designed for. Add-ins' provide avenue for introducing new features, powers and integration hooks to the software. And therefore, with HP QC 10 also this philosophy holds true.

If one wants to avail such exclusive add-ins, then one need to get the license from HP, in order to use the same. Few of the mostly used add-ins' that can be installed on top of HP QC 10 are:

- *HP Quality Center connectivity:* This empowers HP QC 10 to integrate with other automation tools such as HP QTP, HP Loadrunner, etc.
- *HP Quality center system test remote agent:* This enables users to run system test in QC.
- *HP QC client side setup:* This enables users to install all QC components on the client side so that user need not access QC via QC server address but can access it directly through client machine.
- *HP tools add-in:* With this add in, user can integrate HP tools with QC.
- *Microsoft office add-in's:* This add-in enables one to export, import data from or to word documents or .xls files, into QC.
- *Quality center extensions for SAP:* This enables to integrate SAP solutions manager and to integrate SAP business process testing by keeping track of changes.

There are few more add-ins that HP provides especially related with site administrator to facilitate version control, screen recorder and making QC launch browser independent.

All these add-ins can be extracted and deployed once HP QC 10 is installed. Every add-in has its specific set of deployment and installation instructions. All add-ins comes with readme.txt file, reading which user gets the required installation information.

4

HP Quality Center 10: UI, Login and User Management

Chapter Objectives: This chapter will give an overview of

- *HP Quality Center Login*
- *HP QC 10 UI explanation*
- *User management in HP QC 10*

4.1 HP Quality Center Login

After HP QC 10 deployment, the first thing that may come to your mind is *"How to login?"* Here's goes the detailing.

To login, you need to input the address in the browser where HP QC 10 has been deployed. HP QC 10 admin or person who has deployed HP QC 10 can provide the address which needs to be routed through to invoke the software.

After inputting the address in browser address bar, there is a pre-login page that will get displayed.

On that page you would get four entry points:

1. *Quality Center:* Clicking this, you would get HP QC 10 login page.
2. *Site Administrator:* Clicking this, you would get a login page, which is specifically for HP QC 10 site administrators.
3. *Add-ins' page:* As discussed in Chapter 3, this takes you to a different page where description and detailing for all HP QC 10 add-ins are stated.
4. *Readme:* This link takes you to a different page, where all such information about HP QC 10 are stated that a vendor wants its customers to take note of.

Now, coming back to the question of *"How to login through HP QC 10?"*, let us walk through the steps involved for doing so.

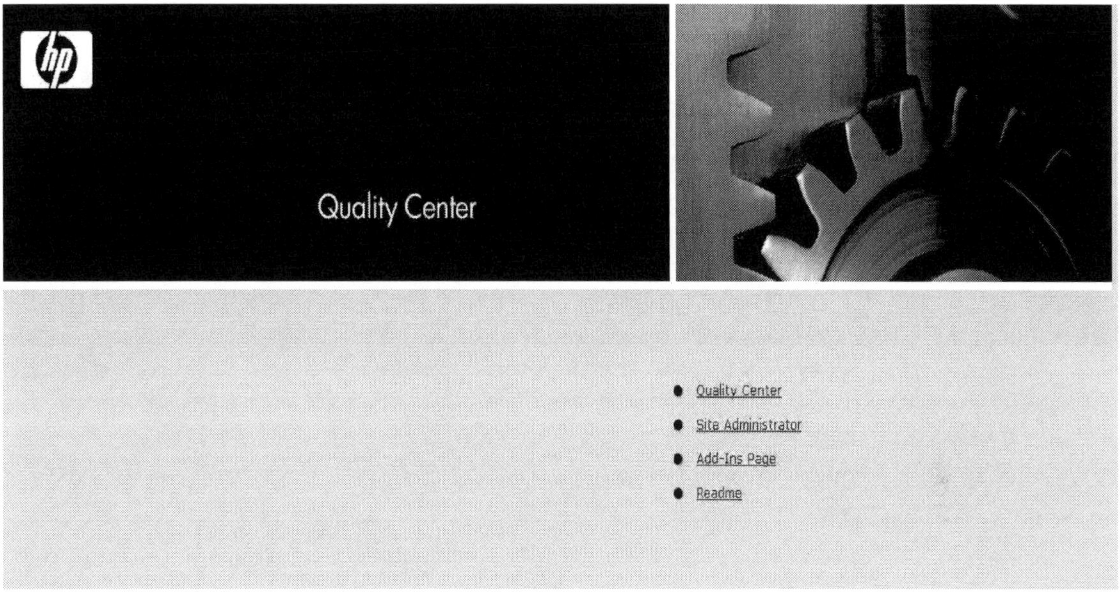

Figure 4.1 *Quality Center 10 Pre-login Page.*

Let us take the route by clicking the Quality Center link. This is the route, which all non- admin users need to take through for their testing and planning work.

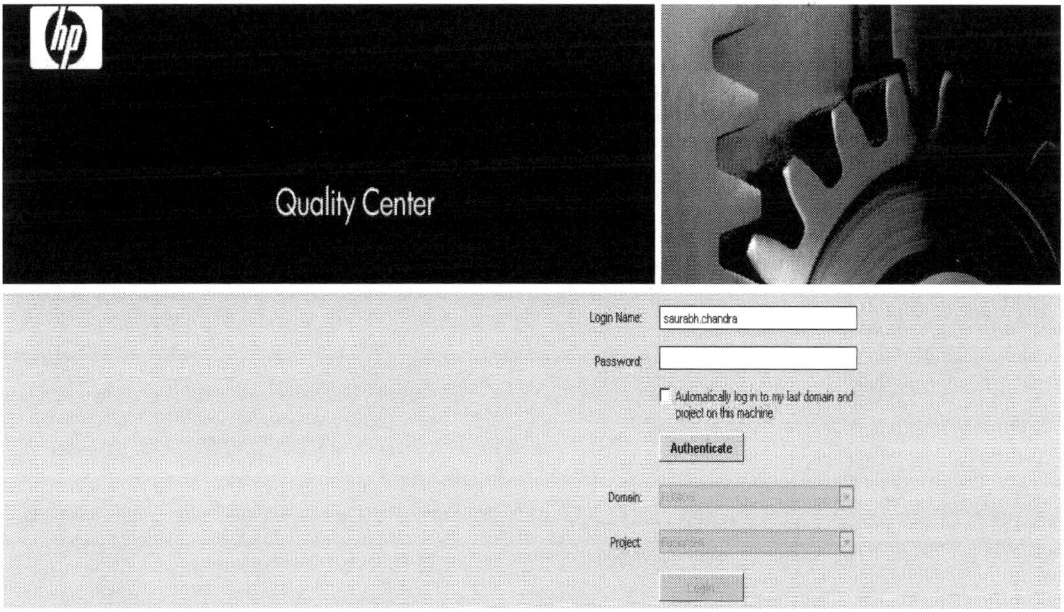

Figure 4.2 *Login to HP QC 10.*

On login page, you can see:

- Login Name:
- Password:
- Domain:
- Project:

All these are created by admin, and after verifying the sanctity of username that one would have applied for, admin provides the access to the specific domain and project. Then, one can view all the files pertaining to the domain, the username is registered for.

Enter all such details and hence you can see HP QC 10 UI.

4.2 HP QC 10 UI Explanation

After entering all the required credentials, you enter your domain and project; you can now see and access files pertaining to that domain.

In below attached screen, you would observe that, I have broken the complete UI into several frames. Let us understand what the attribute of each frame is.

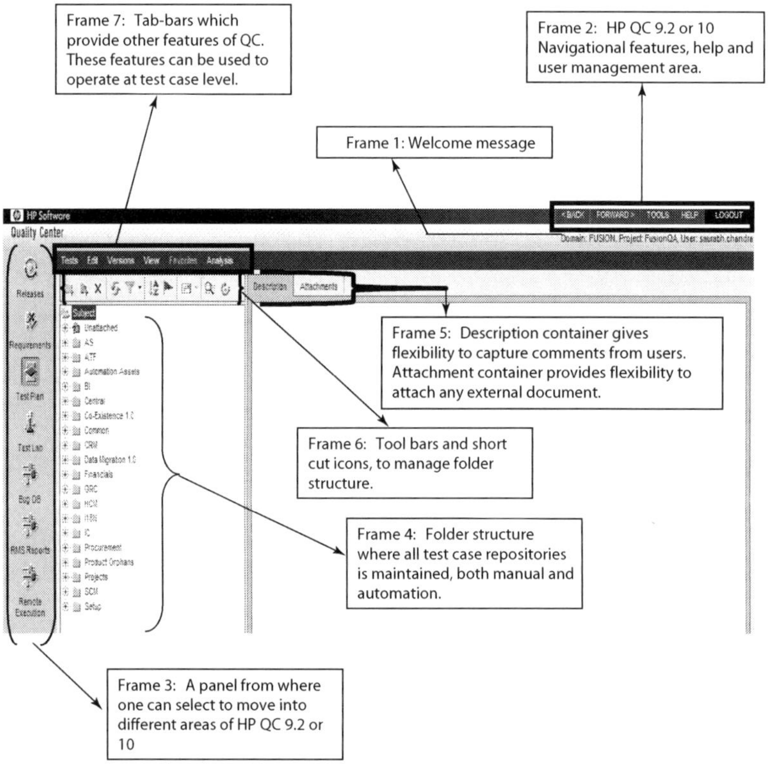

Figure 4.3 *HP QC 10 UI.*

4.2.1 Frame 1: Welcome Bar

Welcome bar, like any other user-friendly software or website, lets you know that you have entered a secured zone, and the respective zone name. Similarly, in case of HP QC 10 also, it lets you know the username with which you have entered and the domain and project, in which you are into.

Figure 4.4 *Welcome Bar.*

4.2.2 Frame 2: HP QC 10 Navigational Bar

- This frame provides flexibility to navigate forward or backward, based on the need. This works based on session cache and the pages that you would have traversed during that session. For example, after you log in to HP QC 10, you click release, requirement, and test plan, in that order. Therefore, on clicking back, the requirement page will come up and on clicking back once again the release page will load. Likewise on clicking forward, other pages in the sequence of forward navigation load.

Figure 4.5 *HP QC 10 Navigational Bar.*

- "Help" provides you with the options as stated in Fig. 4.6.

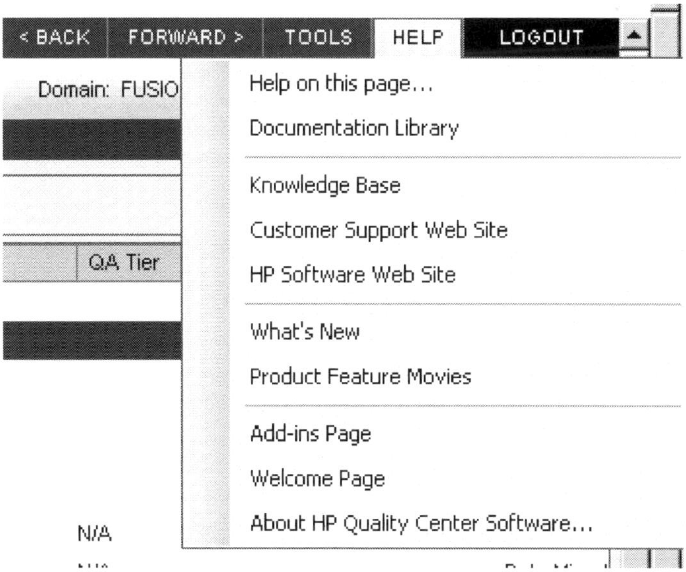

Figure 4.6 *Help Menu Options.*

- *Help on this page:* When this menu item is clicked, another page opens up which provides all the required explanations about the current page that has opened in HP QC 10 at that moment. Therefore, if you navigate on to some other page and click this option, it would give all the required details and explanation of the new page.

Figure 4.7 depicts the UI of the "Help on this page – requirements tree page", "*Help on this page*" option was selected on "Requirements" page.

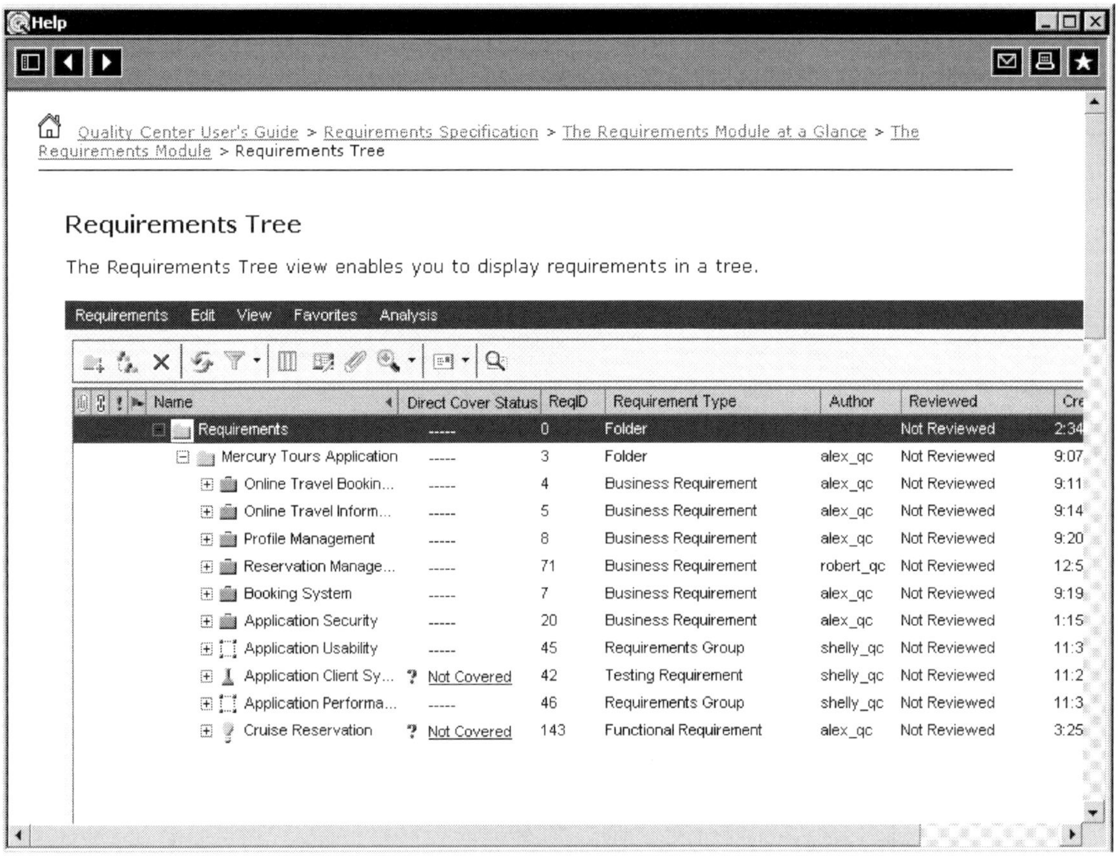

Figure 4.7 *UI of "Help on this page".*

- *Documentation Library:* This section enlists the quick byte about various sections and features of HP QC 10. This can prove to be one of the most useful libraries to furnish or brush up HP QC 10 important features, workings and other details. Figure 4.8 depicts the UI of "Documentation Library".

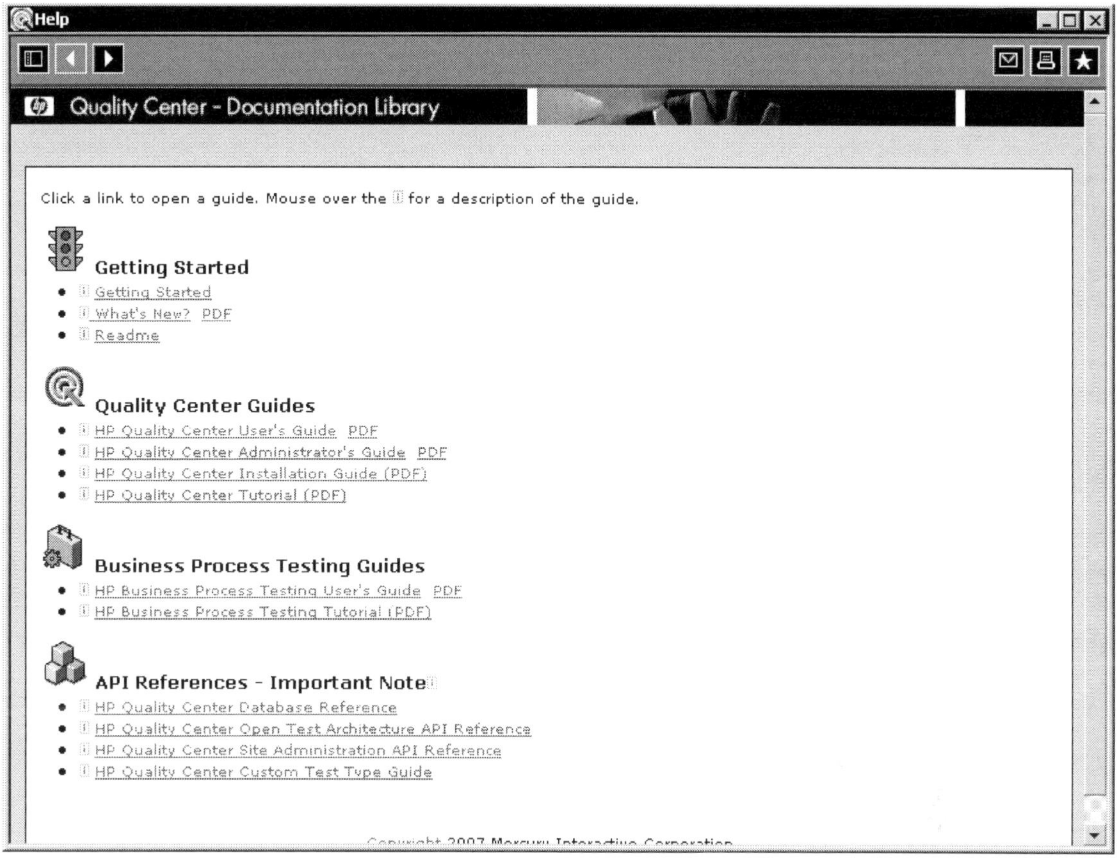

Figure 4.8 *Help ® Documentation Library UI.*

- *Knowledge base, customer support website and HP website* – All these three route to HP domain. If you have valid license then HP website allows you to enter these zones and avail information and support pertaining to any of the three services.
- *What's new:* This section lets you know about what is the latest feature or enhancements that has been plugged in to the latest version of HP QC 10

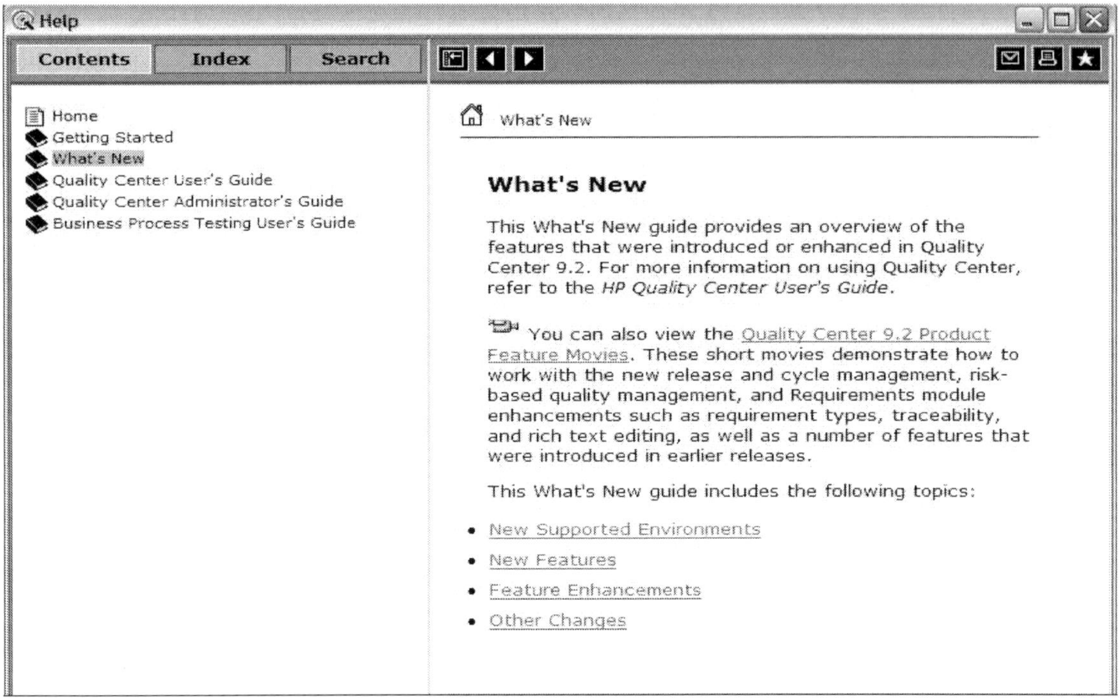

Figure 4.9 *"Help ® What's new" UI.*

- *Product Feature movies:* To facilitate ease in understanding, HP QC 10 provides users with video recording of features and details over best utilization and usage of HP QC 10 features.

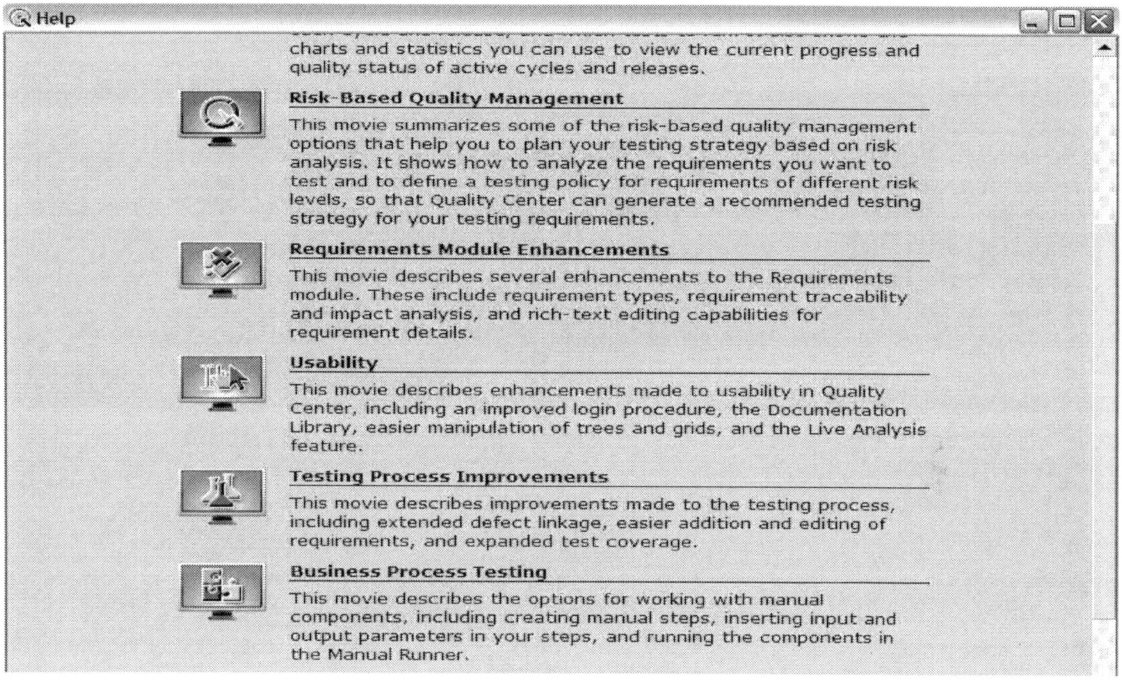

Figure 4.10 "*Help ® Product feature movies*".

- *Add-ins page:* This menu item takes you through the page about the add-ins that HP QC 10 supports. This is similar to what we discussed in Chapter 3.
- *Welcome page:* This takes you to the same first page as displayed in Fig. 4.1.
- *About HP QC 10 software:* This pops up another window as shown in Fig. 4.11 and explains the components and version that HP QC 9.2 and 10 currently uses for that installation. This may change per installation based upon the components installed and add-ins purchased.

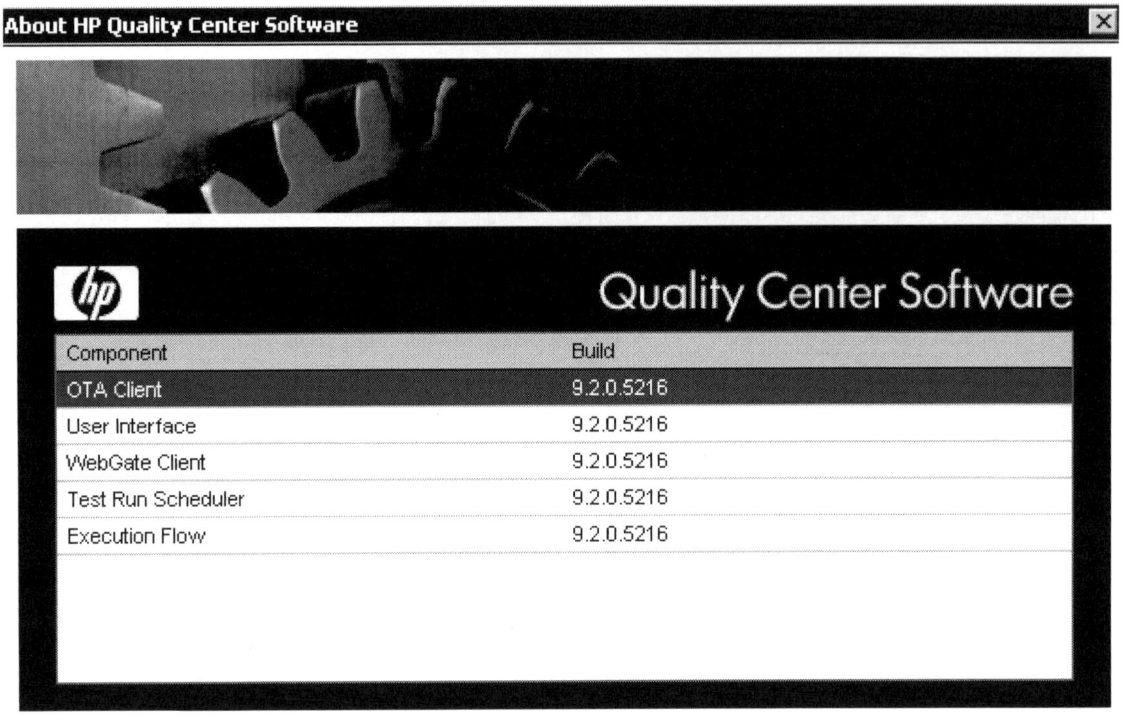

Figure 4.11 *About HP QC 9.2*.

- **Logout:** As the name suggests, this link help users logging out from current domain and project.
- **Tools:** Below displayed menu items are part of tools tab bar.

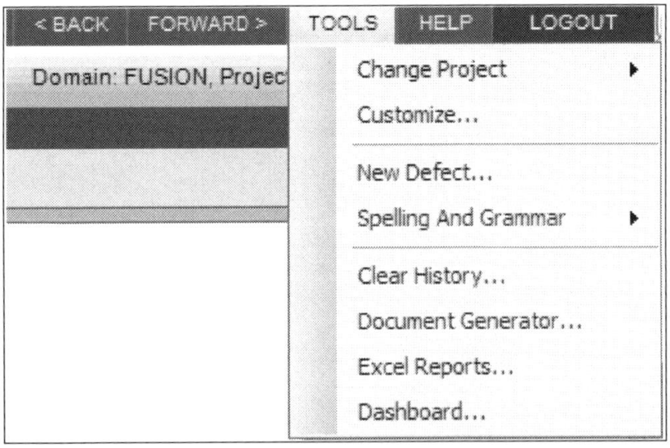

Figure 4.12 *Tools Menu Options.*

- *Change project:* Selecting this option, you will be logged out of the system and will be asked to select another project and domain to enter into.

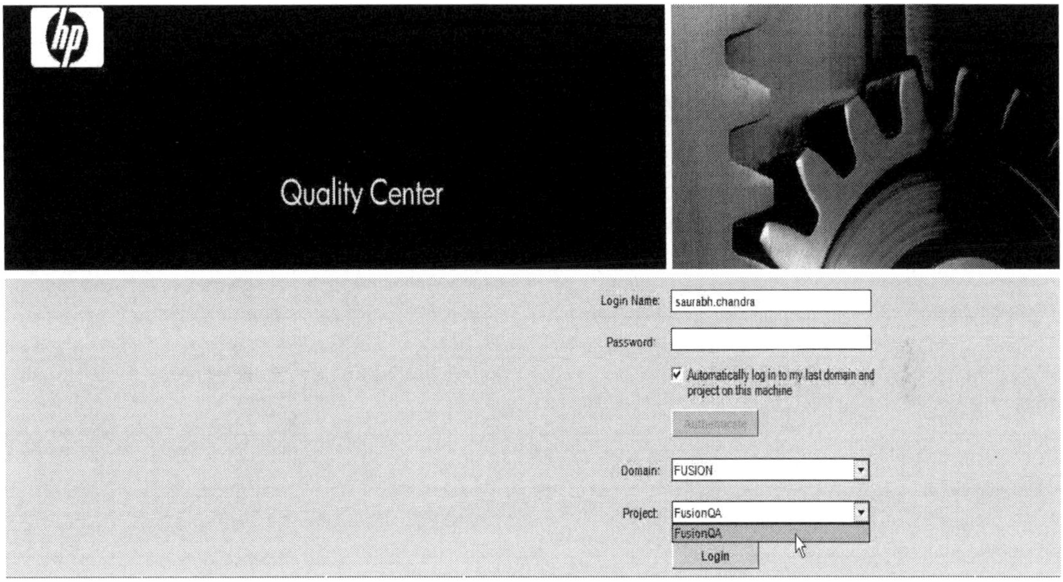

Figure 4.13 *Re-login by Selecting Required Project and Domain.*

- *Customize:* This menu item takes you through the current user profile and based on the privileges that current user profile has, one can perform user management operations.
- *New defects:* This is one such option that in spite of any page that you are into, by selecting this you can log defects against any respective case or requirement.

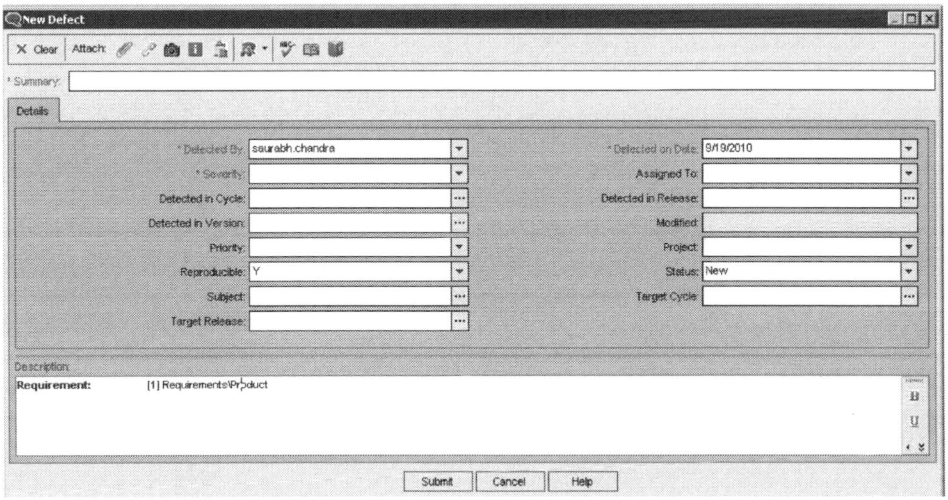

Figure 4.14 *New Defect Window.*

- *Spelling and Grammar:* Place your cursor to the word or statement and accordingly HP QC 10 would verify whether spelling or grammar of required word or statement is correct.
- *Document Generator:* Placing the cursor on the required folder and then choosing this option will ensure that it generates reference document in the below displayed format.

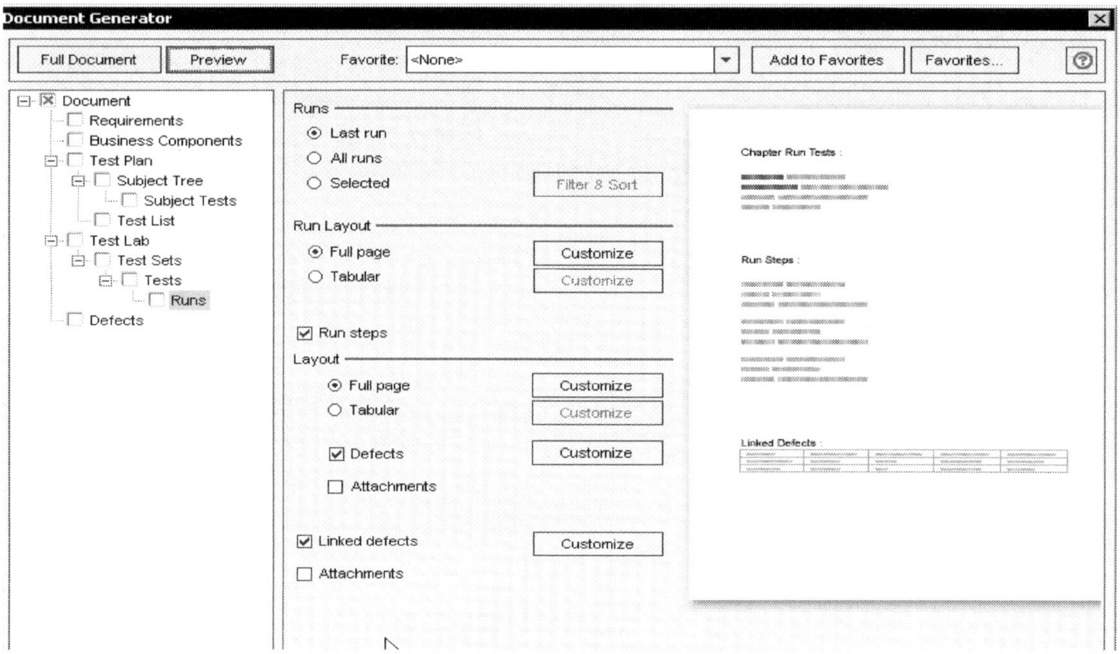

Figure 4.15 *Document Generator Window.*

Clicking "Full document" button on document generator, below window gets displayed. In this window, you can see that the document generator progress bar is displayed. Based on the success of the progress bar, document generation process is tracked and hence document is generated with relevant details.

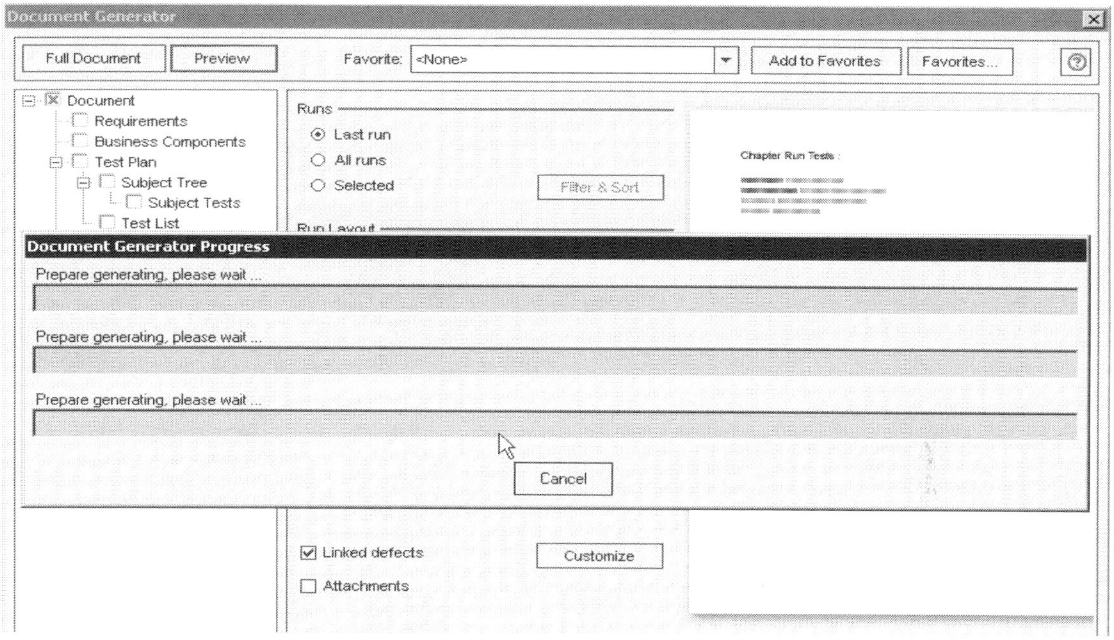

Figure 4.16 *Document Generator Progress Bar Window.*

- *Excel report:* As how document generator helps in generating document for required details stored within HP QC 10, likewise, excel report also helps in transporting HP QC stored data set into .xls report.

  Select any such details required and accordingly, the data set can be exported to .xls format.

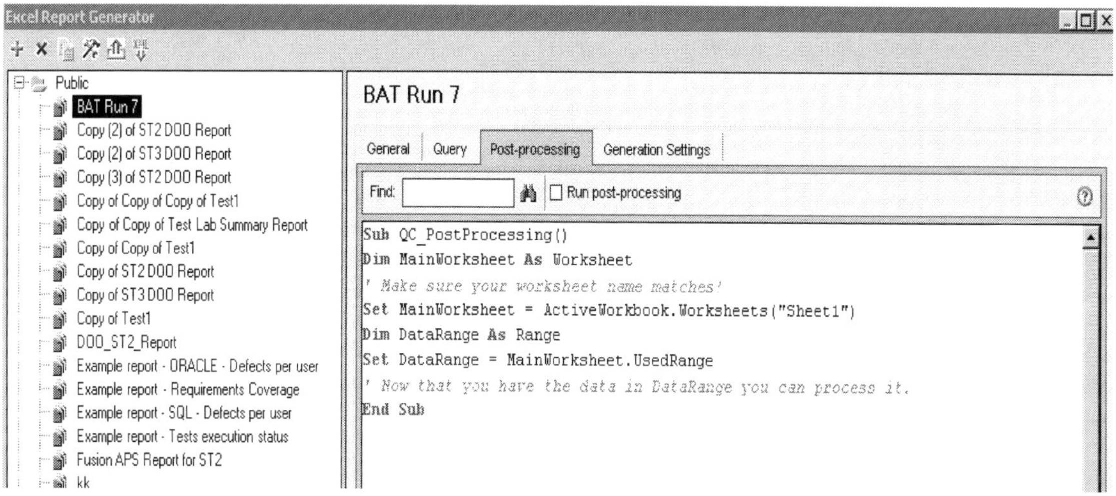

Figure 4.17 *Excel Report UI.*

- *Dashboard:* This particular component is an add-on component that needs to be bought separately from HP. This component helps in tracking application readiness and managing projects and risk in real time scenarios.

4.2.3 Panel to Move into Different Areas of HP QC

The menus reflected in frame 3 are the areas where user can navigate through based on the business requirement one has.

- *Release:* Under this section, one can go and define release and cycle
- *Requirements:* Under this section, one can go and define requirements
- *Test Plan:* Test Plan is an area where one can create test cases and store relevant details pertaining to that test case, either manual or automated.
- *Test lab:* Under this area, one can execute test cases, both manual and automated.

All these areas will be talked through in detail in further chapters.

The other areas that you see in frame 3 snapshot in Fig. 4.3 are customized one. Besides what you see in Fig. 4.18, HP QC 10 vanilla flavor should reflect two more areas, i.e., defect tracking and reports.

Figure 4.18 *Part of Frame 3 as per Fig. 4.3.*

4.2.4 Folder Structure Layout Philosophy

As you can see in Fig. 4.3, tree like structure area is primarily to align all the details in tree like structure, for easy traceability. Tree like structure can be formed based on specific business needs or organisational process.

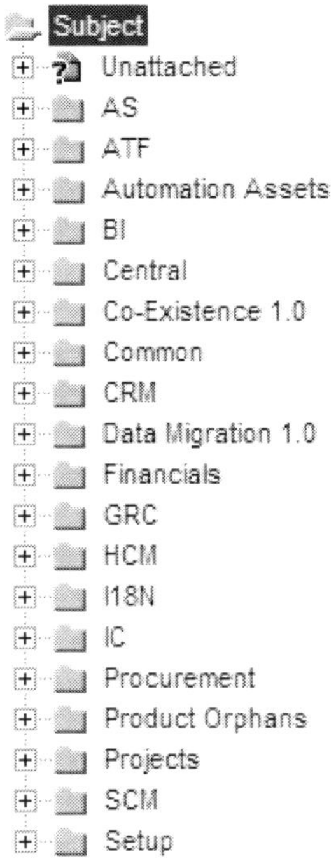

Figure 4.19 *Frame 4 as per Fig. 4.3.*

4.2.5 Description Container Overview

Description and attachment containers provide flexibility to capture user inputs as well as external files. Let us see if any child, under test plan area is selected then how the UI appears.

Figure 4.20 *Frame 5 as per Fig. 4.3.*

4.2.6 Short Cut Icons Overview

This frame is primarily to give users options to exercise few critical operations via so-called shortcut icons.

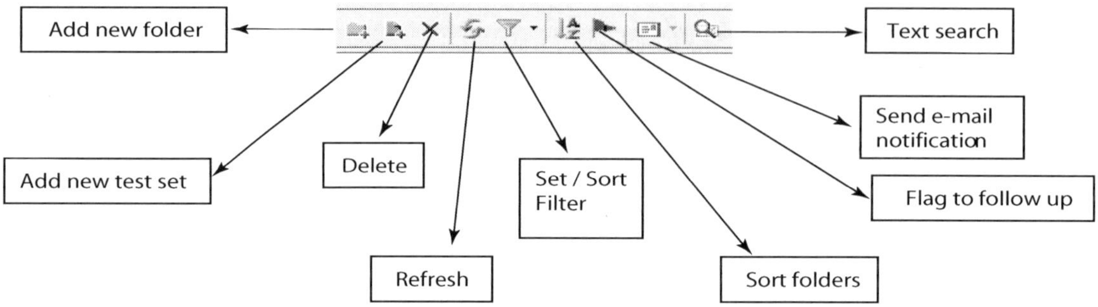

Figure 4.21 *Frame 6 as per Fig 4.3.*

- *Add new folder:* As the name suggests this is a short cut icon to add new folder across HP QC 10, in relevant areas such as test plan, test lab, etc.
- *Add new test set:* As the name suggests, this is a short cut icon to add new test set in test lab area
- *Refresh:* This feature reloads the page and panel with current data set.
- *Set/Sort filter:* This option provides flexibility for setting filter criteria for quick search and sort
- *Sort folders:* This provides an option to sort folder either in A-Z sequence or vice versa.
- *Send e-mail notification:* As the name suggests, select any tests or other detail, and click on this option to send that detail via email attachment to required user. The only caution here is that email client should be configured on both client and server machines.
- *Text search:* This is to search for any text within the tree like structure either in test plan area or test lab area.
- *Flag to follow up:* This is one of the interesting features that you should pay special heed to. Primarily this option is set to trigger an alert. HP QC 10 can generate alerts on these changes:
    - Requirement changes either modify, update or delete
    - Defect changes
    - Test execution status change

4.2.7 Other Short Cut Keys Description and Analysis Tab

Frame 7 again is the short cut keys to navigate to and search tests. The only interesting area in this tab-bar is "analysis", which in turn provides option to generate various kinds of reports.

4.3 User Management In HP QC 10

HP QC 10 provides several levels of access privileges. Primarily, it is the job of the HP QC 10 admin to set the required privileges to specific usernames, depending upon the role and business requirement they need to be used for.

In order to customize user HP QC 10 privileges, go to *"Tools -> Customize"*, below displayed window opens up.

Figure 4.22 *User Management Page.*

Click user properties. This will open up a frame where the username credentials which you have entered, will be displayed. In user properties window, you can change or modify user details, based on the access privilege one holds.

Figure 4.23 *User Properties Window.*

The other link, at the left hand frame, that you see in Fig. 4.23 is of "Project users". On clicking this link, project users window displays where all the users registered within that project are enlisted. The privileges that each user has, also get enlisted.

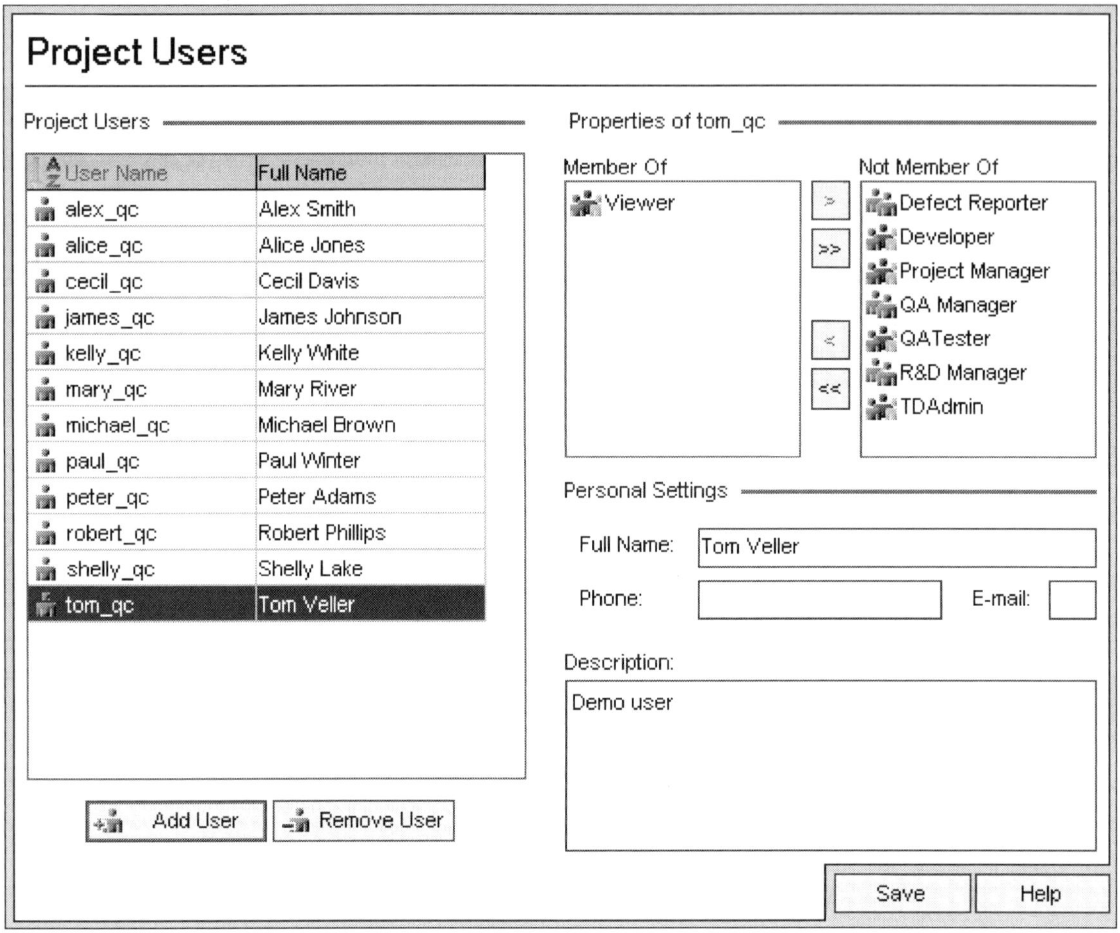

Figure 4.24 *Project Users' Permission Details Page.*

Primarily, there are 5 important types of permissions that can be granted in HP QC 10. Besides these 5, for the rest admin can customize the access permission level and hence grant the same to users.

- *TD Admin:* User with this privilege has full access control over HP QC 10.
- *Project Manager:* This user has full access privilege under Release, requirement, test plan, test lab and defects. This user also has privileges to set alert rules. Additionally, this user can also grant privileges to other project users in his/her domain. This user can also change user id and password for other project users.
- *QA tester:* This user has full privileges under release, requirements, test plan, and test lab. In defects area, this user can add or modify defects and defect links. This user also has privileges

to set alert rules. Additionally, this user can also customize project users and accordingly set or modify their user id and password.

- *Developer:* Such kind of users can only modify attachments or record details in requirements, test plan and test lab. It is worth noting that this user has full permissions in release module. These users can also add and modify defects and defect links. Nonetheless, these users can just change the user id and password for project users.
- *Viewer:* Such kind of users have just *"read only privileges"* in HP QC

HP Quality Center 10: Release and Requirement Management

5

Chapter Objectives: This chapter will give an overview of

- *Release feature*
- *"Requirements" feature*
- *Full frame and attributes — "Cycle"*

5.1 Release Feature

The very first step in planning for a quality release of a product is to identify all required activities and set completion date of each. All such completion dates, when considered in unison, give a final release date.

On the same philosophy, defining release in HP QC 10 helps you tie up all the activities pertaining to that release. All such activities are divided into cycle. Therefore, for each release, there are two major cycles that are created — one is development and the other is testing. It is not mandatory just to have these two, but depending upon the organisational needs, there may be many such activities that need closer tracking, and hence can be termed as cycle.

5.1.1 Define Release in HP QC 10

In this section, let us see how can "release and cycle be defined".

Step 1) Login to QC in the respective domain and project.

Step 2) Click "Release" menu item at the left hand side.

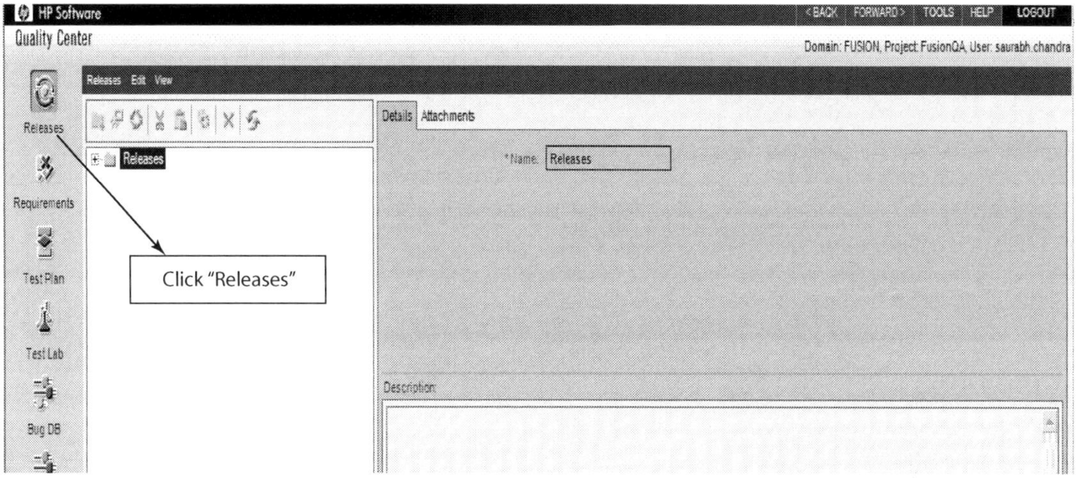

Figure 5.1 *Release Page.*

The page, that you see in Fig. 5.1, comes up. "Releases" folder is displayed on this page. Within that folder, you can create the release name that needs to be tracked.

Please note, "Releases" folder name can be re-named also, but only by HP QC admin.

Step 3) Right click the "Releases" folder, and you would see the menu bar gets populated where you get an option to create new folder. New folder means, within releases folder you want to create a new release.

Note: All such menu options, as displayed in Fig. 5.2 will grey out, if the user does not have the relevant QC privileges and hence can't perform any operation related to grey out field.

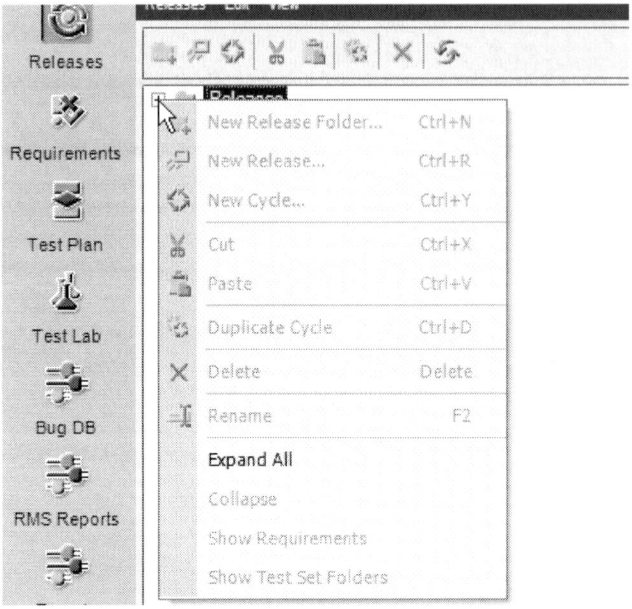

Figure 5.2 *Grey Out Menu Options.*

Step 4) Click "New release folder" option to get new release folder window where you can give the release name. For reference, I'm giving the release folder name as "Fusion".

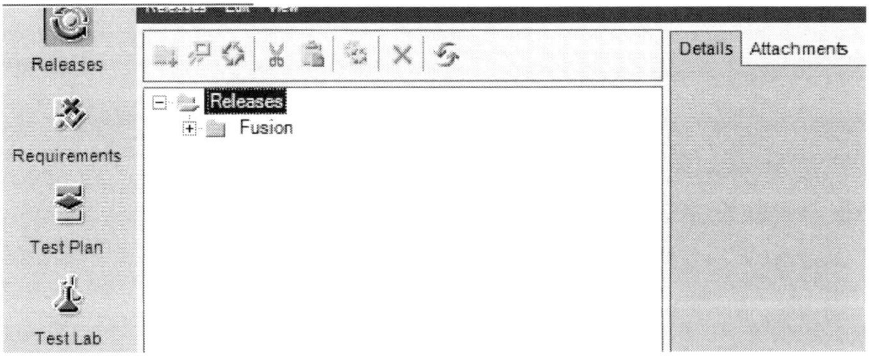

Figure 5.3 *Release Folder Named as "Fusion".*

Step 5) Again right click "Fusion" folder and select "New release". This is to create new release under "Fusion" folder. You can create more than one release. After you create the same, it would look like what is shown in Fig 4.

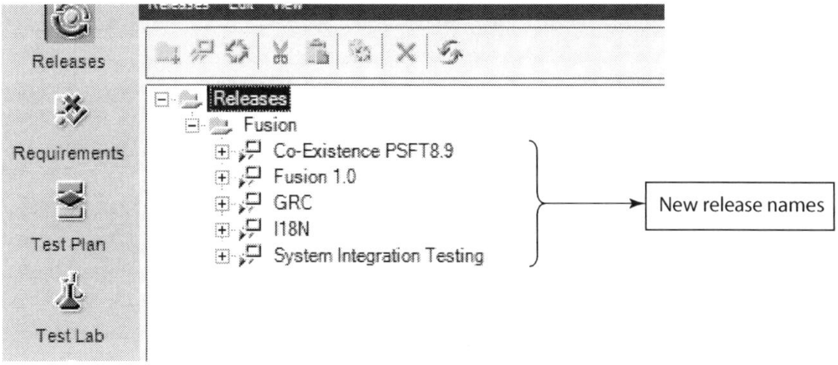

Figure 5.4 *New Releases.*

Step 6) Right click any of the release name and then select "Create cycle". Relevant cycle under that release will be created.

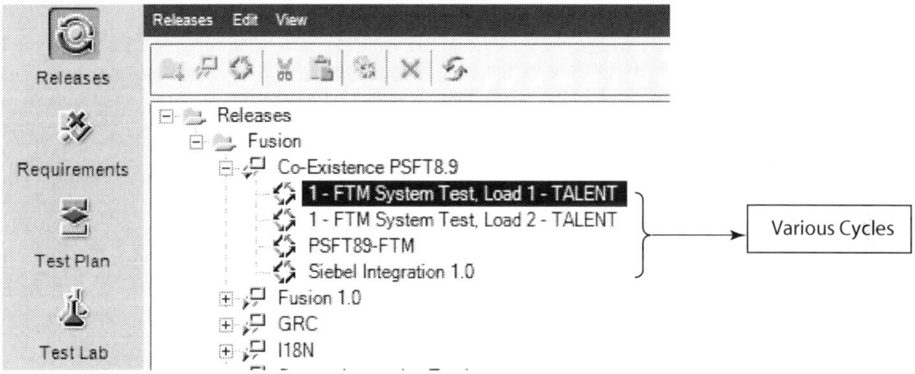

Figure 5.5 *Cycle.*

This equips you with the knowledge of release creation and cycle creation technique in HP QC 10.

5.2 Full Frame and Attributes — "Cycle"

As in Fig. 5.5, the current displayed window is just a partial window, which enlists the names of various "cycle". Let us see the full window and understand other features or detailing that can be clubbed in, with cycle frame.

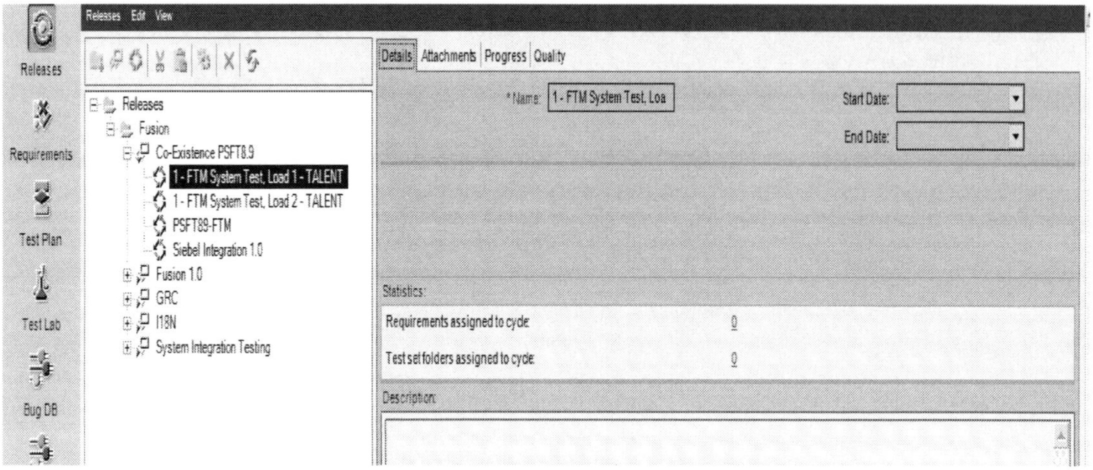

Figure 5.6 *Complete View of "cycle" Frame.*

All the requirements, test cases and defects get associated to the cycle and hence in turn "Release"; therefore, the panel where such events can be tracked is shown in Fig. 5.6.

- **Details** tab, as in Fig. 5.6, shows the start date and end date when this cycle was created. Additionally, it provides number of requirements this cycle holds. It also displays the number of test set in test lab area associated with this cycle.
- **Attachments** tab acts as a container where if you have any other relevant files to associate with cycle, then one can do so under attachments tab.

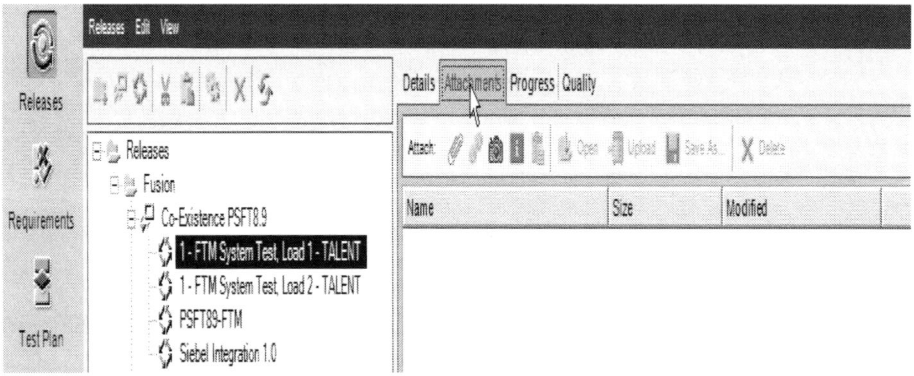

Figure 5.7 *Attachments Tab Details.*

If one does not have the required privileges, then all the tabs in attachment area will grey out and will not allow user to perform any operation.

- **Progress** tab, provides synopsis of the progress of events happening within that cycle.

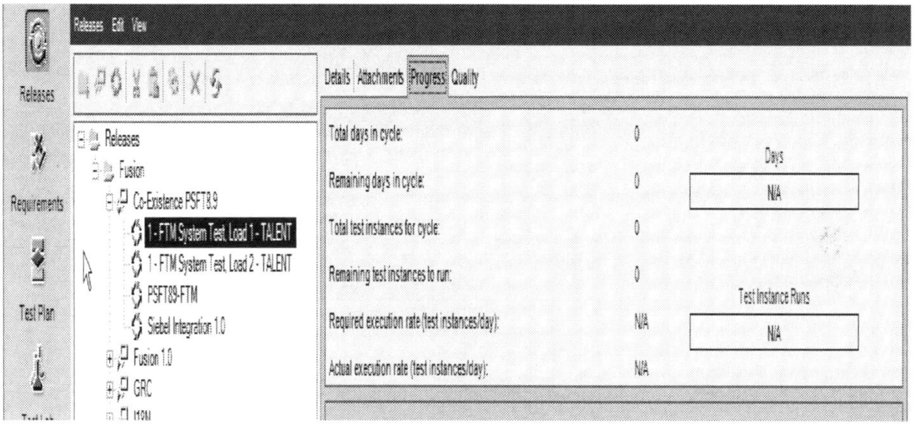

Figure 5.8 *Progress Tab Details.*

This section provides you with these basic answers which management looks for on a daily basis:

- Total days in cycle
- Remaining days in cycle
- Total test instance for cycle
- Remaining test instances to run
- Required execution rate (test instances / day)
- Actual execution rate / day

- **Quality** tab provides detailing about two major data sets:
  - *Defect opening rate:* This depicts total number of bugs found during that cycle
  - *Outstanding defect:* This depicts, out of total bugs found, number that is still open.

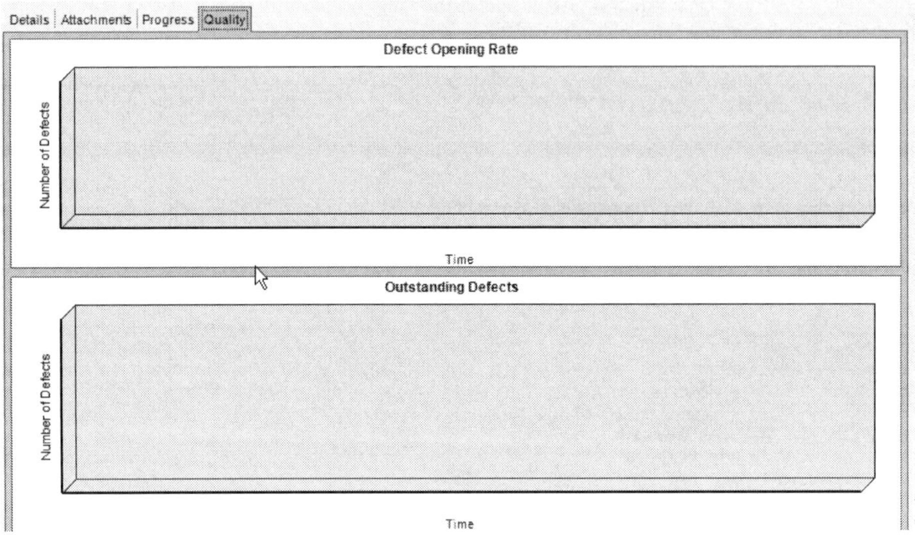

Figure 5.9 *Graph For Quality Tab.*

It may be noted that since there is no data available for this cycle, the graph shown in Fig. 5.9 is empty.

5.3 "Requirements" Feature

This is that area of HP QC 10, where all the strategy, roadmap and finer detailing of complete testing process for a particular cycle and release is stored.

Let us see what all different operations that can be conducted in requirements section of HP QC 10.

5.3.1 Define Requirements

Step 1) Under "Requirements" work area, there is a folder named "Requirements". One can either click "new folder" icon at the top of the image or can right click and select option to create new requirements folder.

Additionally, the parent folder name "Requirements" can be re-named, but only by HP QC admin.

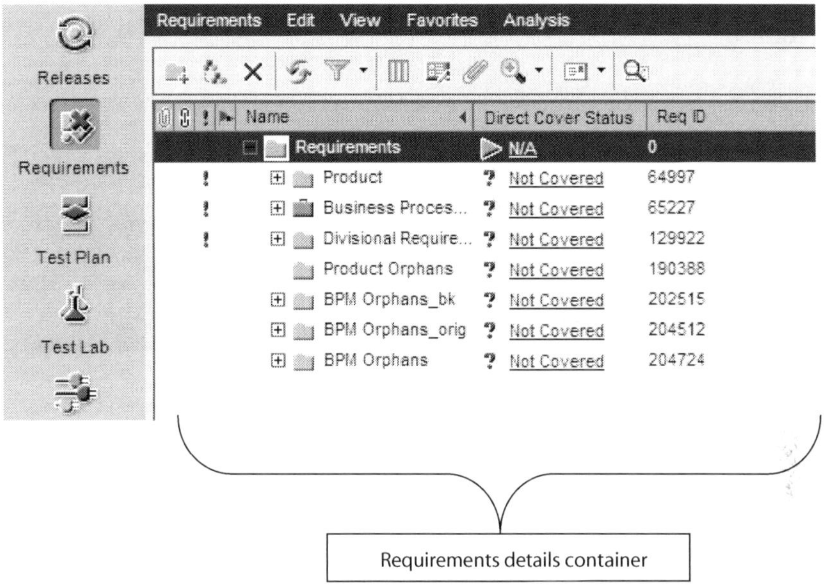

Figure 5.10 *Requirements Work Area View.*

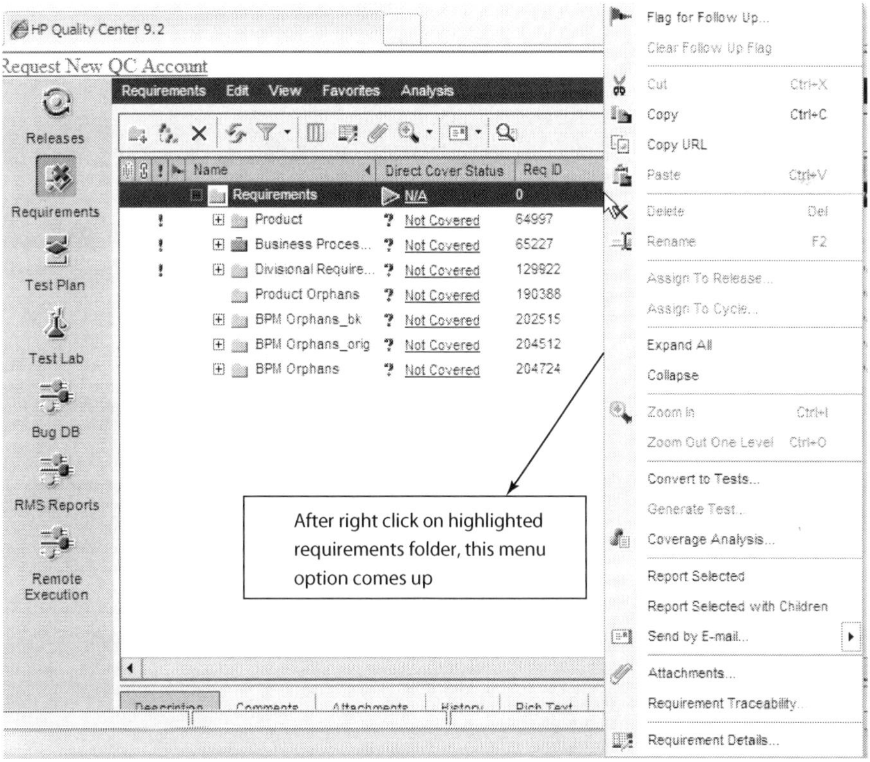

Figure 5.11 *Right Click The "Requirements" Folder and Get Options.*

Step 2) Clicking on "new requirement folder creation" option, below window pops up.

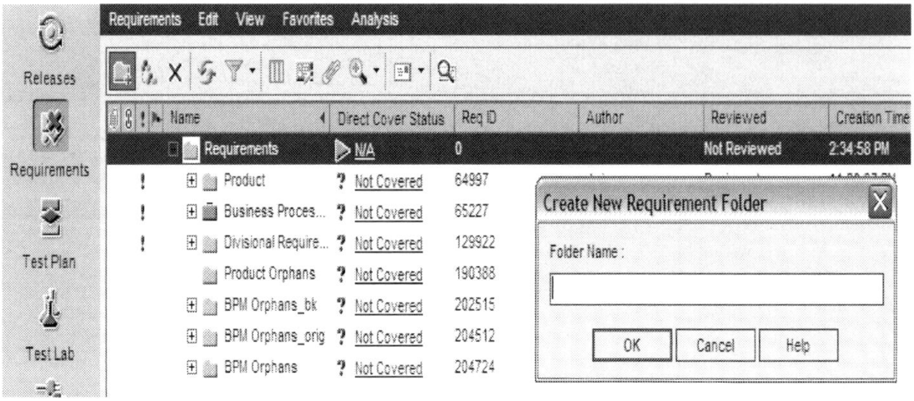

Figure 5.12 *Input Requirement Folder Name.*

Let us keep the requirement name to be RCE (Requirement creation example). Write it and click "OK". You can see RCE folder is created under "Requirements parent directory".

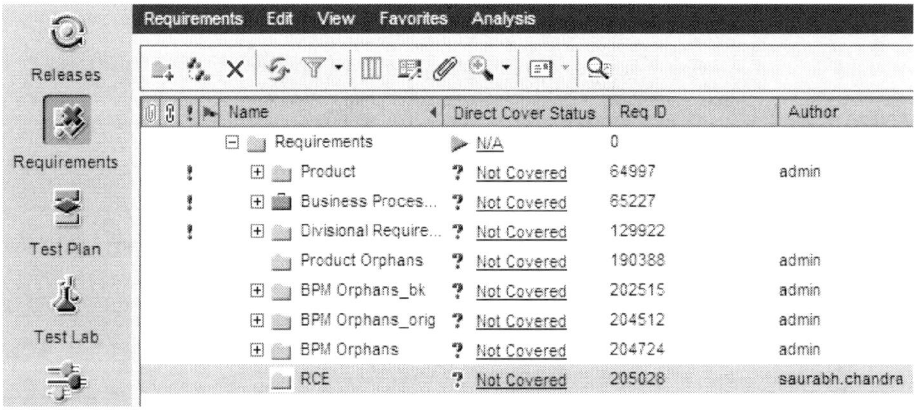

Figure 5.13 *RCE Folder Creation.*

Step 3) Double click the "RCE" folder, and the requirement details window comes up.

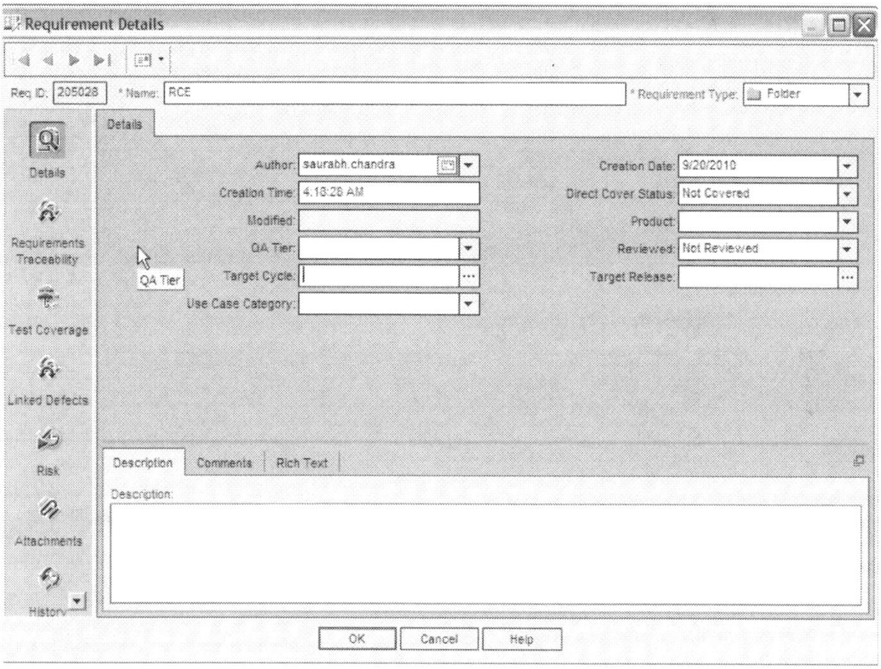

Figure 5.14 *Requirement Details Window.*

Here you would observe that automatically few fields get auto populated.

- Creation time
- Creation date
- Direct cover status
- Reviewed

These fields are populated based on the system default.

For other relevant fields, we need to input details. Important aspect here is that via this window, one can associate relevant cycle and release.

Click "Target Cycle" field. All cycles get auto populated.

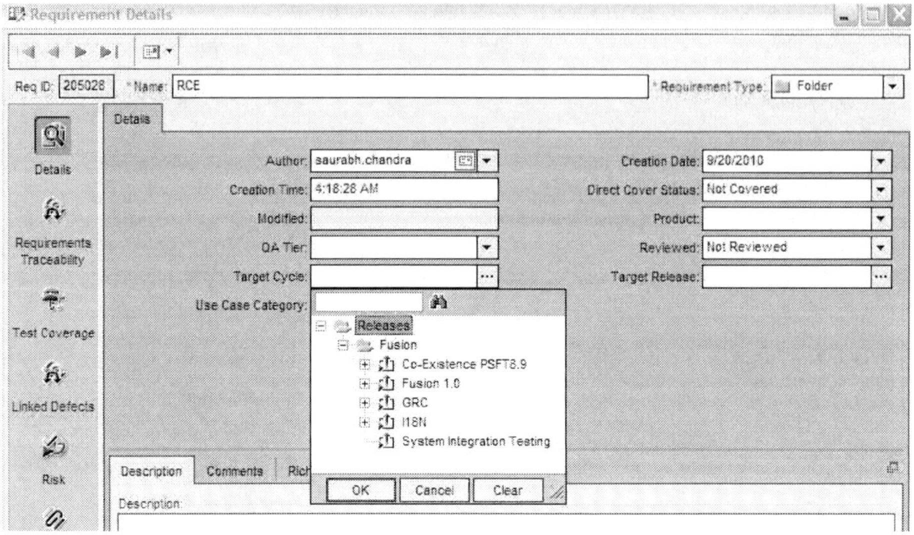

Figure 5.15 *"Target cycle" Option.*

Select one.

Likewise, in "target release" field, select the one you want to associate with this requirement.

Select the checkbox and click ok.

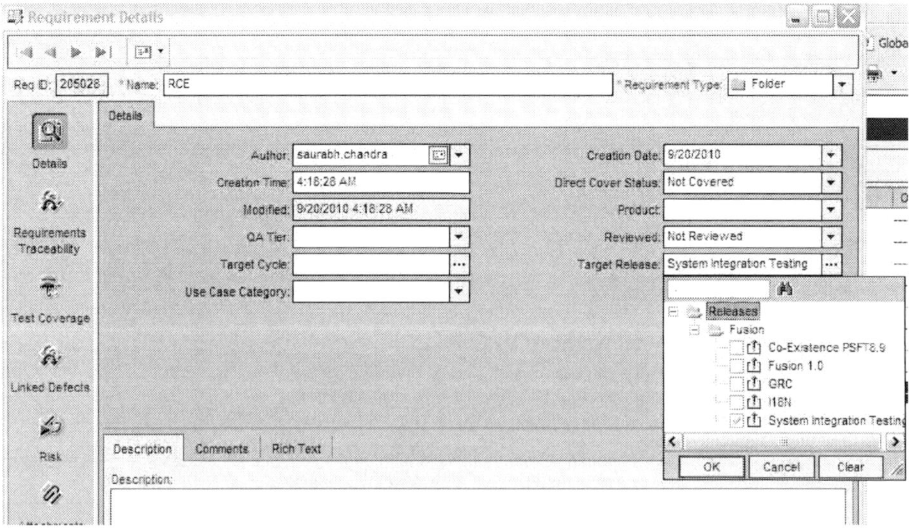

Figure 5.16 *"Target release option" Window.*

Once all these details have got filled in, then you can click “Ok” on requirements details page. The requirements get defined.

Step 4) However, this is not the complete requirement definition that has taken place. In practical situations, you would want to place some child under the defined requirements. Therefore, to create one, choose the icon as displayed below in Fig. 5.17, after selecting the RCE folder as this is that requirement for which you want to generate hierarchy.

Step 5) Click the “create child” icon and another window “create new requirement” comes up. In this window, you need to provide the requirement type. Requirement type can be user defined values that your admin and organisation would have defined.

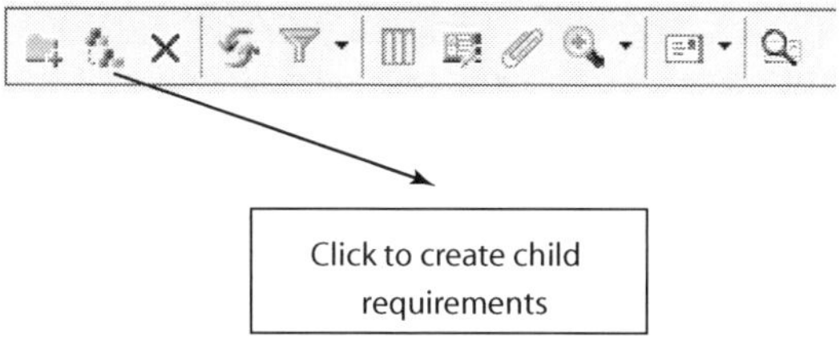

Figure 5.17 *Shortcut Panel.*

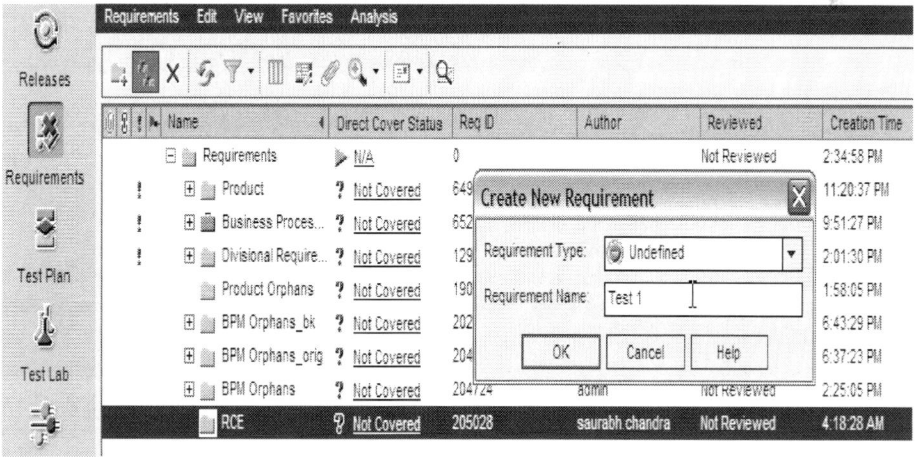

Figure 5.18 *Inputting Value to Create New Requirement Window.*

Click "Ok". Again the same requirement details page would open up where you need to define details as how we walked through in step 3.

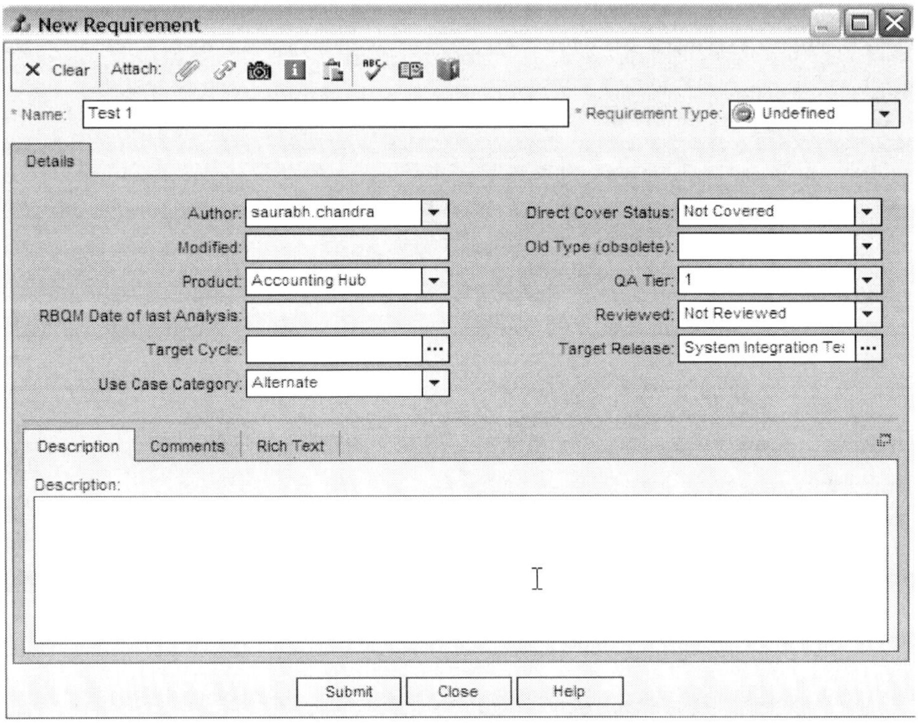

Figure 5.19 *Requirement Details for Child Item "Test 1".*

You can see the tree like structure being populated in the container area of requirements. (Refer Fig. 5.20). Your child item is created.

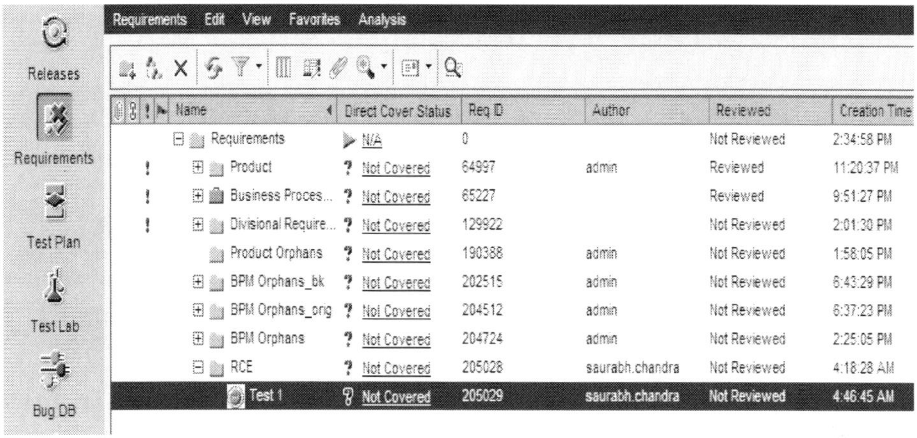

Figure 5.20 *RCE ® Test 1, Tree Like Structure Getting Created.*

5.3.2 View Requirements

In the earlier section, you have seen how to view the requirement history in "requirement details", but the question that would be tickling you is how to view the same after they have got already defined and stored.

Therefore, to view the "created requirements details", you can go to *"View-> Requirement details"*

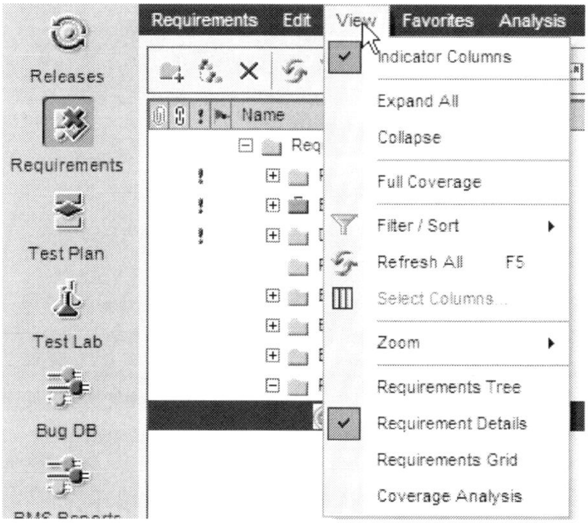

Figure 5.21 *View ® Requirement Details.*

And then, after selecting this option, the window frame changes. Left hand panel shows the selected requirement and right had panel shows the details.

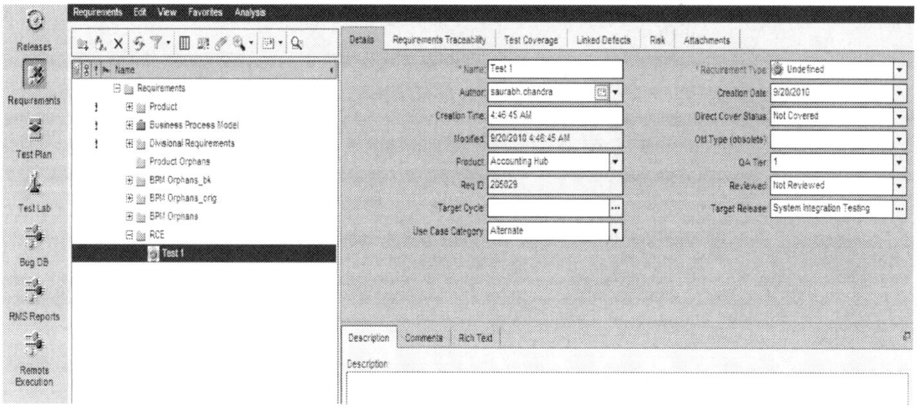

Figure 5.22 *Requirement Details.*

5.3.3 View Requirements → Coverage Analysis

As the data set and progress all are tightly coupled with requirements, therefore under requirements section, HP QC 10 provides the flexibility to have a single view to track the details.

In order to enable that view, you need to go to *"View -> Coverage analysis"* and hence select the same.

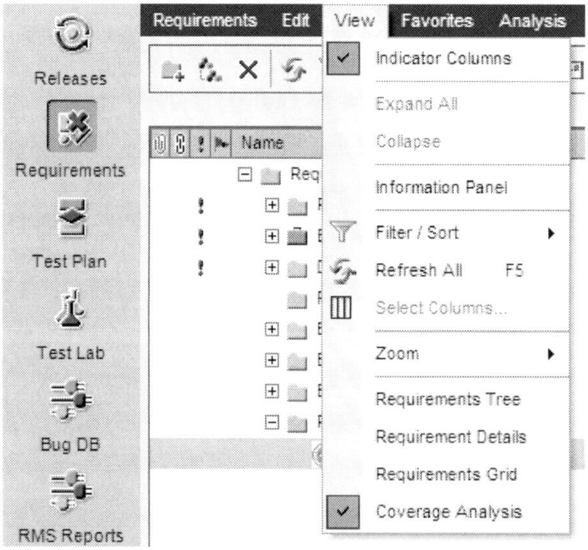

Figure 5.23 *View ® Coverage Analysis for Requirements.*

Coverage analysis window comes up. And this window provides you graphical representation of coverage and progress with respect to the selected requirement.

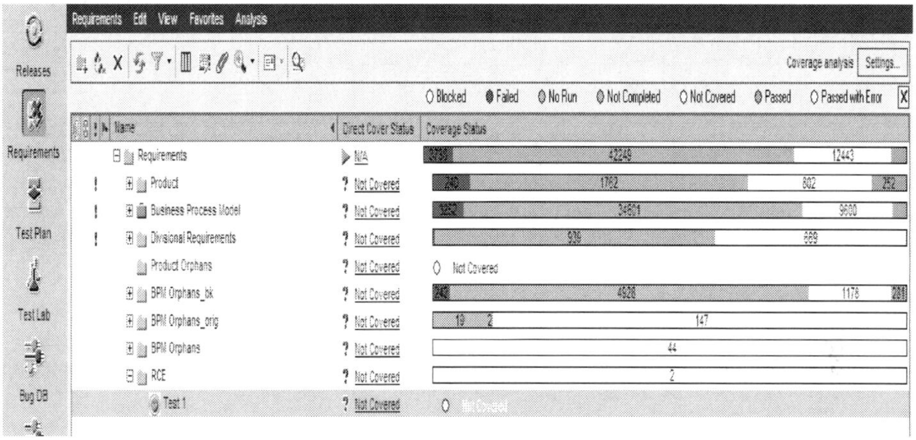

Figure 5.24 *Coverage Analysis Report.*

5.3.4 View → Requirements Grid

One special feature that HP QC 10 provides is the complete view of the requirements via a grid. All details that constitute part of all the defined required can be viewed in a single grid by selecting *"View-> requirements grid".*

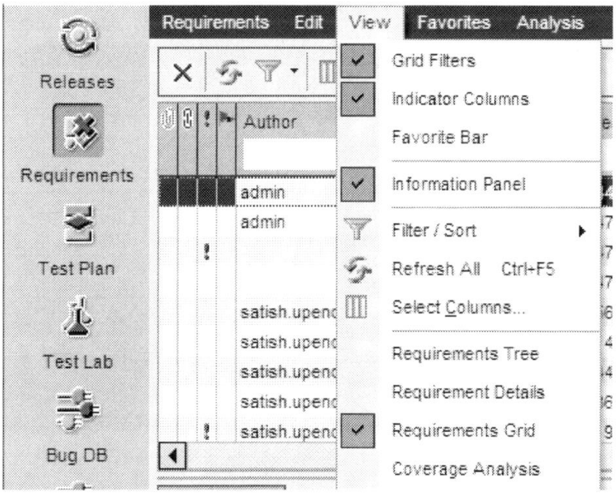

Figure 5.25 *"Requirements grid" Menu Item.*

Below displayed window comes up once "view-> requirements grid" is selected.

Additionally, if you want to configure the view, you can select the field by clicking "select field" option.

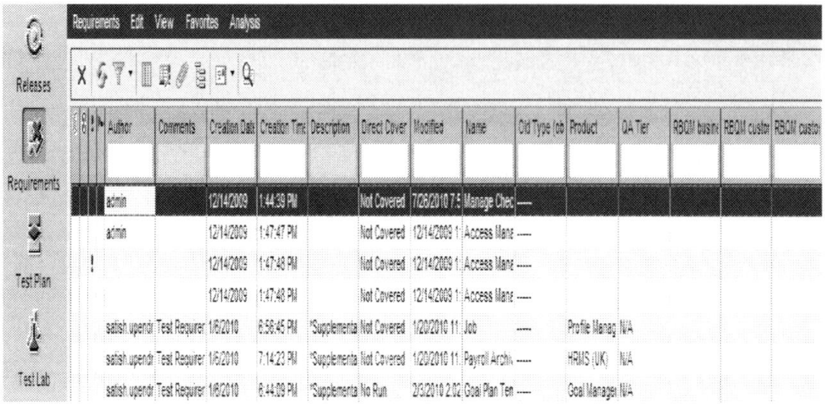

Figure 5.26 *Requirements Grid.*

Whichever value you pull in to the right panel that will get reflected as one of the columns in the requirements grid.

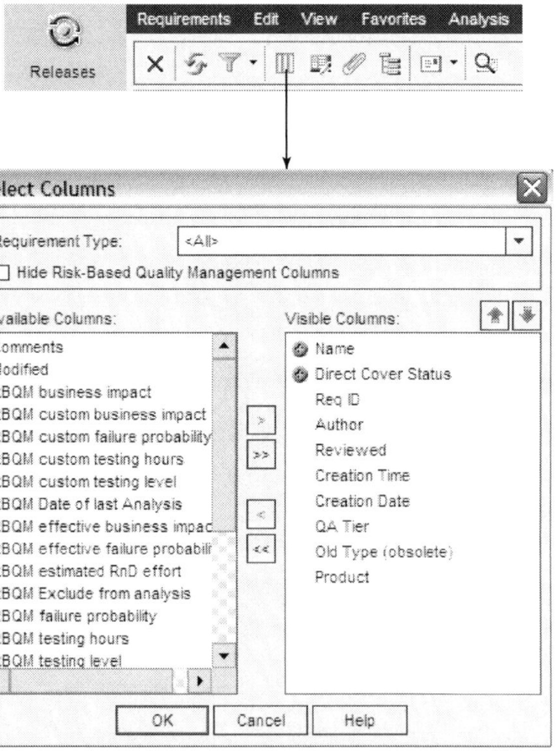

Figure 5.27 *Select Field Option.*

Requirements grid, in Fig. 5.26, provides a single view to know about all exhaustive details about the requirement under check.

6

HP Quality Center 10: Test Planning — Non QC Approach

Chapter Objectives: This chapter will give an overview of

- *Basic Definitions of all the components involved in preparation of "Functional Test Scripts"*
- *Pyramid Model: Co-relation of components of functional test scripts*
- *Input Criteria for "Test Scripts"*
- *Case Study to understand designing and implementing test scripts in real time scenario*

Introduction

One of the most important HP QC 10 features is test script and test case designing and creation process. However, the history and basics of test case designing was prevalent much before the advent of HP QC 10. Therefore, before I touchbase the test case designing feature of HP QC 10, it is essential to understand the basics behind designing test cases. In this chapter, I would take you through the test script and test designing concepts without bringing HP QC 10 in discussion. If you can understand the philosophy behind laying out test case design strategy without HP QC 10, then it will become a seamless ride to understand the same through HP QC 10.

6.1 Overview: Pyramid Model

6.1.1 Definition of "Manual Test Script"

A document, which states all the cases that a tester will traverse while automating the test or while manually executing the test, is known as "Manual Test Script". The minimum bare elements for Manual Test Script should consist of "Test Case ID", "Navigational Step", "Action to Perform", "Expected Output", and "Salient Checkpoint".

6.1.2 Definition of "Test Case"

Collection of individual actions within test scenarios, which are written in most comprehensible manner, is termed as "Test Case".

6.1.3 Correlation amongst Test Case, Test Scenario, Test Script, Feature and Application

Let us try to understand Fig. 6.1.

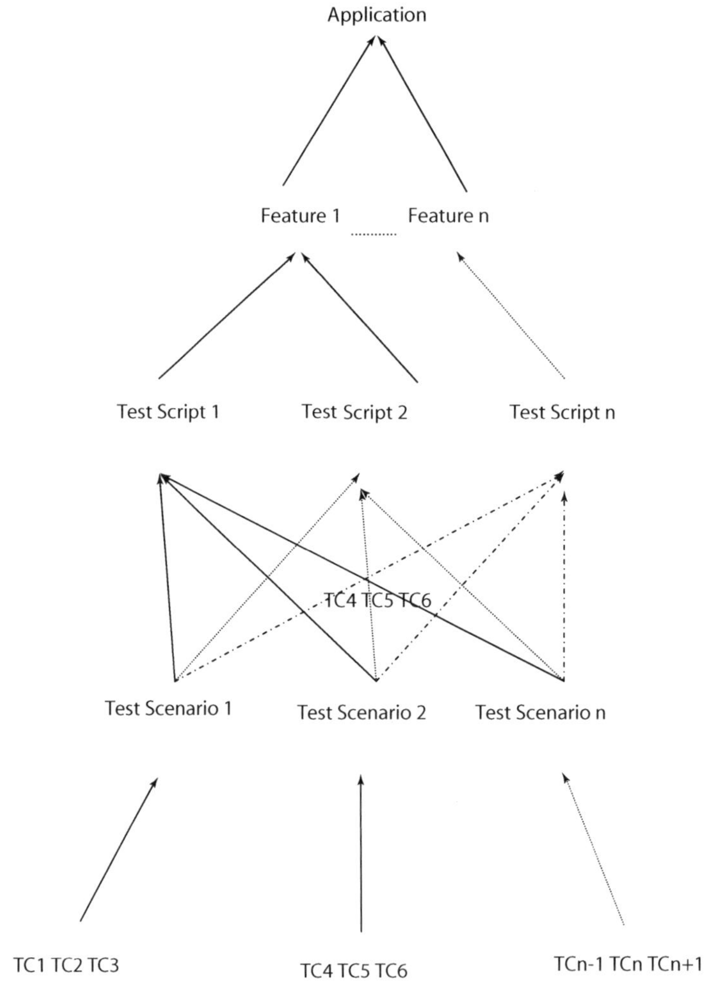

Figure 6.1 *Pyramid Model: Correlation Amongst "Test Case", "Test Script", "Test Scenario", "Feature" and "Application".*

Figure 6.1 explains the correlation between each, i.e., "Test Case", "Test Scenario", "Test Script", "Feature" and "Application".

- Collection of individual actions within test scenarios, which are written in most comprehensible manner, can be termed as "Test Case". Each action corresponds to one test case.
- Compilation of several test cases constitutes a "Test scenario".
- Compilation of several test scenarios constitutes a "Test Script".
- One Test Script is compilation of either one or more important functionalities of the application.
- Compilation of various functionalities can be termed as "Feature" of the application.
- The software product, which either needs to be given to customers or needs to be used in-house or needs to be released into the market, is known as "Application".

Let us take a real time case where these can be defined properly.

Case Study 1: Mr. Paul has developed an application *X*, which has these many features embedded into it.

- Mail Engine
- General News
- Stock Market News

Feature "Mail engine" has these many "functionalities":

- Send/Receive Mail
- Attachments
- Contact Book
- Sent Folder

These functionalities can be prepared as an individual "Test Scripts" having n [where n = {1 to infinity}] no. of test scenarios depicting n no. of cases.

Now, let us see various scenarios for each functionality:

1. Send/Receive Mail
   (a) Sign-in
   (b) Compose and send
   (c) Sent folder contents
   (d) Receive
2. Attachments
   (a) Sign-in
   (b) Compose
   (c) Send and attach files
   (d) Sent folder contents

3. Contact Book
   (a) Sign–in
   (b) Contact book
   (c) Add contact
   (d) Edit contact
4. Sent Folder
   (a) Sign-in
   (b) Compose and send
   (c) Sent folder contents

Clubbing the scenarios under their respective functionality can be termed as one test script.

Therefore in conclusion, in the above case, we can term:
Application name as: Application *X*
Features as: Mail Engine
Functionality as: Send / Receive mail, Attachments, Contact Book, Sent folder
Test Scenarios under functionality send/receive mail as: Sign-in, Compose and send, sent folder contents, receive.

Similarly, let us take the example of another feature named "General news". "General news" has these many functionalities.

- Daily News
- Archive
- Most Read Articles

Again, these functionalities can be prepared as an individual "Test Scripts" having *n* [where *n* = {1 to infinity}] no. of test scenarios depicting *n* no. of cases.

For better clarification, let us define the various scenarios against each functionality:

1. Daily News
   (a) Featured
   (b) Entertainment
   (c) Sports
   (d) Business
2. Archive
   (a) Filter datewise
   (b) Filter Topicwise
   (c) Filter most read articles

3. Most Read Articles
   (a) More

   Therefore, clubbing the scenarios under their respective functionality can be termed as one test script.

Therefore, in conclusion, in the above case, we can term:
Application name as: Application *X*
Features as: General News
Functionality as: Daily News, Archive, Most Read Articles
Test Scenarios under functionality send/receive mail as: Featured, Entertainment, Sports, Business, Filter Date Wise, Filter Topic Wise, Filter most read articles, More

Similarly, coming back to another feature named "Stock Market News", let us define the functionalities:

- Daily News
- Most Traded stock in last 5 days
- World exchange news

It will be a task for you to brainstorm as what can be the test scenario for each and hence conclude what can be termed as Application Name, Feature, Functionality and test scenarios, for feature "Stock Market News".

This, in totality, explains everything about what test script contains and the correlation between each component of *pyramid model* (refer Fig. 6.1). Let us move on to the next section that will talk about identifying input criteria for test script and hence test case.

6.2 Input Criteria for Test Case

The other logical question that will come up to your mind would be "What is the basis for identifying valid test cases or preparing effective test scripts?"

Before apprehending over the above question, let us try understanding the software industry segmentation pertaining to various lines of business.

Software industry basically consists of two different segments of business. Broadly, one can be termed as the "Services industry" and other can be termed as the "Product industry".

Companies that basically take software related work from other vendors, constitute the Services industry. For Ex: Infosys, Tata Consultancy Services, etc.

Product industry comprises those companies, which develop their own product and sell it into global market. For Ex: Microsoft, Oracle, SAP, etc.

As you have gained the basic difference between these two industry segments, it will be more viable to pick up the question as "What is the basis for identifying valid test cases or preparing effective test scripts?"

The basis to identify valid test cases or draft effective test scripts differs in both segmentation of software industry. Let us see the valid scenario for each one in detail.

6.2.1 Software Services Industry

In software services industry, first the business analyst along with account manager and unit head bid for various kinds of work from various customers.

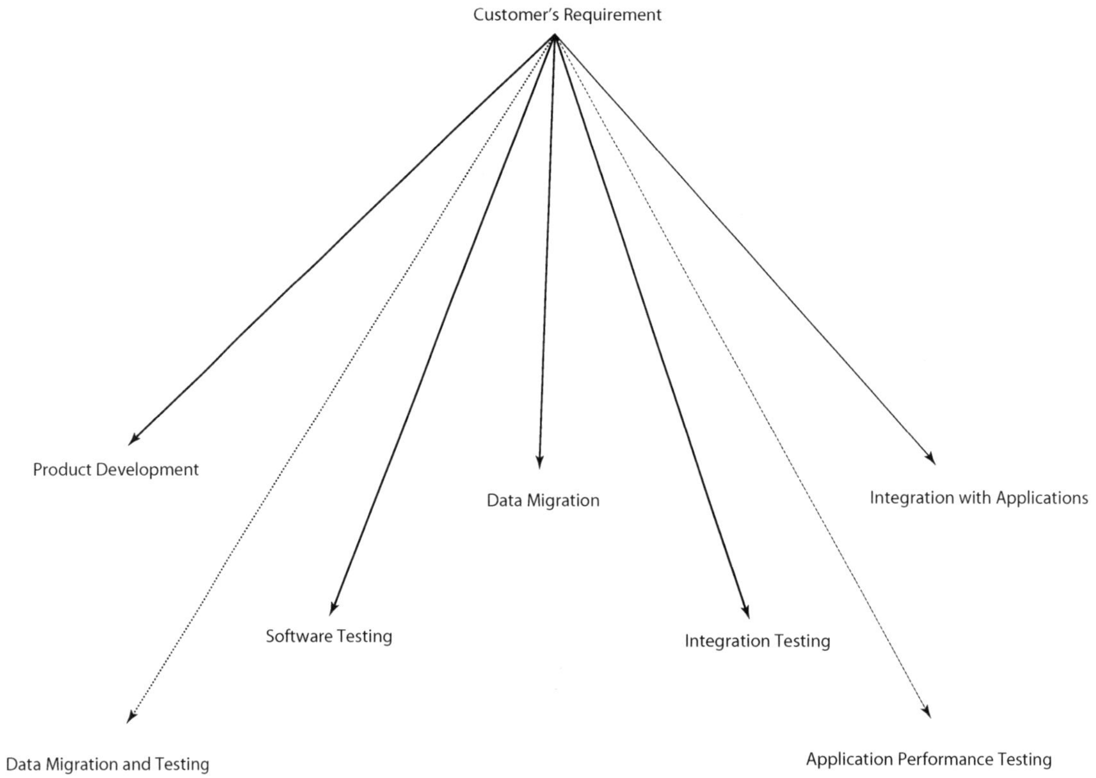

Figure 6.2 *Various Kinds of Customer's Requirement.*

After the bid is converted into deal, services company starts working on "Requirement Gathering" from customers. Let us assume that the deal got finalized for functional testing of an application *A*.

Now the company, which is performing the testing for the customer, would ask about three basic documentations:

- *Use case documentation:* This documentation talks about the cases which user will experience while traversing through the application or software product.
- *Business case documentation:* This documentation contains the business requirements pertaining to application functionality.
- *Functional documentation:* This documentation describes the functional flow of the application or software product.

  Besides these, company would also require:
- *Development environment simulating the production environment:* This is application environment, which simulates the application when deployed into production environment.

However, when business analyst receives the above-said documentation, then accordingly project manager is informed to start working on Test Plan detailing.

Once Test Plan is ready, then the team is provided with all the three documentations and referring to all the three, team drafts the test scripts.

Therefore, Use Case Documentation, Business Case documentation and Functional documentation become the input criteria for drafting test scripts.

6.2.2 Software Product Companies

You are aware that product companies design, implement and release their own products across the global market. Therefore, within this industry, product development life cycle passes through various phases and one of the phases in this complete SDLC is "Product Testing". Of course, product can be tested for both functional domain and performance domain.

For performance domain, the input criterion for test scripts is basically the TDD's, i.e., Technical Design Documents, public API's, approximate performance behavior of each functionality load statistics of the functionalities, load statistics of the application and breakpoint of the application. All these are converted into test cases in order to test the performance of the product thoroughly.

However, for functional testing domain, there are several scenarios that one needs to keep in mind before identifying the input criteria for drafting test script.

- *Scenario 1: Product isn't released*

This scenario talks about a situation where product isn't released into the market and is currently under the development stage. Now, automation strategist or functional manager needs to get the required

"FDD's" and "User Guide" to the tester who would be drafting test scripts. For effective testing, it will also be essential for the manager to prioritize the features and functionalities that need to be drafted first. Accordingly, in each build appropriate test scripts and test cases will be pushed into.

- *Scenario 2: Product is released into the market and is there for some time.*

In this situation, several details become input criteria for test case drafting. First, of course, it will be FDD's along with user guide of that product that a tester would need. In addition to that, tester would also require to analyze customer bugs logged till date and to identify appropriate cases pertaining to various features. Furthermore, if various fixes are released then tester would also require guidance from development team for the areas where regression probability is high. Therefore, in sum, FDD + Userguide + Customer bug analysis + development team input for regressions would suffice the input criteria for drafting appropriate test scripts for this scenario.

- *Scenario 3: Next version of existing product to be released as new product*

In this situation, again tester needs to get the FDD's and user guide for that product. Especially tester would require enhancement documentation which clearly talks about each enhancement. In addition to this, integration point should be specified clearly within FDD's or TDD's and accordingly tester needs to identify valid cases pertaining to those integration points. Furthermore, tester needs to refer to earlier logged bugs of customer for earlier version of the product and from there tester needs to analyze the most usable feature that customer generally uses on regular basis and hence draft cases revolving around those. Nonetheless, tester would also require development team input in terms of knowing about possible regression points. Therefore, for this scenario, in sum, FDD + TDD + Enhancement guide + Customer bugs on earlier release + Integration points + Regression points, would suffice the input criteria for effective test scripts and hence test cases.

6.3 Body of Manual Test Script

From the definition of "Manual Test Script", you would have become aware as how critical this document would be for the organisation. Therefore, it is very important that the whole body of this document should be prepared in a well-structured manner. If this document is well structured then at the time of crisis, this helps organisation to retrieve critical information with much ease.

6.3.1 Understanding Components of "Manual Test Script"

Let us once again refer to case study 1 (section 6.1.3) and hence try understanding all the important components of a "Test Script".

Extension of Case Study 1: Mr. Paul has developed an application X, which has "Mail engine" as one of the features. Mail engine is completely ready, and Mr. Paul wants to get a Manual Test Script for checking one of the functionalities of "Mail engine", named "Send/Receive mail". Therefore, Mr. Paul assigns the task of drafting "Test script" to one of his employees, named Mr. Smith.

Let us see as what is that minimum basic detailing that Manual Test Script document should certainly contain:

Prototype of Manual Test Script

1. **Topic of the Manual Test Script:** As the name suggests, this field contains the topic of "Test Script".
   For example: Send/Receive mail
2. **Test Objective:**
   This field should contain overall objective of testing this feature.
   For example: Objective of this document is to verify and validate the output produced by every action performed against this "Send/Receive mail" functionality of feature "Mail engine". Negative testing should also be performed to validate the "validations" that "Send/Receive mail" functionality should handle.
3. **Author Name:**
   This field should contain the name of the author who is drafting this Manual Test Script.
4. **Date of Creation (Start Date):**
   This field should contain the creation date of this document.
5. **Date of Completion (End Date):**
   This field should contain the completion date of this document.
6. **Release:**
   This field should contain the information about the "Release" cycle for which this test script is valid.
7. **Build:**
   This field should contain the information about both the build number, when test script creation task started and when test script got completed.
8. **Version:**
   This field should contain the latest version of this file. V0 means first draft, V1 means second draft; similarly version *n* {where *n* = 0, 1 to infinity) means *n*th draft.
9. **Author name for current version:**
   This field should contain the name of the author who has last updated this file. Let us say that version 0 was drafted by S. Chandra, V1 by N. Shahi and V2 by V. Ranjan. Then this field will contain name of V. Ranjan.
10. **Priority of this test script:**
    Priority in layman's terms can be defined as the importance of this test script in organisation's viewpoint keeping customer focus in mind. Priority can range from P1 to P4, P1 being the highest and

P4 being the lowest. Business analyst, who has done detailed homework pertaining to customer demands, basically assigns this priority.

11. **Location of supporting files or documentation:**
    This field should contain location for all supporting files such as Use Case Document, Business Case Document and Functional Document.
    Note: Refer to the definition of these documents within section 6.2.1.
12. **Location of this Test Script:**
    This field should contain the current storage location of this file.
13. **Change Record:**
    This field should contain a change record format, which would provide details about all the changes incorporated within this document along with the name of the person who updated the document.

The suggested format to capture change record is:

Tester's Name	***Date of Change***	***Test Case ID***	***Earlier Functionality/ Comment***	***New Functionality/ Comments***	***New Functionality Suggested By***

(b) *Tester's Name:* This field should contain the name of the person who found that change and incorporated within the test script.
(c) *Date of Change:* This field should contain the date when change was incorporated within the test script.
(d) *Test Case ID:* This field should contain the exact case number, which has got replaced or modified.
(e) *Earlier Functionality / Comment:* This field should contain the functionality, which is about to be, replaced or should contain some comments about the change that should be comprehendible enough to understand in later point of time.
(f) *New Functionality/Comment:* This field should contain description about the new functionality that needs to be incorporated within this test script.
(g) *New Functionality Suggested by:* This field should contain either the name of the person or the document or the reference or all, which led to this change.

14. **Reviewer:**
    This field should contain name of the reviewer who gave green signal to go ahead and use this for testing.
15. **Source Control (Y/N):**
    This field should be inputted with either "Yes" or "No" value.

16. **Source Control Location:**

    This field should contain location of source control of this file.

17. **Issue Logs:**

    This section should contain the details about the issue faced while drafting this test script or while traversing this test script during testing.

The suggested format to capture "Issue Log" is:

Tester's Name	***Date of Reporting the Issue***	***Reported Through***	***Issue Description***	***Comments***

(a) *Tester's Name:* This field should contain the name of the person who found that change and incorporated within the test script.

(b) *Date of Reporting the Issue:* This field should contain the exact date when issue was reported.

(c) *Reported Through:* This is an important column. Several organisations have *n* no. of ways to report an issue— for instance either through in-house bug logging tool, third party vendor's bug reporting too, mail, etc. Therefore, this field should contain the name of that mechanism through which bug has been reported.

(d) *Issue Description:* There exists two cases.

- o Case 1: Bug has been reported through bug logging tool and bug id is generated. Then, this field should contain that bug id
- o Case 2: Bug has been reported through mail, than a brief synopsis of issue needs to be provided.

(e) *Comments:* In case tester has any important additional comment to highlight, then this field should be used.

18. **Review comments:**

    This section is required either by automation professional who would be drafting automation scripts or by any third tester who would not have drafted this case but needs to traverse this during build testing. If automation expert or tester finds some anomalies in the stated steps then one should keep a record of the same using this section. This section can be used either as learning or as a checklist for test script author for the team.

The suggested format to capture "Review Comment" is:

Tester's Name	*Date of Reporting*	*Test Case ID*	*Issue Type*	*Issue Description*	*Additional Comments*	*Date of Resolution*

(a) *Tester's Name:* This field should contain name of the person who found that change and incorporated within the test script.

(b) *Date of Reporting:* This field should contain the exact date when issue was reported.

(c) *Test Case ID:* This field should contain the exact test case number where issue percolated.

(d) *Issue Type:* This is an important section. Let us see the most common type of issues and their descriptions, that generally arise in an organisation:

- o Test Case description Issue: Specific test case has not been written properly.
- o Data Issue: The data provided to navigate through the application does not match properly.
- o Flow missing issue: Various test cases are not in sequential integrated fashion as a result navigation breaks.
- o API Issue: Test Case does not talk about the specific API that needs to be executed before proceeding to next flow.
- o Setup Issue: Appropriate setup for the stated test cases has not been provided.

(e) *Issue Description:* This field should contain a synopsis of issue.

(f) *Additional Comments:* In case tester has any important additional comment to highlight, then this field should be used.

(g) *Date of Resolution:* This field should contain the date when appropriate resolution for the issue was found.

19. **Table of Contents:**

This section contains information about any kind of "Dependencies" such as precursor to this test script, screen shots to be studied before designing or executing the cases, etc. In addition to dependencies, this section provides the test scenario within which various test cases are drafted.

The suggested format, to capture test case details, is as follows:

Test Case ID	*Navigational Step*	*Action to Perform*	*Expected Output*	*Salient Checkpoint*	*Comments*

(a) *Test Case ID:* This is the unique id for every test case
(b) *Navigational Steps:* This field contains every minute detail about the step that needs to be navigated.
(c) *Action to Perform:* After detailed navigational step is provided, this field provides information about the action that needs to be performed on that page.
(d) *Expected Output:* After action has been performed, this field should contain details as what will be the outcome of that performed action.
(e) *Salient Checkpoint:* In case, one needs to verify or compare the output with any value, then that detail should be mentioned here.

6.3.2 Case Study to Explain Importance of "Test Script" Components

Now, let us see in real-time scenarios, how the above said "Test Script" format becomes helpful for the organisation, manual tester, automation expert and strategy maker.

Case study 2: With reference to *"Case study 1"* (section 6.1.3) and *"Extension of case study 1"* (section 6.3.1), we know that Mr. Smith is the person who is drafting the test script for the functionality "Send/Receive mail". Now, let us assume that Mr. Smith has drafted the test script between Build 1 and Build 4 of Release 1 of the product development cycle. This script then has been assigned to an automation expert for automation script development. Automation expert started developing this test script from Build 5 onwards. Suddenly, news breaks out that Mr. Smith would be leaving the organisation by the end of Build 5. Therefore, let us see how various situations may arise and how well structured Test Script body helps retrieving the information with much ease.

Situation 1: During build 6, the leader of the team decides that after Mr. Smith, it will be Mr. Rao who would be performing the manual testing against the *"Send/Receive feature of mailing engine"*. Mr. Rao asks his leader for all pre-requisite information based on which he can learn the functionality as well as perform the manual testing.

Resolution: Leader checks the body of "Manual Test Script" and provides Mr. Rao with all kind of pre-requisite details pertaining to this test script. Mr. Rao checks into section "*Location of supporting files or documentation:*" to find out all relevant training documents and required documentation about this feature.

Situation 2: During build 6, automation expert identifies that few of the flows stated within the document does not match with the application against which he is developing the script.

Resolution: Leader gets in touch with the "*Reviewer*" of this document and asks the individual if appropriate review is done before freezing this document. The reply is affirmative. This puts the leader into a baffling situation. Then the leader goes into the "*Change Record*" section of the document and tries to identify if some change request for that feature has come in or not. If change request is there then the next step of the leader is to check if necessary changes have been incorporated within the document or not. Let us say, that necessary changes have also got incorporated within the document.

This makes the leader's case even worse. Now, the leader needs to reason it out only by checking all the documents provided by customers. In order to search for all relevant documentation, the leader needs to go to section "*Location of Supporting files or documentation*". This helps him identify whether this could be a possible application enhancement or a bug.

Situation 3: It is a bad day for Mr. Rao. He comes to office and while rebooting the system, he observes that the system's hard disk crashed. The question now is, from where can he get that test script again? Irrespective of this situation, Mr. Rao does not panick. Why?

Resolution: Mr. Rao does not panic because he knows that he can go to "*Source control*" area of that application and can retrieve all required files, once again.

Situation 4: During final build of mailing engine, management wants to do a quick sanity check of all very important flows.

Resolution: Mr. Rao quickly checks out "*Priority*" of each test script and hence shortlists the P1 scripts for quick sanity of the application. Therefore, rather than reading or performing an extensive research to find out very important scripts, it beomes much easier for a tester to quickly check the priority and shortlist important flows.

These are the most frequently occurring scenarios that almost every software firm encounters on a periodic basis. Therefore, it is very important to maintain the body of "Manual Test Script" with these elements embedded into it. However, it is not necessary that only these elements are used in the body of test script, but teams, depending upon their need, can add or delete elements from the suggested list.

6.4 Real-Time Scenario "Test Script"

With reference to the *"Case study 1"* (section 6.1.3) and *"Extension of case study 1"*(section 6.3.1), we know that Mr. Smith is the person who is drafting the test script for functionality, "Send/Receive mail".

Let us reiterate a part of Case study 1, for which Mr. Smith has designed the test script. Let us try to understand the same as how ideally a test script should look like in a real-time scenario.

Case Study1 (Section 6.1.3): Mr. Paul has developed an application *X*, which has these many features embedded into it.

- Mail Engine
- General News
- Stock Market News

Feature "Mail engine" has these many "functionalities":

- Send/Receive Mail
- Attachments
- Contact Book
- Sent Folder

These functionalities can be prepared as an individual "Test Scripts" having *n* [where *n* = {1 to infinity}] no. of test scenarios depicting *n* no. of cases.

Now, let us see various scenarios for functionality "Send / Receive Mail":

1. Send/Receive mail
   (a) Sign-in
   (b) Compose and send
   (c) Sent Folder contents
   (d) Receive

Now, that you have understood the case, let us see various scenarios, based on which test cases can be drafted.

Scenario 1: Mr. Smith has drafted the test script for the above-mentioned functionality. He has drafted the test script between build 1 and build 4 of release Alpha. Let us see how Mr. Smith has drafted the test script. Let us assume that Mr. Smith has no "changes", "issues" and "dependencies" for this test script.

Functional Test Case Document For Feature "Mail Engine"

Functionality Name: Send / Receive Mail

Test Objective: To check the "Send / Receive" functionality of "Mail Engine"

Author Name: Mr. Smith

Date of Creation: 26-Dec-2007

Date of Completion: 28-Apr-2008

Reviewer: Mr. Hora

Release: Alpha

Build: 1 - 4

Version: 0

Author Name for current version: Mr. Smith

Priority of this test script: P3

Location of supporting files or documentation: \\pc-mrsmith-us\Mail Engine\ Training

Location of this Test Script: \\pc-mrsmith-us\Mail Engine\ Test Script

Source Control: Y

Source Control Location: \\hydmac-1\Visual Safe Source\Project Application 1\Manual Test Case\Mail Engine\ Send / Receive mail.doc

Change Record Section:

Tester's Name	Date Of Change	Test case ID	Earlier Functionality / Comment	New Functionality / Comments	New Functionality suggested By
	N/A	N/A	N/A	N/A	N/A

Issue Logs:

Tester's Name	Date Of Reporting the issue	Reported Through	Issue Description	Comments
	N/A	N/A	N/A	N/A

Review Comments:

Tester's Name	Date of reporting	Test Case ID	Issue Type	Issue Description	Additional Comments	Date of Resolution
	N/A	N/A	N/A	N/A	N/A	N/A

Table of Contents:

2.1 Sign-in

- 2.1.1 URL details

Test Case ID	Navigational Step	Action to Perform	Expected Output	Salient Checkpoint	Comments
2.1.1.1	Enter url: http://abc.com, in IE address bar	Click "go" or press "enter"	Abc.com home page should be displayed		

- 2.1.2 Login Details

Test Case ID	Navigational Step	Action to perform	Expected Output	Salient Checkpoint	Comments
2.1.2.1	Find for button named "mail" on the bottom of the page.	Click "mail".	Mail login page should be displayed		
2.1.2.2	Enter username: mrsmith				
password: india	Click "go" or press "enter"	Mail box for mrsmith should be displayed	Take mrsmith as checkpoint at the right hand side, top of the page.		
2.1.2.3	Find for inbox tab-bar at the left pane.	Click inbox tab-bar	Mail box, including all the mails for mrsmith should be displayed		

2.2 Compose and Send

- 2.2.1 Compose

Test Case ID	Navigational Step	Action to perform	Expected Output	Salient Checkpoint	Comments
2.2.1.1	Find for compose button at the left pane of the window	Click "compose".	A new page with these fields should be displayed. • To: • Subject: The below mentioned tab-bars should be displayed: • Send • Contacts • Spell • Attach		

- 2.2.2 Send

Test Case ID	Navigational Step	Action to perform	Expected Output	Salient Checkpoint	Comments
2.2.2.1	On the new window, place your cursor.	Fill up these fields with the below stated values: To: mrsmith@abc.com Subject: Hello World Body text: Testing this application. Click "Send".	This window should show processing bar and the whole window should get eloped.		

2.3 Sent Folder contents

- 2.3.1 Sent Tab Details

Test Case ID	Navigational Step	Action to Perform	Expected Output	Salient Checkpoint	Comments
2.3.1.1	Find for Sent button at the left pane of the window	Click "sent".	Sent mailbox will get opened.	Check for mail sent by : mrsmith@abc.com having subject: hello world, dated : current date	

2.4 Receive

- 2.4.1 Receive mail details

Test Case ID	Navigational Step	Action to Perform	Expected Output	Salient Checkpoint	Comments
2.4.1.1	Find for inbox button at the left pane of the window	Click inbox.	Sent mailbox will get opened.	Check for mail sent by : mrsmith@abc.com having subject: hello world, dated : current date	

Scenario 2: Let us see a different scenario now. Mr. Smith gets some change request, has encountered few issues, and has some review comments, too. He has got the change request during Build 5 of same release "Alpha".

Let us assume that as per test script in scenario 1, test case id 2.1.1.1 looks like

Note: All the changed areas are highlighted.

Test Case ID	Navigational Step	Action to Perform	Expected Output	Salient Checkpoint	Comments
2.1.1.1	Enter url: http://abc.com	Click "go" or press "enter"	Abc.com home page should be displayed		

- **Let us now see how the new version of test script looks like:**

Functional Test Case Document For Feature "Mail Engine"

Functionality Name: Send / Receive Mail

Test Objective: To check the "Send / Receive" functionality of "Mail Engine"

Author Name: Mr. Smith

Date of Creation: 26-Dec-2007

Date of Completion: 28-Apr-2008

Reviewer: Mr. Hora

Release: Alpha

Build: 1 - 4

Version: 0

Build: 5

Version: 1

Author Name for current version: Mr. Smith

Priority of this test script: P3

Location of supporting files or documentation: \\pc-mrsmith-us\Mail Engine\ Training

Location of this Test Script: \\pc-mrsmith-us\Mail Engine\ Test Script

Source Control: Y

Source Control Location: \\hydmac-1\Visual Safe Source\Project Application 1\Manual Test Case\Mail Engine\ Send / Receive mail.doc

Change Record Section:

Tester's Name	Date Of Change	Test case ID	Earlier Functionality/ Comment	New Functionality/ Comments	New Functionality Suggested By
Mr. Smith	18-May-2008	2.1.2.3	Find for inbox tab-bar at the left pane.	Find for inbox tab-bar above inbox frame.	Santosh (Development Team)

Issue Logs:

Tester's Name	Date Of Reporting the issue	Reported Through	Issue Description	Comments
Mr. Smith	16-May-2008	Bug Reporting Tool	Bug ID: 52 Subject: URL not getting launched in netscape navigator.	See bug id 52 for details.

Review Comments:

Tester's Name	Date of reporting	Test Case ID	Issue Type	Issue Description	Additional Comments	Date of Resolution
Mr. Smith	17-May-2008	2.1.1.1	Data Issue	Explorer / navigator details has not been provided.	URL is getting launched in IE but not in netscape navigator.	17-May-2008

Table of Contents:

2.1 Sign-in

- 2.1.1 URL details

Test Case ID	Navigational Step	Action to Perform	Expected Output	Salient Checkpoint	Comments
2.1.1.1	Enter url: http://abc.com, in IE address bar.	Click go or press enter.	Abc.com home page should be displayed.		

- 2.1.2 Login Details

Test Case ID	Navigational Step	Action to Perform	Expected Output	Salient Checkpoint	Comments
2.1.2.1	Find for button named "mail" on the bottom of the page.	Click "mail".	Mail login page should be displayed.		
2.1.2.2	Enter username: mrsmith password: india	Click "go" or press "enter"	Mail box for mrsmith should be displayed.	Take mrsmith as checkpoint at the right hand side, top of the page.	
2.1.2.3	Find for inbox tab-bar above index frame	Click inbox tab-bar.	Mail box, including all the mails for mrsmith should be displayed.		

2.2 Compose and Send

- 2.2.1 Compose

Test Case ID	Navigational Step	Action to Perform	Expected Output	Salient Checkpoint	Comments
2.2.1.1	Find for compose button at the left pane of the window.	Click compose.	A new page with these fields should be displayed. • To: • Subject: The below-mentioned tab-bars should be displayed: • Send • Contacts • Spell • Attach.		

- 2.2.2 Send

Test Case ID	Navigational Step	Action to Perform	Expected Output	Salient Checkpoint	Comments
2.2.2.1	On the new window, place your cursor.	Fill up these fields with the below stated values: To: mrsmith@abc.com Subject: Hello World Body text: Testing this application. Click "send".	This window should show processing bar and the whole window should get eloped.		

2.3 Sent Folder contents

- 2.3.1 Sent Tab Details

Test Case ID	Navigational Step	Action to Perform	Expected Output	Salient Checkpoint	Comments
2.3.1.1	Find for Sent button at the left pane of the window.	Click "sent".	Sent mailbox will get opened.	Check for mail sent by : mrsmith@abc.com having subject: hello world, dated : current date.	

2.4 Receive

- 2.4.1 Receive mail details

Test Case ID	Navigational Step	Action to Perform	Expected Output	Salient Checkpoint	Comments
2.4.1.1	Find for inbox button at the left pane of the window.	Click inbox.	Sent mailbox will get opened.	Check for mail sent by : mrsmith@abc.com having subject: hello world, dated : current date	

In sum, we saw that how the changes got implemented in the updated test script. The important point to keep a tab upon is that, after the document got updated, for any further testing, this new version would be referred and not the old version.

This completes explanation of most of the complex cases while drafting test script. Now, you are ready to write a test script for any given functionality of any application. What are you waiting for, pick up any website and try writing down a test script for any of the functionality given in that application.

HP Quality Center 10: Test Planning Approach

7

Chapter Objectives: This chapter will give an overview of

- *Test Plan tree in HP QC 10*
- *Creating folder*
- *Create "test"*
- *Understanding "New test" RHS window*

7.1 Test Plan Tree In HP QC 10

In an earlier chapter, we learned the philosophy behind test case designing aspect, independent of HP QC 10. In this chapter, let us walk through the steps of designing using HP QC 10.

Designing test case is one of the most important activities from either manual or automation testing perspective.

However, before designing test case using HP QC 10, the very crucial aspect is to understand the scientific folder structure creation technique in QC. Generally, folder structure nomenclature is very organisation specific, but still to suggest the parent child structure, it is always advisable to keep the highest level denomination as parent and then build the tree further, accordingly.

With few additions, let us refer to the same example as discussed in Chapter 6.

Product family: Automation Asset
Application name as: Financials
Features as: Mail Engine
Functionality as: Send / Receive mail, Attachments, Contact Book, Sent folder
Test scenarios under functionality send/receive mail as: Sign-in, Compose and send
Test script (Sign-in) : Login
Test script (Compose): Inbox, compose, save, send

The folder structure snapshot in HP QC 10 looks like as displayed in Fig. 7.1.

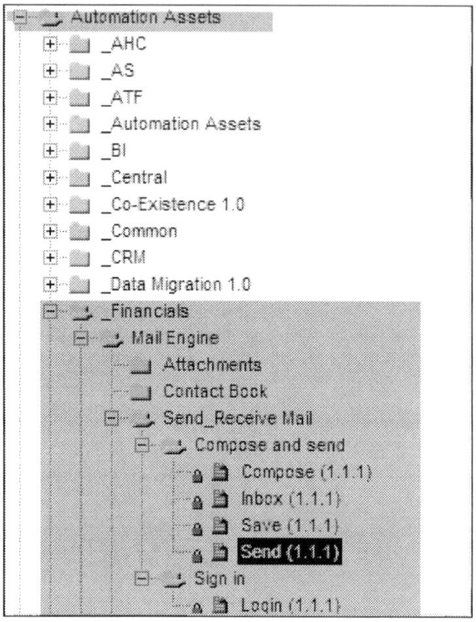

Figure 7.1 *Snapshot Folder Structure Layout in HP QC 10.*

7.2 Creating Folder

To create a folder, one needs to follow the below-mentioned steps.

Step 1) Login to QC, in your specific "project" and "domain".

Step 2) Come to the "test plan" area.

Step 3) In test plan area, under root QC folder, which is named "Subject" here as shown in the below screen shot, create a new folder. To create a new folder, you need to click on "new folder" icon.

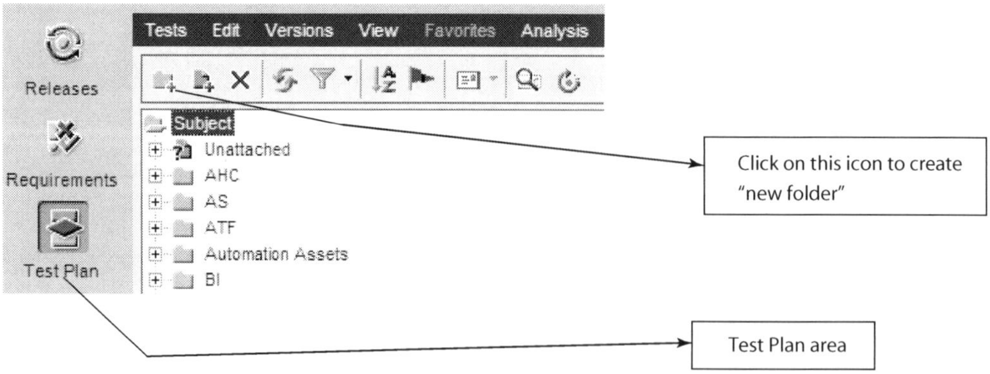

Figure 7.2 *New Folder Creation Icon.*

Clicking "new folder" icon, folder name window comes up, where one needs to input "Name" value.

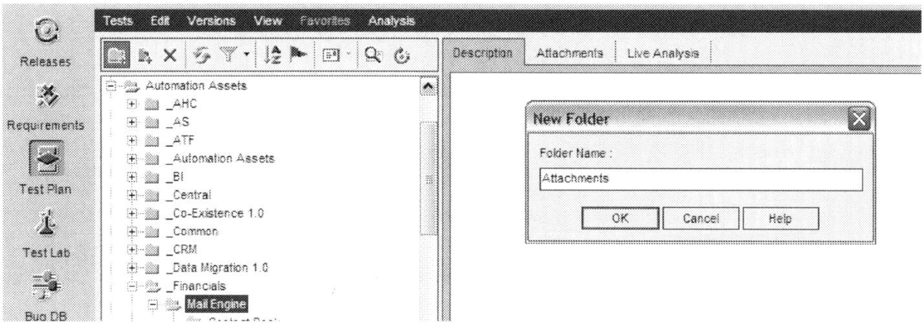

Figure 7.3 *Folder Name.*

After inputting the name, click "Ok".

Step 4) Selecting "OK" in Fig. 7.3, creates a new folder.

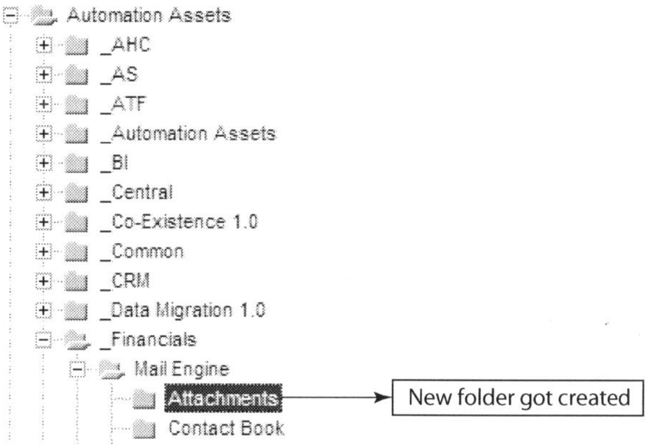

Figure 7.4 *Creation of Attachments Folder.*

7.3 Create "Test"

"Test" here in QC means an area which contains collection of test cases. Therefore, according to the pyramid model, as discussed in an earlier chapter, this can also be termed as "Test Scenario". But for sake of QC understanding, throughout the discussion, we will term it as "Test".

Let us see the steps involved in order to create a "Test":

Step 1) One needs to select a folder under which test needs to be stored; then click "New Test" icon.

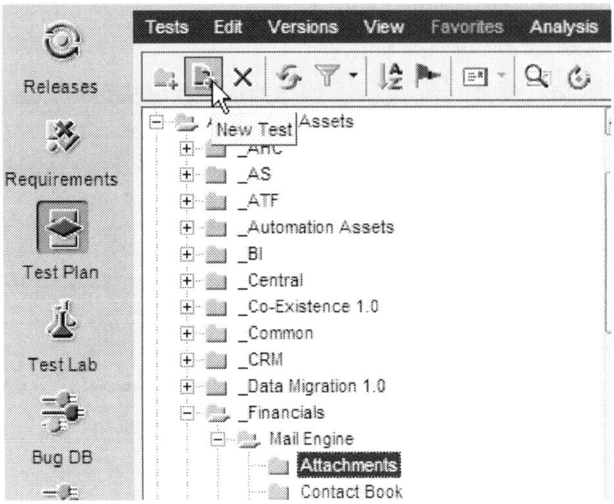

Figure 7.5 *"New Test".*

Step 2) On clicking the "New Test" icon, below displayed window comes up.

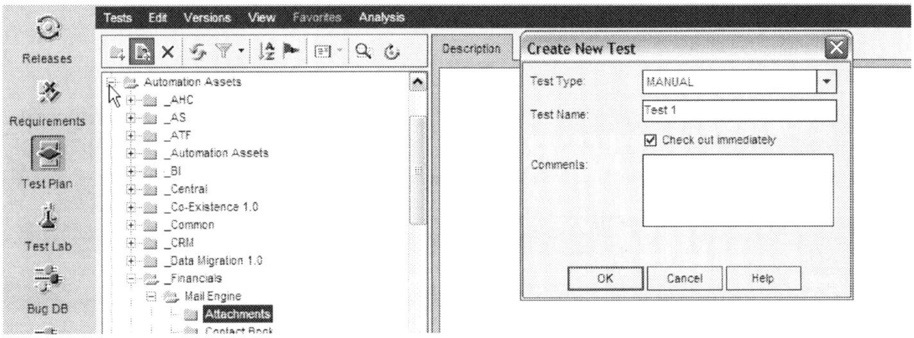

Figure 7.6 *Create New Test Window.*

You can see "Test Type" is already populated as "Manual". Hence, if you are creating manual test, you can leave it as it is; else the other options that this window provides are as displayed in Fig. 7.7.

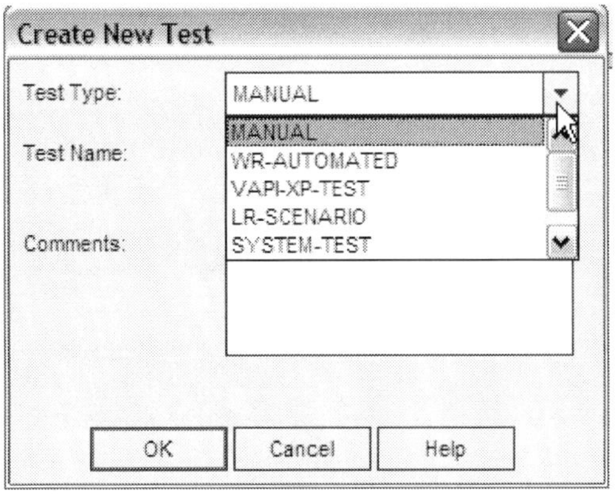

Figure 7.7 *Menu Items for "test type" in New Test Window.*

The value in the menu items can be defined or customized by the QC admin, based on organisational need.

Under comments section, user can input any comment, which can be referred later for clarity.

Step 3) Click "Ok" on "Create New Test" window. Another window comes up, which again can be customized based on the organisational needs, such as, if you want this test to be associated with any product or category, then all such relational information can be kept intact within this new window.

Additionally, this window can be bypassed, as well.

Step 4) Going further step 3, new test gets created.

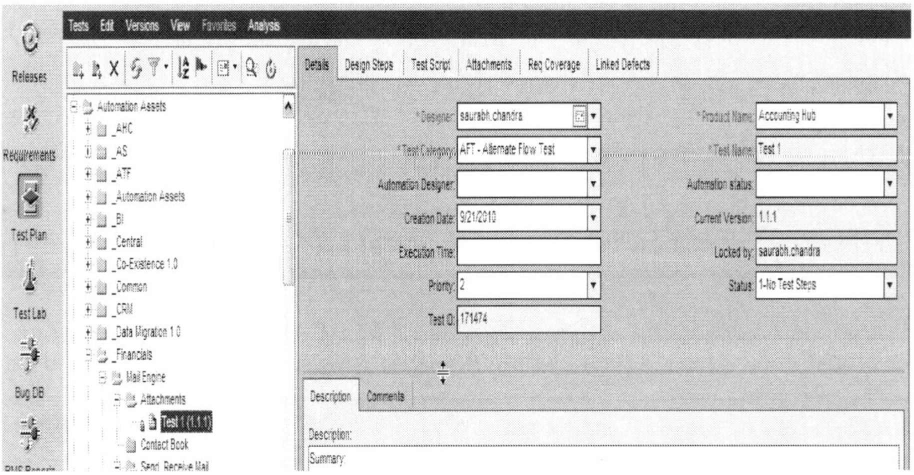

Figure 7.8 *New Test Created.*

7.4 Understanding "New Test" RHS Window

As you can observe in Fig. 7.8, that there's a different window that has got attached with the newly created test. Therefore, before going ahead, let us understand attributes of each tab one by one.

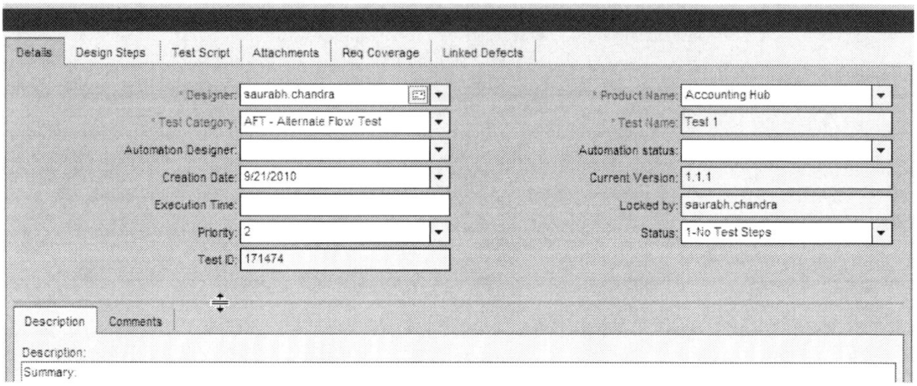

Figure 7.9 *"New test" Associated Tab-bars.*

7.4.1 Details

As displayed in Fig. 7.9, under details section, user needs to input all such details that define this test explicitly. Definition of few important fields is:

- *Designer:* This is the name of the person who has created this test.
- *Test category:* User needs to define the category of the test such as basic test, regression test, etc.
- *Automation designer:* If this test goes through automation, then the name of the person automating this test, should come here.
- *Creation date:* This is the date of creation of this test. This field gets auto populated as it takes the system date, for the very first time, when the panel was invoked.
- *Product name:* Here user needs to input name of any such product with which this test needs to be associated with.
- *Test name:* This is the logical name of the test that user needs to input.
- *Automation status:* If case test is under automation then the current automation status of the test should be inputted here. It can be either developed, under development, under review, etc. based on the status, current automation activity is at, at that point in time.

7.4.2 Design Steps

Design steps aka test case – This is the most critical section, which contributes towards designing the test case. In this section, I will walk you through such features which would help designing the test cases effectively and efficiently. During this journey, we will also discuss as how to reference tests with "Requirements" and in turn "Cycle" and "Release".

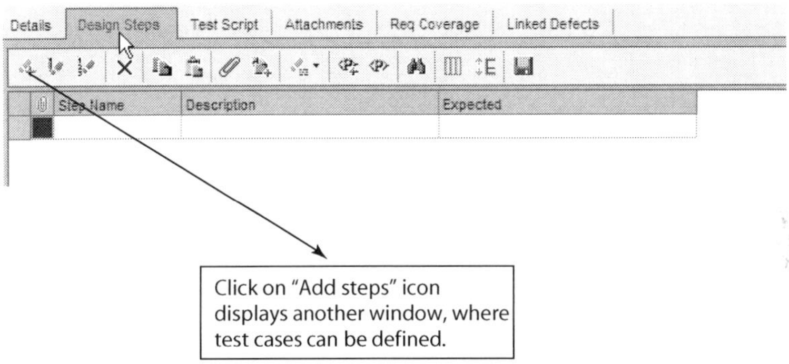

Figure 7.10 *Design Steps Window.*

Clicking "Add steps" window, "Design step editor" window comes up.

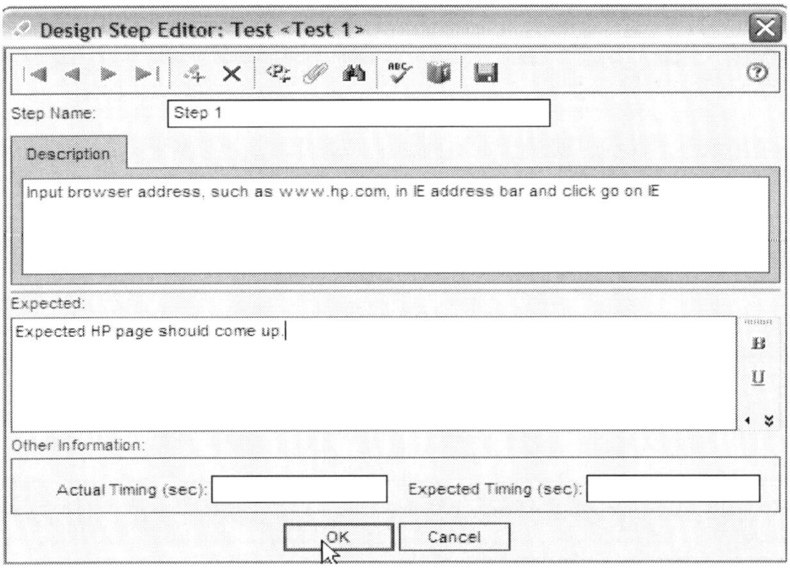

Figure 7.11 *Design Steps Editor.*

Under description, user needs to input the exact navigational path that tester should traverse, while testing the application.

Under expected section – user needs to input the expected outcome of the action that should come up after traversing the step stated in description section.

Click "Ok" and you would see the design step window getting populated with the steps.

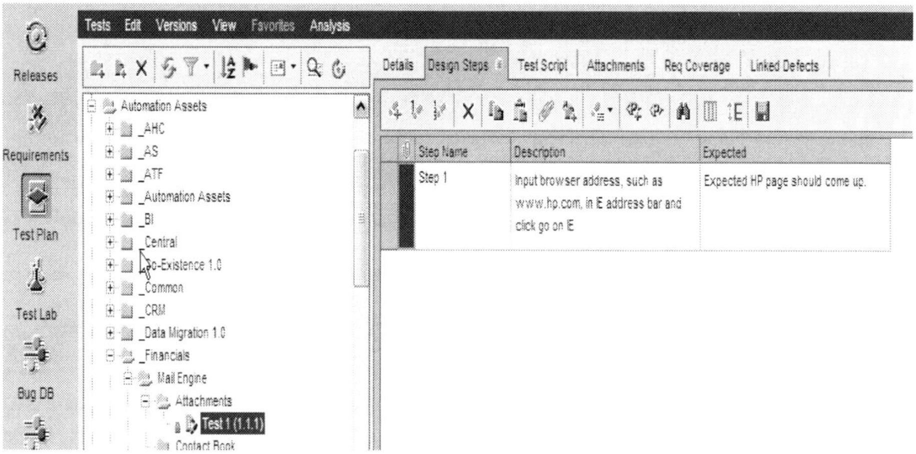

Figure 7.12 *Steps Reflected.*

Now, let us understand the design steps tab-bar features.

- **Edit step:**

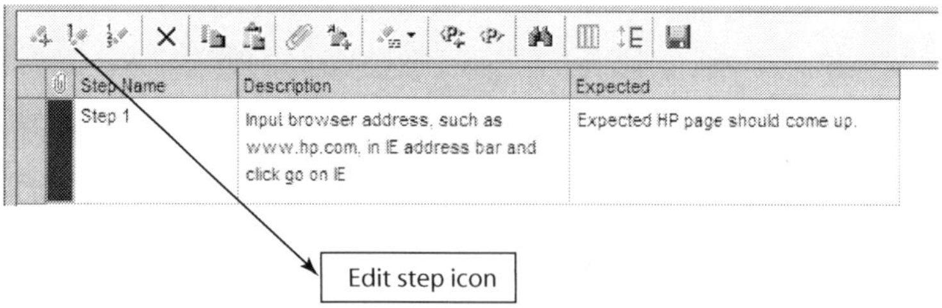

Figure 7.13 *Edit Step Button,*

On clicking this icon again "Design step editor", as shown in Fig. 7.11, shows up and user can change texts accordingly here. Additionally, if you don't want to go to design steps then by double clicking the case displayed on "design steps" window, you can edit texts directly.

- **Renumber steps:** If you have more than one step and at any point in time if you want to re-number them, then the displayed icon in Fig. 7.13 should be clicked. Additionally, you can also edit texts by double clicking on the "Step name" column of design steps window.

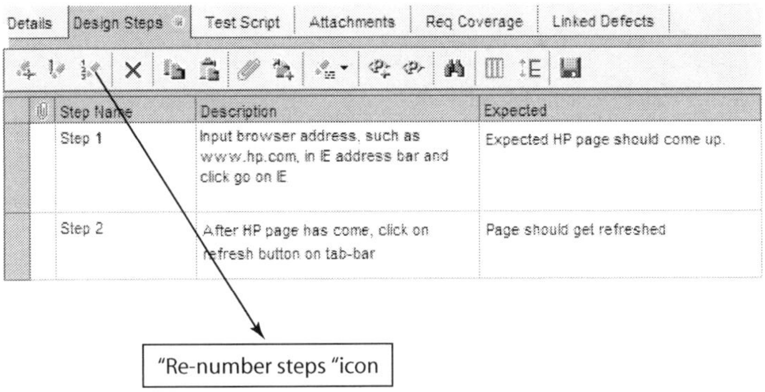

Figure 7.14 *Re-number Steps.*

- **Delete:** As the name suggests, delete can be used to delete any of the steps row by row.

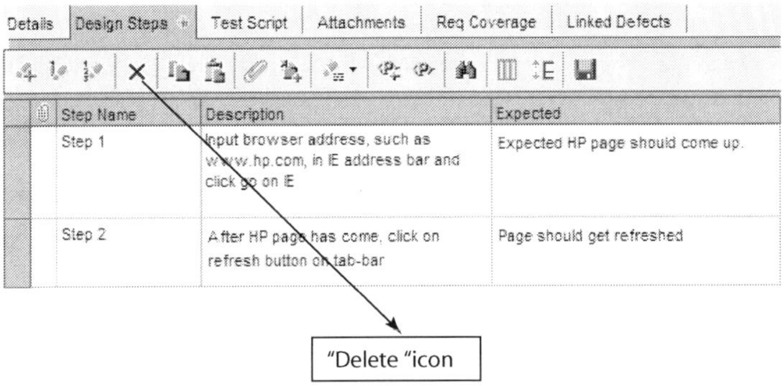

Figure 7.15 *"Delete" icon.*

- **Copy and paste steps:** This sounds very easy but ideally this is very intriguing. Indeed, while exercising this option for the first time, I was baffled for about 20 minutes.

Then I realized the technique of copying steps.

Of course, this needs to be shared with you.

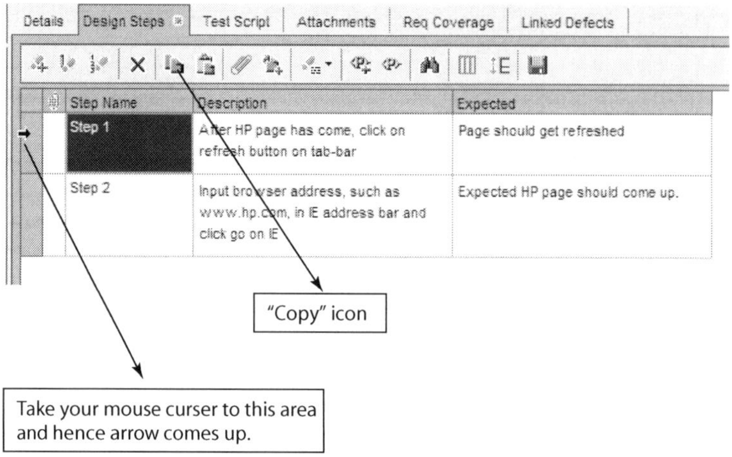

Figure 7.16 *Copy "icon".*

Step 1) As shown in Fig. 7.16, place your cursor at that bay area. Cursor icon gets changed to arrow.

Step 2) Click the left hand side of mouse and complete row gets highlighted, which in other words has got selected, as displayed in Fig. 7.17.

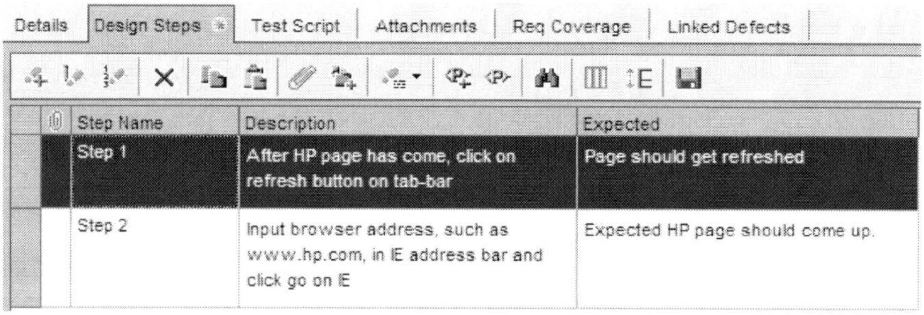

Figure 7.17 *Select a Row.*

Step 3) Press shift and bring mouse cursor to the next step and then press the left side button on mouse. The other row also gets selected.

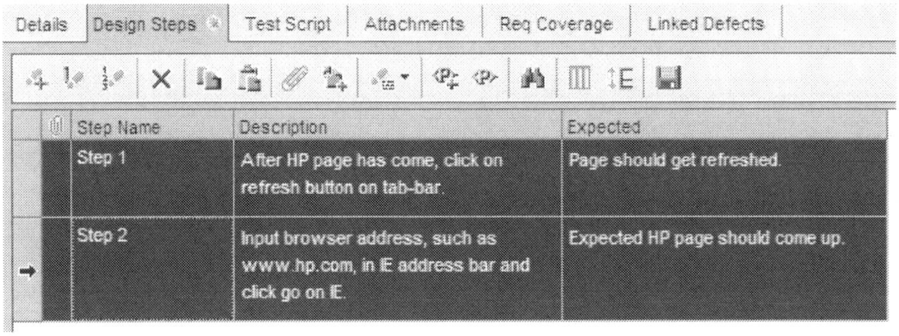

Figure 7.18 *Multiple Row Selection.*

Step 4) Click copy icon on HP QC 10 tab-bar.

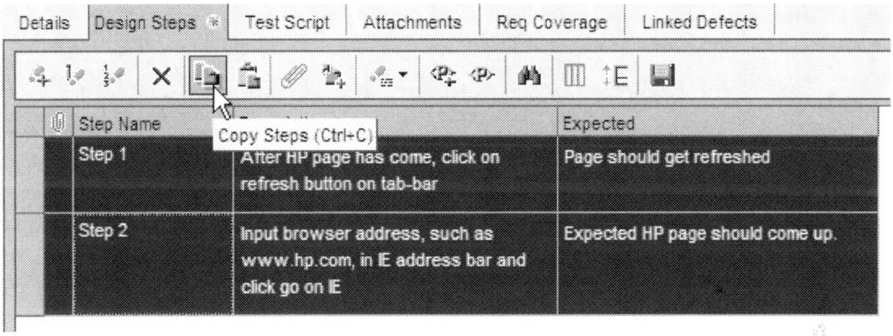

Figure 7.19 *Copy Steps.*

Step 5) Place the cursor at the step where you want to paste this data. For reference, let us place it at step 2, as per HP QC 10 window.

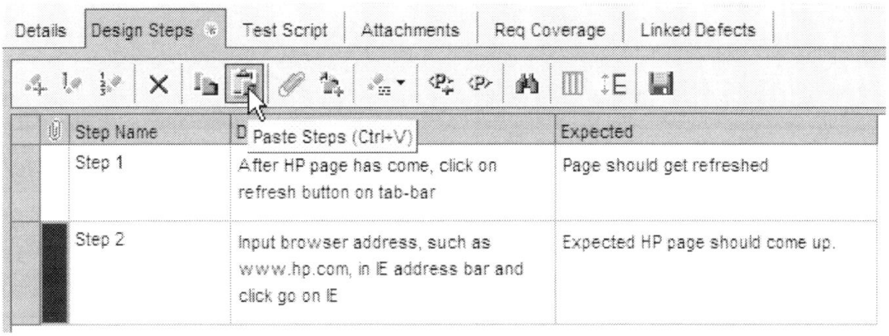

Figure 7.20 *Paste Steps.*

Step 6) The steps get pasted in 3rd and fourth row (as per Fig. 7.21), which earlier was null in Fig. 7.20.

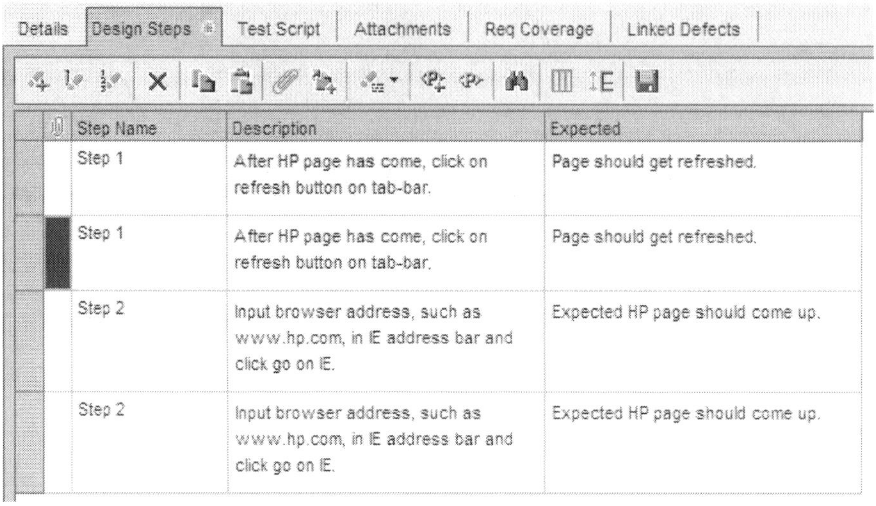

Figure 7.21 *Paste Steps.example*

After pasting, in Fig. 7.21, you can observe that the steps numbering has got skewed, and step number becomes repetitive. In order to correct this, you can select all the steps and then click on "re-numbering steps" icon.

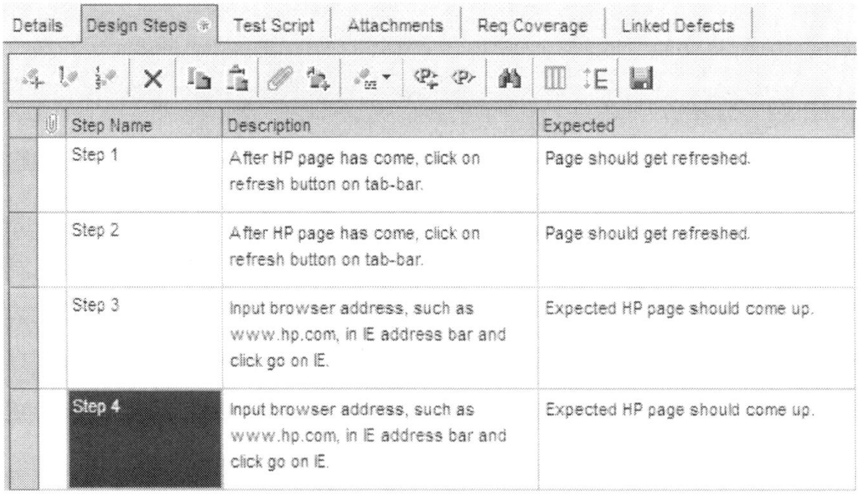

Figure 7.22 *Renumbering Steps.*

- **Attachments:**
  As the name suggests, this feature is used to attach any such file, URL, etc. which may be relevant enough to be stored against this "test".

Let us see how much flexibility attachment window provides to users.

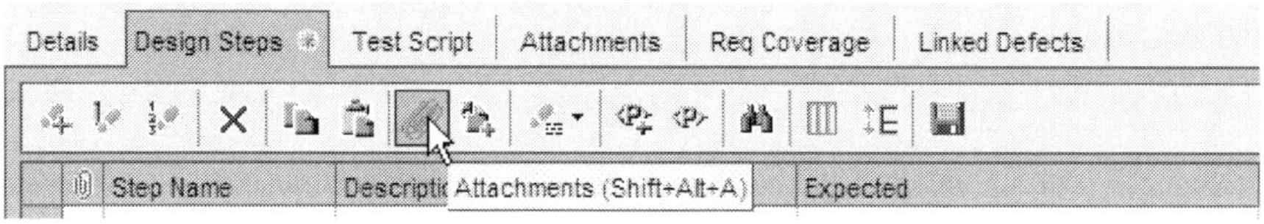

Figure 7.23 *Attachments Window Icon.*

Clicking "attachments" icon, another window comes up as shown in Fig. 7.24.

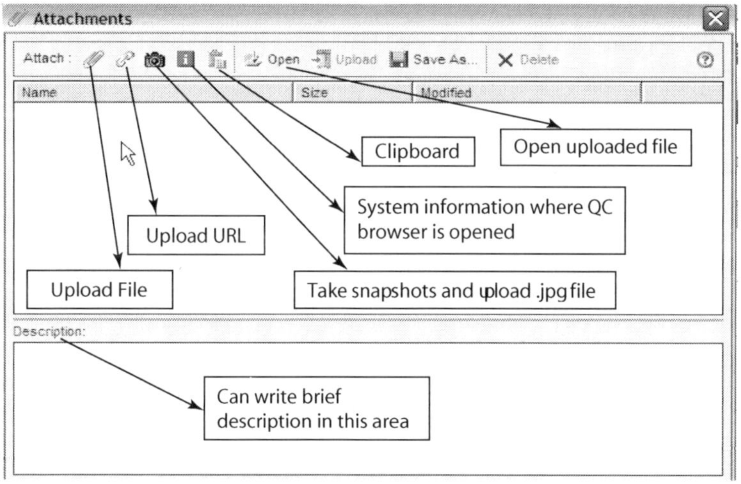

Figure 7.24 *Attachments Window.*

As per Fig. 7.23, all the mentioned types of attachment facilities are given in QC. Interesting part is the "i" icon, which is there to provide system information. System information details can't be attached against the open "test' but can only be viewed.

Let us see how system information window looks like, after "i" icon is clicked:

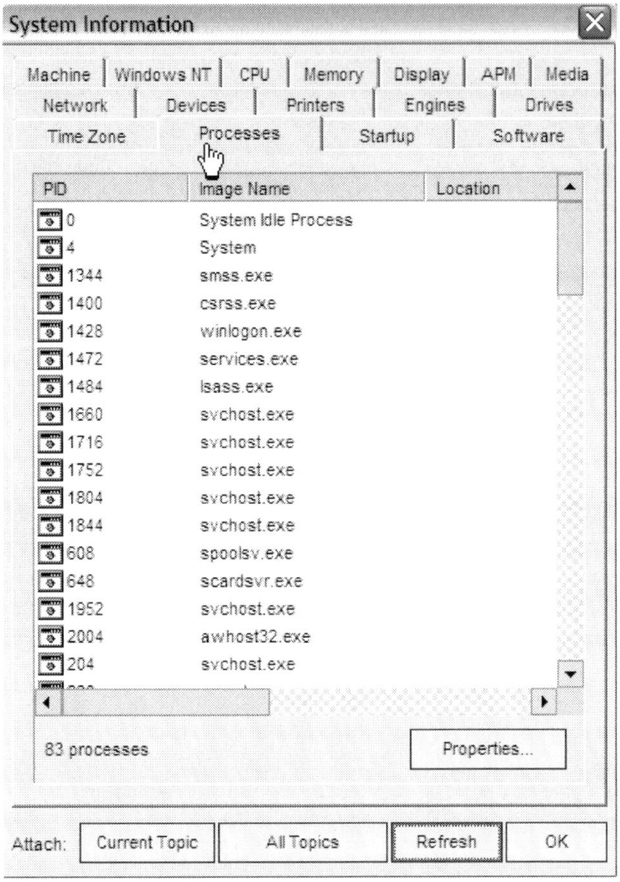

Figure 7.25 *Click "i" and Get This Window.*

In this window, you can see the tab-bars – one can get all such information about the machine at which HP QC 10 is invoked.

- **Call to test**

  This can be termed as one of the most important features of Hp QC 10. Let us first understand a scenario in which let us say you have 5 independent tests and from sixth one, you realize that few of first five tests need to be re-used or should be embedded as part of the sixth test. Is it that you would re-write all the steps once again in the sixth test or can the already existing test steps be pulled in as a reference in the sixth test.

HP QC 10 gives the facility to call the test which needs to be re-used via a feature named *"Call to test"*.

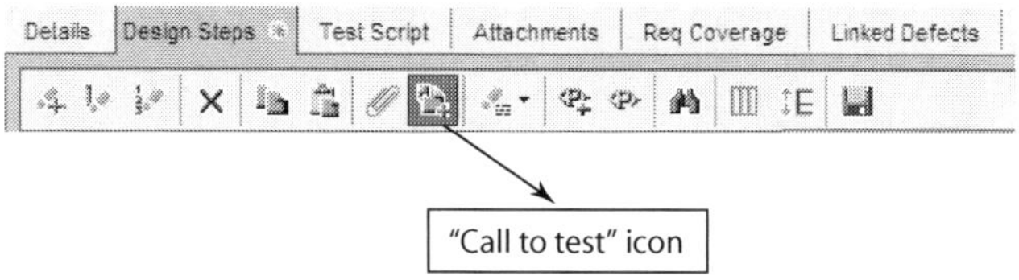

Figure 7.26 *"Call to Test" Icon.*

Let us see how this works.

Step 1) Place the cursor at the line where you would want to call the test from other folder and hence click on the icon i.e., "Call to test".

Step 2) The below displayed window pops up. Select the path from where the test needs to be called.

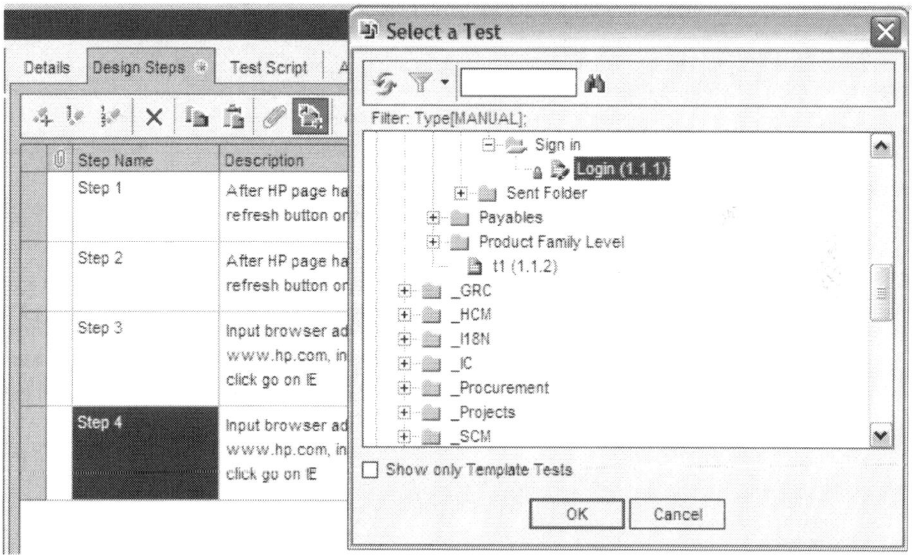

Figure 7.27 *Select a Test.*

Here you can observe at the bottom of the frame that there's an option *"Show only template tests"*. What this means is that if this option is un-checked then all the tests till last child level get displayed. But if the option is checked then it would only show the parent folder of the test (refer Fig. 7.28) but not the actual test.

After the test got shortlisted, click "Ok" on Fig. 7.27 window.

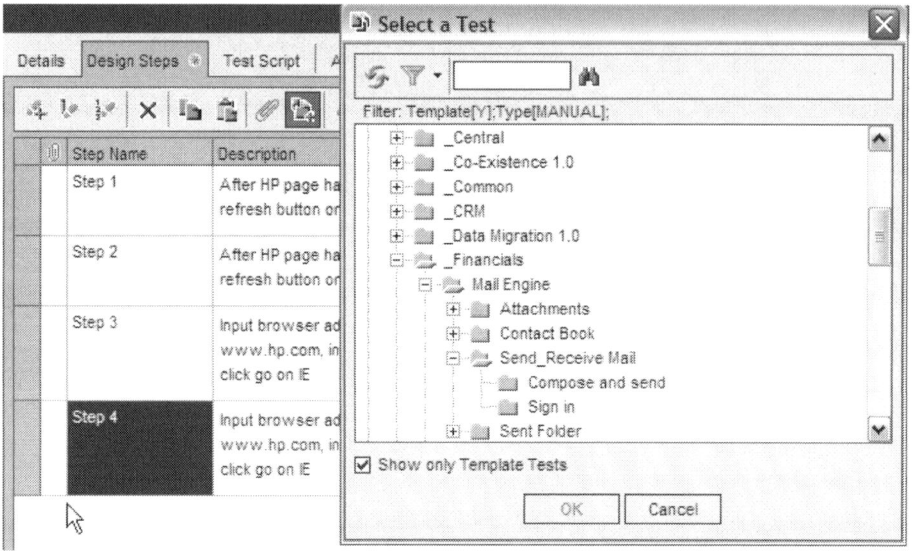

Figure 7.28 *Only Parent Folder Visible but No Test.*

Step 3) Test gets associated to the one from where this was called, at the stated step, i.e., the last step as in the below displayed screen.

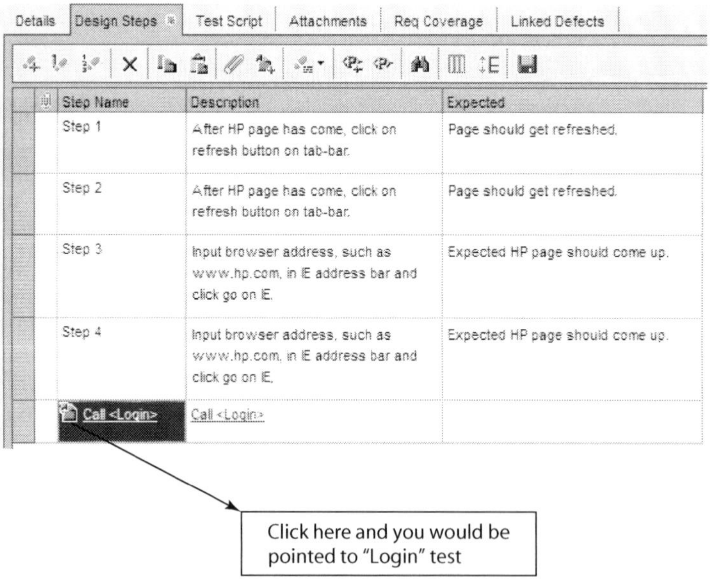

Figure 7.29 *Test is Called.*

If you would click on the arrow icon as pointed in Fig. 7.29, you would be pointed to the "Login test". Important point is that "call to test" is one such feature that can prove to be very useful, primarily because automation people by virtue of their responsibility, generally, do not know about the in-depth functionality of the test. Therefore, if there are tests being called via another test, for an automation engineer to dig in all such tests without having a structured mechanism becomes very difficult, and hence leads to coding deficiencies. However, such feature of this kind of pointers in HP QC 10 makes it easier to identify called test and hence re-use code. This in turn helps in saving lots of development efforts and makes maintenance easier, too.

Since the fundamental behind call to test lies upon the theory of "call by reference", if the reference test is changed, one need not go to all tests and change steps. The change will come into effect at all the called tests.

- **Generate Script:** This area is used when the manual test needs to be converted to automated test. We will touchbase upon this in detail in Chapter 8.

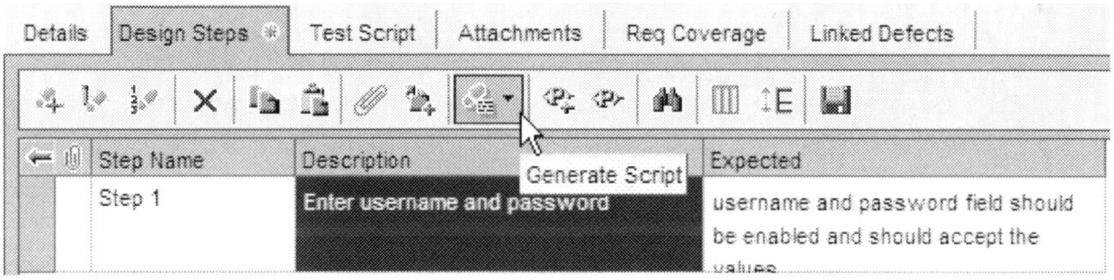

Figure 7.30 *Generate Script Icon.*

- **Insert Parameter:**

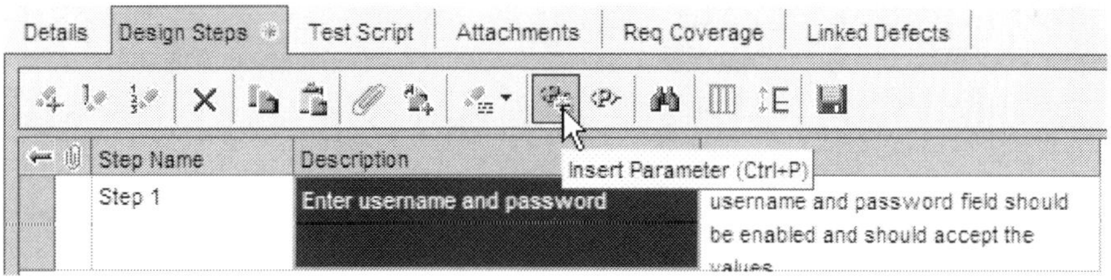

Figure 7.31 *Insert Parameter.*

This is one of the most important and thoughtful features provided by the tool. Parameter inserting is a technique where, if user feels that few strings are generic enough and may be changed based on business transactions, such strings or statements should be parameterized. Usefulness of such parameterization of strings comes in two ways:

- While traversing the flow manually, user knows that changing data set for parameterized event is rational.
- During automation coding, these test cases become input criteria, hence automation engineers come to know easily which all values to be parameterized in their code.

Let us see how this works. In Fig. 7.31, step 1, you can observe that username and password need to be entered as part of the manual testing action. Therefore, by definition, it means that username and password values are those, which can be changed based on access permission to the application. Hence, these should be highlighted as parameterized events.

Step 1) Double click the step where you have values to be parameterized. "Design Step Editor" window comes up.

Select the word or statement that needs to be parameterized and you would observe that "P+, insert parameter" icon gets enabled.

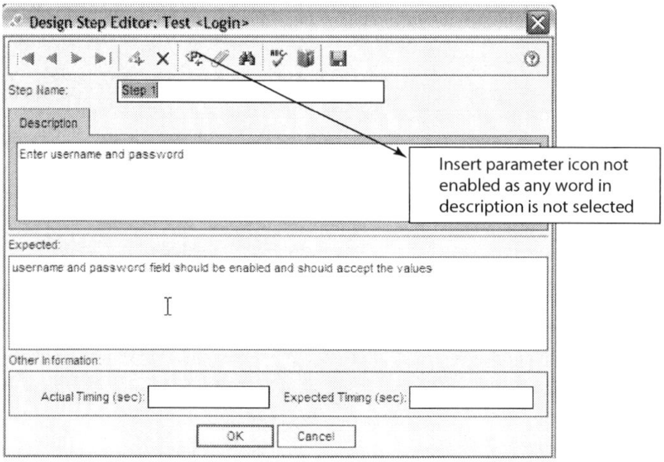

Figure 7.32 *Design Step Editor.*

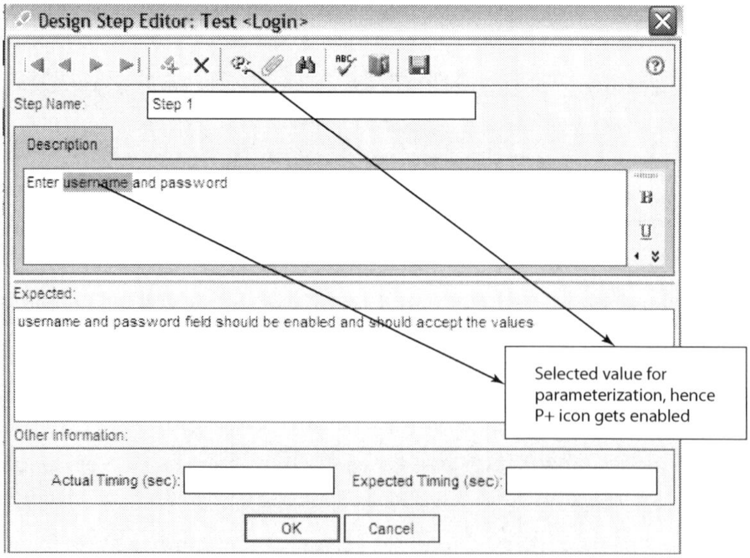

Figure 7.33 *"Insert Parameter Icon Gets Enabled".*

Step 2) Click "Insert Parameter" icon on "Design Step Editor" window. Parameter properties window comes up. Insert "Parameter Name" and click ok.

The word becomes parameterized.

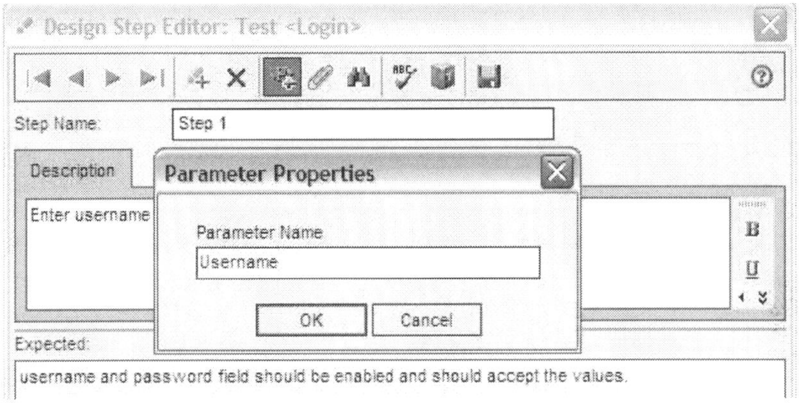

Figure 7.34 *Parameter Name.*

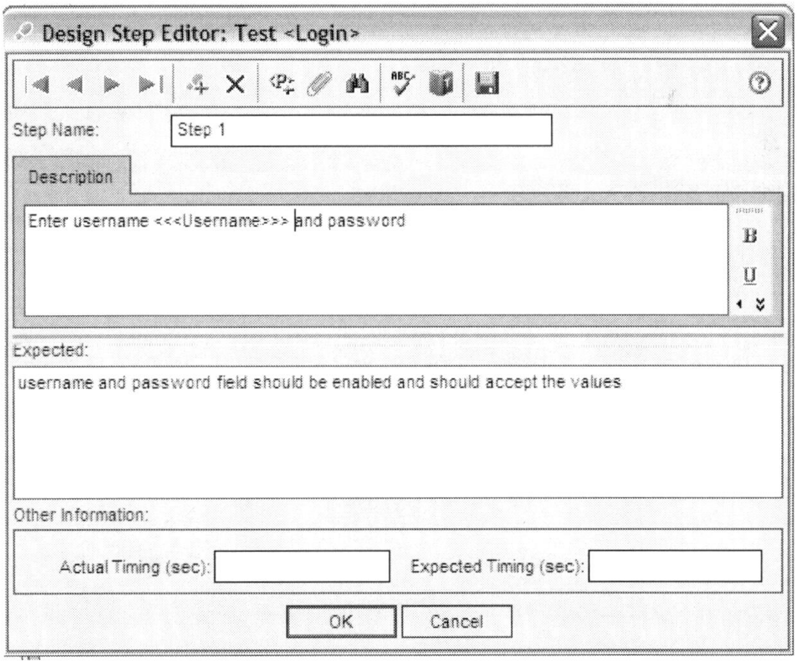

Figure 7.35 *Parameterized Value.*

Click "Ok"

Step 3) Parameterized value gets associated with the test step.

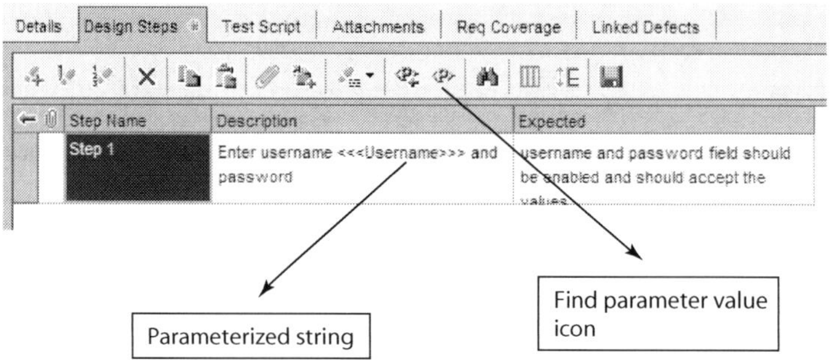

Figure 7.36 *Test Case Showing Parameterized String.*

Important point here is that you can't add parameter to the parameter value.

The other interesting feature is the <P> icon, near to insert parameter (<P+>) icon, as shown in Fig. 7.36. The usage of this <P> icon is that where ever you have parameterized string, select that step and click on <P>, it would pop up "current test parameters" window (Fig. 7.37) with the value that would have got assigned to the parameterized value.

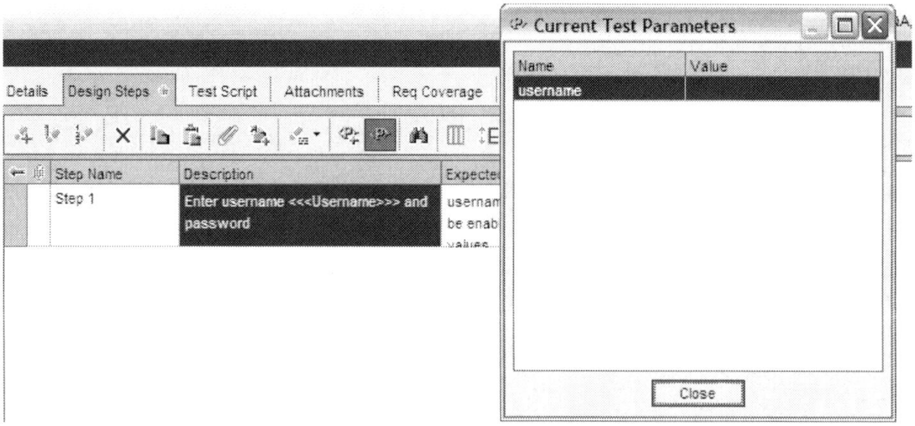

Figure 7.37 *Find Parameter Value Screen.*

- **Find text:**

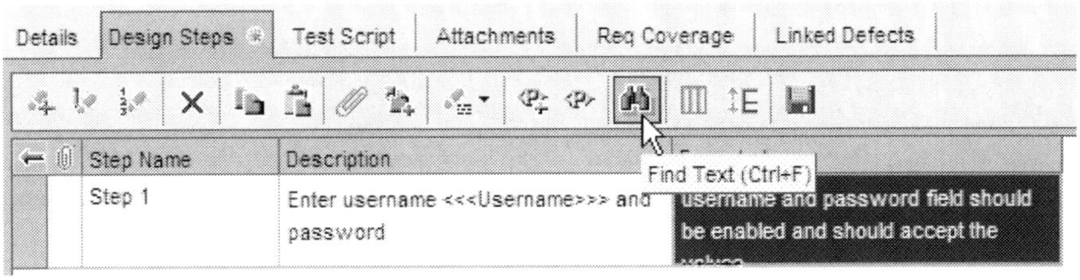

Figure 7.38 *Find Text Icon.*

I never thought that any "Find text" component to be so insightful. Let's see what component comes up when "Find text" binocular shaped icon is clicked.

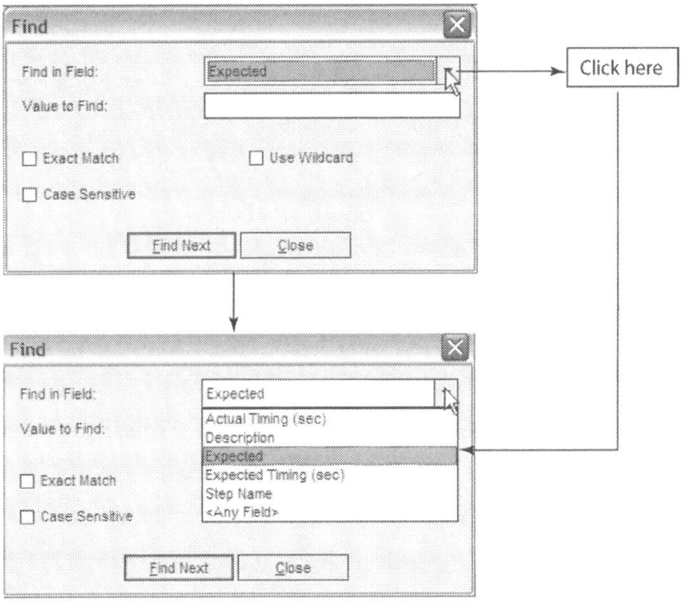

Figure 7.39 *Find Window.*

As you can see in Fig. 7.39, there are numerous query criteria based on which texts can be searched.

- **Select Columns:**

Using this feature, one can select column that one requires.

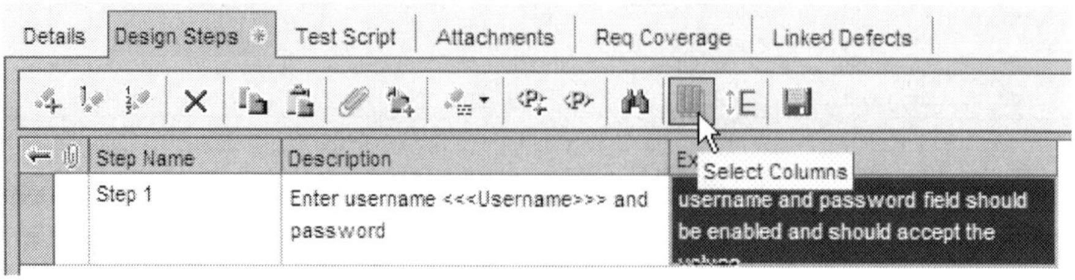

Figure 7.40 *Select Column.*

Click on "select columns" and a grid opens (Fig. 7.41).You can pull to the right grid whichever values you feel the need to be part of the column, and that will become visible as one of the columns in the test case table.

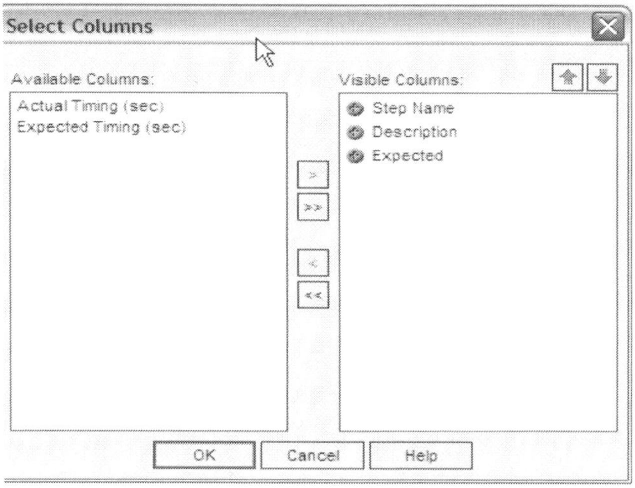

Figure 7.41 *Select Values to Make it Visible Columns.*

- **Adjust Row Height**

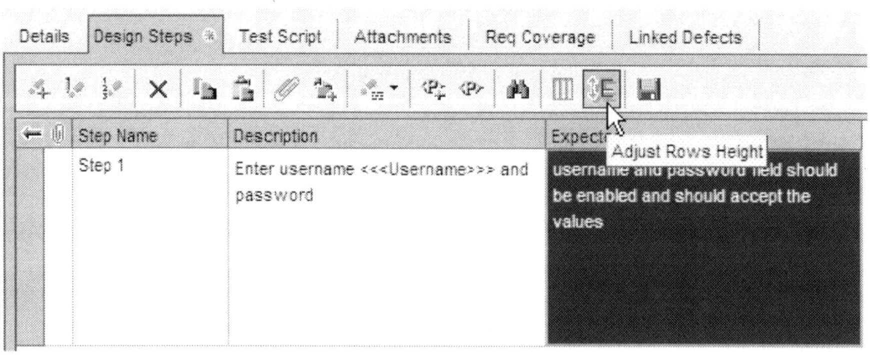

Figure 7.42 *Adjust Row Height Icon.*

We can term this feature to be required for cosmetic changes. The usefulness of the feature is that as you can see in the Fig. 7.42 that height of the row is much more than required then clicking on this, it would get adjusted as shown in Fig. 7.43.

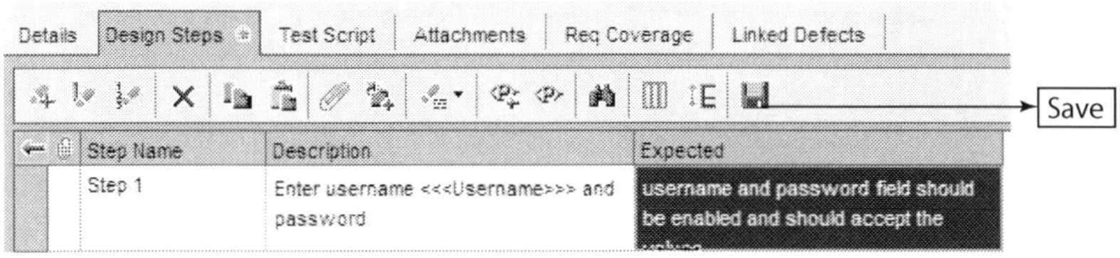

Figure 7.43 *Adjusted Height after Clicking "Adjust Rows Height".*

- **Save:**
  And the last icon, "save" (Fig. 7.43) — this is used just to save and commit all your inputs and changes.

7.4.3 Attachments

Attachments feature is exactly the same as what we discussed in "Design steps – attachment" section. The only difference between test step level and here at test level is that under test step level, this feature is used to attach relevant external documents at test step level but at "Attachments" level, external documents are attached at test level.

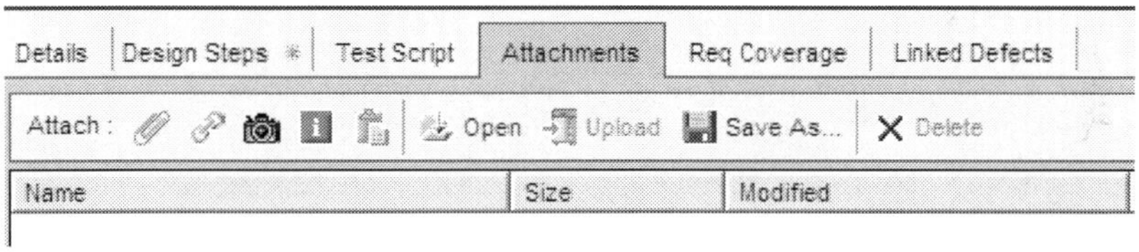

Figure 7.44 *Attachments Level.*

7.4.4 Requirement Coverage

In this section, we will see how to attach tests to requirements. As you can observe that tests are attached to requirements and requirements already were attached to cycle, which in turn was attached to release. Therefore, with this you understand all these details are tightly coupled, and hence the testing business process tracking becomes highly efficient.

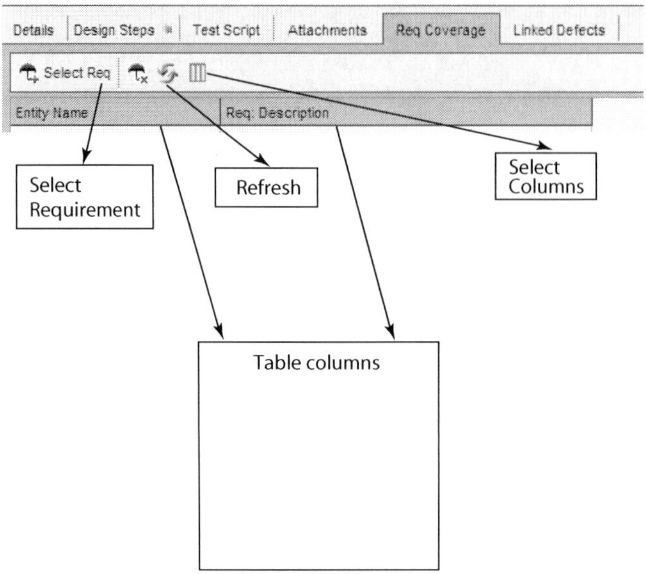

Figure 7.45 *Requirement Coverage Area.*

- **Select Requirement (Fig. 7.45):** Clicking this option, a new window comes up where at right hand side, users gets the facility to browse through the QC requirement level folder structure and hence select one, as the need.

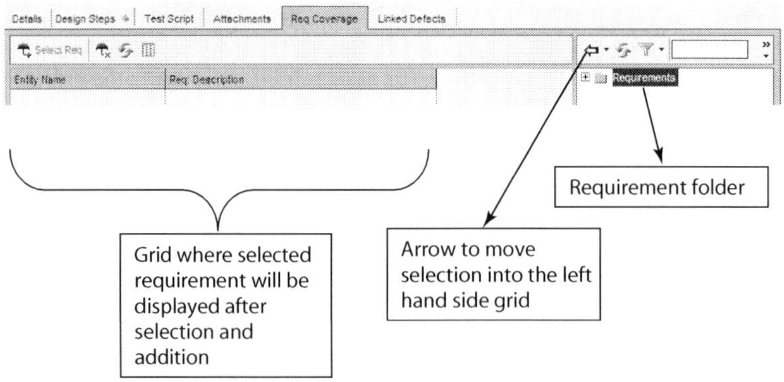

Figure 7.46 *Select Requirement.*

7.4.5 Linked Defects

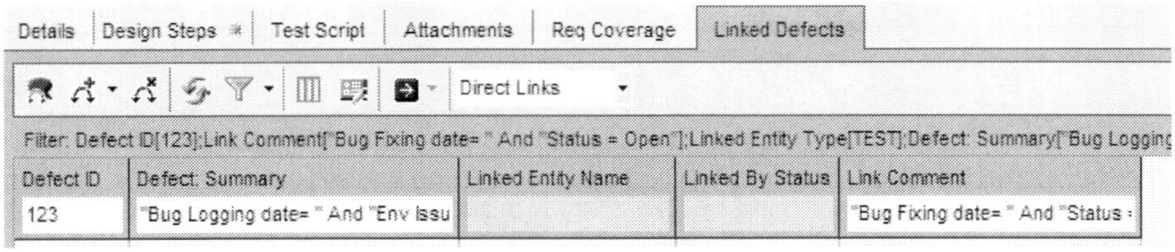

Figure 7.47 *Linked Defects Window.*

The application issues found during testing can be attached at this level, which is "Linked defects". Users have the flexibility to link bugs with various status and entity name. Additionally, users can also link one defect to another. All-in-all, this panel can be used for defect logging, tracking and management.

You would be wondering, why we didn't discuss "Test Scripts" area. It is primarily because "Test Script area" is specifically used for automation script management. Therefore, before discussing this area, in next chapter I will walk you through basics of HP QTP 9.5 and then, in further chapter, I will walk you through the concepts behind "Test Script" feature.

8

HP Quality Center 10: Quick Bytes

Chapter Objectives: This chapter will give an overview of

- *What is HP- QTP?*
- *"HP QTP Add-In's" Concept*
- *HP QTP Window*
- *Folder option to reference important resources path*
- *OR Basics and OR Types*
- *Binding two separate scripts in QTP*
- *Passing variables between two individual scripts*
- *Parameterization through Data Table*
- *Establishing HP QC 9.2 or 10 connection through HP QTP*

Introduction

To appreciate the discussion in further chapters, it was very essential to let you know in a brief about HP QTP features and how few of these integrate with HP QC . With this basic overview, at least, the essence and basic understanding of areas discussed in further chapters will become quite easy to understand. However, I would strongly recommend to purchase and read the book named *Automation Testing* by Saurabh Chandra, published by McGraw-Hill India, as it has in-depth detailing about how QTP works and what is the real-time usage of all important features of HP QTP 9.5 and 10.0.

Additionally, please note that throughout this chapter, whole subject matter discussed is valid for both HP QTP 9.5 and 10. As a result, I would be denoting the tool simply as HP QTP. On the similar lines, whole subject matter discussed within, related with HP QC, is valid for both 9.2 and 10.0 version. Hence, I would be denoting the tool as HP QC.

8.1 What is HP QTP?

"Quick Test Professional", widely known as HP QTP, is a functional automation tool that is used for performing the functional as well as regression testing. The approach or philosophy against which HP QTP is based upon is known as "Keyword Driven Approach".

"Keyword Driven Approach", is an approach that separates most of programming from data. This helps companies to put in a test strategy where a code skeleton can be built in before application gets developed. In addition, this also enables, not so proficient coders, to understand the underlying assumptions of the code through "Keyword View" and hence tweak the code in a more effective and efficient way.

The operational mechanics of the tool is to capture "Graphical User Interface (GUI)" operations during recording mode and then playback accordingly from next time onwards when tool is set into execution mode. In recording mode, the tool generates code-set for those functionalities that are traversed manually.

8.1.1 Version

As any software has its version to track enhancements and categorize differences between earlier development codeline and the latest codeline of the software, HP QTP also has a version which is one of the latest offerings by HP i.e., 10.

It is very critical to know the version of the automation tool, especially when it has to be integrated with some other software such as HP QC. Compatibility check should be done before buying license of two such tools, where you have a plan to make them work in tandem.

8.2 "HP QTP Add-In" CONCEPT

It is highly recommended to know the importance of Add-in, in HP QTP . Hence, the first question that you should ask is:

What is "HP QTP Add-In"?

Several different environments have various different objects, which "out of the box HP QTP tool" may not be able to recognize successfully. In addition, "out of the box HP QTP methods" might not be relevant enough to operate on these objects. In order to make such objects get recognized by the tool and have specific methods to operate on them, HP provides an additional plugin to the tool. This additional plugin is known as "Add-In".

The window, which displays all the add-ins are known as "Add-In Manager". Furthermore, add-in manager window gives power to user to select/de-select required add-ins as per the need.

Furthermore, when HP QTP 10.0 is integrated with HP QC 10.0, then while launching the tool, it is recommended that add-ins' selection are always checked. Otherwise, script once recorded with one set of add-in, if executed using another set of add-in, will not work.

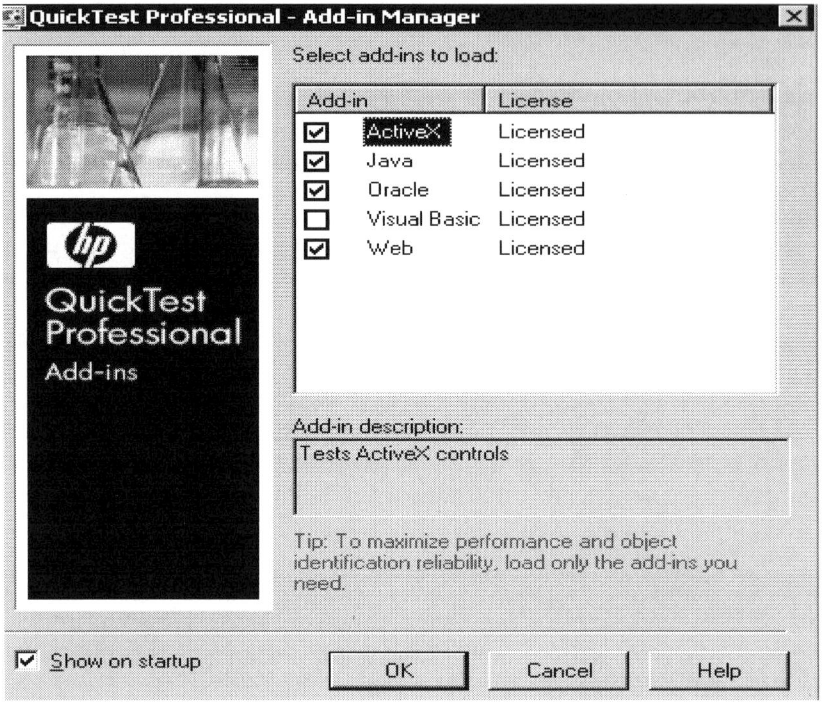

Figure 8.1 *Add-in Manager Window.*

In order to ensure that add-in page always opens up while launching it from HP QC or otherwise, enable the below stated option in HP QTP tools settings, which will do the job.

"QTP ->Tools -> Options -> General". Check option **"Display Add-In Manager on startup".**

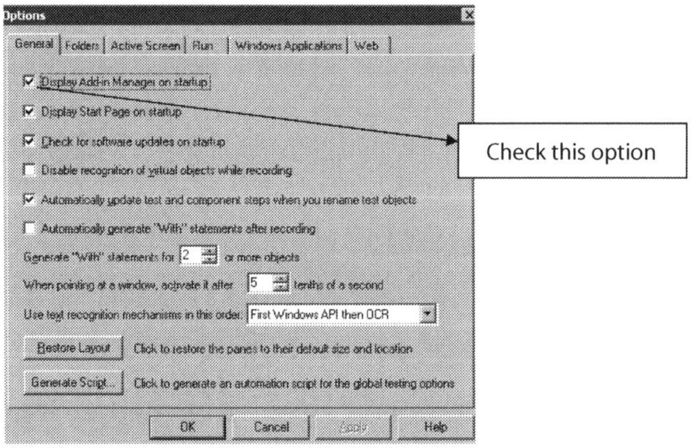

Figure 8.2 *Check Add-in Manger Window.*

8.3 HP QTP Window

HP QTP window is divided into several sections. Refer to Fig. 8.3 for details. The sections are:

- Title Bar
- Menu Bar
- Window for selected Pane
- Expert View window
- Keyword view tab
- Data Table
- Tabs for other panes

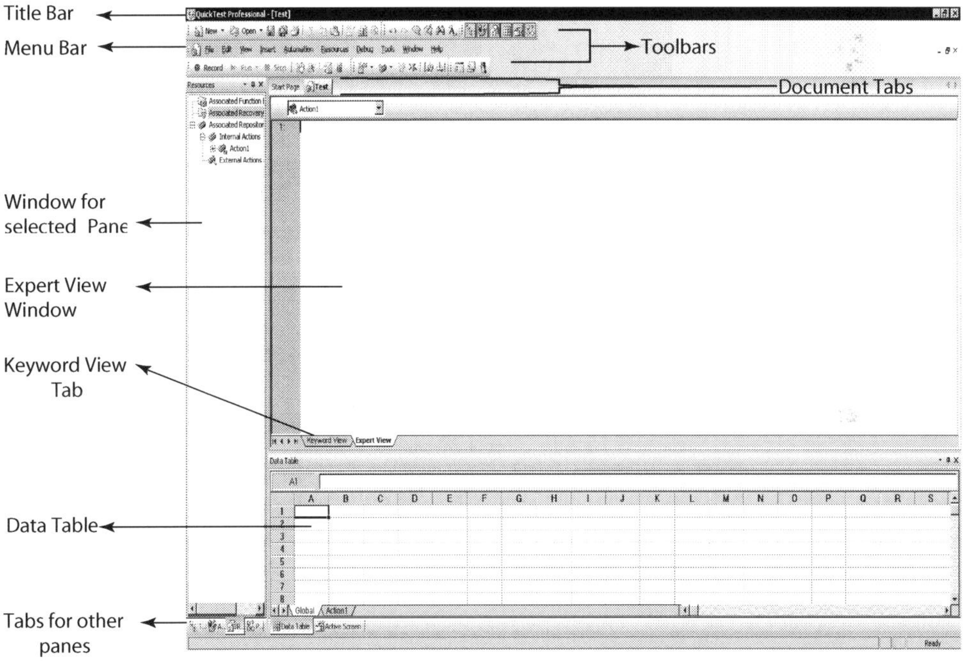

Figure 8.3 *HP QTP Window Explanation.*

Let me give you a brief explanation about few of the displayed area, which are not self-explanatory.

- *Title Bar*

  It displays the name of the active document or script. In addition, if the active script hasn't been saved, then an * (asterix) mark is displayed in the title bar.

- *Menu bar*

  This section displays the menu of HP QTP . There are in total 11 different menus, which contain several sub-menus.

- *Tabs for other panes*

  There are several panes under **"View"** menu of HP QTP . Every time when any one of them is selected, it starts reflecting in **"Tabs for other panes section".**
- *Window for selected pane*

  Whatever pane is selected under "Tabs for other section" area, the required window for that pane gets displayed, in "Window for selected pane".
- Data Table

  This is the area where various data sets are stored and hence are used within the scripts. This section has both global and per-action data table worksheet.

8.3.1 Understanding Important Attributes of HP QTP

HP QTP , as you know, is a very powerful functional test automation tool. Powerful, because of some fantastic features of it, which help HP QTP earn this coveted status in the IT industry.

Let us try understanding attributes of few of the most important features of HP QTP .

- *Expert View*

This view gets ported into HP QC 9.2 or 10.0, when QTP is integrated with QC. Advantage that HP QC 9.2 or 10.0 gives here is that without even launching HP QTP, user can see the expert view platform and codes through QC.

This view, in HP QTP, is such a view where code-level detailing is displayed. Using this view, users can edit existing step, insert new step and do various other activities in terms of debugging the already recorded steps or can even record and code a new test altogether.

In order to explain this section in detail, let me first walk you through a scenario.

Let us say that through HP QTP , the below displayed steps need to be recorded:

Step 1) Launch IE

Step 2) Sync the IE window.

Step 3) Enter www.hp.com, in the browser address window

Step 4) Input "Printers" under search field

Step 5) Click submit

Step 6) Sync the search result page

Step 7) Close the window.

User records the steps through HP QTP.

Corresponding HP QTP code line for the same is:

Step 1) SystemUtil.Run "C:\Program Files\Internet Explorer\iexplore.exe","","M:\","open"

Step 2) Browser("Customize Your Settings").Page("Customize Your Settings").Sync

Step 3) Browser("Customize Your Settings").Navigate "http://www.hp.com/"

Step 4) Browser("HP United States - Computers,").Page("HP United States - Computers,").WebEdit("qt").Set "printers"

Step 5) Browser("HP United States - Computers,").Page("HP United States - Computers,").WebEdit("qt").Submit

Step 6) Browser("Search HP US - Search").Page("Search HP US - Search").Sync

Step 7) Browser("Customize Your Settings").CloseAllTabs

These codelines, if you would refer to the below figure, gets generated in *"Expert view"*

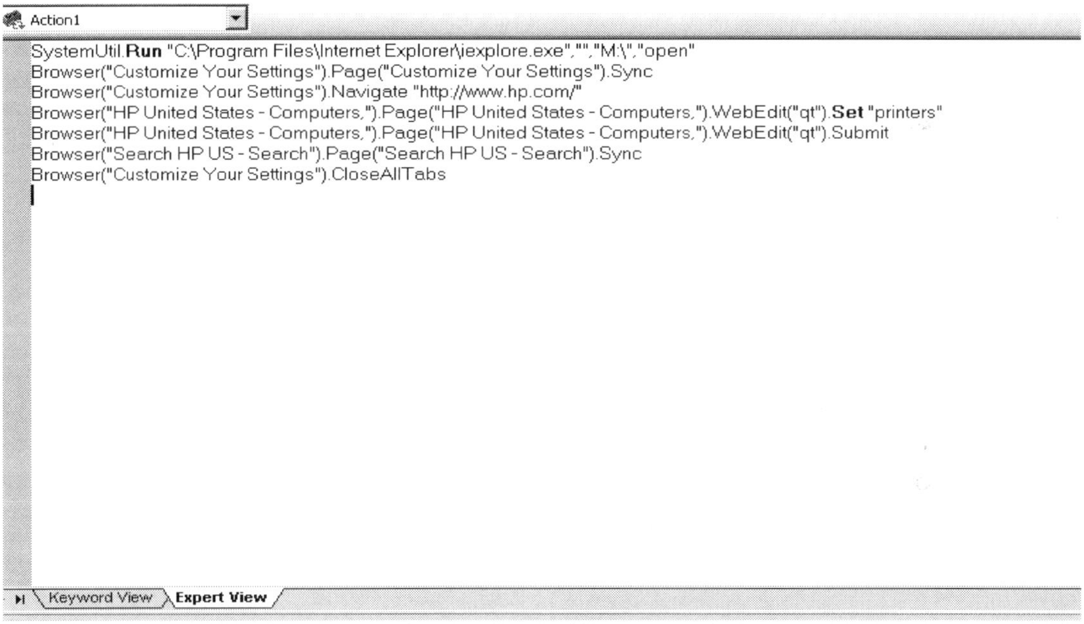

Figure 8.4 *Expert View.*

- *Keyword View*

  This view enables you to create and view the steps of your test in a keyword driven modular table format.

For the steps discussed within the expert view section, let us see how keyword view layout would be.

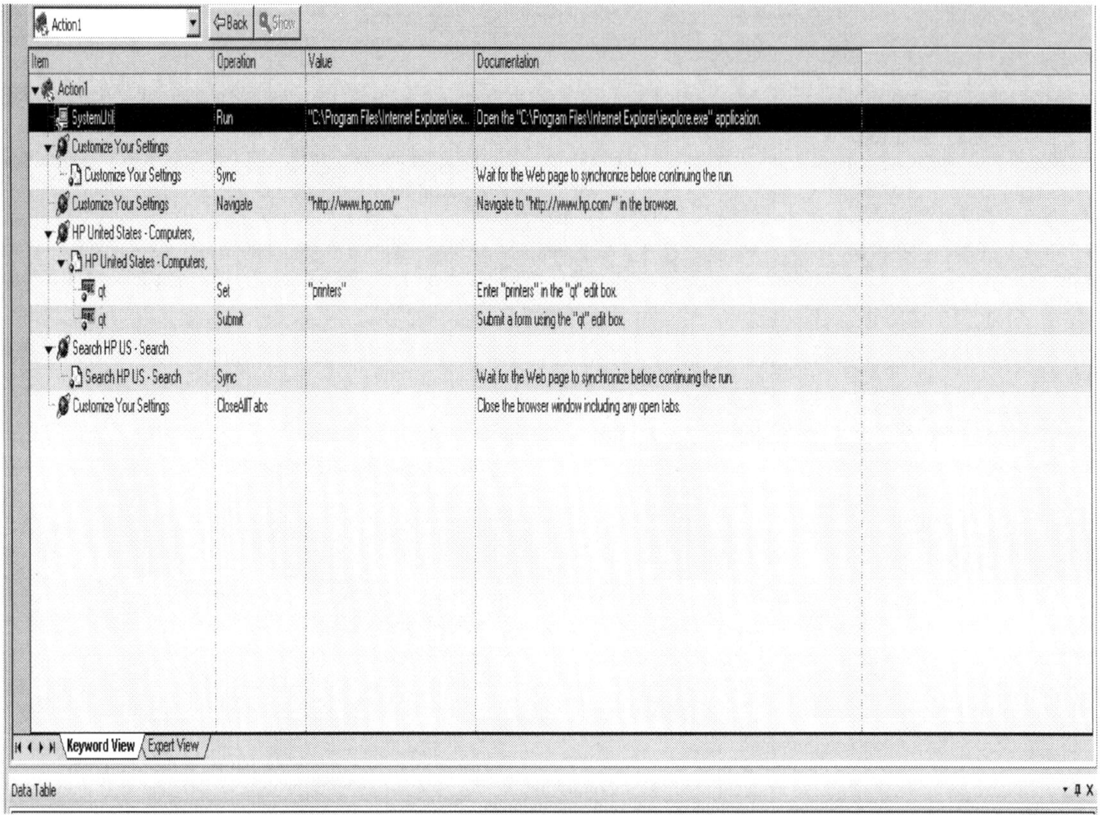

Figure 8.5 *Tabular Format in "Keyword View".*

Like expert view, if HP QTP is integrated with HP QC 9.2 or 10.0, then keyword view can be referenced in QC itself, without launching HP QTP .

- *Active Screen:*

During the recording session, HP QTP "Active Screen" feature captures the screen shot of the recorded screen. After recording gets stopped and if one wants to see the recorded step and its subsequent screen, through "Active Screen" feature this facility is made available to the user.

In order to populate active screen in **"Tabs for other panes"** section, go to "QTP -> View-> and select "Active screen".

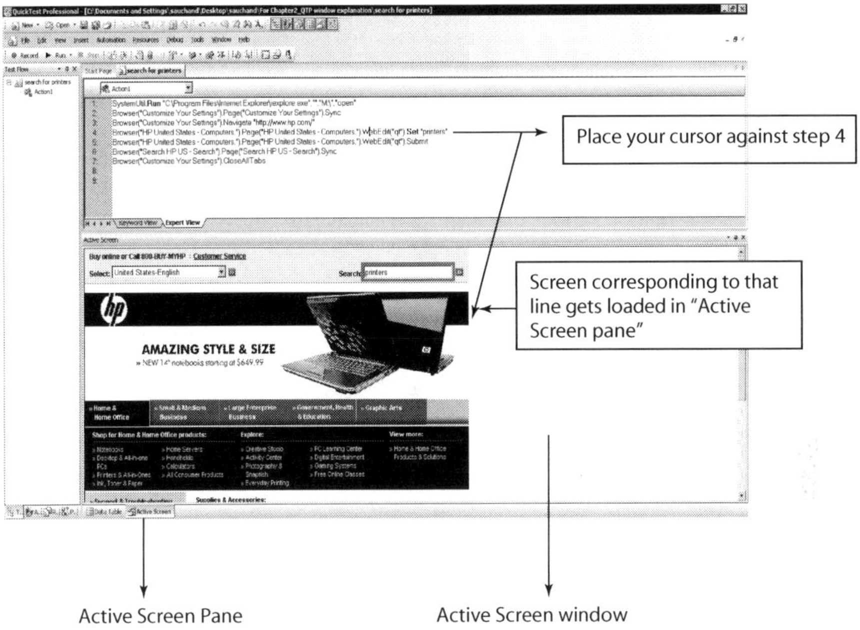

Figure 8.6 *"Active Screen" Window.*

Important point here is that if HP QTP is integrated with HP QC 10.0, then without launching QTP, in QC, this active screen can be viewed as how expert view and keyword view, can be referenced.

- *Test Flow Pane*

  In order to populate "Test Flow" pane in "Tabs for other panes" section, goto **"QTP -> View->** and select **"Test Flow".**

  It is the pane where all the actions within that test get reflected. Furthermore, in this pane, the actions are reflected into hierarchical fashion.

- *Resources Pane*

  As the name suggests, this is a feature from where one can manage all the resources associated to a current test. When I say all the resources that mean Local OR, Shared OR, function libraries and Recovery scenarios.

  In order to populate **"Resources"** pane in **"Tabs for other panes"** section, go to **"QTP -> View->** and select **"Resources".**

- *Missing Resources Pane*

  In order to populate **"Missing Resources"** pane in **"Tabs for other panes"** section, go to **"QTP -> View->** and select **"Missing Resources".** (*Refer 5.2.1.f for better understanding*)

The major attribute of missing resources pane is that whenever a test is opened in HP QTP and if any of the resources stated within the test are not mapped to the test, then the same gets captured and displayed through missing resources pane.

Missing resources can include highlighting missing resources messages about calls to missing actions, missing function libraries, missing recovery scenarios, a missing XML file used to store environment variables, unmapped shared object repositories, and parameters that are connected to shared object repositories.

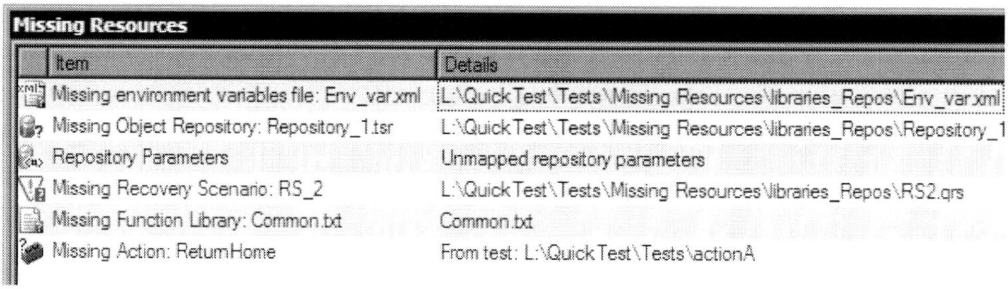

Figure 8.7 *Missing Resources Pane.*

All these features are very critical when HP QTP is being used for automation using HP QC 9.2 or 10 . The most important aspect of this knowledge comes into play when automation framework needs to be designed to store scripts of various types, such as single test case script, functions, libraries, etc. Not knowing in-depth about all such areas and then designing and rolling framework, can prove to be very costly for organisation.

Therefore, thorough understanding of these attributes is mandatory before anyone thinks of laying automation framework, using HP QTP and HP QC .

8.4 Folder Option to Reference Important Resources Path

HP QTP has some out-of-the-box global settings, which is machine specific and is not user specific. Changing these settings, at times, changes the appearance of quick test.

As an example, if you choose not to launch add-in manager at start up, then you will not be seeing that add-in manager window at startup.

However, at times, user feels the need to change the settings either because of the business need or for customizing UI and coding need.

One such business need is when you are storing all your libraries, files, etc., in HP QC 9.2 or 10. To have proper handshake between all scripts and related files, you need to configure the path in the tools setting permanently. And that can be done using the below displayed section.

In order to invoke the global setting option, go to **QTP -> Tools -> Options**

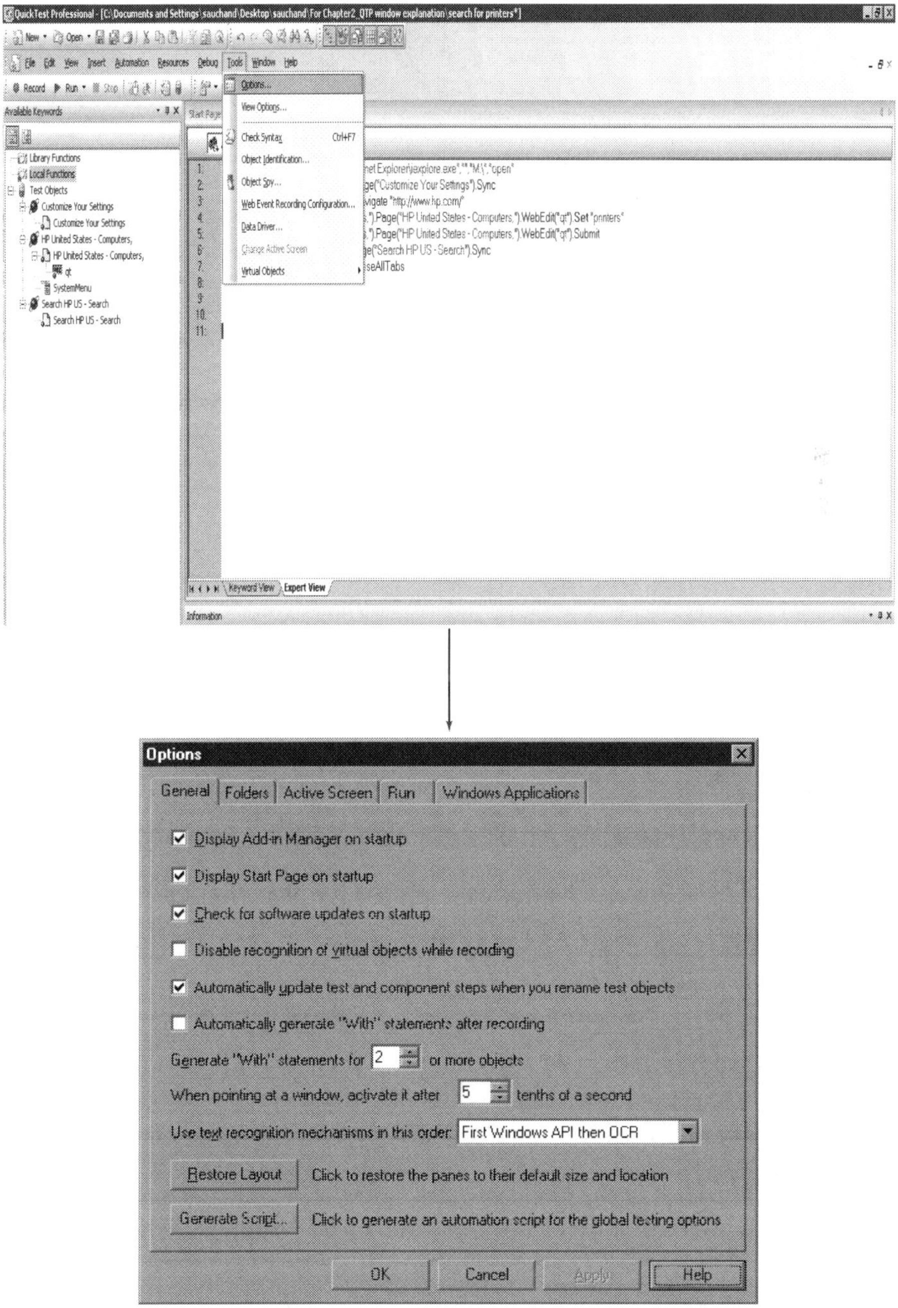

Figure 8.8 *Options, General Setting Window.*

- **Folders Option**: Coming to second tab-bar within options window leads to "Folders Option" section.

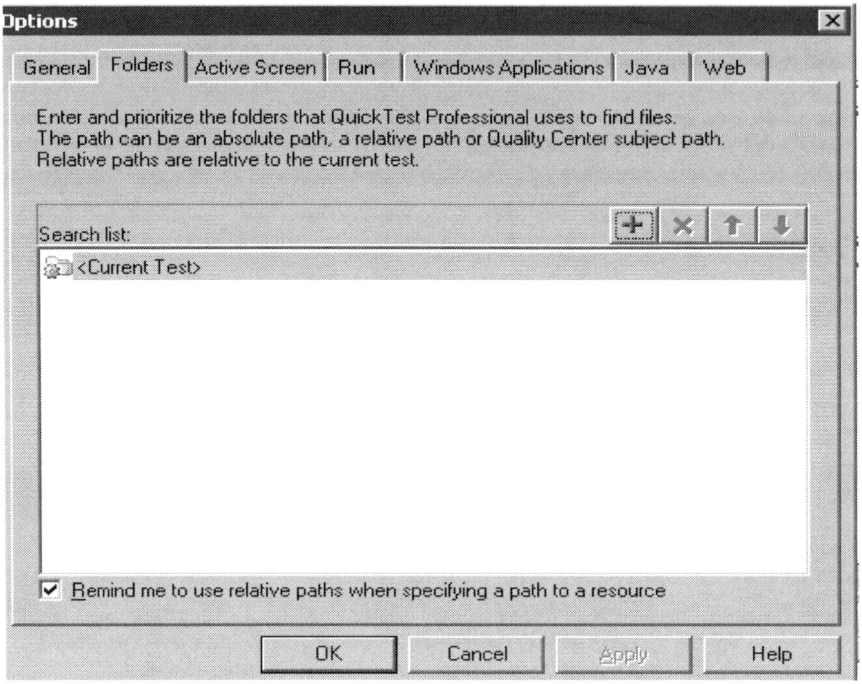

Figure 8.9 *Snapshot of "Folders" Section Under "Options" Window.*

Folders section provides an option to users to add the path of all such resources, which during the development or execution needs to be used by various tests. In such a scenario, HP QTP automatically searches for these files within the folders section and hence utilizes the same during execution of various associated tests. This becomes really an efficient methodology to practice when QTP is integrated with QC and then all files are stored at specific path in QC . Therefore, configuring that global path and making tool learn this throughout, helps in increasing development or execution efficiency.

8.5 OR Basics and OR Types

There are two different types of Object Repositories that can be associated with tests. Let us try understanding both the types:

1. Local Object Repository
2. Shared Object Repository

8.5.1 Local Object Repository

Any set of objects, when are recorded for a single action and are accessed only through that action, then that object storage mechanism is known as "Local Object Repository" storage mechanism.

- When to use "Local Object Repository"?
  - When the object description for a particular object type does not change so often.
  - When the functionality to be automated is kind of pretty much single action test.
  - When for an application you do not have many tests to automate.

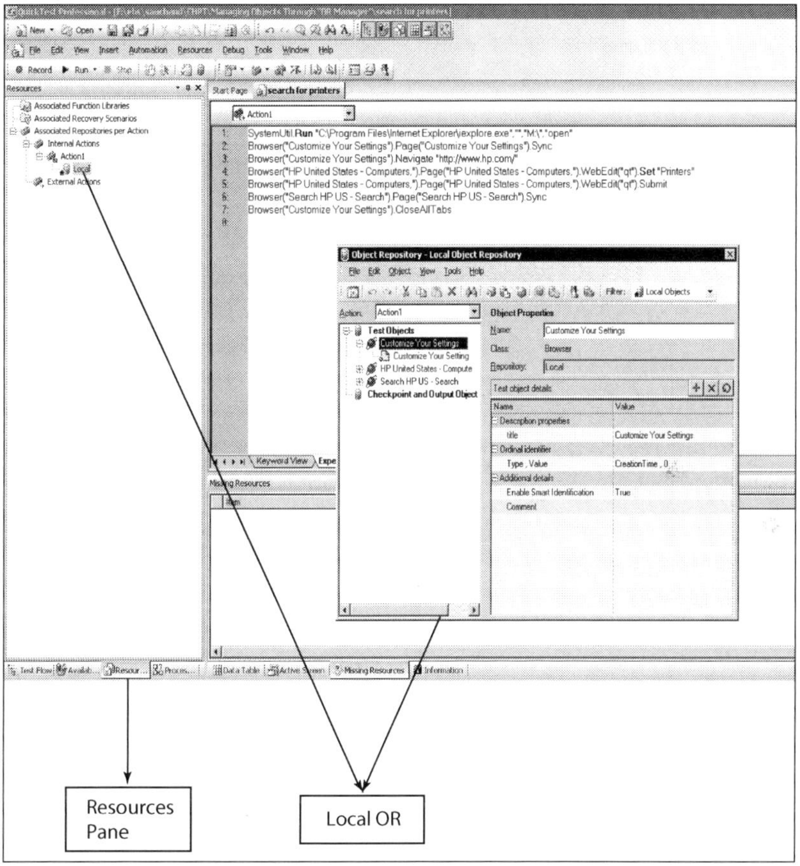

Figure 8.10 *Local OR.*

8.5.2 Shared Object Repository

When the description of the object needs to be shared amongst several actions or tests, then objects are stored in a file, which is termed as "Shared Object Repository" file. The same is used by all the tests. The extension of this file is ".tsr".

Attribute of "Shared Object Repository" is that the common objects, across scripts/actions in a test, are not duplicated in shared object repository. However, the same is not true for "Local Object Repository".

- When to use "Shared Object Repository"?
    - When several tests or actions within a test use similar object description and the object description for that particular object type changes very often.
    - When the functionality to be automated consists of collection of scripts, which in turn have many common objects amongst each.
    - When for an application you have many tests to automate.
    - When re-usability of tests is very high within your working scenario.

In order to generate shared OR, one either has to import Local OR into a packet using OR manager or use an existing shared OR to contain newly recorded objects of a new script in existing shared OR. Shared object file extension is .tsr and hence is shared OR.

Let us see pictorially in brief, how to create shared OR .

Step 1) Local OR gets recorded automatically during script recording. Opening Local OR file and then selecting the option as displayed in the below Fig. 8.11, i.e., *"Export and Replace Local Objects"*, will transport all objects into a file having .tsr extension. That file is shared OR file. You can save that file at your preferred location and hence add it to the script wherever to be used.

Refer to Figs. 8.11, 8.12, and 8.13 to understand the sequence.

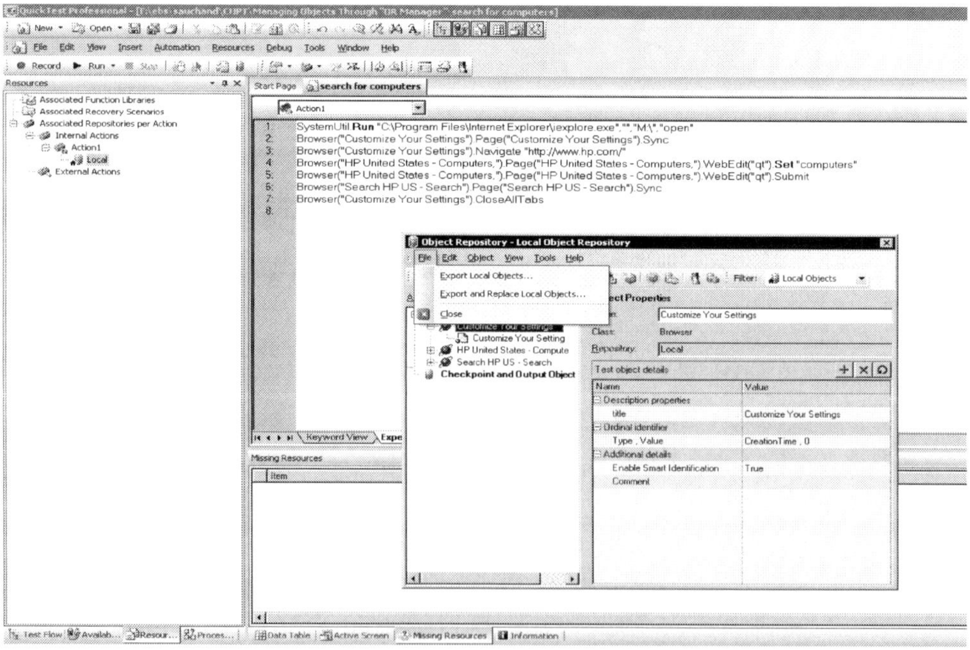

Figure 8.11 *Export Local OR.*

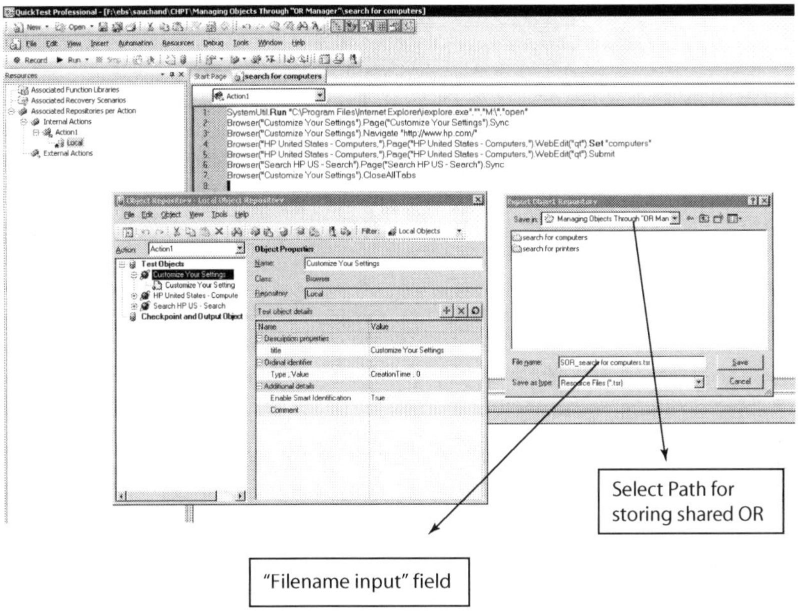

Figure 8.12 *Store Local OR into .tsr Extension File.*

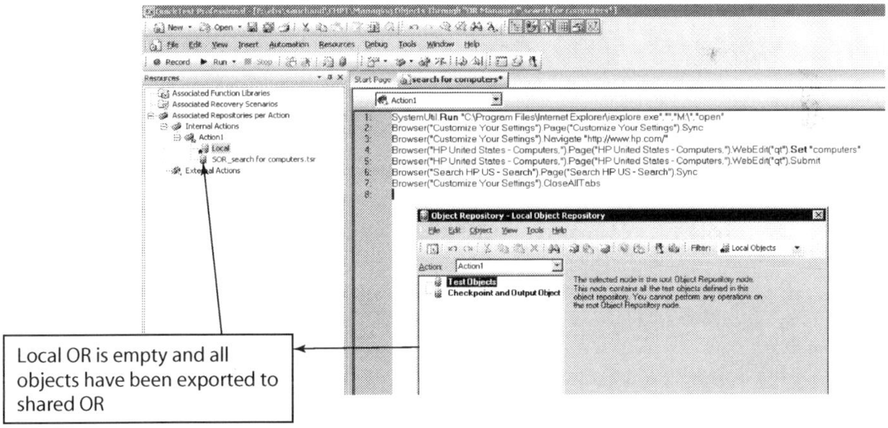

Figure 8.13 *Shared OR Created and Attached to the Script.*

8.5.3 Which OR to be Used in QC?

The important question here is which repository type to be used, when using the QC+QTP infrastructure.

The answer is that it does not depend on QC+QTP integration infrastructure, but the real answer depends upon the script execution mechanics that organisation is planning for. To elaborate further on this, if organisation plans to execute same script against four different environment applications or techstack concurrently, then shared object repository is not advisable. But if organisation plans to use good number of scripts to be run sequentially and not concurrently against various environments flavors then shared object repository is highly recommended.

8.6 Binding Two Separate Scripts In QTP

If you have two individual scripts that you want to bind together, then QTP provides various techniques to do so. In Fig. 8.14, such features have been shown as encircled. These are described further.

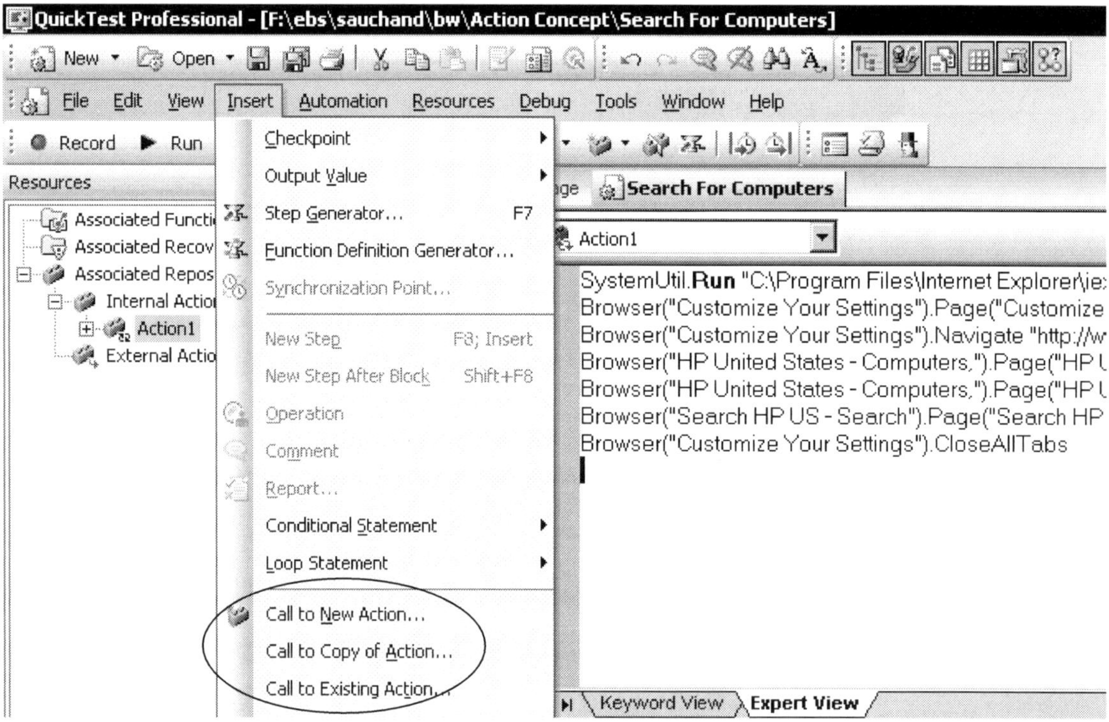

Figure 8.14 *Techniques to Bind Two Individual Scripts.*

- **Call to new action:**
  This is used to create any new action. After assigning the attributes for this newly created action, one can save it. Newly created action, through this method does not contain any code line. This is used simply to create an empty action file having certain assigned attributes. After creating new action, one can start recording the cases, accordingly within this action.

- **Call to copy of action:**
  Using this feature, whatever action you are trying to call, a copy of that action gets associated with the test.
  After inserting call to copy of action, if the action gets modified than the new changes done in the parent action, will not get reflected within the inserted action.
  This option is used when you know that already existing scripts can be re-used to a certain extent and later you can build over and above the same. Using this option makes the action and associated data table, editable.
- **Call to existing action:**
  Unlike call to copy, in call to existing feature, the script that you call gets associated to the called script but acts on the theory of "call by reference". If parent script gets changed then in the called script also that change is visible.
  As per QC+QTP integration is concerned, these features are one of the most valuable features to learn. On almost everyday basis, user would feel the need to bind two individual scripts into one and thus anyone of these features, accordingly, need to be used.

8.7 Passing Variables Between Two Individual Scripts

You have seen how to bind scripts. Now, let us see another case here.

Suppose you have two test cases in QC, where in output of one test case has to become input to another test case. Now, when you are executing test case manually, it is still fine because you can write down the output of one test case on paper and then while executing second test case, can input the same wherever required. But the same if has to be emulated in automation scenario between two individual scripts, then an important feature named, I/P – O/P feature comes to use. Here, output of first script is captured in a variable and that variable is stored in the "Output Parameter" section of first script. Now this variable value has to be inputted to the second script; therefore, this variable is now stored in "Input Parameter" section of second script. In this way, communication between two different scripts gets established when it comes to passing variable value.

When you are working with QTP using QC integration infrastructure, this scenario again will be the most frequently occurring scenario. Thus knowing the technique behind I/P-O/P parameter passing, reduces the operational intricacies to manifold. Hence, it exhibits great boost to development efficiency.

In order to open the parameters window, you need to open script and go to **"File-> Settings"**.
Parameters Tab-bar:

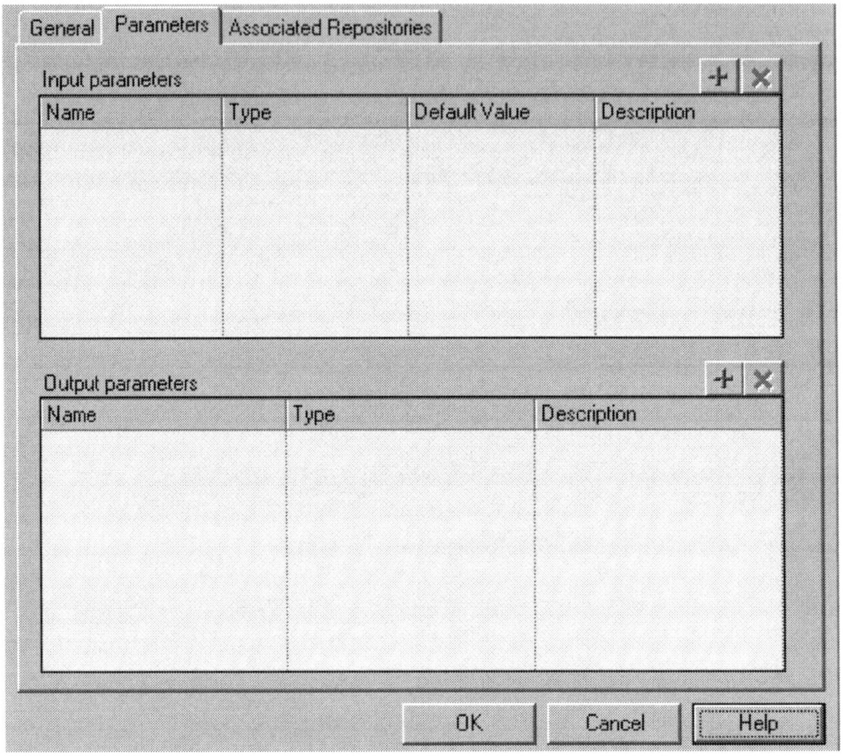

Figure 8.15 *Enlarged View of "Parameters" Window.*

Under this you can see "Input Parameters" section and "Output Parameters" section.

- Input parameters are those parameters, which if defined at the test level, then the variable values can be used across action from top to bottom level with respect to action hierarchy.
- Output parameters are those, which return a value to the action within which output parameters have been defined and those values can be used in later associated actions.

  Let us see a code snippet, to understand the usage of input and output parameters.

Scenario is that within a transaction, one has to enter the amount for two different materials and then automatically total amount would be evaluated by the application.

Let us say "Amount 1" and "Amount 2" are the input amount and hence, these are the input parameters. "Total Amount" is the output parameter for which tool will capture the value and will store in the output parameter which will return the values to the required action.

.Set parameter is the internal QTP method that helps in calling parameter variable value within the script codeline.

Browser("A").Page("B").WebEdit("Material 1").Set Parameter("Amount 1")

Browser("A").Page("B").WebEdit("Material 2").Set Parameter("Amount 2")

Browser("A").Page("B").WebButton("Enter").Click

NumTableRows = Browser("A").Page("B").WebTable("Orders").RowCount

Parameter("TotalAmount") = Browser("A").Page("B").WebTable("Orders").GetCellData (NumTableRows,"Total")

8.8 Parameterization Through Data Table

Parameterization through data table is one of the most widely used concepts within automation fraternity. In fact, it would not be wrong to state that this is one of the most powerful techniques to modularize your script to handle n{where n = 1 to infinity} no. of data sets through single or limited lines of code.

<u>For better understanding of this concept, let us consider a test case here:</u>

Step 1) Launch IE

Step 2) Sync the IE window.

Step 3) Enter www.hp.com, in the browser address window

Step 4) Input "computers" under search field

Step 5) Click submit

Step 6) Sync the search result page

Step 7) Close the window

In the above discussed step 4, you can see that "computers" is the keyword that is being inputted. Now if the similar search for keyword "printers", "laptops" and "personal computers" have to be performed, then is it that step 4 needs to be recorded 4 times or is it that from step 1 to step 7 needs to be recorded 4 times?

Well, I can say, yes, if you want your code to look unintelligent and ineffective, then you can record the above steps for different cases for 4 times.

However, the other alternative is through intelligent coding, i.e., embedding parameterization through data table technique within the code line. This technique neither demands to record step 4 for 4 times not does this demand to record all the steps from step 1 to step 7, for 4 times.

Only the steps mentioned within the test case will be recorded once, and the rest will be dealt through data table parameterization technique.

Let's see the mechanism and code line for embedding data table parameterization technique.

<u>Method I</u>: Using **QTP -> Tools -> Data driver**

Step 1) Record the above test case but only once. Code generated would be:

SystemUtil.Run "C:\Program Files\Internet Explorer\iexplore.exe","","M:\","open"

Browser("Customize Your Settings").Page("Customize Your Settings").Sync

Browser("Customize Your Settings").Navigate <u>http://www.hp.com/</u>

Browser("HP United States - Computers,").Page("HP United States - Computers,").WebEdit("qt").Set "computers"

Browser("HP United States - Computers,").Page("HP United States - Computers,").WebEdit("qt").Submit

Browser("Search HP US - Search").Page("Search HP US - Search").Sync

Browser("Customize Your Settings").CloseAllTabs

Step 2) Pick up below stated line and highlight keyword "computers"

Browser("HP United States - Computers,").Page("HP United States - Computers,").WebEdit("qt").Set "computers"

Step 3) Go to **QTP -> Tools -> Data Driver**

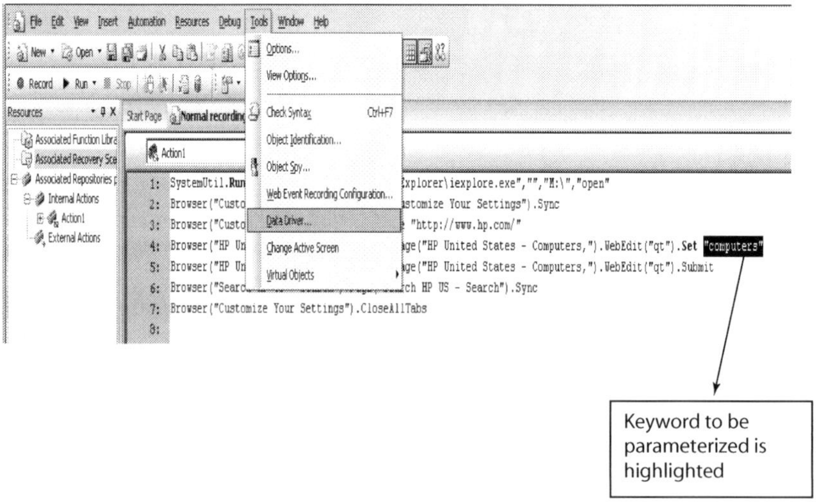

Figure 8.16 *Invoke Data Driver.*

Step 4) Data driver window gets displayed.

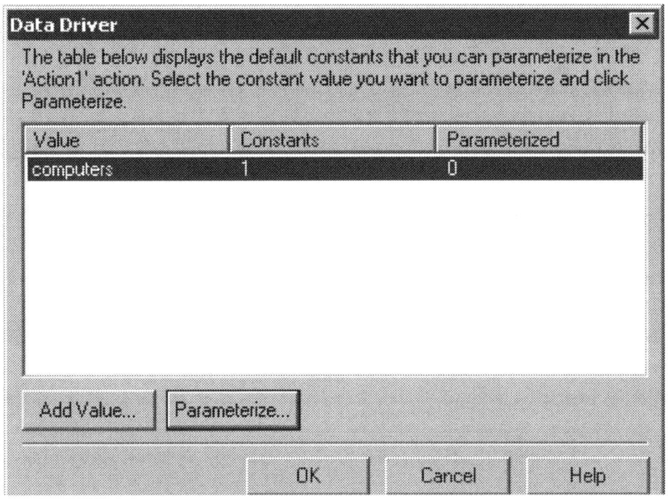

Figure 8.17 *Data Driver Window.*

Click "Parameterize" on the data driver window.

Step 5) "Select parameterization type" window gets displayed.

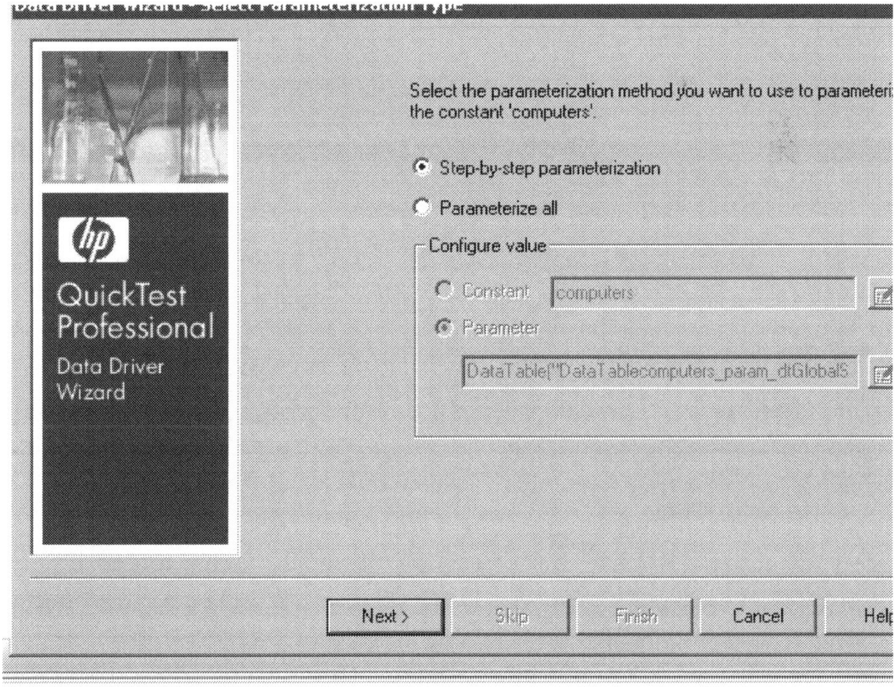

Figure 8.18 *Select Parameterization Type Window.*

You can see the two radio boxes on the "select parameterization type" window.

- *Parameterize all*

  This needs to be selected if you have all the constants listed within the data driver window and you want to parameterize all at one go.
- *Step-by-step parameterization*

  This needs to be selected when you have more than one value listed within data driver window and you want to parameterize all one by one.

Let's choose "Step-by-step parameterization" option and click "Next".

Step 6) A window comes up, which displays the values that is getting parameterized along with other parameterization details. As in Fig. 8.19, the data has been stored within global sheet.

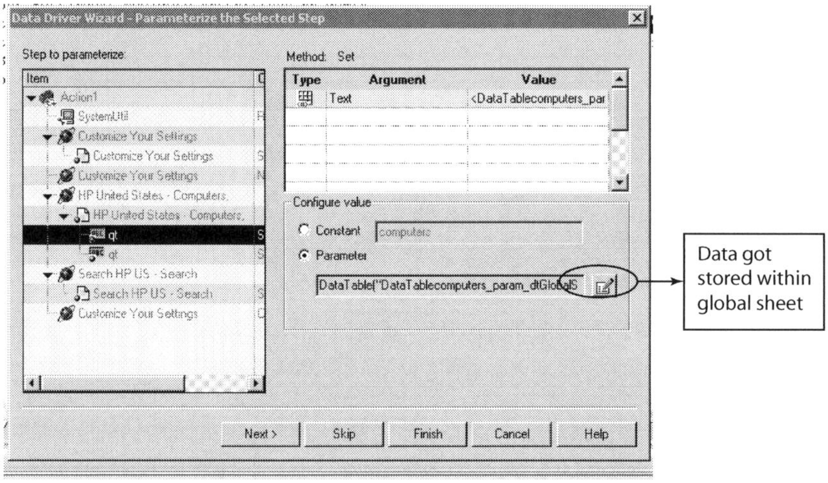

Figure 8.19 *Value Getting Parameterized.*

Click "Finish". Close the data driver wizard. And this completes your parameterization.

Step 7) The code against which parameterization technique was performed gets converted into new parameterized line. New line looks like:

Browser("HP United States - Computers,").Page("HP United States - Computers,").WebEdit("qt"). Set DataTable("DataTablecomputers_param_dtGlobalSheet", dtGlobalSheet)

The meaning for this newly generated code is that the value, which is inputted within the field "qt" under page "("HP United States - Computers,")" and browser "("HP United States - Computers,")", has been parameterized into global sheet. The name of the column, which stores the parameterized value, is "DataTablecomputers_param_dtGlobalSheet".

Here if one feels like changing the name of the column, certainly it can be done.

To perform so, double click the column name within the global sheet. A window "change parameter name" would come up where you can input the new column name. Let us keep the new column name as "Search_keyword". Replace the old column name within the codeline to "Search_keyword". The new code line now looks like:

Browser("HP United States - Computers,").Page("HP United States - Computers,").WebEdit("qt"). Set DataTable("Search_keyword_dtGlobalSheet", dtGlobalSheet)

After inserting the required parameterization techniques, let's see how HP QTP UI looks like.

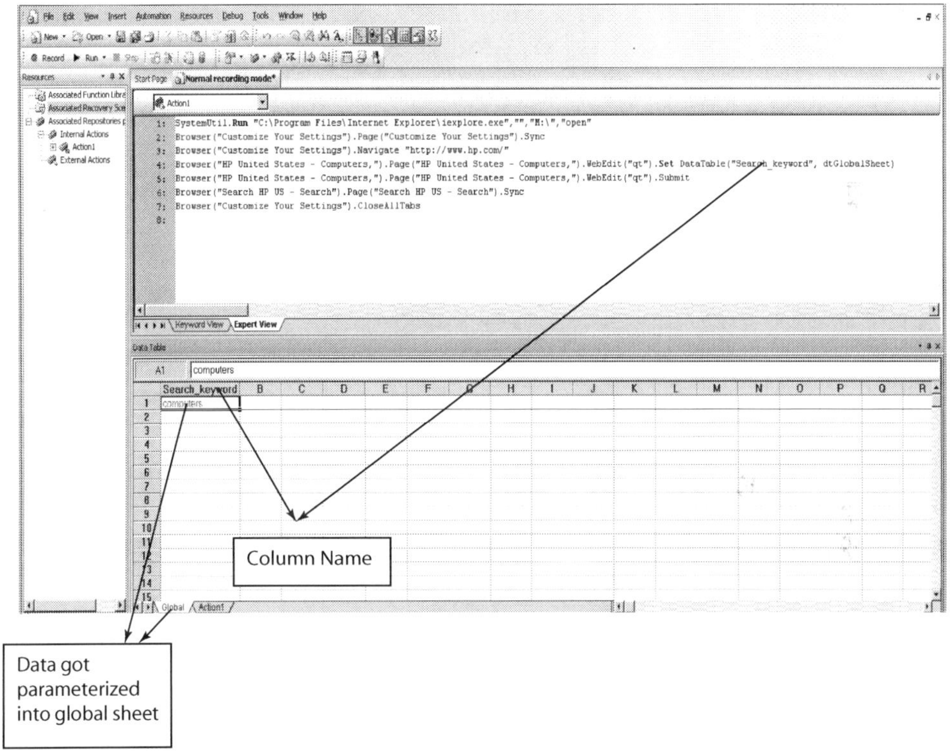

Figure 8.20 *HP QTP Layout After Parameterization is Complete.*

Now, the other requirement to tackle is how to make use of the same code for performing search operation against other keywords, i.e. "printers", "laptops" and "personal computers"?

The answer is, don't stop at seven 7. Move ahead to further steps.

Step 8) Under "Search_keyword" column, enter other values i.e. "printers", "laptops" and "personal computers".

Step 9) Go to **File -> settings -> Run**. Select the option **"Run on all rows".** Selecting this option ensures that tool traverses the code line for those many iterations for which data set is available within the rows. Therefore, with this logic, for our discussed case, the total number of iterations would be 4.

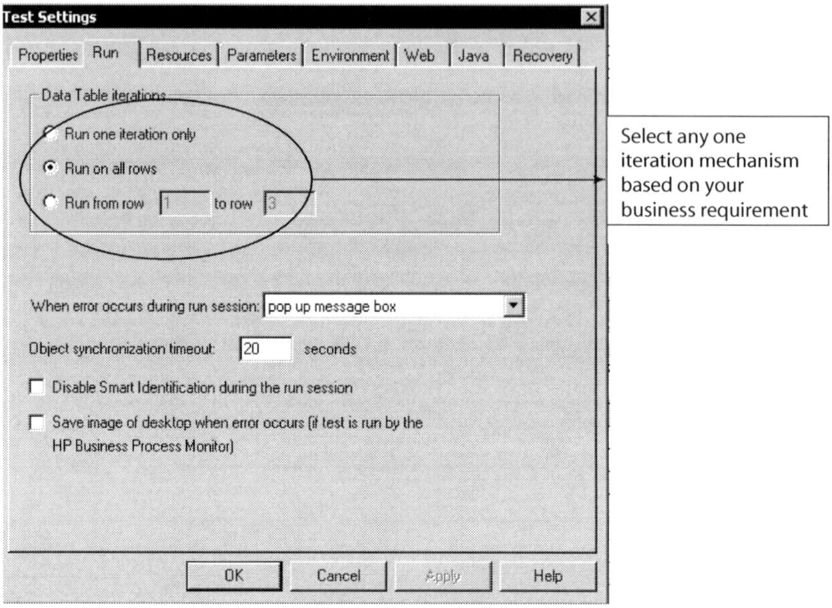

Figure 8.21 *Run Settings for Data Table Iterations.*

Select **"OK"** and kick off the execution. Your code line is ready to be traversed across all the row values within the data table.

An important point while selecting any of these options is that when any of the run options are selected then during execution, next iteration starts after completing the last line of the script and again starts off from first line of the script. Therefore, the only area to ensure is that do check the initial condition and end condition of the script so that your code, while completing one iteration and going on another, does not stop in-between.

The result file, as displayed in Fig. 8.22, displays results for all the 4 iterations.

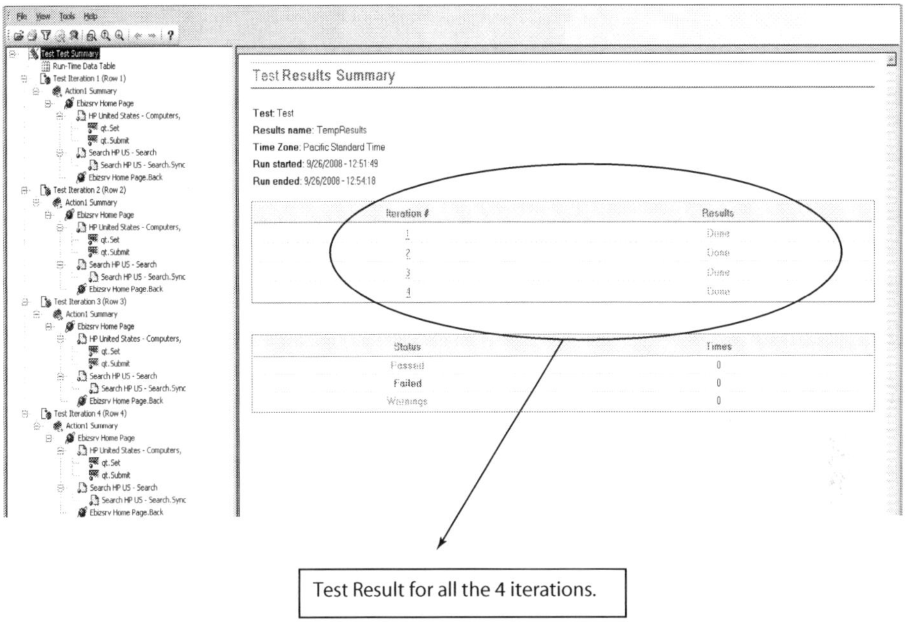

Figure 8.22 *Test Result for All The Iterations.*

8.8.1 Definition Global Sheet and Local sheet

Let me put down two very famous questions that, during my working tenure, have been asked by many professionals.

- *What is Global sheet and Local sheet according to the action sheet?*
  They are basically .xls files worksheet, which is embedded within HP QTP interface. These worksheets are basically required if one wants to parameterize a value for either random numbers or for having "*n* {where *n* = 1 to infinity}" number of iterations for set of code or for capturing an output value during runtime. In addition to these worksheets, one can even output or export the runtime values to external worksheets or .xls files. Furthermore, this doesn't restrict HP QTP from referring to additional .xls file, which can be stored outside HP QTP.

- What is the most important difference between these two worksheets?

  Global worksheet values: The values stored within the global sheet can be used across various scripts within a suite.
  Per Action or local worksheet values: The values stored within this sheet are local only to that script or action.

8.9 Establishing HP QC 9.2 or 10.0 Connection Through HP QTP

There are two ways in which HP QTP can be launched, when integrated with HP QC. One via QC, and another is directly and then establishing connection to HP QC.

Let me walk you through the steps to show how to establish connection to QC via HP QTP.

Step 1) Launch QTP and click the highlighted icon "Quality Center Connection".

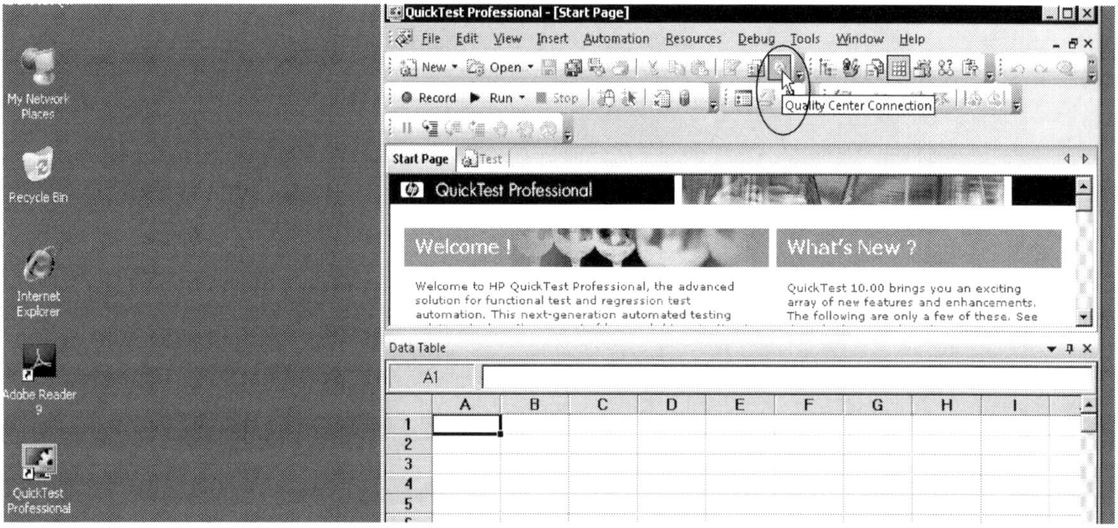

Figure 8.23 *Quality Center Connection Icon.*

Step 2) Quality center server connection window will come up. Enter the address where HP QC is installed.

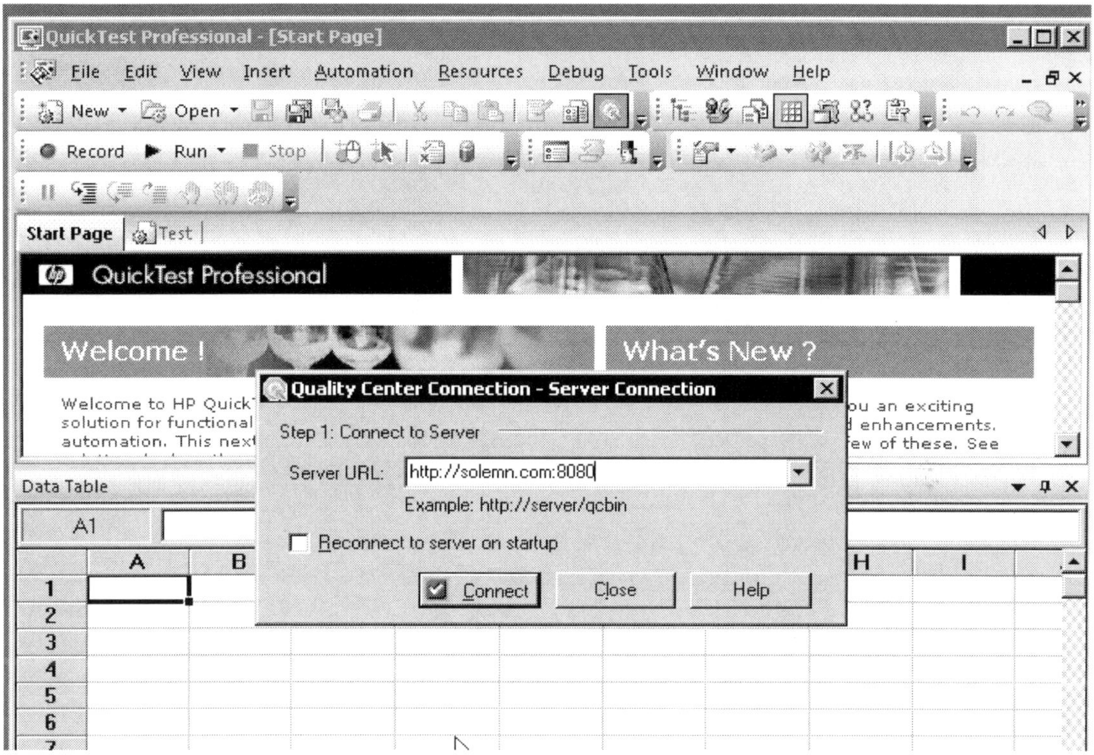

Figure 8.24 *QC Connection Server Window.*

Step 3) Click "Connect" button and give required login credentials and thus, connection gets established. From here on, you can access all directories stored on HP QC pertaining to your domain and project.

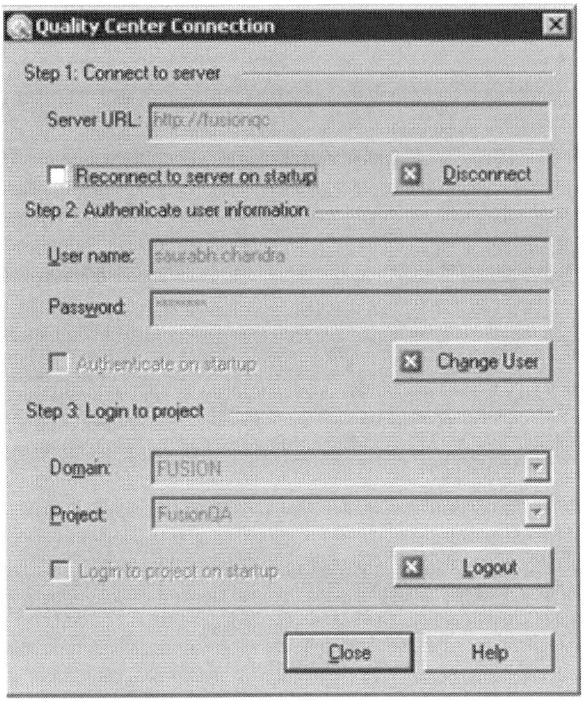

Figure 8.25 *QC Connection Window.*

This equips you with very basic understanding of HP QTP and HP QC 9.2 or 10.0 integration mechanics. However, again I would like to re-iterate that in order to learn the HP QTP in detail, the book recommended is "Automation Testing by Saurabh Chandra", published by McGraw-Hill, India. Must grab!!

HP Quality Centre 10: Automating Tests and Execution Methodology

9

Chapter Objectives: This chapter will give an overview of

- *Test Planning - Automation*
- *HP QC 10 integration with automation tool*
- *Planning automation script*
- *Test Lab*
- *Manual Execution*
- *Automation Execution — Tips*

9.1 Test Planning — Automation

One of the most critical aspects of HP QC is the ability to store automation scripts and keep it tightly coupled with the corresponding manual test case. Till now, we have seen how release, requirements, test, test cases, bug defects are closely tied up to each other. In this section, you will see how manual test case gets converted to automation test script and is also closely coupled with all the required modules.

9.2 HP QC 10 Integration with Automation Tool

Before we talk about the automation attribute support by HP QC 10, it is very critical to understand that HP QC 10 does not support codeline development aspect of automation, but just ensures storage and logical integration of developed automation script with its associated requirements such as test cases, tests, requirement documentation, cycle, release, cycle and defects.

Another question that may be tickling your mind is:

Which all tool does HP QC 10 support?

Answer to this one is that primarily, it does not support tools which are not owned by HP.

Few of such tools that can be integrated with HP QC 10 are WinRunner, Quick Test Professional, LoadRunner, VAPI-XP-test, etc.

For ease of understanding, all examples that I would be taking you through will be using HP QTP+HP QC 10 integration. To have in-depth knowledge about QTP, I would strongly recommend you to go through the book "*Automation Testing*" by Saurabh Chandra, published by McGraw-Hill.

Therefore, before I discuss further, important point always to keep in mind is that, HP QC 10 is just a scientific storage area with some powers to integrate HP QTP tool and is not in itself an automation tool. HP QC 10, as I said earlier, is a "Test Management Tool".

Like manual test cases, automation test scripts are also stored under "Test Plan" area.

The first thing to understand under test plan area is the icon which demarcates between automation test script and test case. Manual test case has only one special typical icon but automation test script icon changes based on the tool that is being used with HP QC 10.

Few of the automation tool icons that get associated with automation test scripts are:

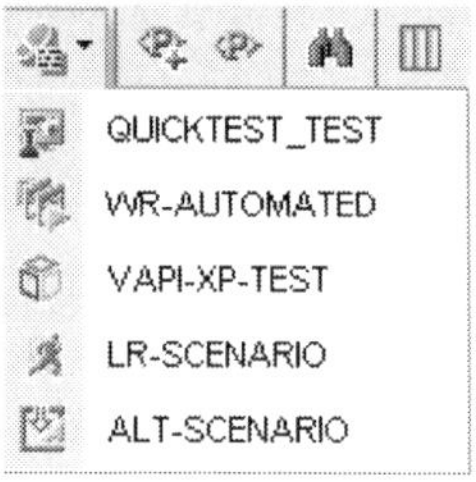

Figure 9.1 *Automation Test Script Icon.*

9.3 Planning Automation Script

Let us study the various steps involved in planning for automated test using HP QC 10 and HP QTP 9.5 or 10.0

Step 1) The first step to facilitate automation using HP QC 10 is to reach to the test case in "Test Plan" area. You open any of the parent folder and traverse to test case level.

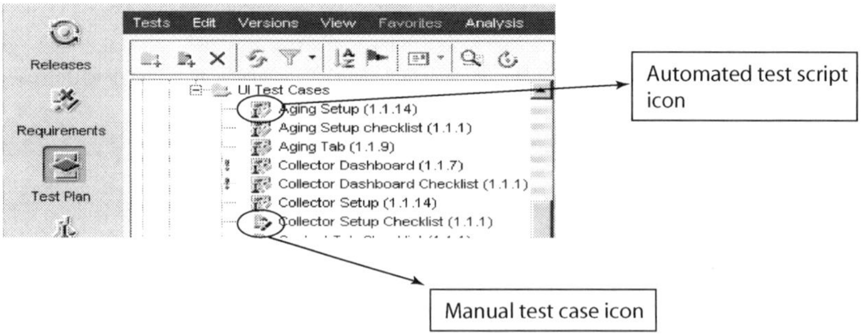

Figure 9.2 *Traversing to Test Case*

- *Automated test script icon:* These are already automated test cases and hence, the icon is getting displayed as "HP QTP automation icon"
- *Manual test case icon:* By default, this icon gets attached to the test case when one is designed and saved in HP QC 10

Step 2) Let us select the manual test case, name "collector setup checklist", as displayed in Fig. 103.

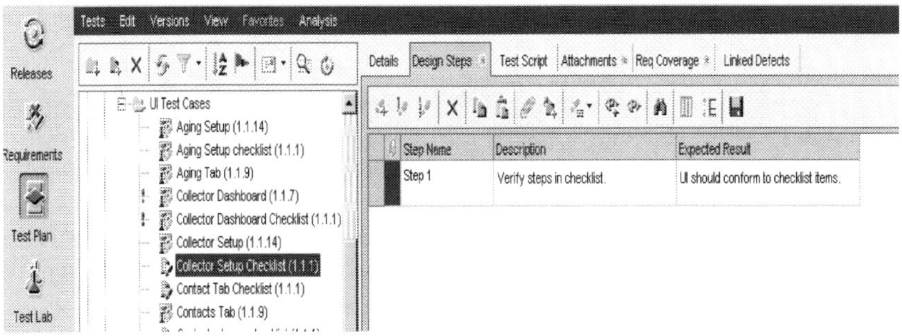

Figure 9.3 *Test Case to be Automated.*

Step 3) Go to "Design steps" and expand the menu item for "Generate script" icon. Select "QUICK-TEST_TEST".

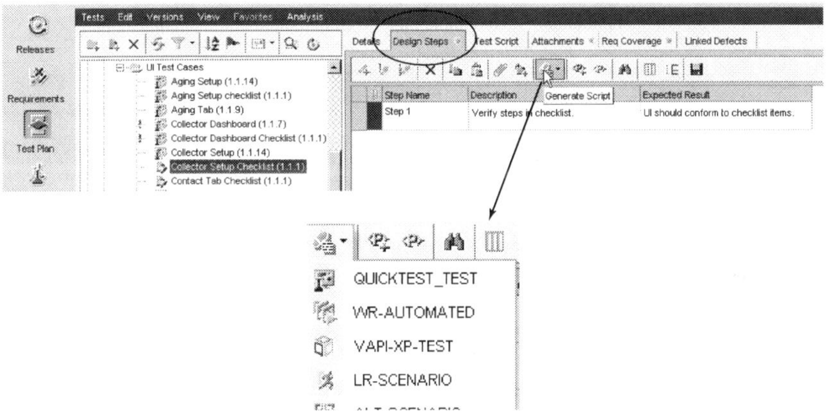

Figure 9.4 *Generate Script.*

Step 4) You would observe that test case icon would change:

- from manual" "to QTP script " "

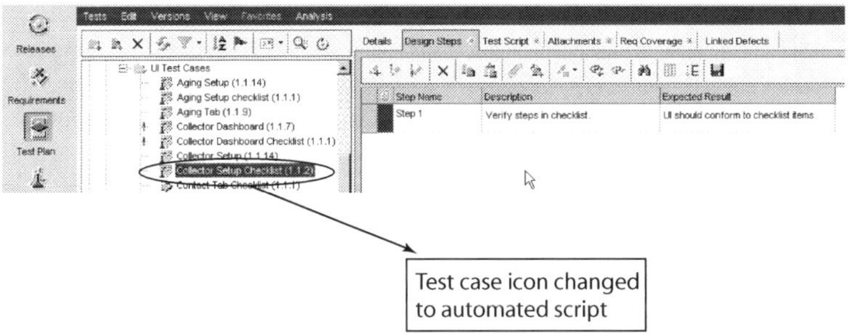

Figure 9.5 *Test Case Icon Changed to Automated Test Script.*

Step 5) Click "test script" tab-bar.

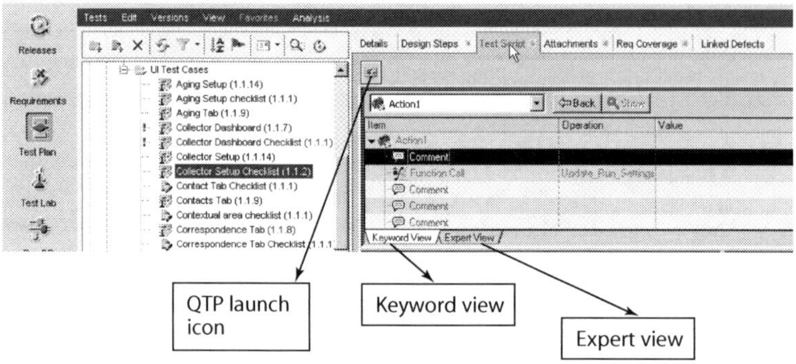

Figure 9.6 *"Test-Script" Tab-bar.*

You would observe that another frame at right hand side has opened up. This right hand frame is the automation panel, where you can see the codeline, if already generated and saved.

- *Keyword view:* This view in HP QTP provides details about coded steps but in a specific keyword fashion and hence is known as keyword view. HP QC 10 has ported this QTP feature in its UI and hence gives advantage to user to walk through those keyword statements via HP QC 10 itself.
- *Expert view:* Unlike keyword view, expert view provides detail code preview. This platform of HP QTP tool is also integrated with HP QC 10 and without launching QTP, user gets an advantage to review ones' code via QC itself.

  Another interesting point here is that, before script coding starts, if QC expert view is opened then user would observe that the manual test steps have got ported in QTP codeline as ***"reporter.reportevent ( ) method",*** having start and end messages. This QTP native method helps in echoing user logs in the result log file.

  This porting feature is one of the attributes of HP QC 10, which if configured, ports the test step in the displayed codeline under ***reporter.reportevent methods.*** Good practice says that all ideally in the result log, one should capture the start event of a step and end event of the step, which HP QC 10 gives the facility by default.

  As an example:

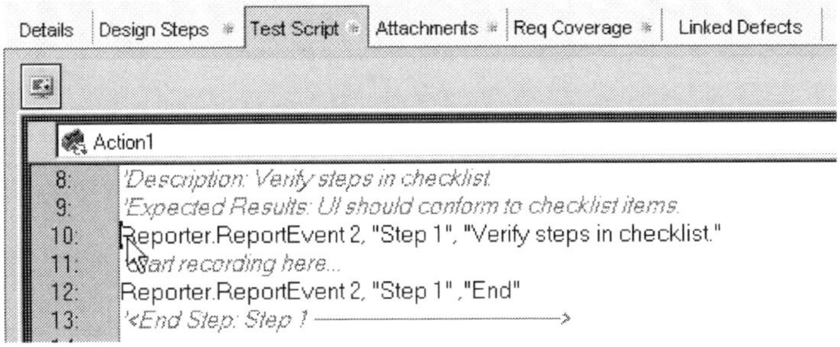

When QTP traverses the first ***reporter.reportevent*** statement then in log, a message will be captured which will mean that "test case step *"verify steps in checklist"* started .

And once the last statement is executed, then the log will capture the message that *"step 1 execution ends"*. Between this start and end block, codelines pertaining to functionality involved within this step should be coded.

- *QTP Launch icon:* The interesting part here is that, you can view these automation script icon or automation tool view under test script tab-bar, only if HP QC 10 is launched on a machine which has HP QTP installed and nonetheless, if HP QC 10 is configured with HP QTP 9.5 or 10.0. Otherwise, in spite of the fact that script would already have got coded, test script tab-bar would be blank and all icons displayed would be manual icon.

Step 6) Launch QTP using launch icon.

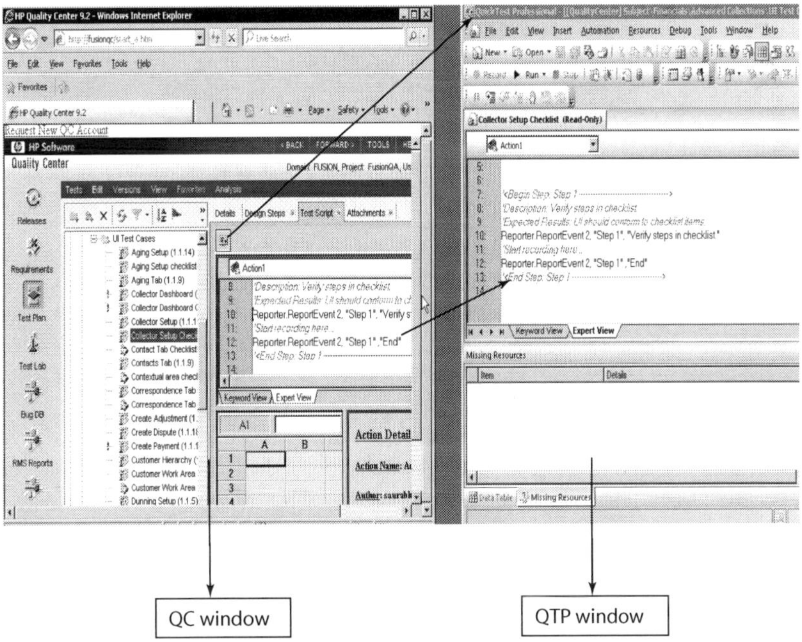

Figure 9.7 *Launch QTP from QC.*

Here you would observe that the codelines that got generated automatically in QC expert view, has got ported to QTP platform, once QTP was launched.

User needs to code on the QTP platform and then save the script. Once script is saved then saved code can also be viewed in HP QC 10 "expert view" panel.

Wasn't it simple? And yes, this completes the knowledge of test planning and scripting using HP QC 10 and HP QTP 9.5 or 10.0

Therefore, you now possess the complete knowledge for the usage of the most critical feature of HP QC 10 i.e., automating tests.

9.4 Test Lab

Till now, we have seen how to build requirements, cases and scripts. In sum, till now we have understood how to build up a repository, which if tested then will give good return of investment (ROI) to the product and company per se.

Therefore, the question that arises is, where is that area where all such real time execution activity should take place? And the answer is "Test Lab".

Test lab is such an area within HP QC 10, where user gets the flexibility to store execution outcome of all kinds of test cases, i.e., both manual and automation.

Let us see how to operate in this area.

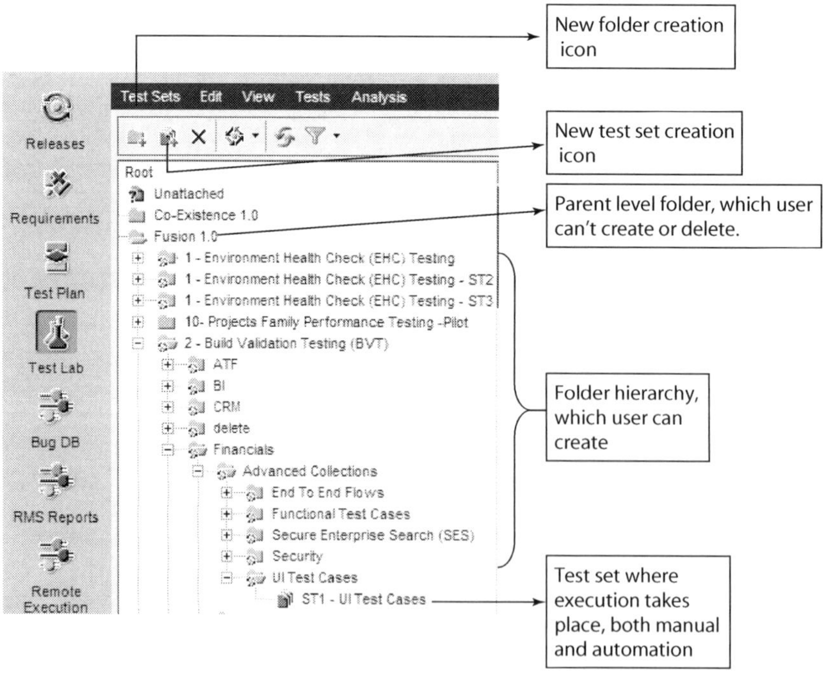

Figure 9.8 *Test Lab.*

As per Fig. 9.8, you can see that there are two icons— "new folder" and "new test set". "New folder" icon is used to create folders and parent child hierarchy. "New test set" icon is used to create the area where execution outcomes will be stored.

Creation of folder hierarchy depends upon the business need and requirement. Ideally, it should be created with a thumb rule, i.e., easy categorisation and logical sequencing, so that any time in future; if one has to look back to results, then digging into folders with logical structuring will make the route easier.

Another tip is to keep test set name very logical and real.

To make it more aligned, generally folder structure in test plan and test lab area should be kept similar.

9.5 Manual Execution

Manual execution is a four step process.

- □ Folder creation
- □ Test set creation
- □ Calling tests
- □ Executing tests and recording results

Step 1) Folder Creation

To create folder, one needs to select the parent hierarchy, under which folder needs to be created.

Once parent folder is identified, click "New folder" icon.

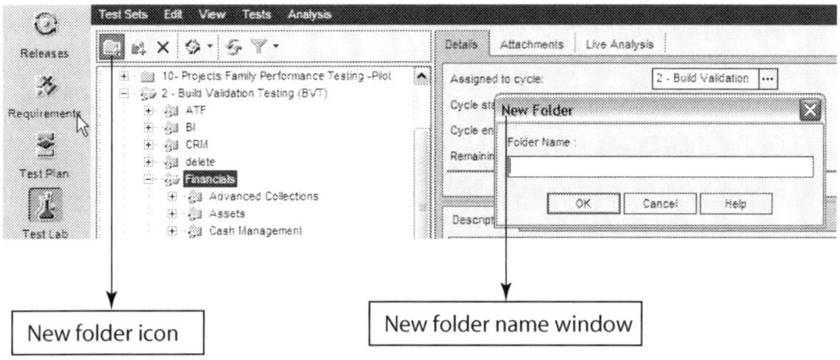

Figure 9.9 *Folder Creation.*

In this case, under "Build Validation Test -> Financials", we are creating a folder named " Manual execution example"

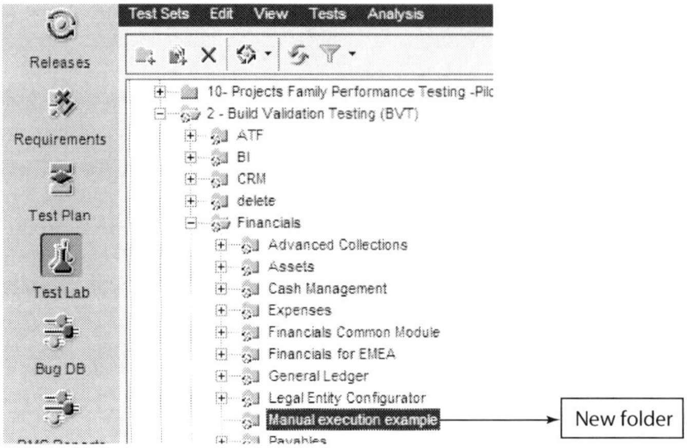

Figure 9.10 *New Folder.*

Step 2) Test set creation

Select the newly created folder and click "New test set" icon. "New test set" window comes up.

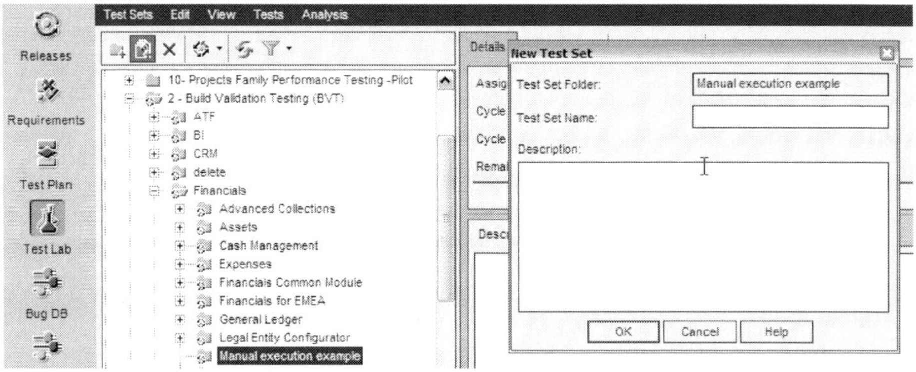

Figure 9.11 *New Test Set.*

Enter test set name and provide description.

Lets' keep the test set name to be "manual execution". Click "ok" on the "New test set" window.

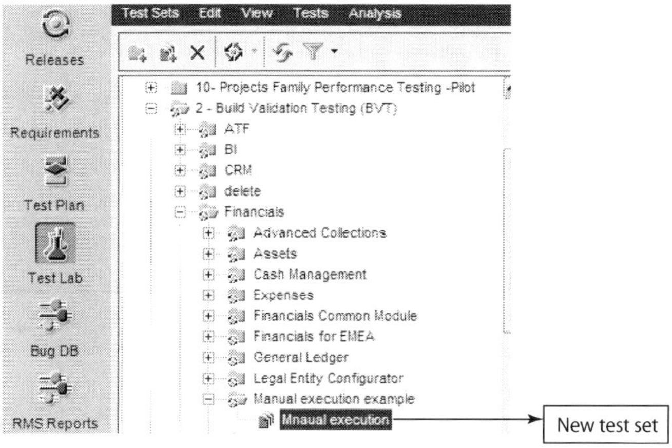

Figure 9.12 *New Test Set Created.*

Step 3) Calling tests

You might be thinking that you have all the folder structure ready and you have also created the area where test execution needs to happen. But million dollar question is from where to call tests and how to call tests.

Let us see the complete HP QC 10 window that comes while creating test set and hence understand the integration and usage of the complete view.

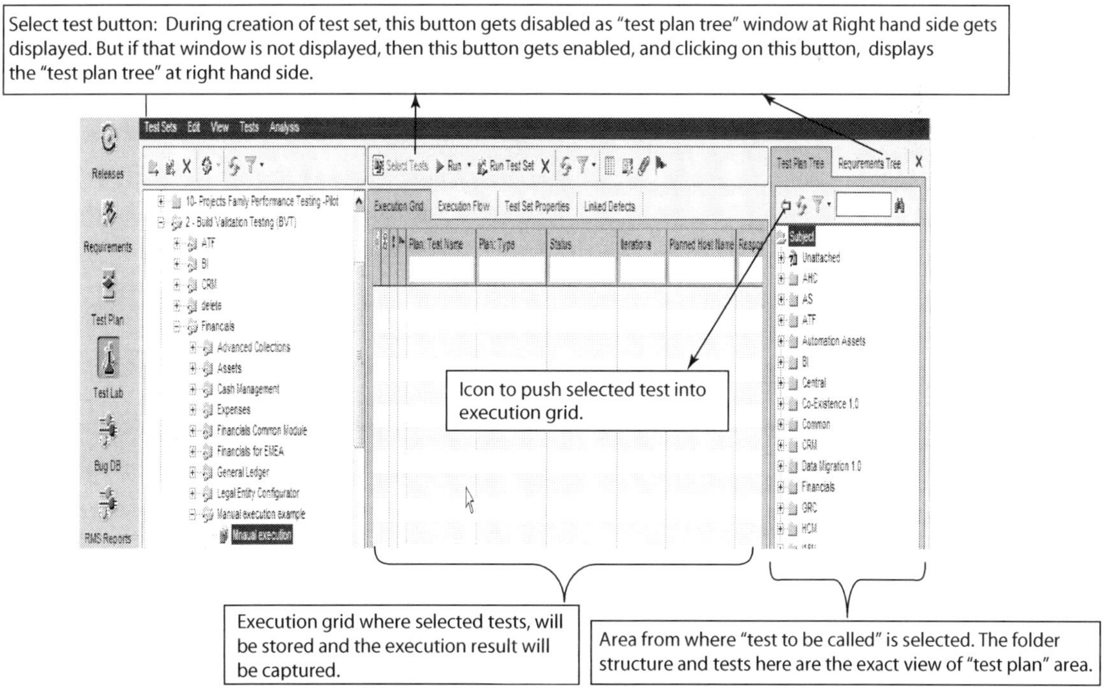

Figure 9.13 *Calling Test Mechanism.*

Now, select test from "Test Plan Tree" displayed at the right hand side in Fig. 9.13 and click the icon, which pushes selected test into execution grid.

Few important tips for selecting tests:

- You can select multiple tests by pressing **"Cntrl"** key on the keyboard.
- If you want to call all tests within a specific folder, just select the folder and click on the push test arrow icon. All tests within that folder will come into execution grid.
- If you have defined any parameter, then while adding tests to the execution grid, a parameter value definition will come, where you need to provide the value to be used for defined parameter.

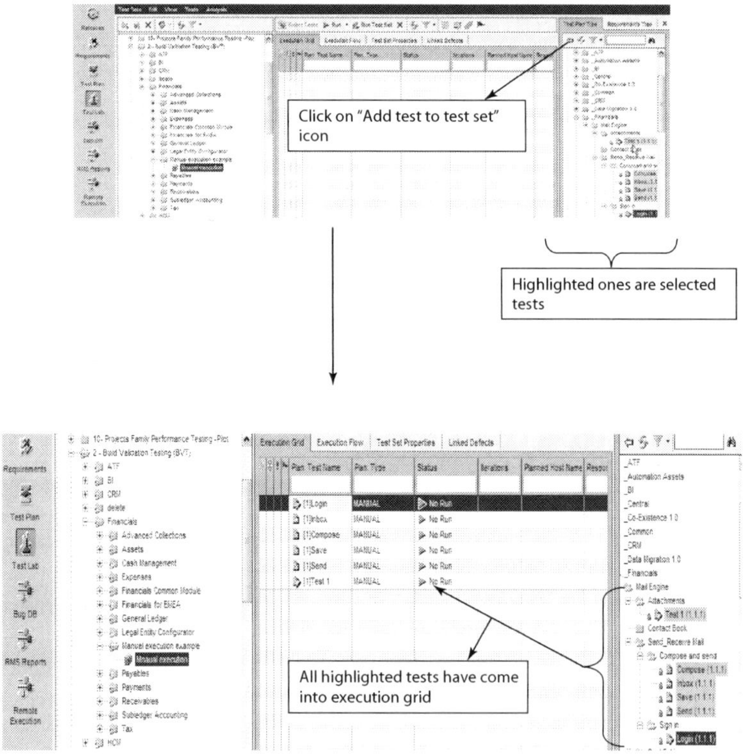

Figure 9.14 *Adding Tests to Execution Grid.*

You can observe that all the six tests highlighted in right frame, have now come into execution grid. Besides execution grid, you can also observe that there are three other tabs on the screen:

- Execution flow
- Test set properties
- Linked defects

  Lets' see what attribute does each feature exhibit and how can this be useful for users.

- Execution Flow:

This is one of the most useful features of HP QC 10, which gives user the power to define the sequence in which test cases or flows should get executed.

This becomes of prime importance when you kick off automated runs using remote server execution. Using this feature, one can define the sequence of automated runs and the unattended runs happen in that sequence.

The view shown in Fig. 9.15 is created automatically when you add tests to the grid. The displayed view, points that none of the flows is currently having any dependencies and each can be executed one by one in any sequence.

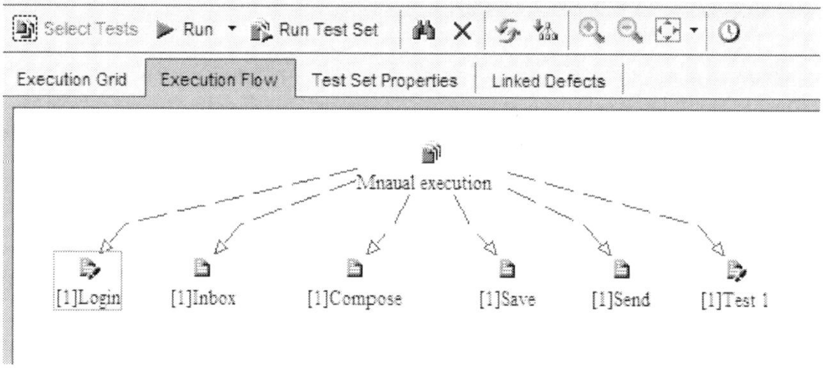

Figure 9.15 *Execution Flow View.*

In order to create dependencies, double click on any test and a "run schedule" window comes up. Lets double click the "Login" script.

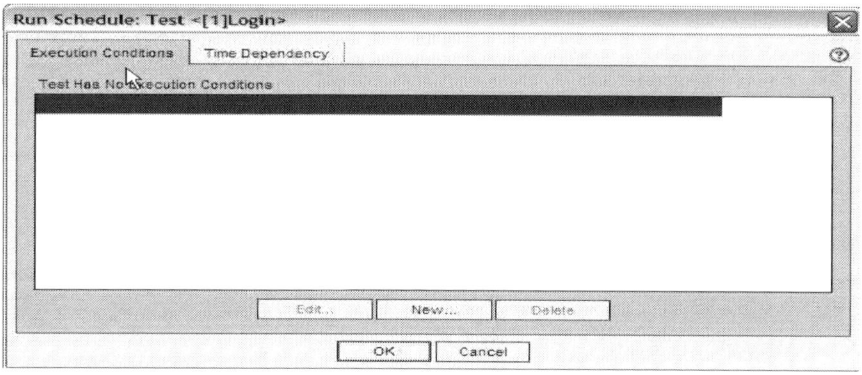

Figure 9.16 *"Run Schedule Window".*

Under execution condition, you can see there's no defined condition for "Login" script.

Click "New" and hence, "New execution condition" window comes up. Refer to Fig 9.17 where you can define the condition when one script should get triggered.

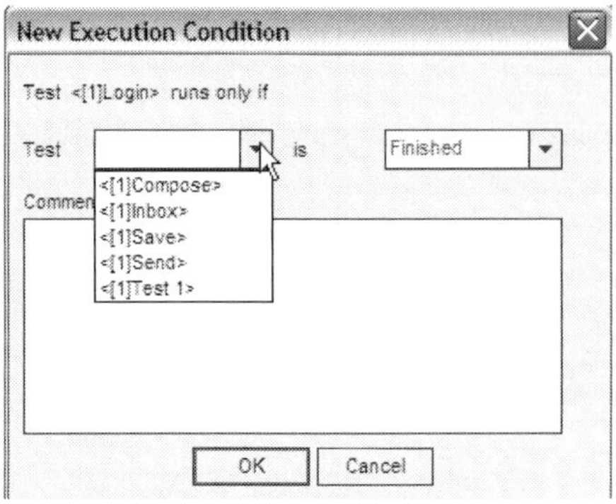

Figure 9.17 *Define Dependencies.*

Likewise, if you think that there should be a sequence in which tests need to be executed, then you can define the same in execution flow grid (Fig. 9.15).

To define the sequence in the execution grid, you just need to drag and pull the arrow in the sequence in which you want tests to be executed. Refer to Fig. 9.18, to understand the difference between the non-defined flows and sequence-defined flows.

No sequence defined – test can run one by one in any sequnce

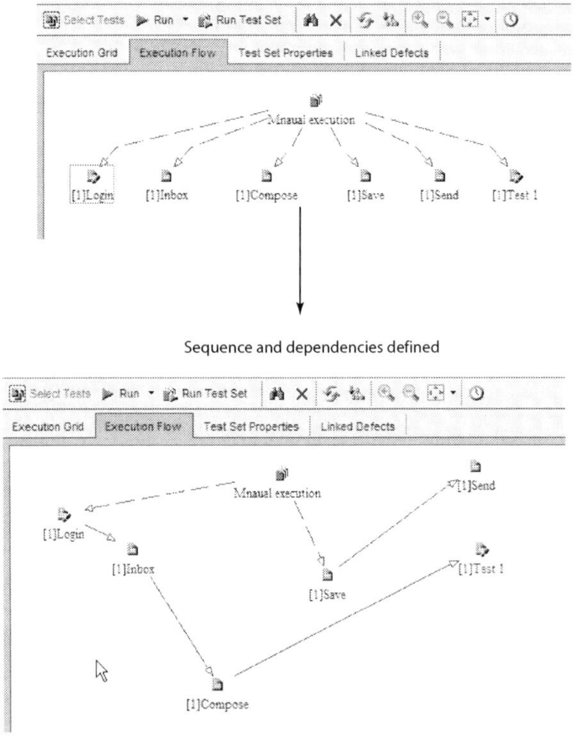

Figure 9.18 *Sequenced vs Non-sequenced Flow.*

Sequence and dependencies defined

You can define the flowchart where dependencies have been defined, just by dragging the cursor and start from the script which needs to be executed first, and drop the cursor at the script which needs to be followed after that. Thus you can create any sequence, you may feel like. But the only limitation of this grid is that it does not allow you to define iterative dependencies.

How to read this flowchart:

- Login and Save can be executed in parallel in any sequence.
- Login, inbox, compose, and test – these scripts can be executed only in the sequence defined.
- Likewise, send can be executed only if save is complete.
- Test set properties.

  Test set properties allow you to define conditions for complete test set, which if any test within that set meet, then trigger will be initiated for required action.

Test set properties -> Notification:

This feature allows users to set the condition as stated in Fig. 9.19. Select the option and give the email id in the "To" field, whenever the condition is met, trigger will be raised.

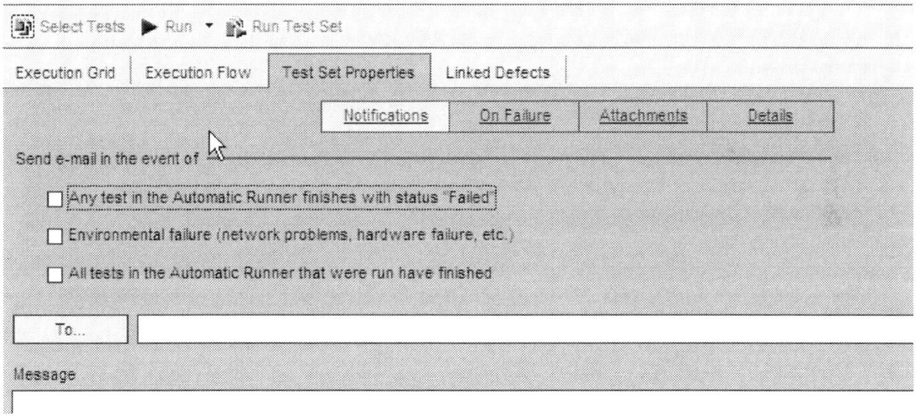

Figure 9.19 *Test Set Properties à Notification.*

Test set properties -> On failure:

As you can see, this feature is primarily used for automated test run. Here, you can give iterative

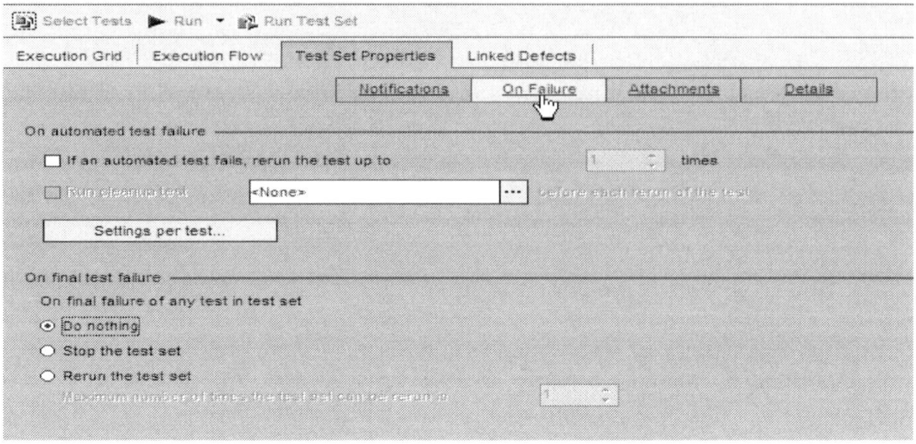

Figure 9.20 *Test Set Properties à on Failure.*

instructions, if any automated test run fails. Accordingly, this also allows you to have a condition on failure at each test script level, by using the button "setting per test".

- Attachment and details:

  As discussed in earlier chapters, this section acts as the repository to store details, pertaining to this test set.

Step 4) Executing tests

Once your tests are there in execution grid, you need to execute them, either one by one or in a batch. To execute is also known as "Run test cases". To run test cases, there are two methods, which can be used to execute test cases:

- *Run every single case one-by-one:* With this option, individual tests get executed. In the execution grid, status gets populated for that respective test. And once execution of the individual test is complete, then control comes back to execution grid.
- *Run all the flows in the test set:* With this option, HP QC 10 allows users to bundle all the tests in the test set, to execute sequentially, without triggering execution event for individual test. In this method, all tests in a test set get queued up and one by one, tests get fired and hence status gets captured in the execution grid. This continues, until execution of all the tests in the test set is complete. Additionally, if one has defined a condition or sequence of the flow, then by selecting this option, flows will get populated based on the sequencing and conditions defined.

  Let us see the execution methodology for each case:

Step 1) Select the case in the execution grid and click "Run".

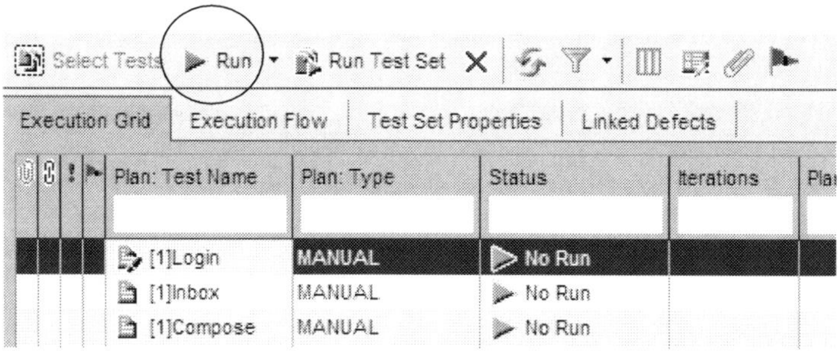

Figure 9.21 *Select Script and Click "Run".*

"Manual Run" window comes up.

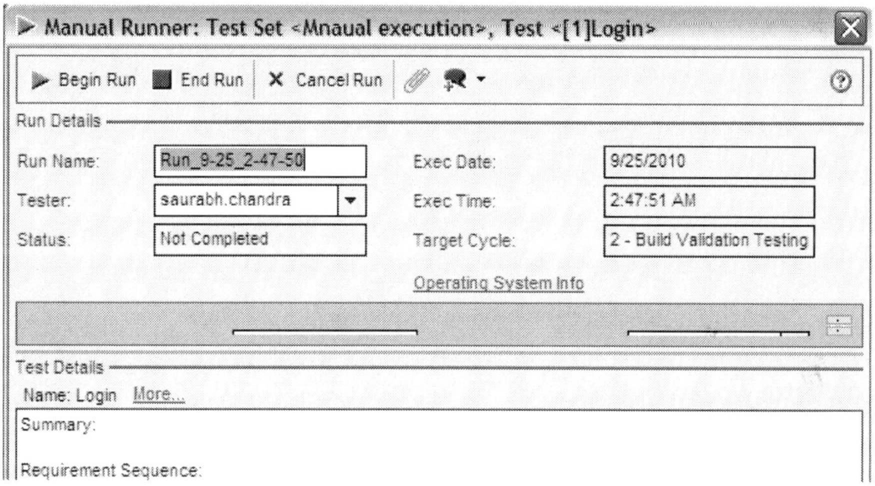

Figure 9.22 *Manual Run Window.*

Step 2) Click "Begin Run". "Manual Runner" window gets populated with test case description.

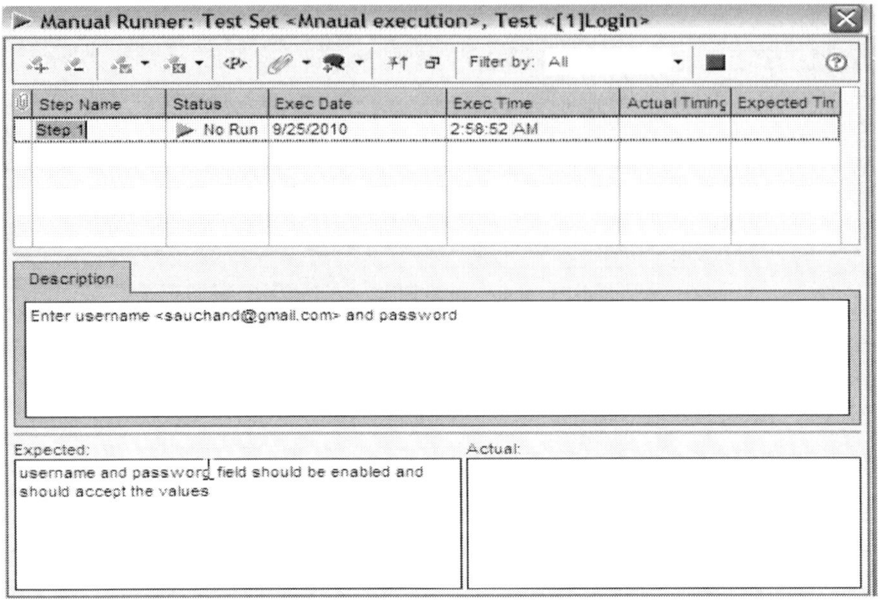

Figure 9.23 *Execution Window.*

Whatever is stated in the "description", user needs to perform the same in the application and the outcome of the testing should match the details cited under "Expected" panel.

Once this exercise is done, then user has to input his/her observation in "Actual" field. If the outcome is positive, i.e., it matches to what is expected, then status is "Passed" (Fig. 9.24); else status should be toggled to "Failed".

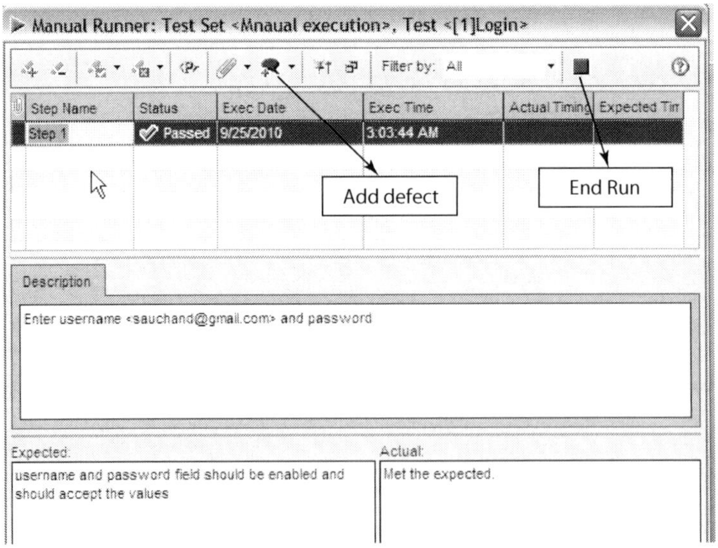

Figure 9.24 *Test Case "Passed".*

If during execution user finds any anomalies then that needs to be researched well and hence concluded whether the anomaly is a bug or some knowledge issue.

If it is a bug, then user needs to click "Add defects" button and hence log the defect with all the required explanation.

In either case, once the execution of this test case is completed and required status is set, then "End run" button needs to be clicked. This is the stage where the result outcome of the test is committed in the execution grid.

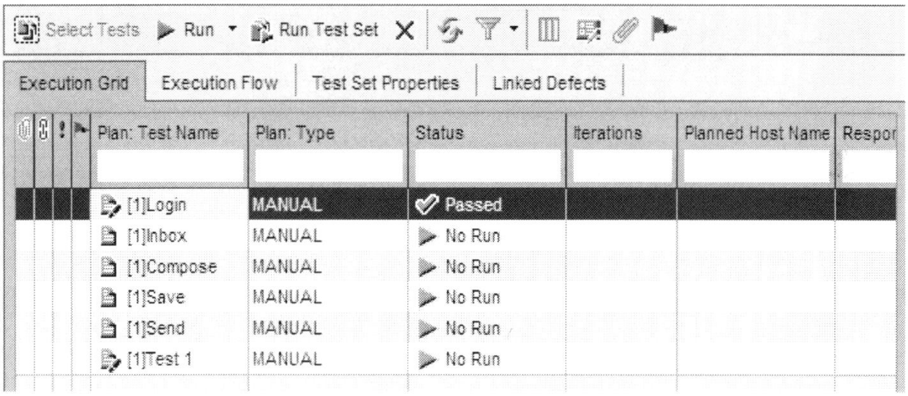

Figure 9.25 *Passed Status Gets Committed in Execution Grid.*

Important tip here is that in the "status" drop down menu, organisation can define its own statuses as well. HO QC 10 gives the flexibility of customization of almost the entire drop down values, present in the execution grid.

Step 1) You need not select any test case but rather just need to click on the option at the tab-bar level i.e., "Run test set". Another window pops up, where you need to select any one of the options. Here one of the options says that cases need to be executed in the order of alignment in the execution grid, and another one states, to execute the same in the order as how the dependencies have been defined in the "execution flow" area. Otherwise, selecting the first option in the window displayed in Fig. 9.26, dependencies can be overwritten. For our understanding, we will select the first one and go ahead further.

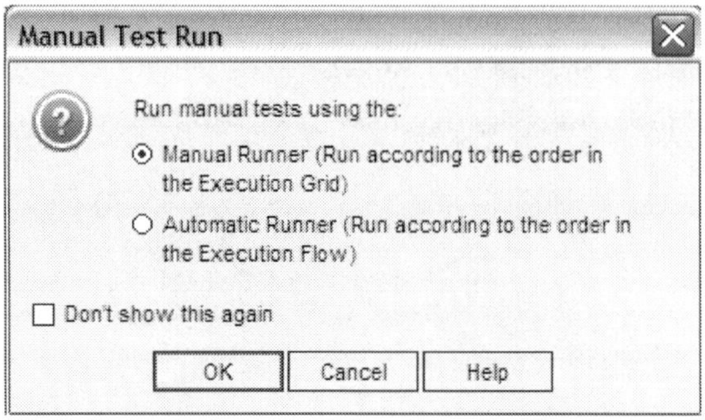

Figure 9.26 *Manual Test Run.*

Step 2) "Manual Runner" window comes up.

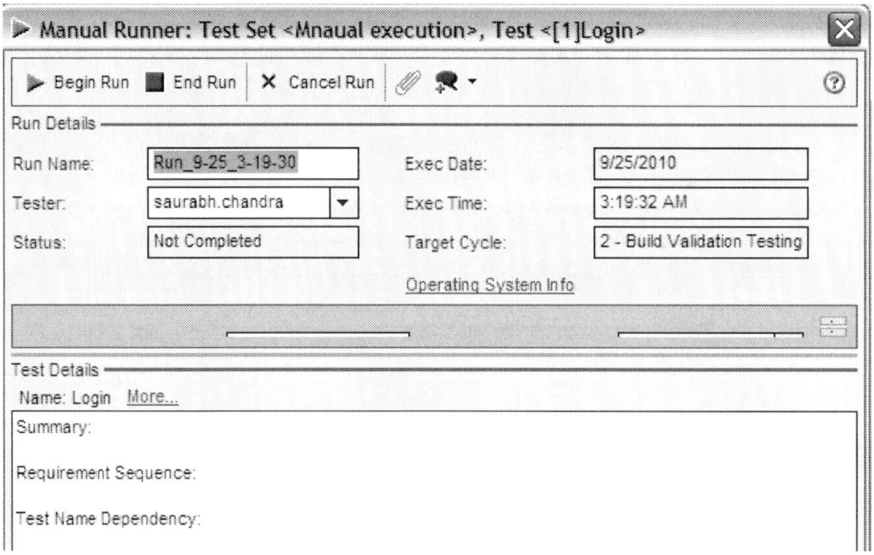

Figure 9.27 *Manual Runner Window.*

Step 3) Click "Begin Run" and execution window comes, as what we have already seen in Fig. 9.23.

Step 4) We will mark the test as per the execution exercise as what we discussed in step 2 of "*Run every single case one-by-one*".

The only difference between these two run approaches is that:

- In "*Run every single case one-by-one*" after one test is executed and "end run" is clicked then "Manual Runner" window gets closed and outcome gets committed in execution grid. However,
- In "*Run all the flows in the test set*" after execution of one test case is done and "End run" is clicked, the again the system would prompt the loading of another test in the test set. This continues at every click of "End run" until all the tests in execution grid get executed.

9.6 Automation Execution — Tips

Automation execution steps remain almost the same as how manual execution has been explained as in the above section, with few differences.

1. It should be ensured that the automation execution is exercised only on those machines where automation tool is installed and hence, is integrated with HP QC 10.
2. Automation scripts only need to be pulled into execution grid for automation execution.
3. Clicking "Run" or "Run test set" would ensure that execution starts unlike manual run.
4. In case, if there's an array of servers tied up, then remote execution capabilities to facilitate parallel execution can also be pulled up.

9.6.1 Automation Run

Automation execution or run can be performed in three ways. (a) By kicking off run by launching scripts, from test "plan area"; (b) by kicking off scripts from execution grid in "test lab" area; and (c) by launching QTP, establishing QC connection, pulling off scripts from required folder and then kicking off run.

For the first and the last case, i.e., kicking off scripts from test plan area and kicking off scripts by establishing connection to QC via QTP, it is highly recommended that if the purpose of the script execution is internal stabilization and not organisational reporting, then result file for that test should always be stored in "Temporary folder". For your ease of understanding, let me explain the scenario pictorially to show what it actually means:

Step 1) Launch script in QTP via QC.

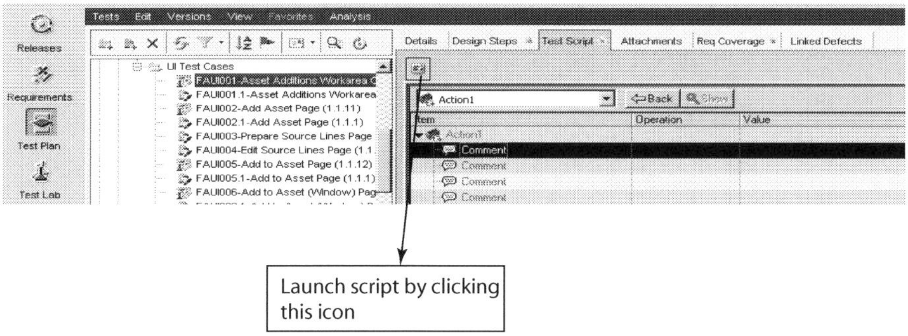

Figure 9.28 *Launch Script.*

Step 2) Click "Run" on HP QTP 9.5 or 10.0 and on the "Run" window, you would see two options:

- *New run results in QC project:* This option means that if you want to latch your result file in any of the already created test set, then under test set drop down, you should select the required test set. However, as discussed above, this should be exercised only if run result needs to be saved for organisational reporting and analysis purpose. Saving it in test set means that on QC server, these log files get stored. Therefore, each log file takes some server space. Hence, if one would start storing all such log files, which may not be of much use and benefit to business, then unnecessary cluttering of space happens and therefore, this kind of storage mechanism is discouraged, unless there is a business demand.
- *Temporary run results folder (not saved in the project):* This is the temporary folder which I was referring to, in my earlier discussion. If you select this option it means that the latest result file log will be stored in the temporary folder of the machine where this execution is happening, temporarily for that session till the time your QTP is open. Since, the philosophy of this storage mechanism is that in temporary folder, only one log file will be stored always and that also the latest one, therefore, there's never a scenario where unnecessary space gets wasted on the physical machine. Hence, for any internal stabilization or execution purpose, this option is highly recommended.

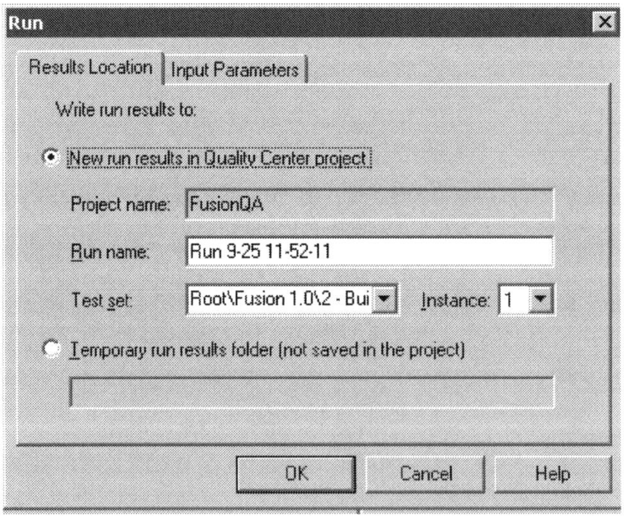

Figure 9.29 *Run Window.*

Now let's see how this works in case where script can be kicked off through test lab.

Step 1) Go to the "Test lab", select the required test set. User can either select the scripts within execution grid of selected test set or if test set already contains the scripts, then user is ready to kick off the runs.

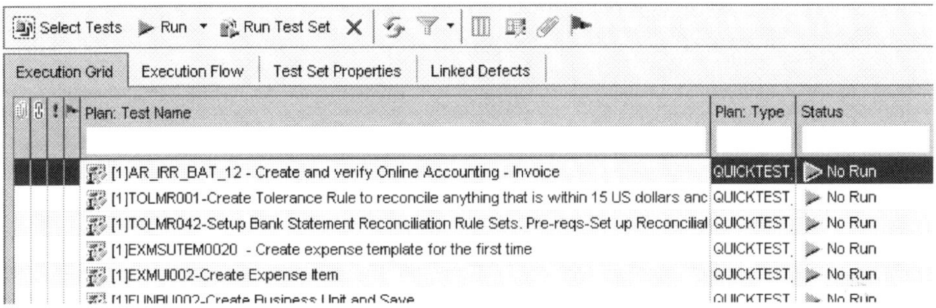

Figure 9.30 *Execution Grid Populated with Automated Scripts.*

Initially, when tests are added, then the status of run is "No Run".

Hence, as discussed in manual execution discussion section, either you can select a test and click "Run", or do not select any test but click "Run test set". With either of the above options, "Automatic Runner" window comes up.

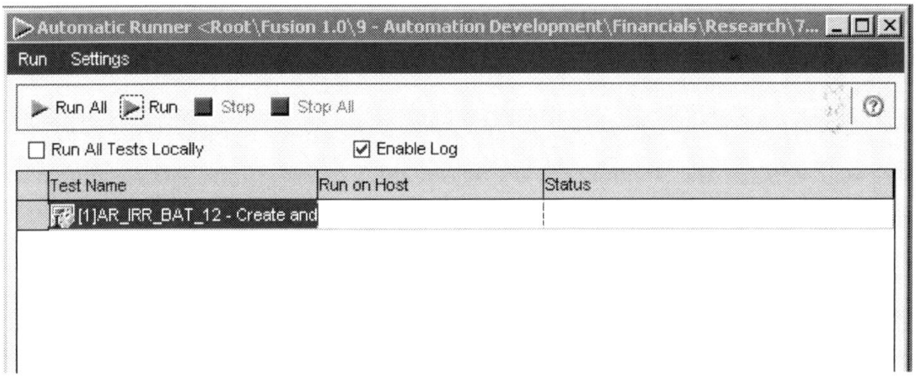

Figure 9.31 *Automatic Runner.*

Based on run type or test selection, all the tests get populated in automatic runner window. Here again you have a choice to either run a single test individually by selecting "Run", or run all tests sequentially by selecting "Run all".

Nonetheless, if you have embedded design flow sequence and dependencies for scripts within this test set, then accordingly run will happen.

Step 2) After run gets over, in the execution grid of the test set under play results get latched. Primarily, in automation three statuses get latched:

- *Passed:* This means script passed successfully.
- *Failed:* This means script failed.
- *Not completed:* There are two cases in which this status gets latched. One, this status gets latched if user has defined execution time limit and script isn't complete within that time limit. Another scenario is that in between the execution, if user stops the execution.

As displayed in Fig. 9.32, this is how automation run results are displayed in the execution grid.

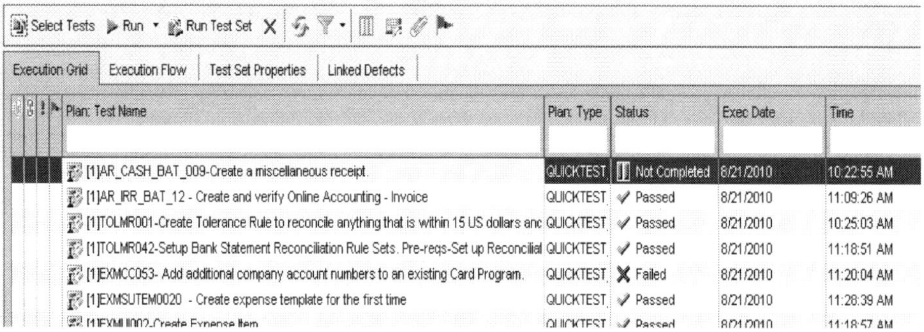

Figure 9.32 *Automation Run Results.*

9.6.2 Result File Viewing

Another question that may be tickling you is that, if user hasn't stored the run result in the temporary folder but latched in the HP QC area, how can one access the run result file?

Let us see the steps to view results.

Step 1) Select the test, in a specific test set, for which result needs to be viewed.

According to Fig. 9.33, the highlighted one at the left panel is the test set and the tests are lying under execution grid, where run results get latched.

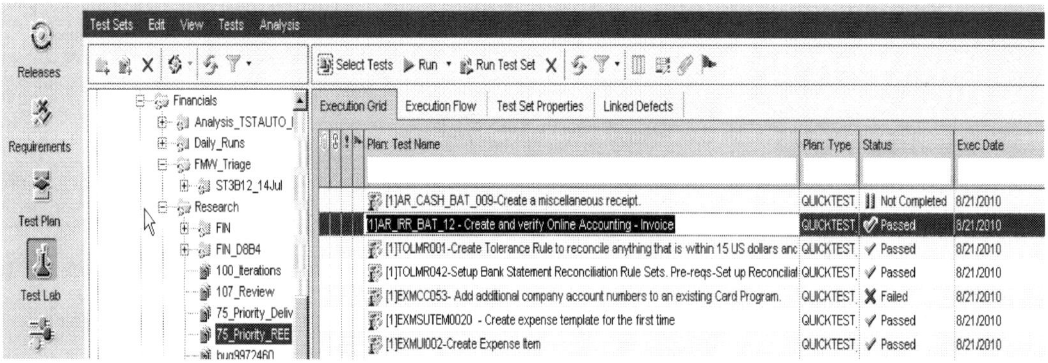

Figure 9.33 *Test Selection to View Run Result.*

Step 2) Double click the selected test.

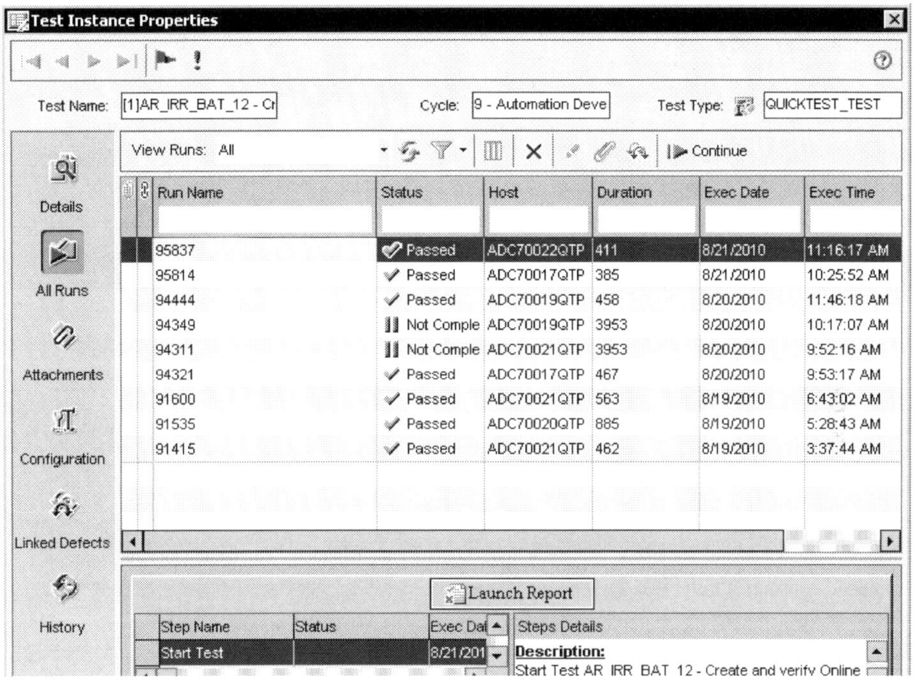

Figure 9.34 *Select Test for Which Result File Needs to be Viewed.*

Select the "Run Name". Topmost will be the latest with the one at the bottom most being the oldest.

Test highlighted in Fig. 9.34 is the selected one. Selected test gets highlighted. Click "Launch Report" and hence result file is launched as shown in Fig. 9.35.

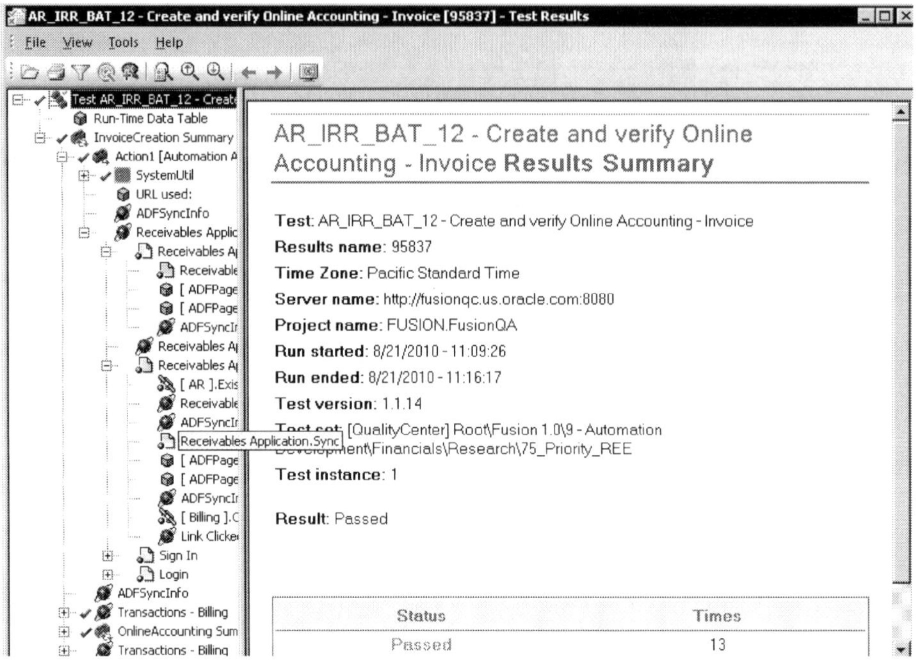

Figure 9.35 *Run Result Report.*

9.6.3 Run History

This feature provides run history for the tests, either for manual or automation execution. To view run history of any flow, one can double click the test and the below displayed window opens, where run result, history and details are captured for all the runs happened for that case in the current test set. Point to note here is that if the same test is executed in three different test sets, it is not possible to have a single history view of this test. You will have to go into each test set, double click the test, and view the run history and details.

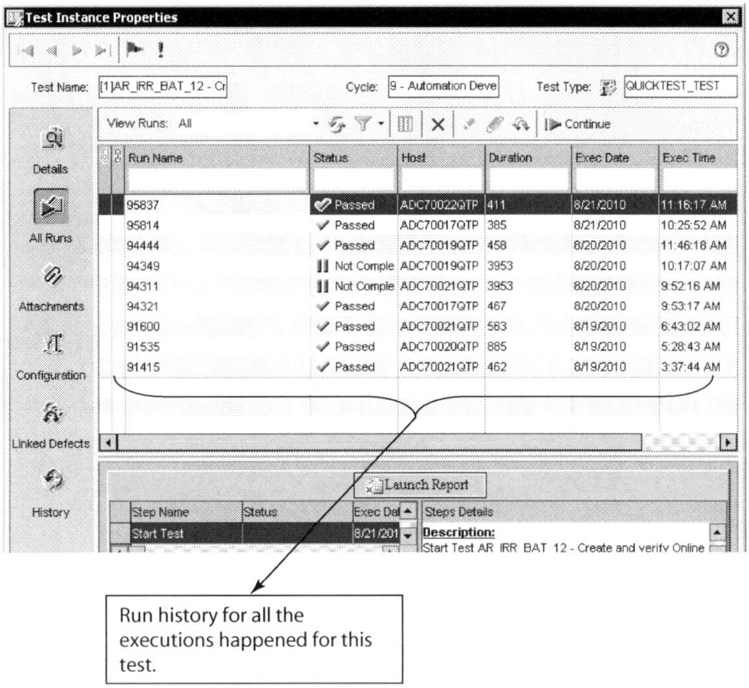

Figure 9.36 *Run History Window.*

It is important to note here is that the first one in the grid is the latest execution, and lower it runs in the row, older the executions are. Thus, the last one in the grid is the oldest execution result for this test.

This brings you to a point, where you can term yourself to be a master on HP QC 10 usage.

HP Quality Center 10: Automation Framework — Pre-Implementation Design Approach and Strategy

10

Chapter Objectives: This chapter will give an overview of

- *Framework – Existence, Definition and Advantages*
- *Automation Framework Design Approach*

Introduction

Framework— the most daunting task and work for any experienced professionals. All companies look for people who have expertise in laying out automation framework. The word in itself displays the horizon of this task. To understand the intensity, just imagine that you have no such processes and team, and from scratch you need to set up complete automation standards and processes. The scope of discussion on framework is immense. In this chapter, I will walk you through four most critical paths that should be considered, while planning to establish a working framework pertaining to any automation tool.

In the next 3 chapters, I will walk you through a working design and technique to lay down automation framework.

10.1 Framework — Existence, Definition and Advantages

While studying in school or college, you would remember teachers and parents used to tell everyone of us that we need to be disciplined, be systematic in our approach of study, prioritize what is more important to gain knowledge and hence get marks during exams. Several such inputs, in sum, used to point out that there should be some strategy in place, which should be followed for long term in order to derive success.

Now let's emulate this philosophy in technical domain. Therefore, before any development or technical activity starts, there should be some template, process and guidelines based on which activities should start. This is one of the most time taking areas for any organisations, because unless you have expertise and experience, you can't lay out a definitive path. Process of laying out a definitive path in any domain is known as a Framework.

Advantages of a framework are:

1. Common path is followed by many; hence chances of confusion is less.
2. Tracking and forecasting of task becomes easier; hence slippages can be avoided.
3. Maintainability of files, resources become streamlined; hence chances of loosing or digging data is lesser.
4. Productivity forecast becomes easier as a pattern of sequence and speed can be gauged.
5. Repeatability and sustainability aspect becomes much higher as there is a common statement followed by everyone.
6. Maturity of process or system becomes easier.
7. Predictability of results become more cogent.
8. Imparting continuous improvement messages and plug-ins across board becomes efficient and effective.
9. In case of any error crept in, impact analysis of the system becomes easier and additionally, weeding out error also becomes easier.
10. Nonetheless, with systematic and scientific framework, quality of task or work packet is always predictable.

However, every good thing comes with a baggage; and the baggage that "Framework" formulation and adaption brings with it is that if the person designing the framework is not open minded and improvement adaptive, then in spite of having several great perspectives and ideas floating across, framework may not come out to be very mature and effective. Therefore, MNC's nowadays resort to highly experienced experts, who in software industry is known as "Architects". Of course, as the name suggests, a lot depends on these architects.

10.2 Automation Framework Design Approach

There is an array of needs that should be planned before one starts with automation development. Primarily, automation framework is a scientific simulation for operations that would be required during automation development and execution journey. It is one of the most critical paths that several industry heads nowadays looks for, but due to shortage of such professionals, it becomes difficult to get one. I'll be unfolding the four most essential areas that one should consider while designing automation framework.

There are several such aspects that differ in nature but are very critical to be considered while planning a framework for automation development.

1 Streamlining input requirements for automation through structured test script or case designing and planning strategy.
2. Controlling variables for better automation scoping and leveraging productivity.
3. Best practices during automation development.
4. Probable issue identification, segregation, and tracking mechanism.

10.2.1 Test Script and Test Case Designing and Planning Strategy

To appreciate the discussion in this Chapter, I would urge readers to have basic know-how about HP QC 9.2, which has been discussed in previous chapters.

There are few situations that arise in designing test cases in real time scenario. Let us see few of the most occurring real time scenarios.

- *Situation 1:* Test case is being designed by people, who do not have technical depth of automation.
- *Situation 2:* Test case is being designed by people who would be designing the automation test case also.
- *Situation 3:* Test case is being designed by people who have technical depth but will not automate.

These are three famous situations that the software industry across globe generally faces. Therefore, the industry is often intrigued by the question, "For effective test script designing which one to opt for?"

However, looking deeper into the aspect of this question, it's the responsibility of the QA and Automation Architect to understand the sensitivity behind this question and hence understand that for all the scenarios that we are talking about in the above cases are people dependent. This should ideally be minimized to the maximum possible extent. Therefore, to make it less prone to biasing of people, there should be certain standards that should be followed strictly while designing test cases. And if such scientific rules are in place then any situation as mentioned in the above cases can be exercised and still the quality of test cases would come out to be apt enough for automation.

Let us see those guidelines, which should always be followed by the manual test script designer:

- Use Organisation specific template or HP QC template:
  - If there is no such central system like HP QC then:

  Several organisations have their standard template, which they would have drafted keeping both automation and manual testing perspective in mind. Hence, one should always use the same, while drafting a test script within their organisation. Test script should be written against the company based "Test script" template.
  - If there is a central tool, i.e., HP QC 9.2:

  In such a case, one has no other choice but to stick with the template as provided in the tool.

- Details to be provided with 100% accuracy

  All detailed navigational steps, data to be entered and expected results should be provided, assuming that someone who does not have working knowledge against that product will automate this Test script.

  Example: In the below attached page, let us say you have to search for "Solemn Products".
- Wrong test case: Open "Solemn" website and search for "Solemn Products".
- Correct Test Case:
  - **Step1)** Invoke www.thesolemn.com by putting this link into the browser address bar
  - **Step 2)** Input "Solemn Products" in the "secure search" text field at the top right hand side of the page.

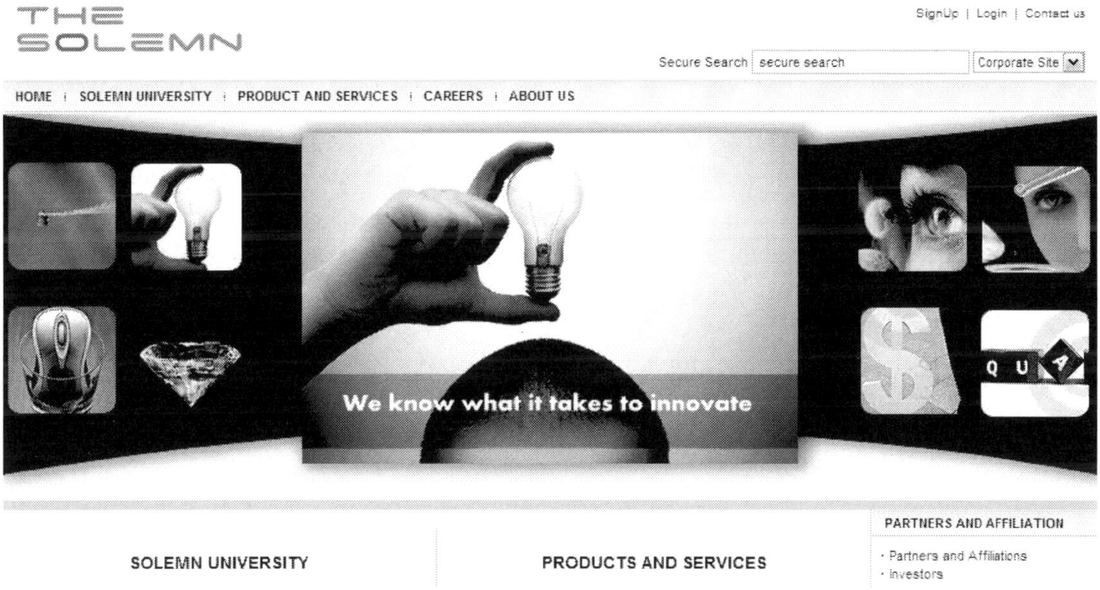

Figure 10.1 *Secure Search Text Field UI.*

- Dependency details:

  All the "Test Scripts", given for automation should be independent. In case, there is any dependency on any other scripts then that should be mentioned appropriately within the given Test script, dependency section. Dependent Test script Name and Automation status of the same should be provided within the "Test script" to be automated.
- **Example**: Let us say one test case in "Solemn" website talks about buying license for a product. Another test case talks about viewing of license history, including its expiry tracking.

In such a case, the first case to be automated, obviously would be buying license. Once License number is generated, that test case ends there.

Then second case gets automated i.e. to verify the history details. Now, in this second case, at manual test case level, there should be one area where it should be notified that, this test case is extension of first test case. Indeed, the same should also be quoted at automation script level so that in case any new member picks up the case, s/he is not lost.

Additional benefit of such detailing is that, if multiple people are working on automation of test cases, and if someone encounters such test case where dependency is quoted and if the same has already been developed by other team member, then in such a case redundancy of work can be avoided by re-usability of existing codeline.

- Date specific details:

  Either Test script should quote specifically that the date to be selected while automating the case should be SYS_DATE (system date) or should contain exact date, quoting whether it is back date, current date or future date.

Example: Let us say you are buying some licensed product from "Solemn". The constraint is that you can't buy license at back date. Now, when you automate such case, the day you are automating, you can input specific date in mm/dd/yy format and the case would run successfully on that day. But on later dates, the code will fail as that date would become back date. Therefore, in test case, it is very critical that test case designer explains date in very specific manner and say whether to input SYS_DATE, while automating or back date to check validity of transaction or future date. All such cases, as and when business scenario demands should be inputted.

- Login URL's and browser details:

  Test script should contain the required login URL's and the browser details where that application will work.

Example: Applications developed and deployed across two socket layers— one is secured and another one is non-secured. HTTP layer is non-secured and HTTPS layer is secured. Now, when the test case designer, is writing about invocation of URL then one should always give complete URL and should not assume that automation designer would know which URL to use.

Additionally, there are several instances where few applications work on one browser but do not work on another browser. In such a case, it should be explicitly written in test case against which browser application works and if required, against which browser, automation is expected.

- Mandatory field details:

  At times within application, several mandatory fields get populated automatically. Test script should have details about data set of all such fields. This is required because during automation it is advisable to re-enter values within such mandatory fields irrespective of the fact that data is getting auto-populated.

Example: In several applications such as account "Sign up" page, if you are updating your information then several of mandatory fields get auto populated. Such fields should be exclusively talked about in test case so that automation designer has the flexibility to choose about coding aspects during development.

- Inherited "Test script":

There are such instances that someone else would have drafted the test script. Hence the same would not have got reviewed till next few builds. And suddenly, one day, it is given for automation. Therefore, for such cases where there is an already drafted test script, functional expert or test script current owner should execute the test script manually against the current build and then should give it to automation team for required automation. This ensures that the data and validations, quoted within the test script are correct and current.

Example: Let us say, in some banking site when test case designer is writing test cases, only name and date are mandatory fields to query for already committed transactions. Test case designer completes the test script in next three months and passes it on to automation designer. Unfortunately, in three months, an additional mandatory field of account no. is also added within the application. Now, unless test case designer talks about such change it will baffle the automation designer. In real-time scenario, there can be two cases i.e., either test case designer also does not know about this, or test case designer knows about this. If test case designer knows about this, then it is test case designer's responsibility to reach out to automation developer and inform him about the up gradation that test case would require.

- Changes against completed "Test script" to be shared with automation counterparts:
  At times, development teams come up with the new data set/ functionality after one has completed drafting the Test script. In addition, the same has been handed over for Automation script creation. Now, if the person drafted the test script and automating the test is same, then there will not be a problem of clarity. However, if person drafting the case and automating the case are different, then it is very crucial that the time when functional expert came to know about the change, with delay should pass the same to automation counterpart and hence update the test script. This helps in avoiding any discrepancies in future. In addition, this helps in saving huge amount of time and effort which otherwise would have got wasted if automation counterpart had not known about this change.
- Single "Test script" in various sub-parts:
  At times, in various organisations, a team starts developing the test script and once it reaches to certain stage, then rather than waiting for completion provides the same for in tandem automation. By the time the automation of that part is over, new cases are pumped in, and thus the cycle continues. In such cases, the most important factor to keep a gage upon is to ensure that all parts

of Test script details, data and validations are in sync with each other. In addition, every sub-part should be drafted keeping in mind the data flow structure of already drafted part. In sum, data flow integrity is mandatory from beginning till end irrespective of sub parts of single test script.

Example: We need to do fund transfer via some banking site. Fund transfer is constituted of three step processes.

Step 1) Check amount

Step 2) Add payee

Step 3) Do fund transfer and capture transaction number

Due to time constraint, organisation takes a call to deploy three people to write test cases for these three steps. However, these three steps are part of single test script.

Now, it is the responsibility of all three different test case designers, who are independently writing these three steps, to highlight within the test script as which data is commonly used across three steps and that only to be used while writing test case. Additionally, when they are passing these three test cases to automation designer, they need to ensure that exit criteria of Step 1 becomes input criteria for Step 2, which in turn is the input for Step 3. Unless this is not controlled, it will become nightmare for automation designer to understand data integrity across test cases and flow sequencing. And this will lead to weak and shabby coding and hence robustness and intelligence of code will be lost.

- Bug numbers to be quoted in "Test script":

  In continuation of case 9, in various organisations, cases arise where in between automation or drafting test script, some showstopper issues are encountered. However, because of these showstopper issues, probably few of the further flows might get interrupted but not all. Therefore, in order to go ahead with further test script designing and automation, test script owner should write down the issue details within the test script adjacent to impacted test case itself. This becomes easier for automation expert to handle and code for the same whenever it gets resolved. The further code that automation expert would write will have a logic to incorporate the scenario when gets resolved. Hence, this helps in saving re-work and debugging in future.
- LDT files, sql files, API's:

  There are several scenarios where in auto population of data set for a particular flow happens only when required files are executed against that application. Unless, that file is executed, further navigation is not possible. Therefore, in such scenarios if the required details along with files are not provided, then for automation expert it becomes difficult to understand whether this is an issue or the automation counterpart has missed out something in earlier steps. This in turn costs a lot in terms of time and effort. Therefore, to avoid such discrepancies, all required files should be provided along with the Test script, to automation engineer.

- Back End table names:
  Test script should contain exact table names in case back end interaction needs to be recorded.
- Highlighting "Parameterizable data" sets:

  All the required data sets that need to be parameterized should be highlighted within the Test script.

Example: Let us say, in the displayed screen, one needs to automate "Sign in" functionality. But the requirement is that this automation script needs to run multiple times in a day. Hence, while writing test case, the test case designer should highlight such values which if parameterized, the script becomes re-runnable.

Figure 10.2 *Parameterization Example.*

This is the most critical aspect of automation development framework, which from the industry experience I have seen, is generally missed out. As Newton rightly said, "every action has an equal and opposite reaction", this theory comes to life when you think that better the requirement better the automation code, and faster the development time and quality.

10.2.2 Controlling Variables for Better Automation Scoping and Leveraging Productivity

Automation development is an activity which is dependent upon many variables. By variables, I mean the environment under test, functional dependencies, functional requirement dependencies, bug fix rate, automation tool deficiencies, enhancements and impacts, and the team's technical prowess. The idea is to keep all such variables into account while planning for automation. Let us see all such variables their impact one-by-one:

- *Functional Requirement* – From the discussion in above section, now you understand how badly automation development activity can be impacted if functional requirements are not drafted appropriately.
- *Environment under test* – This is the application environment against which automation needs to happen. Therefore, it is very crucial to get an answer for the below-mentioned areas:
- On which techstack is the application hosted?
    - Techstack against which environment hosted means, whether it is hosted on Linux box or Solaris or Tru 64, etc.
- What is the patching time for the environment?
    - Patching time for environment means that there are several fixes that need to be pushed into the environment. It is not done at any random time. There has to be a defined time frame. Therefore, patching time is that time when environment is pulled down and fixes go in.
- What is the load that environment can withstand with respect to concurrent users?
    - Assume there are 10 automation designers working on development activity. During that, these 10 automation designer have two tasks in parallel, i.e., to develop the tests, and in parallel execute them. Therefore, with this scenario, you can see that each automation engineer is accessing 2 sessions of the environment under test at a single point in time. If there are total of 10 people involved in such activity, then at any point in time, at least 20 concurrent sessions are being worked upon the environment under test. Hence, before automation development starts, this kind of calculation needs to be derived and hence get the environment configured accordingly to handle that much of load.
- Is there any intermittent issue that is faced by the environment in normal occurrence?
    - Several times, it is observed that when an event gets triggered, then before reaching to the server connection gets lost. This may be due to several reasons. Rather than knowing those reasons, the first step is to know whether this happens or not. And if this happens, then beforehand itself, environment owner needs to be made aware of this situation so that s/he can start capturing such issues and hence capture a pattern of such an occurrence. This will help in root cause analysis as well as permanent fix.
- *Functional dependencies* – There are several such functionality or pages that may be temporary within the application. Automation designer should know beforehand of all such areas either to code accordingly so that tomorrow if right UI is passed on, then code revamp is not much or not to code that at priority and keep that for future consideration.
- *Test case complexity* – As you know every test case may not be equally complex. Some may be less complex, some average, and some high. The most critical part is to understand the complexity definition in absolute terms. For example, one needs to deduce that less complex

cases take approximately 3 hrs to automate (including all odds), average takes 8 hrs (including all odds), and highly complex cases take 2 working days (including all odds). This is very critical to understand while putting a blueprint plan to chase automation. This helps you derive number of resources and number of days required for work packet completion, and plan for mitigations. Indeed, this also helps you forecast the technical challenges that team may need to cater to during development activity. Knowing about this factor helps in productivity gauging and improvement.

- *Functional intermittent issues* – There are several such functionalities which throw intermittent errors and may not be reproducible at will. The idea is to understand all such areas and then utilize the automation codeline to gauge and reproduce a pattern which otherwise if done manually, will not be possible. Accordingly, knowing about such areas helps in putting exceptions in the code in such a manner that it caters to error scenario, as well as once patched then without code revamp will be good enough a codeline to cater to correct scenario too.
- *Functional enhancements* – Like intermittent issues, even impact of functional enhancements, if not known beforehand can be huge. Assume an automation designer starts automating a case; after reaching 50% completion, he understands that it's a showstopper scenario to go ahead further due to some pending enhancement fix. Therefore, impact here is that time is lost; effort is also lost as the case couldn't be completed, and we don't even know whether utilizing the half developed case will add any value to the product as such or not. If these areas were known earlier, automation development could have been planned in a way that the time and effort could have been channelized in other activities which would add value to automation.
- *Bug fixing rate* – It is very critical that before automation development starts, one should put a service level agreement with all required parties who would be involved with fixing issues faced during the journey of automation development. This service level agreement formulation is critical; else, rate of development would drop. The worst part is not because of poor productivity but due to third party derailments. However, the irony is that, it would not reflect badly on any such third parties but would reflect badly on the automation team. Therefore, it is the task of the leader or architect to have right level of agreement with development team, performance team, and operations team to provide fixes within stipulated timeline.
- *Automation tool deficiency* – There are several such situations which may or may not be known in the beginning but should certainly be kept into account throughout development activity and that is to find out tool deficiency to automate certain technology stack or pages or objects. These also become a critical part in bigger planning when it comes about un-attended automation runs. Because of such gaps, un-attended runs may not become possible for the organisation and a part of automation benefit can be missed out. Therefore, keeping a keen eye, knowing about such issues helps in faster resolution of such issues and hence lead to seamless execution or development.

- *Team's technical prowess* – Last but not the least, this aspect should always be taken into account when you give a realistic estimation of your development completion activity. Additionally, this is one such area which should be accounted for continuous improvement.
- *Future need of automation codeline* – It is very critical to understand what the future need of the codeline under development is. As an example, in few organisations, the codeline needs to be used just for 3-4 months. In few it has a much bigger life. Likewise, in few organisations, the need is to use these across platforms via parallel execution. Therefore, based on business need, complexity of coding would increase and hence budgeting would change. Hence, it is very critical for a manager or architect to understand about the same and then put a plan into perspective.

Indeed, all the above-said factors become critical input points while planning for completion of automation work packet. Indeed, I have witnessed myself, if these are not known and well thought off, there is an impact which can cost one's job as a manager as well. Therefore, now since, I have unfolded the mystery behind most critical aspects that could derail automation completion deadline, I would assume all my readers to take maximum benefit out of this.

10.2.3 Best Practices During Automation Development

This stage is very critical when you are planning for automation development activity. Of course, at this stage all challenges may not be known, but the most certain ones are known. When I say most certain ones are known, I'm saying it based on the above discussions we have had. If you try digging out answers for the abovesaid discussion, then almost you parse the complete detailing and challenges that one would witness during automation development. Hence, based on such homework and research, one should start designing a common approach for codeline development. Again, I would ask my readers not to get confused with automation coding guidelines. Automation coding guidelines is a superset for "best practices – automation coding", which will be discussed in detail in further chapters.

In this chapter, we will be discussing about best practices – automation coding, that should be planned as a common standard against any automation tool. I'll be explaining the detailing by taking example through HP QTP 9.5 tool.

1. **Environment URL not to be hardcoded** – When tool records, by default environment URL's get hardcoded in the program. Programmatically, data and code need to be separated. Advantage is that the same script can be used across multiple platforms just by passing URL's and not by changing any codeline.

   <u>Real-time usage:</u>

Let us say you have one of your applications deployed on 8080 port and later the port needs to be changed for the same application. In that case, you may need to find out all such areas in the codeline, where you may have to replace 8080 port with new one. Hence, to avoid such future risks, it is advisable that you don't hard code environment URL, but try its parameterization by segregating code and data in the code.

Code Snippet:

```
Dim Login
'Login=inputbox("Enter Login Name:", "URL Providing Window")
'DataTable.GetSheet ("Action1").SetCurrentRow (35)
DataTable.SetCurrentRow (cint(parameter("RowNumber")))
Login=DataTable.Value("Login",dtLocalSheet)
systemutil.Run "C:\Program Files\Internet Explorer\iexplore.exe", Login
```

<u>Code snippet explanation:</u>

Above code snippet says that:

Line 1: Declare variable name login

Line 2: Login variable name will be an input dialogue box, where the window name of that dialogue box would be "Enter login name" and text box will be with name "URL providing window"

Line 3 and Line 4: Setting the data table row

Line 5: The value of the variable "Login" is to be picked up from data table, from column "Login". Note, this column contains environment URL information. Therefore, in future after code development is complete, in case one needs to change environment URL information, changing the same in data table column would suffice the code need. Hence, you can see code and data has got separated.

Line 6: Launch internet explorer and enter "Login" value in the address bar to launch required environment.

2. **Use "Parameterization" technique** – This is used to segregate code and data so that in future if data gets changed then there isn't much rework at code level. As an example, to create a login function where in dashboard link value, login credentials, tab-bar areas to enter into – all are passed into data table sheet and code would pick up required values by handshaking with data table. This is the most effective way to segregate data and code. One needs to program the script in a way that all data set is stored in datatable, which can be changed on need basis and values are passed through variable in the codeline.

<u>Real-time usage:</u>

Let us take a retail application, where invoices are created in bunch of hundreds and thousands on daily basis. Simulate this condition via automation codeline. In such a event the codeline should have intelligence to run a single set of program for number of times. The data to be picked while executing the program should be segregated and kept outside code such as data table. Two benefits we derive of this: first is that, now hundreds of different data set can be plugged outside code and this can be done by a non-technical person also, and hence code can be kicked off. Dependency to execute code is minimized. Secondly, later in future, if there is a need to execute automated tests using some specific data set to reproduce a pattern, one need not go into code to change the data set. This can be done easily via data table.

<u>Code snippet example:</u>

```
If DataTable.Value("Product",dtLocalSheet) = "AP" Then
Browser("Application Index Page").Page("Login").WebEdit("Class Name:=WebEdit","html tag:=INPUT","type:= text","name := j_username").Set DataTable.Value("UserName",dtLocalSheet)
Browser("Application Index Page").Page("Login").WebEdit("Class Name:=WebEdit","html tag:=INPUT","type:= password","name := j_password").Set DataTable.Value("Password",dtLocalSheet)
Browser("Application Index Page").Page("Login").WebButton("Submit").Click
Reporter.ReportEvent micDone, "Logged In As: ",DataTable.Value("UserName",dtLocalSheet)
```

A1 Dashboard

	Link	UserName	Password	Login
1	Dashboard	ACCOUNTS_PAYABLE_SUPERVISOR_VISION_OPERATIONS	Welcome1	http://fusionsystemtest-a-fin.us.oracle.com/payables/faces/in
2	Invoices Setup Aging Periods	ACCOUNTS_PAYABLE_SUPERVISOR_VISION_OPERATIONS	Welcome1	http://fusionsystemtest-a-fin.us.oracle.com/payables/faces/in
3	Payment Process Request Templates	ACCOUNTS_PAYABLE_SUPERVISOR_VISION_OPERATIONS	Welcome1	http://fusionsystemtest-a-fin.us.oracle.com/payables/faces/in
4	Invoices	ACCOUNTS_PAYABLE_SUPERVISOR_VISION_OPERATIONS	Welcome1	http://fusionsystemtest-a-fin.us.oracle.com/payables/faces/in
5	ISP Invoices	ACCOUNTS_PAYABLE_SUPERVISOR_VISION_OPERATIONS	Welcome1	http://fusionsystemtest-a-fin.us.oracle.com/payables/faces/in
6	Payments	ACCOUNTS_PAYABLE_SUPERVISOR_VISION_OPERATIONS	Welcome1	http://fusionsystemtest-a-fin.us.oracle.com/payables/faces/in
7	Invoices Setup Reporting Entities	ACCOUNTS_PAYABLE_SUPERVISOR_VISION_OPERATIONS	Welcome1	http://fusionsystemtest-a-fin.us.oracle.com/payables/faces/in

<u>Code snippet explanation:</u>

Line 1: If value being looked by the program is AP then in datatable under "product" column, look for AP.

Line 2: In data table, look for username

Line 3: In data table look for password

Line 4: Click on "Submit" button

Line 5: Report in result log that "Logged in as <Username, as picked by data table>"

3. **Script decoupling technique** – This is one of the most valuable methodologies practiced during test script creation. This also can be termed as one of the most useful techniques for code re-usability.

<u>**How this works:**</u> Identify the most frequently and commonly occurring page. Create a standalone script for the scenario discussed within that page. Try handling all the required exceptions and data sets interaction on that page. Once this kind of script is ready, float it across all the automation designers. Let them know what you have embedded within the script. Therefore, wherever they use this page, the same script can be plugged and played.

Important point to note is that such scripts should be called by the codeline using "Call by reference" methodology unless highly impossible. This method repeats for all such functionalities or pages that needs to be repetitively used by all automation engineer working on that module. This enhances code re-usability and decrease development time of each automation developer, too.

Advantages of this methodology:

- *Code reusability:* As explained above, one code snippet can be re-used by multiple folks around and hence saves development effort.
- *Minimizes the impact:* In future if some enhancements have been pushed for such pages, by changing or upgrading the codeline at parent file, automatically all inventory will be updated as the script has been called using "Call by Reference" methodology.

Real-time usage:

Generally, login pages are such pages which are used across application, and as per business need may change from time to time. Therefore, it is always advisable to decouple login page script and hence call it across inventory using "Call by Reference".

Code snippet example:

RunAction "Action1 [Automation \Solemn\Product Level\Payments\Common Lib\Scripts\Solemn_DisableCookie_Login]", oneIteration,4

DataTable.SetCurrentRow (cint(parameter("RowNumber")))

Code snippet explanation:

Line 1: There's a script at location *Automation \Solemn\Product Level\Payments\Common Lib\Scripts* - with name "*Solemn_DisableCookie_Login*"

Call this script via the given path. This script has data table attached to it. While execution, pick up data set that is there in Row 4.

Line 2: Set the Row 4 as stated in Line 1, when ever Line 1 is called for execution.

4. **Code to handle primary key values** – There are several instances in the application where for each new transaction, input parameter needs to be primary key value or in layman's term, should be unique.

Example: Username creation, bank account creation, invoice number creation, etc. During recording, tool records the current punched-in value, and that is hardcoded in the code. When the script is executed next time, the same codeline will fail as the value is already punched into the application during recording of the codeline. Therefore, to make scripts re-runnable across instances, program needs to be embedded wherein, in each run, unique value is generated on the fly, embedded with required string in the code, and used at all required places in the apps.

How to handle such scenarios:

The most famous technique used across the industry is time stamp capturing on the fly. Capture the combination of system hour, minute and second and hence wrap it up as a digit and suffix it with required string. Therefore, the complete string becomes unique in every run.

Real-Time usage:

When you create your username for any email account, the same username can't be used again for that email client. If one has to create a script for registering or creating a username, the username value that the user would have inputted at first go, will not work if the code is executed more than one time. Therefore, it is the work of an engineer to identify all such primary keys and code accordingly for all such areas, maintaining individuality..

Code snippet example

```
Dim v_filename
v_filename = DataTable.Value("g_Rerun_Folder_Path",dtLocalSheet) & DataTable.Value("g_Rerun_File_Name",dtLocalSheet)
Call fn_fin_cleanGlobal(v_filename)
Call fn_fin_declare_extern_functions()
Call fn_fin_setGlobal (v_filename,"PARAMETERS","g_Rerun",minute(now)&second(now))
g_Rerun=fn_fin_getGlobal (v_filename,"PARAMETERS","g_Rerun")
```

Code snippet explanation:

Line 1: Declare variable "v_filename".
Line 2: Path of the folder where all dynamically generated keys are stored.
Line 3: Call function that cleans the global variable value.
Line 4: Generate unique random number and set the global variable with that value.
Line 5: In the variable "g_rerun", store the unique value.

5 **Parameter value passing technique across scripts** – The technique to handle a scenario like, a transaction id generated in one script requiring to be passed across various scripts, is known as parameter passing technique. Here, programmatically parameter is defined, then assigned as output variable in one script , where this value is generated; it is then defined as input variable in another script, where this is used. After performing this, then required code is inserted for handshaking between two scripts.

Real-Time usage:

Let us take an example of banking transaction. As you know, when you do funds transfer, there's a transaction id that gets generated. In order to query for history details of that transaction, you need to input transaction id. Now, for the discussed scenario, if performing funds transfer is one script and querying for committed transaction is another script, then in such a case when transaction id gets generated in the first script, there should be a mechanism by which the variable value should get passed on to the second script. Otherwise, the second script either will not work or in it the complete scenario from fund transfer transaction needs to be scripted.

Therefore, it is very crucial that automation engineers are given heads up to start capturing such ID's that have relevance and can be passed on to other scripts to tie several script transactional flow together.

6. **Function declaration and definition** — Any automated tool gives you feature to design functions and this should be highly encouraged within the coding domain either automation or development. As you already know the several benefits of functions, one major benefit to the organisation is lesser development time through code re-usability and lesser maintenance overhead.

Real-time usage via eyes of QTP:

QTP allows users to use their function which is user defined. Therefore, in several instances where one feels that the action type will be used at several places, such action needs to be coded as function and that wrapper is called within scripts wherever required. These functions are written in VB.Net codeline.

Code snippet:

fn_fin_cell_check - Checks particular cell value in "Table"

```
############################################################
Public Function fn_fin_cell_check(browsername,pagename,adftablename, rownum,colnum,expectedval)
Dim rowcount,actualval,position
rowcount =Browser(browsername).Page(pagename).Table(adftablename).GetROProperty("rows")
If rowcount <> "" Then
  Reporter.ReportEvent micPass,"Table Query","Table: "&adftablename&" return results"
  actualval =Browser(browsername).Page(pagename).Table(adftablename).CellValue(rownum,colnum)
  If expectedval <> "NOT_NULL" Then
      position=Instr(actualval,expectedval)
      If position > 0 Then
      Reporter.ReportEvent micPass,"Table Cell Query","Cell Value In Table At Row:"&rownum&" column:"&colnum&" Successfully Displays: "&expectedval
      Else
      Reporter.ReportEvent micFail,"Table Cell Query","Cell Value in table At Row:"&rownum&" column:"&colnum&" Fails To Display: "&expectedval&". Actually It Displays: "&actualval
      MsgBox "TableCellQuery:"&"CellValueintableAtRow:"&rownum&"column:"&colnum&" Fails To Display: "&expectedval&". Actually It Displays: "&actualval
      End If
```

```
Else
If actualval <> "" Then
Reporter.ReportEvent micPass,"Table Cell Query","Cell Value In Table At Row:"&rownum&" column:"&colnum&" Successfully Displays: "&actualval
Else
Reporter.ReportEvent micFail,"Table Cell Query","Cell Value in table At Row:"&rownum&" column:"&colnum&" Fails To Display: "&expectedval&". Actually It Displays: "&actualval
MsgBox "Table Cell Query: "&"Cell Value in table At Row:"&rownum&" column:"&colnum&" Fails To Display: "&expectedval&". Actually It Displays: "&actualval
    End If
  End If
Else
  Reporter.ReportEvent micFail,"Table Query","Table: "&adftablename&" DOESNT Returned Any Results As Expected"
  MsgBox "Table: "&adftablename&" DOESNT Returned Any Results As Expected"
End If
End Function
```

Code snippet explanation:

This function is trying to validate a value in a table which has multiple rows and columns. This code traverses through each row and column combination, and tries to verify whether the expected value is available or not.

In the next chapter, several such common functions, that are a must before coding starts, will be discussed.

7. **To capture values generated at run time** – There are several instances where transaction ID's get generated once a transaction is completed. This primarily happens in banking domain applications, retail applications, etc. It should be mandated beforehand to automation designer not to hard code such transactional messages; else the codeline will fail in next iterative run. Therefore, the best method to capture such events is via the code logic which would capture such transactional events on the fly during the code execution. After capturing, there should be a procedure to pass the captured transactional message in the result log. In this way one can ensure whether transaction got committed and also if required then one can dig in the transaction number from result log.
8. **Descriptive programming** – One of the most powerful aspects of automation coding is descriptive coding. Generally, all automation tools support one platform or the other; for example, QTP supports VB language, WinRunner supported "C" like TSL language, Selenium supports Java, etc. Therefore, the benefit that automation designer can derive is that without going with simple

playback and record, one can also plug in direct codeline into the automation script. This non-dependent codeline is known as descriptive programming technique.

Real-time usage:

There are several instances where an object when interacts with server, then the long id or html name of the object gets generated based on the session id of that particular transaction event. In such a case, object id changes at each access. To code and control the dynamic nature of object ID description, it becomes highly important to parse and control every line of such tags that get dynamically generated. In order to do so, "descriptive programming" is one of the most powerful techniques.

Code snippet with example:

Else If DataTable.Value("Product",dtLocalSheet) = "AR" Then

Browser("Payables Application Index Page").Page("Receivables Application_2").Link("Payments").Click

Browser("Application Index Page").Page("Receivables Application Index").ADFSync(50000)

Browser("Application Index Page").Page("Receivables Application Index").ADFPanelTabbed("pt1").SelectTab "Payments"

Browser("Application Index Page").Page("Receivables Application Index").ADFSync(50000)

Reporter.ReportEvent micDone, "Tab Clicked: ",DataTable.Value("Tab",dtLocalSheet)&" Tab"

**Below mentioned is the descriptive programming code snippet , where object property, which is of "Link Type", is written down in a single line and appropriate condition value is being picked up from data table –

Browser("Application Index Page").Page("Receivables Application Index").Link("Class name:=Link","html tag := A","class:=af_goLink","text:= "& DataTable.Value("Link",dtLocalSheet)).Click

As you can see, the required object property is written as part of codeline, which otherwise in above codelines is not the case. Since all such properties of objects have been pulled into the codeline, it is possible to wild card several such arguments which may be created dynamically by the session ID's. Doing so makes object recognition less susceptive to failures in spite of changes.

9. **Wild carding technique** – In continuation to the scenario explained in point 8 above, there are several instances where the physical description of objects may change from one value to another. In order to handle such fluctuations, wild carding technique is plugged in within the code.

Practically, it is very difficult to say which object to wild card during the development and which one not to. This is something that comes with experience of the automation engineer and the engineer over the application under test. The most important event when such changes can be thought for is during automation test execution. This is the time when various objects show such fluctuations and accordingly they should be wild carded not simply recorded.

Code snippet:

Original object property description - setpt1:USma:0:MAt1:1:pt1:BuSrch1:1:pnlProp:isActive
Wild Carded object property descriotion –
*.*pt1.*:USma:0:Mat.*:.*:pt1:BuSrch1:1:pnlProp:is.**

10. **Capturing and echoing outcome in log files** – As a good practice, it should be mandated to the engineers before development starts that for all transactional event, once committed or processed, there should be a code to echo the event outcome. Additionally, wherever necessary, code needs to be embedded to capture and compare the run time value with the expected value and echo the result in the log file. This is done using conditional loop involving some functions.

Code snippet:

```
If Status <> "Payment Created" Then
  Reporter.ReportEvent micPass,"PPR Status","PPR Status on actual page is: "&actual_Val
Else
  Reporter.ReportEvent micFail,"PPR Status","PPR Status on actual page is: "&actual_Val
End If
```

Code snippet explanation:

Line 1: If and else conditional loop is triggered, where line 1 says if status is equal to "Payment created" then

Line 2: Latch pass message in the log file that echoes "PPR status on actual page is *<PPR no captured during run time>*

Line 3: Else

Line 4: Latch fail message in the log file that echoes ""PPR status on actual page is *<PPR no captured during run time>*

10.2.4 Probable Issue Identification, Segregation and Tracking Mechanism

This was one such area which I never felt that would be so relevant to plan for before automation development or automation execution kicks off. But with practical perspective, today I can say that this can be one of the most critical segregations and planning that one could think as a part of Automation framework strategy.

Central idea here is to identify all such failure types that one expects to encounter during journey of automation development and execution. Of course, this could be a daunting task as you would have a question that how can one think of issues when work in itself hasn't started. And that is where the experience and expertise when coupled with vision, counts. Once such failure points are jotted down then the next level of work is to define the service level agreement with all required development, operations and infrastructure team.

Let us see all such issue areas that generally are encountered during the journey of automation development and execution stage.

Functional Issue: Any functional failure encountered can be termed as functional issue.

If the nature of such issue is critical then development should provide immediate fix within agreed time limit. Accordingly for all such cases, architect or automation head need to have a service level agreement where definitions of various functional failures need to be defined and accordingly ETA (expected time of arrival) of the fix should be agreed upon.

Example: Click "submit" button, at times transaction gets submitted and at times does not This is an example of intermittent functional issue.

-For intermittent functional issue: Development team needs to step up to identify the root cause analysis of such failures and provide a fix on priority.

Seed data issue: If any application has already seed data entered as part of vanilla configuration, and later in further builds that data is missing then this is known as seed data issue. In such a case, operations and development team should be questioned as there is a possibility that wrong data packet has got sourced in within the application and such discrepancies can cost development a lot in further builds, if not ironed out immediately.

Example: By default customer name which is being used across invoices transaction is missing in later builds.

Object mismatch issue: All the UI objects on the application during automation development are recognized with unique properties. When those properties differ than what has been recorded then such kinds of failures are known as object mismatch issue.

In case of such failures, development team should justify the change and revert back to original name unless is a strategic change.

Example: In build three name of submit button is "submit". In build four it has become "submit transaction". This deviation can be termed as object mismatch issue.

Failure due to enhancement: By the nature of software development activity, there will be certain builds throughout the development lifecycle, when some new features would get introduced. Now, if this enhancement is introduced in between the automated sequence then the change would make already developed scripts fail. Such failures are termed as failed due to enhancement. Central idea is to get this change reported as issue and get a buy in if this is the final deployment or still it's in progression phase. If it is into progression stage then automation development should be halted else the ne enhancement should be embedded within the existing code line.

Environment issue: In real-time scenarios, you would observe that after clicking specific transactional event, "server disconnect" error pops up. Such kinds of issue are generally under the purview of operations team to correct and hence are termed as environment issue.

Automation head needs to streamline definition of issue type under environment issue category and accordingly agree upon as what termed critical needs to be fixed on priority within agreed time limit and likewise, accordingly as priority and severity of the cases decrease, ETA for the fix can be little bit longer.

Intermittent environment related issue: When any environment issue comes at one point in time, but does not get reproduced on will, such issues can be termed as intermittent environment issue. Accordingly, service level agreement for defining severity and ETA should be set with required operations team.

Script coding issue: If the script fails due to coding deficiency then such issues can be termed as script coding issue. This should always be termed as highly critical issue and should be fixed as and when found.

Tool issue: Several times, during development one may observe that applications do not get recognized by the tool. Accordingly few of the features may not be very suitable for the testing perspective and hence need to be enhanced. All such cases are termed as tool related issues and should be addressed to tool vendors.

Tool object identification issue: During the journey of automation development, you would observe that there are several instances where objects are not getting recorded or playback by the tool. Such instances are termed as "Tool object identification issue". Accordingly, such types of issues should be reported to tool vendor for immediate fix.

Environment performance issue: Last but not the least, if the automation development starts at an early phase of development cycle, then there are chances that application performance may not be that great or may be fluctuating throughout the day. In such a case, the impact on automation codeline is immense as in spite of best synchronization techniques embedded within the codeline, it becomes difficult to define a bandwidth of such synchronization until which code should handle fluctuating performance. Such kind of occurrence can be termed as environment performance issue.

Besides setting service level agreement on the prioritization and ETA for the fix, the other most important aspect of this planning is to account for bundling similar issue type using some deliminator or tag. The tag helps in filtering out reports or studying the data set, more effectively and precisely.

HP Quality Center 10: Automation Framework Implementation Using HP QC 9.2/10 + HP QTP 9.5/10 Integration — Part 1

11

Chapter Objectives: This chapter will give an overview of

- *Introduction*
- *Principle behind automation framework*
- *File Storage design principles*
- *Scope and Naming Conventions (Folders, Files and Variables)*
- *Scripting and Coding Standards*

Introduction

This along with next two chapters will take you through the real-time working model of functional automation testing framework. This working model involves layout structure using HP QC 9.2/10 and HP QTP 9.5/10. This is the first time when in any book real time simulation of automation framework is being walked through from scratch. Several professionals, directors and architects have asked me this question during my professional journey, and hence this prompted me to pen down the framework. This automation framework that I'm talking about here facilitates performing the automation development and execution for functional testing domain. Though, I'm taking into account functional tool HP QTP while laying out this framework, but using the discussed principles, the framework can be applied for any functional tool, too.

Additionally, the concepts discussed within the chapter, hold valid for both HP QTP 9.5, 10.0 and HP QC 9.2, 10 versions.

11.1 Principle Behind Automation Framework

In this chapter, I will take you through the journey of laying out automation framework involving QC9.2/10 and QTP 9.5/10. Please note this is real-time simulation of how framework is laid out in MNC's.

There are certain benefits that need to be derived out of framework. In order to retain those benefits, one needs to start thinking about it from the beginning, before inception of framework. In other words, we can mark those benefits as pillars and start putting structure into place. Those pillars aka principles that should be kept intact are:

- Re-runnability of tests
- Re-usability of tests
- Easy maintainability of tests
- Easy integration of tests
- Seamless handshaking when tests are bonded together
- Astute integration of all files
- Flexibility of interchanging or exchanging files at the time of need
- Easier and effective code development
- Ensure parallel execution of tests at the same time across concurrent systems

11.1.1 Pre-requisite

Let us see those pre-requisite, which should be into place before laying out the automation framework.

1. QTP 9.5/10 tool should be deployed on shared Windows 2003 server
2. QC 9.2/10 tool should be deployed and integrated with HP QTP 9.5/10
3. Shared drive should be mapped on machines where QTP 9.5/10 is deployed. Am giving it a name of "Q:\\drive"

Definitions:

- **Product Family (PF)** = Conglomeration of several small products. Example- Financials is a product family but payables can be one of the products under Financials.
- **Product** = One single product in a product family. Example- Under Financials product family, Payables is one product.

Throughout our discussion, we will refer "Financials" as product family and "Accounting Hub, Payables, etc." as products.

11.2 File Storage Design Principles

The first area to think about is that since we need to integrate QTP 9.5/10 files with QC 9.2 /10 management software, hence a very systematic file storage principle needs to be designed. To derive maximum benefit of file storage structure, while designing the same, the below mentioned principles should be kept into account:

- Re-usability of files should be possible
- Re-runnability of the files should be possible
- Parallel execution of tests should be possible
- Extensibility of files and tests should be possible
- Clear segregation of all kinds of files should be possible
- Global function file demarcation
- Local function file demarcation
- Data file to be stored scientifically so that later on in future, finding correct data files to their respective files should not be a problem
- Sql file scientific demarcation
- Re-usable .vbs files which should be at product family level and product level.

Now, you can understand that besides what has been talked about above, additionally, in sum, the challenges behind laying out File storage structure is that:

- Each test case should correspond to each script
- Easy identification of tests should be possible
- Bundling of test script should be made possible
- Clear demarcation and storage principle should be laid out for all the global and local supportive files

Let us see the design principles abiding by which file storage should be laid out.

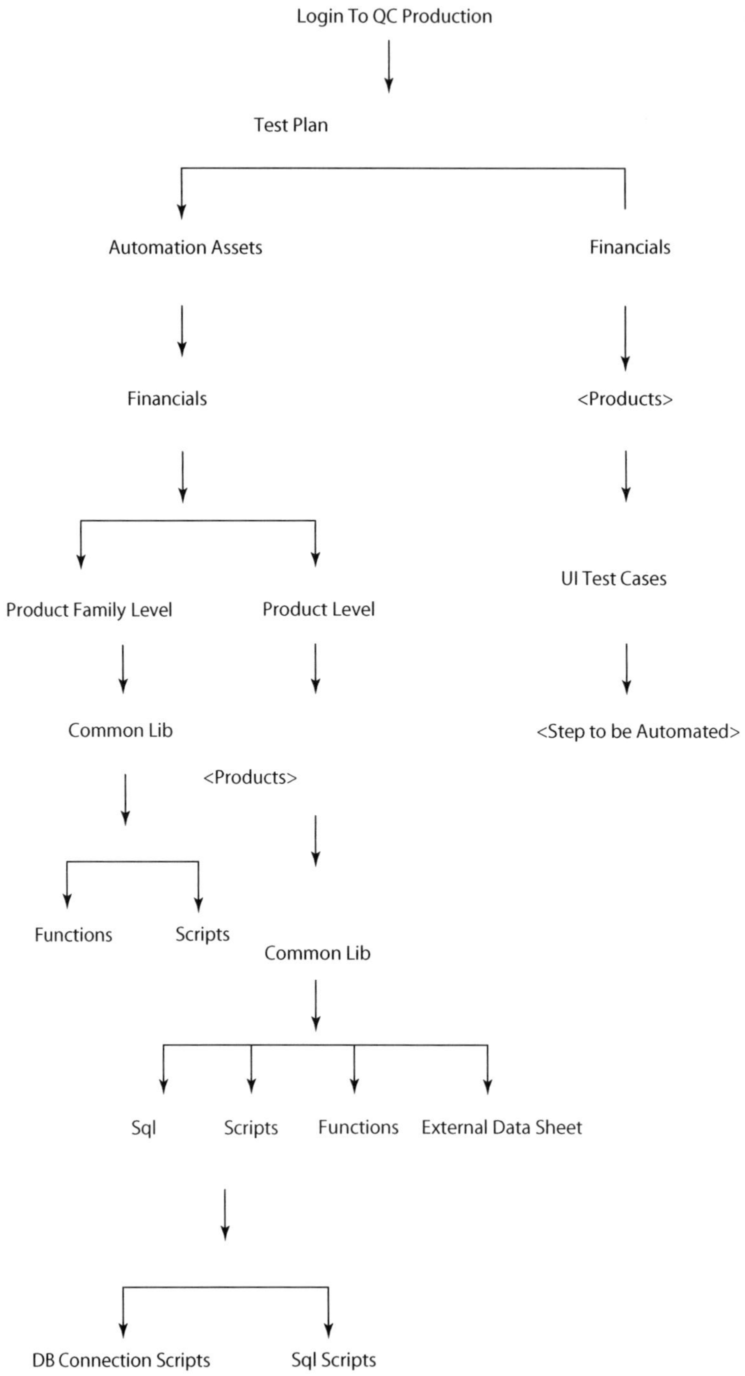

Figure 11.1 *File Storage Design and Structure on QC 9.2/10.*

This design, once you enter to the "Test Plan" area, gets segregated into two other areas:

Test Plan -> Automation Assets: This area primarily does not hold any test plan but is an empty area but is being developed to keep all global files, function files and supportive files in a structured manner so that easy segregation of all such file types is achievable, even at later point of time when inventory grows huge.

- *Test Plan -> Financials:* This is product family area where all the manual test cases are stored. Mapping to these manual test cases, individual test scripts need to be churned out.

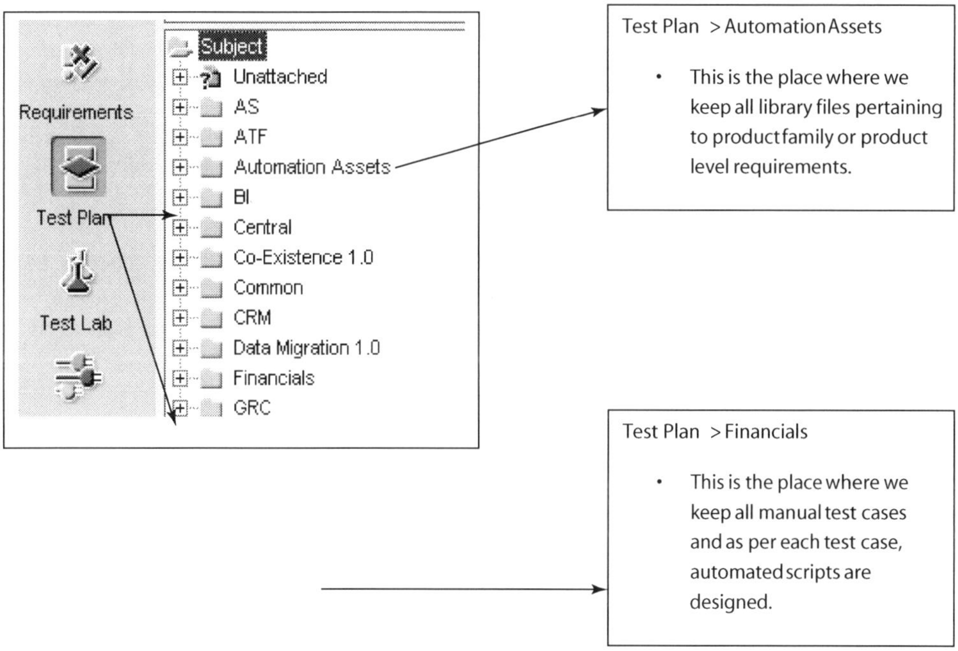

Figure 11.2 *Folder Segregation Explanation as per Line Diagram in Fig. 11.1.*

11.2.1 Definitions of Folders Under "Test Plan -> Automation Assets -> <Product Family>"

- Files stored at mentioned location has scope across product family level:
  QC-> Test Plan -> Automation Assets -> Financials-> Product Family Level–> Common Lib

Explanation: The files stored at product family level means that the entire product family, which includes "n" no. of products, can use these files. Therefore, a mandatory process should be floated around to each team member that any file that they intend to keep there should be useful and global enough to contribute to entire product family.

- *Common Lib -> Functions :* This folder contains one generic .vbs file, which contains functions common to whole product family.
- *Common Lib -> Scripts :* This folder contains various generic re-usable scripts, which can be used across product family level.

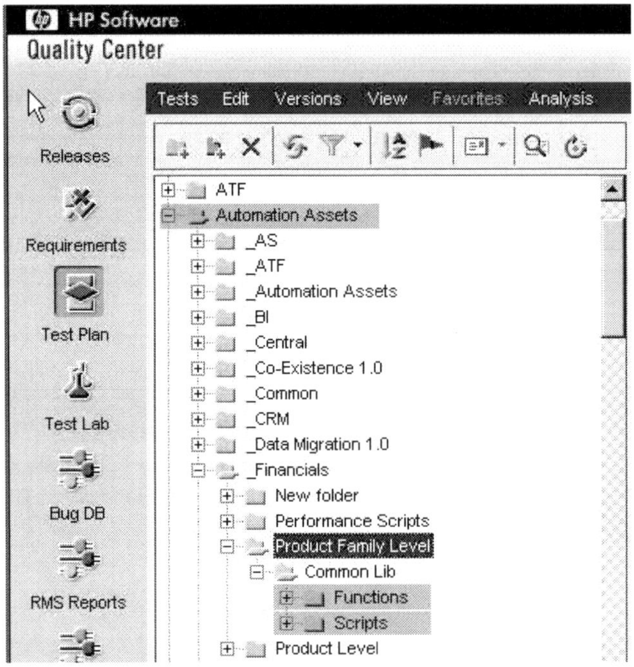

Figure 11.3 *HP QC Snapshot for Folders at Automation Asset Level.*

□ Files stored at mentioned location has scope limited to specific products only:

QC-> Test Plan -> Automation Assets -> Financials-> Product Level–> <Products>

Explanation: All relevant product names should be stated here. The files stored under each product should be pretty much local to that product only. In case, if anyone still needs to re-use part of this script or file, then one should first copy the file to the respective product area and hence tweak it to accommodate to their needs.

QC-> Test Plan -> Automation Assets -> Financials-> Product Level–> <Products> -> Common Lib

Explanation: This is that area where all such files should be stored which could act as global file for their respective product but not for entire product family. Various such file types that become part of common library are:

- Sql:
  - *Common Lib -> Sql -> DB Connection Script:* This folder contains a generic script that the respective product within a product family uses to establish DB connection. This script will be generic enough where one can enter the relevant details based on that product needs.
  - *Common Lib -> Sql -> Sql Script:* Here some product specific generic sql scripts should be stored. As an example, Sql scripts to push 100 users in customer table.
- Scripts:
  - *Common Lib -> Scripts:* This is the folder where all common QTP scripts pertaining to that product need to be stored.
- Functions:
  - *Common Lib -> Functions:* This is the folder where.vbs file needs to be stored, which would contain product specific common functions.
- External Data Sheet:
  - *Common Lib -> External Data Sheet:* Several times in automation, situation comes when external files need to be used either to call for data set or to export data set. Therefore, this is the folder, where all external data sheet needs to be stored – such as .xls sheet, .vbs sheet, .txt, .xml, etc.

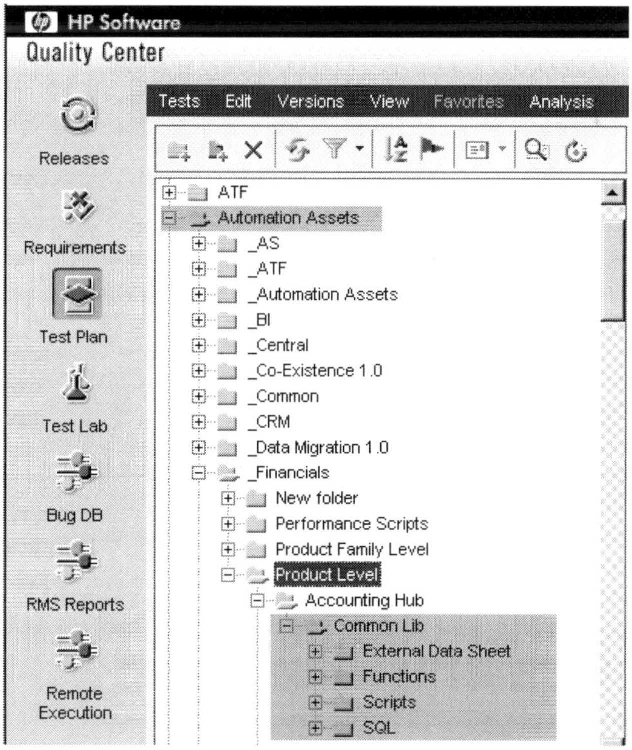

Figure 11.4 *HP QC 9.2/10 Depiction for Automation Asset -> Product Level Folder.*

11.2.2 Definitions of Folders Under "Test Plan -> <Product Family>"

This is the area where all the manual test cases pertaining to entire product family should be stored. Let us see how the folder structure layout should look like.

- *Test Plan -> Financials -> <Product>:* Here, all the products related folders need to be created. Under automation asset, product folder — the product folder names should be exactly the same as what is mentioned here in Test Plan -> Financials -> <Product>.
- *Test Plan -> Financials -> <Product> -> UI Test Cases:* All the test cases pertaining to respective product should be stored here.
- *Test Plan -> Financials -> <Product> -> UI Test Cases-> <Steps to be automated>:* Ideally, UI test cases and steps to be automated are the same level structure, but just for easy explanation, am keeping it in this segregated fashion. At this level, when we change the script type from manual to automation, then manual test scripts will generate the automated test file as well.

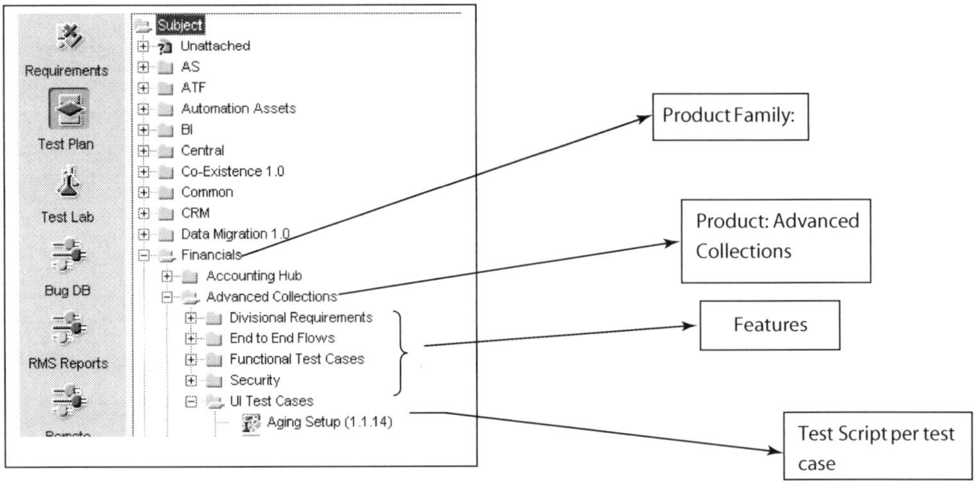

Figure 11.5 *HP QC 9.2/10 Depiction for Test Plan -> Product Family Level Folders.*

The best part of this architectural design is that for both product family and product level folders, this architecture is extendable. When I say extendable, what it means is that assume there are few recovery scenarios that needs to be coded at product family level then this can easily be accommodated. As common lib is the place where all such files are stored, therefore adding one more level for recovery scenario will not be difficult at the time of need. ***Test Plan-> Automation Assets -> <Product Family name> -> Product Family Level -> Common Lib -> Recovery scenario***

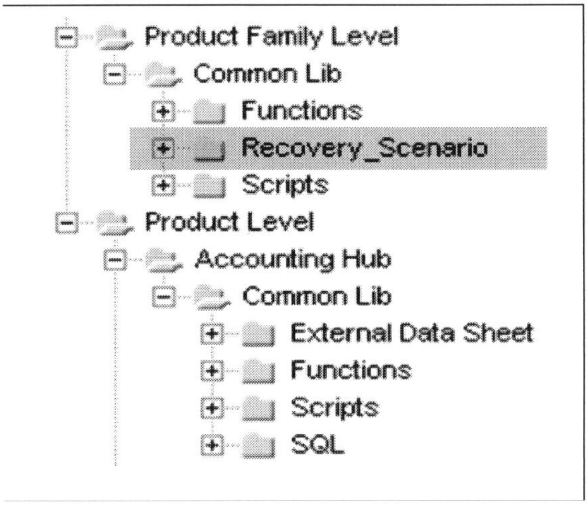

Figure 11.6 *Recovery Scenario Folder Added.*

Likewise, the same can also be added under common lib folder at product level. Indeed, addition of new areas can also be done at several parent levels as and when the business or requirement grows. And the best part is that in spite of this extension, there will always be a clarity regarding files, their relevance and their layout. Already stored files are also kept intact without loosing their definition or path.

Now, let us see, after plugging the line diagram Fig. 11.1 concept , in HP QC 9.2/10 then how HP QC 9.2/10 layout looks like.

Folder segregation explanation as per line diagram in Fig. 11.1.

11.3 Scope and Naming Conventions (Folders, Files and Variables)

Once the folder structure and coding standard are developed, the other most critical aspect is naming convention that needs to be designed and abided by, always for various types of files. Benefit of naming convention comes into picture when many people are developing across modules at in the same time and then to avoid any confusion, all of them use the same protocol to name the files accordingly. Additionally, this also helps management to view or dig in to the files across modules based on these naming conventions and hence dependency upon people gets minimized.

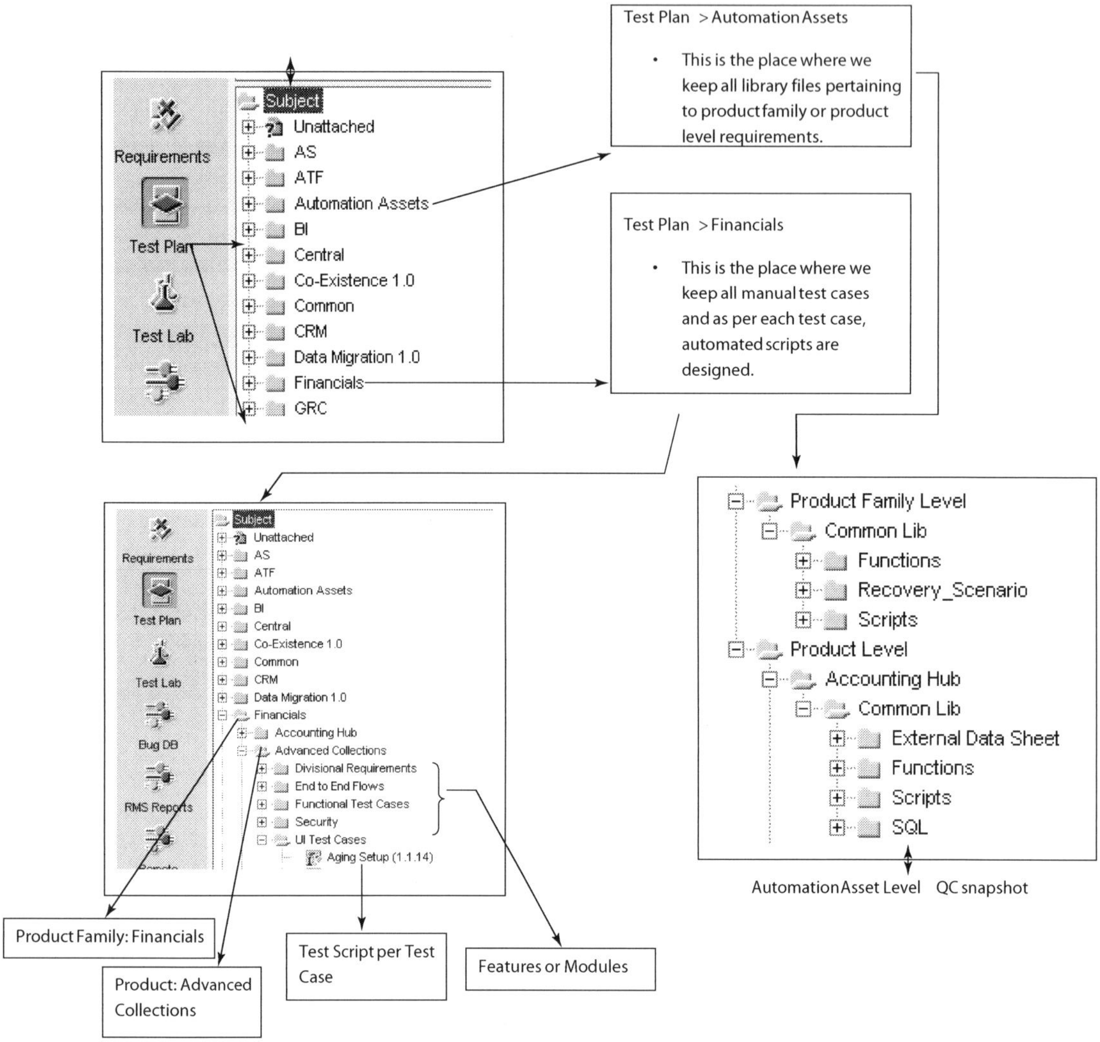

Figure 11.7 *HP QC 9.2/10 – Integrated Depiction of Folder Layout as Per Structure Explained in Line Diagram, Fig. 11.1.*

11.3.1 Naming Convention for Variables While Coding

If a variable is used across different automated tests, then you must declare it as global variable. If the scope of variable is within local script then variables should be declared as local variable.

1. Local Variable should be prefixed with "v_" such as "v_<Variable Name>".
2. Global variable should be prefixed with "g_" such as "g_<Variable Name>".
3. Statistics Variables should be prefixed with "s_" such as "s_<Variable Name>"
4. While passing parameter (Both Input and Output) from one script to another and setting the parameter variable name within script, one must use the same in the mentioned format:
   "V_<VAR>_FROM_ACTION#<(1,2,3..n)>" (if global G_ and if static S_)
5. Naming convention of .ini file should be **"<Flow Name>_param.ini".** Flow name depends on user as what one decides to keep. Tip here is — If the same .ini file is being used across scripts, then keeping logical flow name would help user in tracking correct .ini file throughout.

11.3.2 Naming Convention for Files to be Used at "Divisional level"

Divisional level here means there are several product families under one division.

- At Divisional Level:

  Divisional centralized custom functions are all lower case and prefixed with <division name>.

Example: <division name>_login, denotes that this is login function that can be used for any products across product family under the given division.

11.3.3 Naming Convention for Files Stored at "Product Family level"

- For Function:
  a. There should be just one .VBS file at location:
     QC-> Test Plan -> Automation Assets -> Financials-> Product Family Level–> Common Lib ->Functions
     Naming convention of this file should be: **"<Product family name>_Lib.vbs"**
  b. Every function at product family level should be prefixed with **'fn_<product family short name>'**.
     Example: Let us say if short name for product family is "fin" then function name should be **"fn_fin_<function name>"**
- For Re-usable Scripts:
  As you already know from folder structure layout design that location to store these types of script is:
  QC-> Test Plan -> Automation Assets -> Financials-> Product Family Level–> Common Lib ->Scripts:
  a. For every re-usable scenario, there should be standalone script. No two scenarios should be clubbed into one script.

Example: Login is one script, Logout is another script, etc.

a. Script name should always have prefix as **"<product family short name>_<script name>"**
   Example: Let us say product family short name is "Fin" and script is "login" script then script name should be "Fin_Login"

11.3.4 Naming Convention for Files Stored at "Product Family level"

Note: Folders for all the below discussed areas can be found at location:

QC-> Test Plan -> Automation Assets -> Financials-> Product Level–> <Products> ->Common Lib ->

- For Functions:
  a. For each product, there should be just one .VBS file at location:
     QC-> Test Plan -> Automation Assets -> Financials-> Product Level-> <Products> ->Common Lib -> Functions

  In this .vbs file, as and when new functions requirement comes, they should be added here. Naming convention of this file should be:

  "<Product family short name>_<product Name>_Lib.vbs"

  Example: Let us say product family short name is "Fin" and product name is "AP" the function library name is **"Fin_AP_Lib.vbs"**

  a. Every function that is being coded in the function library, should be defined as **'fn_<product name>_<feature name>'**.

Example: Let us say product name is "ap" and feature name is "create supplier" then "Function name" should be **"fn_ap_CreateSupplier"**

- For Re-usable Scripts:
  a For every re-usable scenario or for scenarios which are pretty much repetitive in that product, there should be a standalone script for each. No two scenarios should be clubbed into one script.
  b. Example: bank Creation is one script, Invoice creation is another script, etc.
  c. Naming convention for such kind of scripts should be: **"<Product Name>_<Feature Name>"**

  Example: Let us say product name is "ap" and feature name is "supplier creation" then re-usable script name should be: **ap_SupplierCreation**

- For Sql Files:
  a. For SQL Files, naming convention should be:
     <Product>_<UI Test Case Name>_<Sql File name>.sql

  Example: ap_ap001CreateSupplier_CreateSuppName.sql

- External Data Files:
  a. If you plan to use external data files, then naming convention is:
     <Product>_UI Test Case name_<data file name>
     Example: ap_ap001CreateSupplier_SuppNameValues.xls

11.4 At Automation Asset Level, How to Attach "Re-Usable Scripts" and "Functions" in QC

Until here, you are aware of the *"test plan -> automation asset"* layout at which functions and re-usable scripts need to be stored. But in order to save and store the same in HP QC 9.2/10 is a procedure in itself. Let us walk through this procedure now. In this section, let us see how you can record and save the file using HP QC 9.2/10 + HP QTP 9.5/10 integration.

Below mentioned are the procedural steps that one should perform in order to store product level scripts and functions, at automation asset level. The benefit of performing the below mentioned steps is that this structure would support parallel execution, without any issues. Else, there can be several such issues that may come up, if one does not lay out the design pragmatically and hence the common script or function may not be used concurrently across several scripts during parallel execution.

11.4.1 Methodology to Attach Re-usable Scripts in QC at Automation Asset Level

Step 1) Open **QTP from desktop -> Establish QC connection** through "QC Connection" tab-bar on QTP

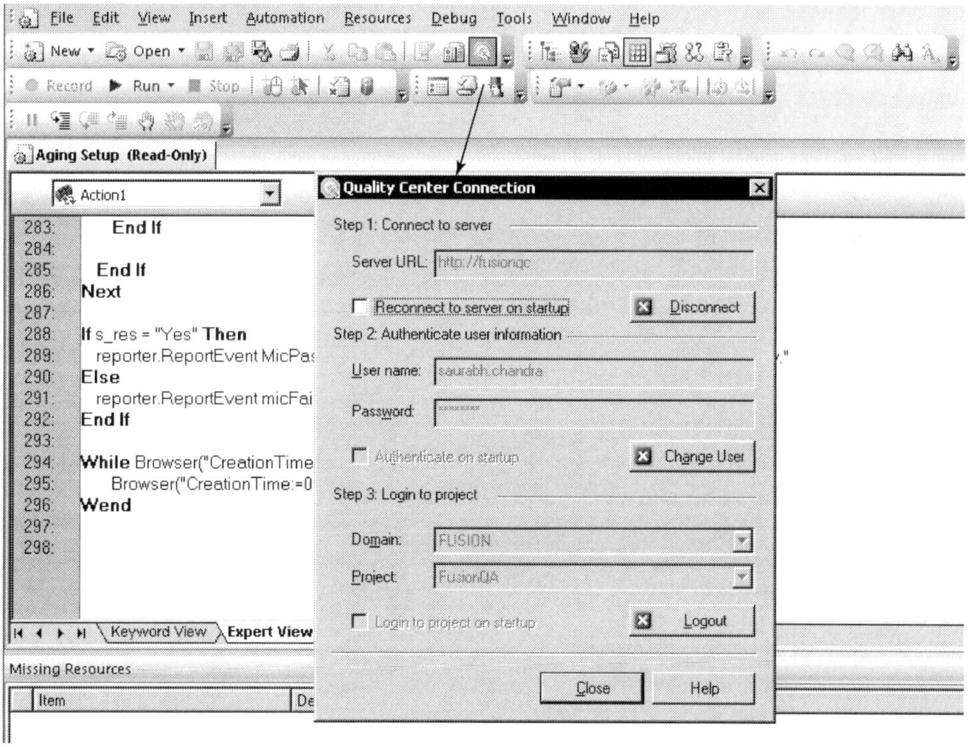

Figure 11.8 *Establishing QC 9.2/10 Connection Via QTP 9.5/10.*

Step 2) Record your script.

Step 3) Stabilize your script by executing it into *"Temporary Run Results Folder"*.

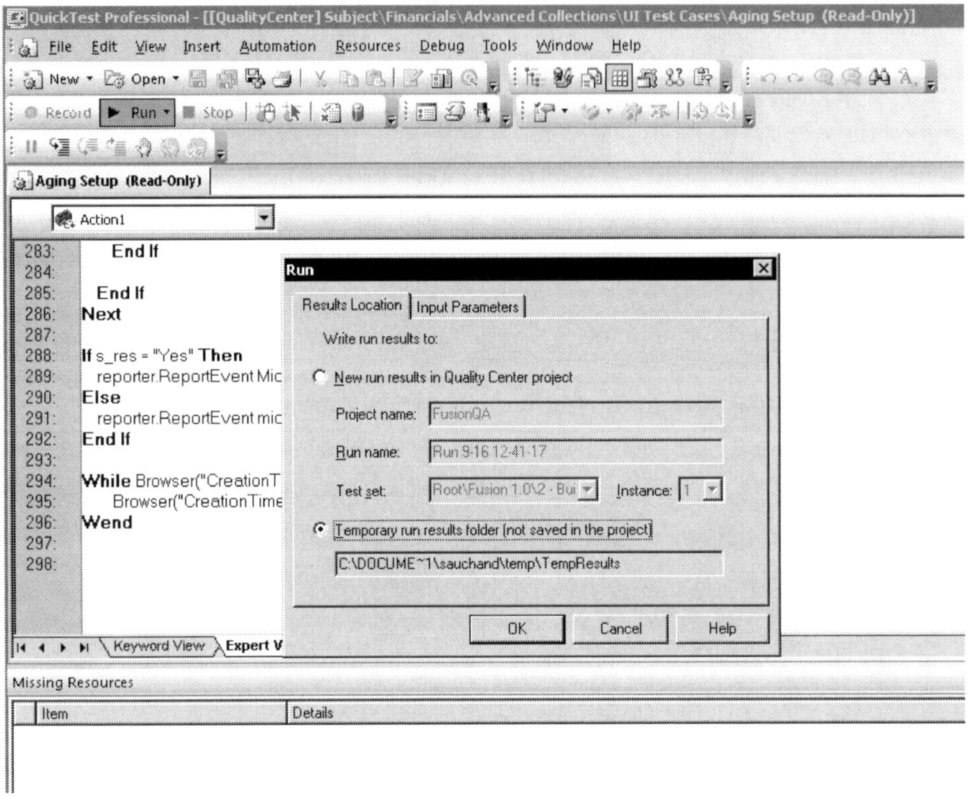

Figure 11.9 *Temporary Run Result Folder.*

Step 4) Save your script in QC at location:

QC-> Test Plan -> Automation Assets -> Financials-> Product Family Level–> Common Lib->Scripts

Step 5) After saving it, launch QC.

Step 6) Go to the location at which you have stored the script i.e.,

QC-> Test Plan -> Automation Assets -> Financials-> Product Family Level–> Common Lib->Scripts

Step 7) Select Script.

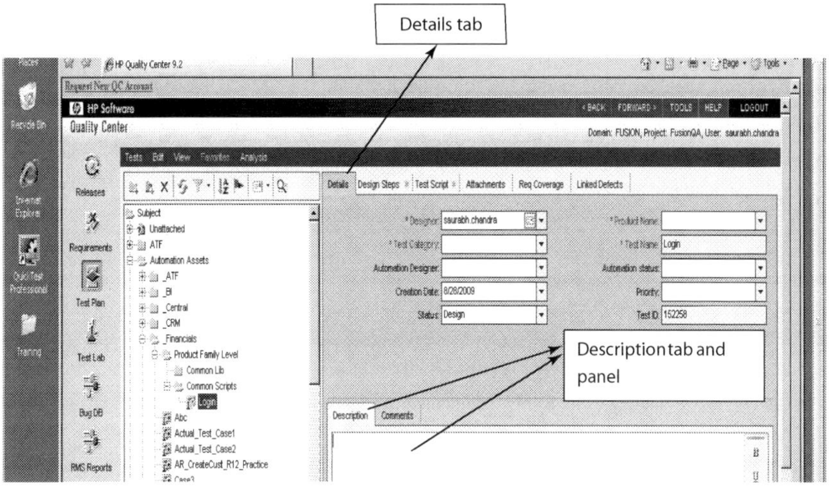

Figure 11.10 *Login Script Selected.*

Step 8) Select **"Details"** tab-bar, under that script.

Fill in, the details:

(a) *Test category:* < Any category that you would have segregated for this test>

(b) *Automation Designer:* < Name of the engineer who would be coding for this test >

(c) *Product name:* <Product Name>

(d) *Automation Status:* <Required automation status> i.e., ready or review, etc.

(e) *Priority:*

You would choose "1" if it is highly used test.

You would choose "2" if it is medium used test

You would choose "3" if it is remotely used test

Under **"Description"** panel**,** give a brief description, as what this script does.

Step 9) Click on **"Design Steps".**

Add one new step and under **"Description"** write down brief description as what this script does. Under **"Expected Results",** write down what is the output of this script.

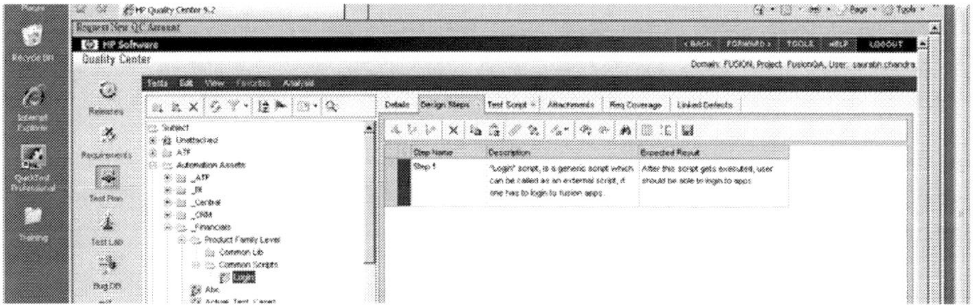

Figure 11.11 *Design Steps Area in QC.*

Step 10) If applicable, under **"Attachments"**, attach any screenshot to showcase what this script does.

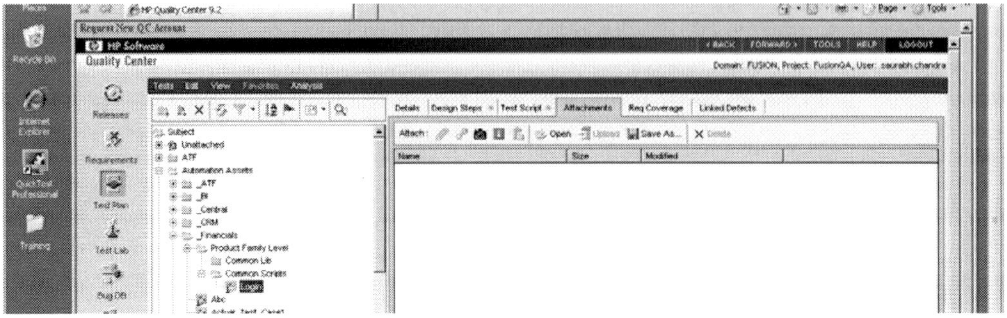

Figure 11.12 *Attachments Area in QC.*

11.4.2 Methodology to Attach Function in QC at Automation Asset Level

Step 1) Open **QTP from desktop -> Establish QC connection** through "QC Connection" tab-bar on QTP.

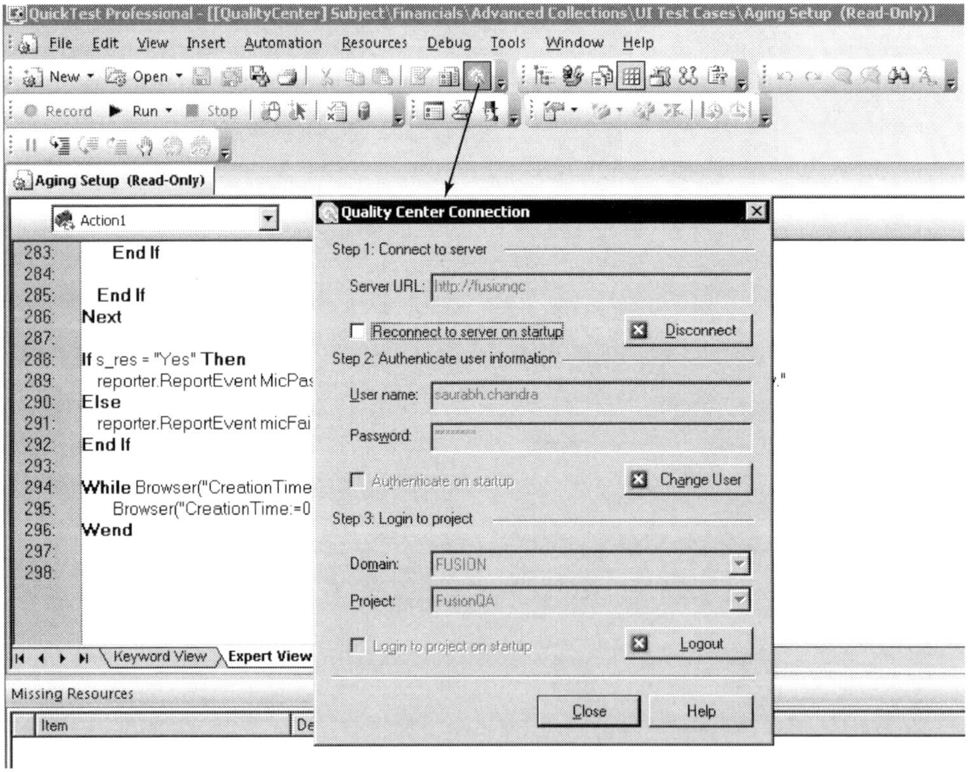

Figure 11.13 *Establishing QC 9.2/10 Connection via QTP 9.5/10.*

Step 2) Open function through QTP.

Step 3) Click **"QTP->File->Save as"**, go to QC file system and save the function at:

QC-> Test Plan -> Automation Assets -> Financials-> Product Family Level–> <Products> -> Common Lib-> Functions

Step 4) After function is saved in QC, it would be visible under **"Attachments"** tab of QC.

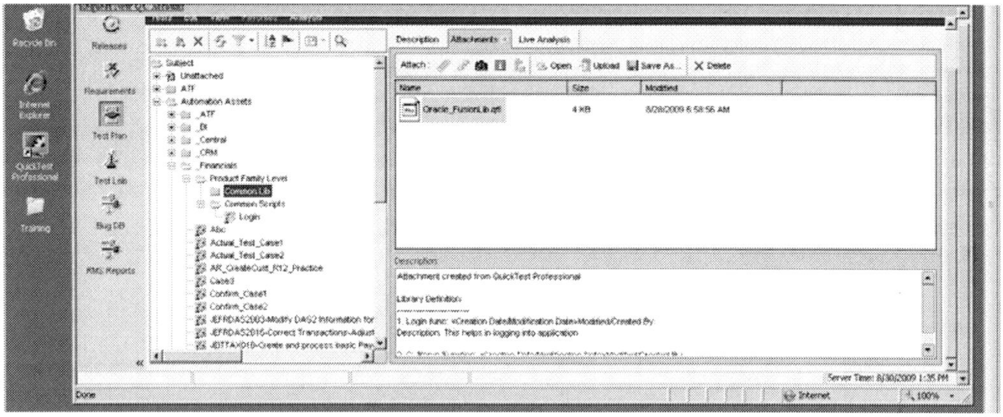

Figure 11.14 *Attachments Area in QC, With Function, .qfl File Attached.*

Whenever, you add any new function to any existing .vbs file, then as a process one should be asked to update **"Attachments -> Description"** section, with the following updates:

<S.No>) <Function Name>: <Creation Date/Modification Date>_<Modified By name/Created By name>

Description: *<Brief description of this function>*

Example:

1) Login: 30-Aug-10_Saurabh Chandra

Description: *This helps in logging to application.*

11.5 Scripting and Coding Standards

For the stability and repeatability of any code, it is very critical that some common standards are followed by the team working on automation. In this section, we will discuss such coding standards that should be exercised when automation coding using QC 9.2/10 and QTP 9.5/10 happens. QTP 9.5/10 supports VB; therefore, below mentioned standards will encapsulate the basic VB coding technique that must be abided by in order to maintain faster development and ensure repeatability of the QTP automated tests.

Let us also try understanding the basic difference between coding standards discussed here and automation development standards discussed in an earlier chapter. In an earlier chapter, we have talked about best practices that should be taken into account to roll out any automation tool. However, here we are specifically talking about QTP coding standards to be followed when we are integrating automation development and execution process via QC 9.2/10.

11.5.1 Standards

1. Each test case should have its associated automated script. If the functionality changes and one needs to upgrade or change the manual script, then the automated script at the same level, will have to go through the required change, without having an extra copy created for the upgraded one.

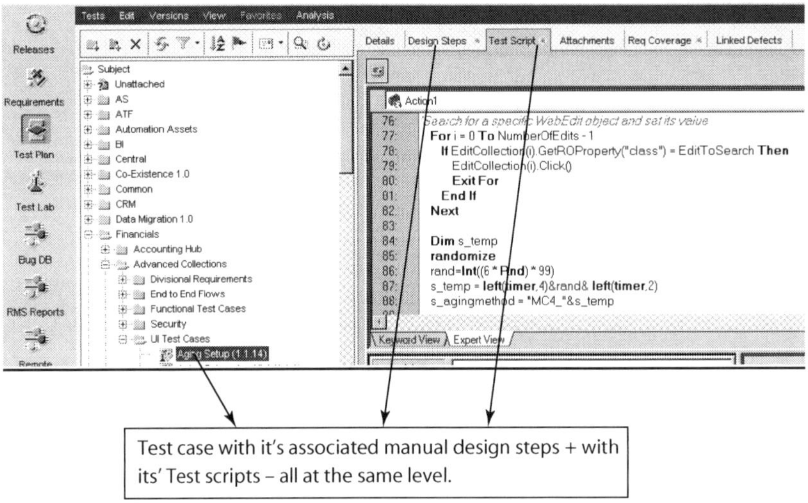

Figure 11.15 *Test Case and Test Script at the Same Level.*

2. Do not hardcode anything that is instance- or environment-specific in the automated tests.
   For example: The environment URL may be deployed at different port today. In future, that port gets changed. Hence, this data set comes into the category which may change build by build when hardware configuration changes. Therefore, such data set should never be hardcoded but should be either segregated via data sheet or handled through dynamic variables values, which user can input and play around during run time.
3. Use wild card wherever you observe that html name may fluctuate but not fully. Additionally, wild carding technique should also be used at several other fluctuating layers where obj description changes, may not fully but partially.
   For example, Let us see a case where *"html name"* of a button is submit and across build it fluctuates between "submit" and "submit all". Since you know that "Submit" word generally is static, one should wild card "submit" object name as ".*Submit.*" .Wrapping it up, wild carding technique will now ensure that the script would not fail till the time this "submit" string is found and additionally, whatever prefixed or suffixed with submit, will get filtered down and bypassed. Therefore, this reduces script failure vulnerability, as well.

4. Insert checkpoints to verify critical application behavior or data.

   Example: Whenever login page is opened, username field should be editable. Therefore, script should have checkpoint or other verification technique embedded in the code to validate such scenarios, which at manual side could have been verified through naked eyes.

5. Add comments throughout the automated test to clearly describe what action the automated test is performing.

   Example:

   To clear temporary Internet files--Comment

   Set WshShell = CreateObject("WScript.Shell")

   WshShell.run "RunDll32.exe InetCpl.cpl,ClearMyTracksByProcess 8"

   To clear browsing cookies--Comment

   WshShell.run "RunDll32.exe InetCpl.cpl,ClearMyTracksByProcess 2"

   To Clear Browsing History--Comment

   WshShell.run "RunDll32.exe InetCpl.cpl,ClearMyTracksByProcess 1"

   The comments become more critical if there's any complex function or different mode of recording of scripting is inserted within script codeline. Usefulness and relevance of inserting steps is easy maintainability and readability of scripts.

6. Create reusable automated tests, always. What this means is that while scripting one should always think with a futuristic perspective that whether any data needs to be parameterized; is there any other condition which is not prevalent but will be good to be handled in the code— considering these points can make the script re-usable across various data set of that scenario, and accordingly can also help in being re-usable to several other modules.

7. Do not record scenarios for performing blind queries. Query for specific data unless the test case specifically requires a blind query. Let us understand this through an example of banking application. There you get an option to search transactions using stated search criteria. If you don't give search criteria and just click on search to dig in complete history then query time becomes very high. If you give some values based on which search needs to be performed, query time is comparatively much less. Hence, during automation coding, it is always advisable to give some query criteria while querying for any data set.

8. Ensure that your automated tests do not depend on any desktop or client settings (e.g. DSN set up). Remove all such dependencies, which are related to desktop or machine configuration from the script. Otherwise, your script will become local to be played back on that machine only and this is not efficient coding mechanics.

9. Checkpoints in your automated tests should clearly state what you are verifying and what the expected and actual results are. Then, the captured outcome must be captured in the test results log file.

For example:
If s_res = "Yes" Then
reporter.ReportEvent MicPass, "Aging Method: "&s_agingmethod, " Created Successfully."
Else
reporter.ReportEvent micFail, "Aging Method: "&s_agingmethod, " Not Created."216
**reporter.Reportevent is a QTP method that helps in echoing output in the result log.

10. All scripts should be re-runnable. Use rerun parameter **"*g_rerun*"** to make scripts rerunnable. This *g_rerun* parameter can act as a variable and using time stamp capturing mechanics, values can be captured in *g_rerun* variable. Another way to populate *g_rerun* variable can be referenced in Chapter 12. Usage of this technique is that if you want to use any sequential event of data set, which are tightly coupled together then for each run, this can act as an identifier and can create and bind all such data set, in tandem.
11 *"Reporter.ReportEvent* keyword should always be used if there's any notification that needs to be passed to result log especially in the event of passed condition, failed condition or message notifications.
12. There are several such file extensions that can be used for function, but to keep a common protocol, one should always use ".vbs" extension file for function library.
13. It is highly advisable not to give user-defined function the same name as what is there for built-in functions list, in the Step Generator. For an example, QTP native function is **"click"**, which has some definition attached to it by software itself. Now user should not try having a function with the same name **"click"** and then define its operation based on their will. This should be avoided unless highly justifiable.
14. **"Call"** keyword to be used for calling function from library.
    e.g., Call fn_function_name(argument list).
15. Function should return at least one value.
16. At the end of the function or action, one should use **"Nothing"** keyword, which in VBScript is used to disassociate an object variable from any actual object. You can use the Set statement to assign **"Nothing"** to an object variable. For example:
    Set <MyObject> = Nothing
17. In whichever action, variables need to be used, that action should contain keyword *'Option Explicit'* at the beginning of 'Action' under test.
    'Option Explicit' forces the programmer to declare all variables, rather than letting them be implicitly declared during their first use.
    This enforces good programming practices and avoids ambiguity of variable scope.
    Explicitly user has to declare variables *"Dim"*, *"Public"* or *"Private"* types.

This brings us to the completion of the first part of our discussion on automation framework. Next chapter is the continuation to this one; hence let us see the other new areas that constitute part of further automation framework concept.

HP Quality Center 10: Automation Framework Implementation Using HP QC 9.2/10 + HP QTP 9.5/10 Integration — Part 2

12

Chapter Objectives: This chapter will give an overview of

- *Global re-run parameter definition and working mechanism*
- *Automation development life cycle*

Introduction

This is in continuation to the earlier discussion over automation framework. In this chapter, global re-run parameter usage and implementation methodology will be discussed. Additionally, this chapter will also cater to the very basic question that will be there in any engineer's mind, i.e. "I'm familiar with the discussion in the chapter but from where can I find the sequential summary of the steps to start the automation development using QC 9.2/10 + QTP 9.5/10 integration."

Note: The concepts discussed here are valid for both HP QTP 9.5, 10 and HP QC 9.2, 10 versions.

12.1 Global Re-Run Parameter Definition and Working Mechanism

Let us take a real time case where the functionality of the application is to "create a customer" and then attach a bank to that customer. Here bank also needs to be created new. Then create an invoice with the same customer name and validate the invoice.

In this scenario, the primary keys are customer name, bank account, and invoice number, which means that one value when submitted can't be used again. To simulate such a case in automation, where re-runnability is kept intact, it is very critical that whenever the code runs altogether a new customer, bank, and invoice get created.

This is where the relevance of "*g_rerun*" parameter comes, where at the end of customer name, "*g_rerun*" variable will be suffixed. Likewise, with the bank name and with the invoice number such dynamic variable value gets suffixed.

Example: If customer name is "Saurabh", then the complete string will be "Saurabh&_&g_rerun"

As "*g_rerun*" is a variable, whatever value is generated at the run time for *g_rerun*, that value will get stamped to "Saurabh" as a suffix.

Now the question is, how can we ensure that the value that gets generated for "*g_rerun*" in every run is new and unique? Therefore, the first mechanism to ensure this is via time stamp but more robust technique is what has been explained below.

Let us say that you have an "Action" or script, where you need to insert and utilize "*g_rerun*". Now, let us see those steps which would be required to generate "*g_rerun*" variable value and hence utilizes it within the required script.

12.1.1 How Can I Generate Unique Value Using "*g_rerun*" Variable?

1. You need to ensure that "*g_rerun*" function is associated with the QTP tests. If not, then go to ***"File-> Test Settings-> Resources"*** and associate the function library which contains "*g_rerun*" function.

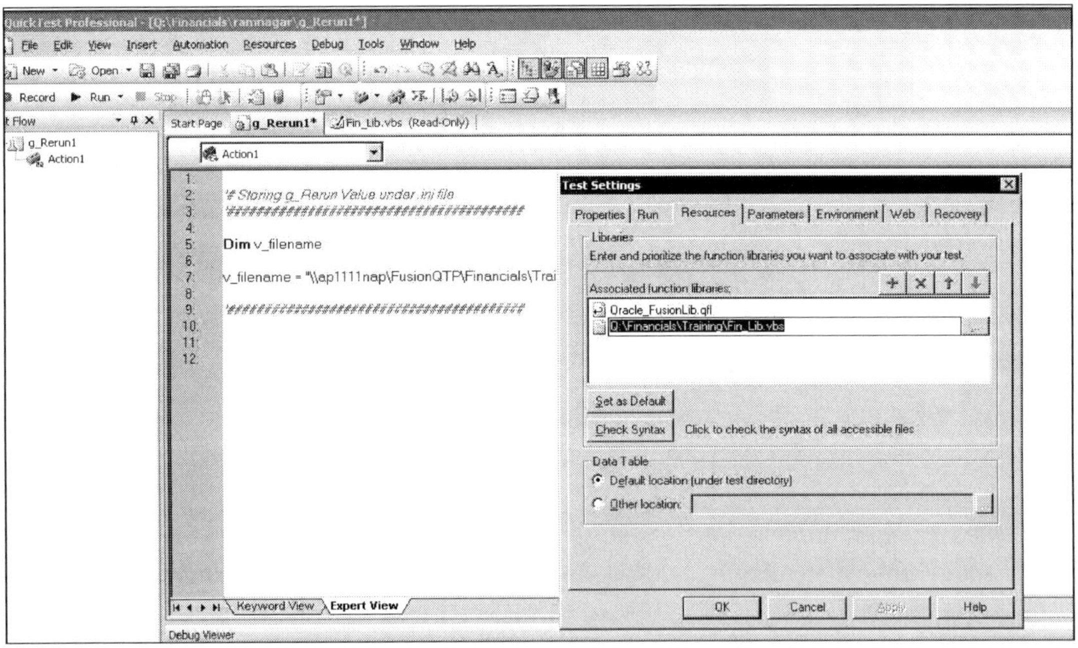

Figure 12.1 *Associating "g_rerun" Function to the Script.*

2. In the script, declare the path of the file where "*g_rerun*" variable value will get stored.
   Code snippet
   Dim v_filename
   v_filename = "\\ap1111nap\FusionQTP\Financials\Training" & "\qtpparam.ini"
   Point to note is that naming convention of .ini file should be **"<Flow Name>_param.ini".** Tip here is: if the same .ini file is being used across scripts, then keeping logical flow name would help user in tracking correct .ini file, even if run session breaks in between.

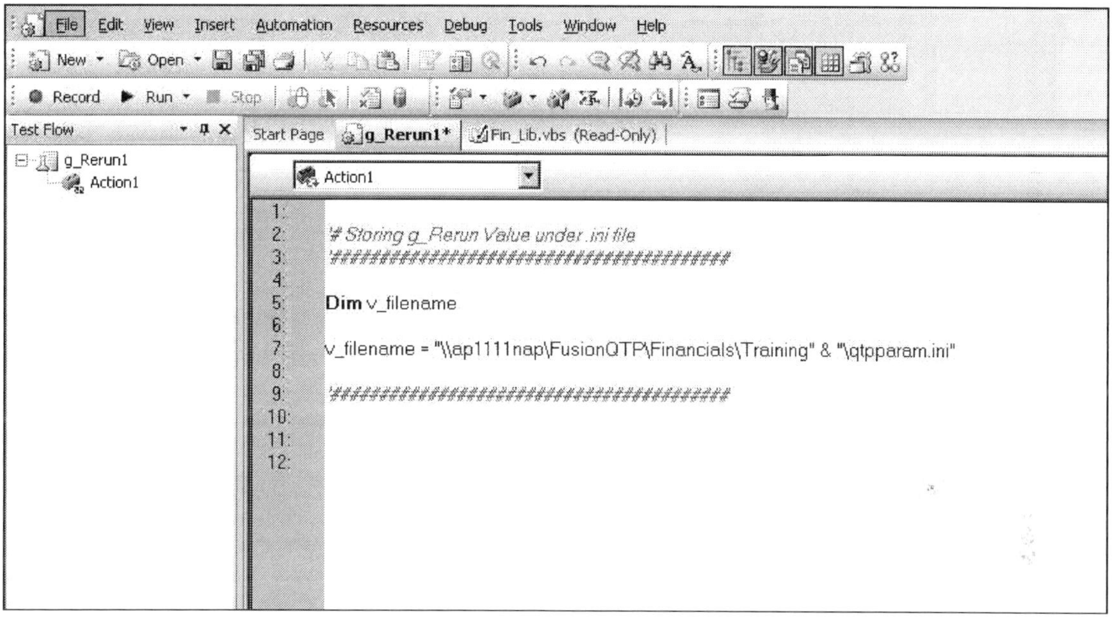

Figure 12.2 *Path Declaration Where "g_rerun" Variable Value will be Stored.*

3. The script where "*g_rerun*" variable value needs to be generated and utilized, call function **"fn_fin_cleanGlobal(v_filename)"**. This function helps in removing already existing .ini file, if there's any. However, if you want to utilize the existing ".ini", you may choose not to call and execute this function. .ini file once deleted can't be retrieved back.

Example:

'# Removes existing ini file, if any existing under the required path
Call fn_fin_cleanGlobal(v_filename) Definition of this function can be found in Chapter 13.

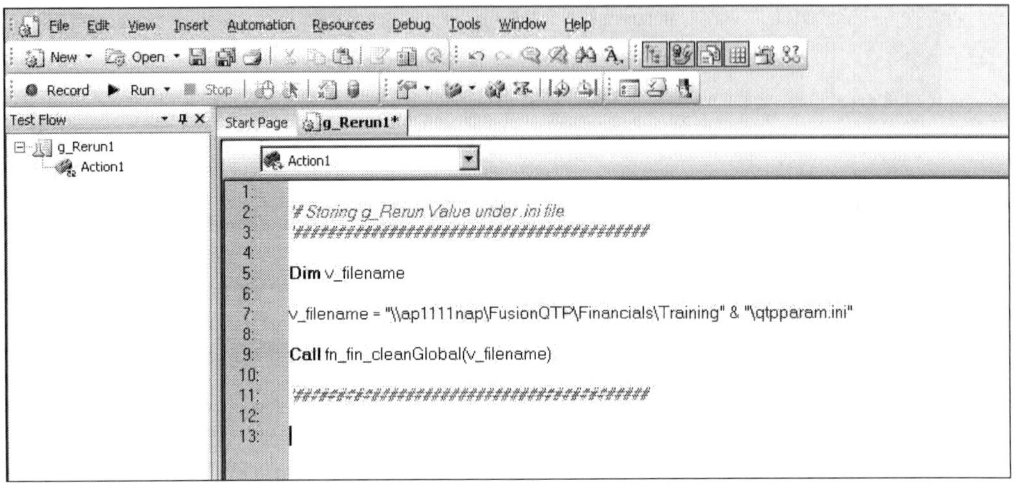

Figure 12.3 *Code Snippet to Clean All Existing .ini Files.*

4. .ini file contains several variables. Therefore, to declare and initialize all those, you will have to call function *"fn_fin_declare_extern_functions()"*, in the script under use. Definition of this function can be found in Chapter 13.

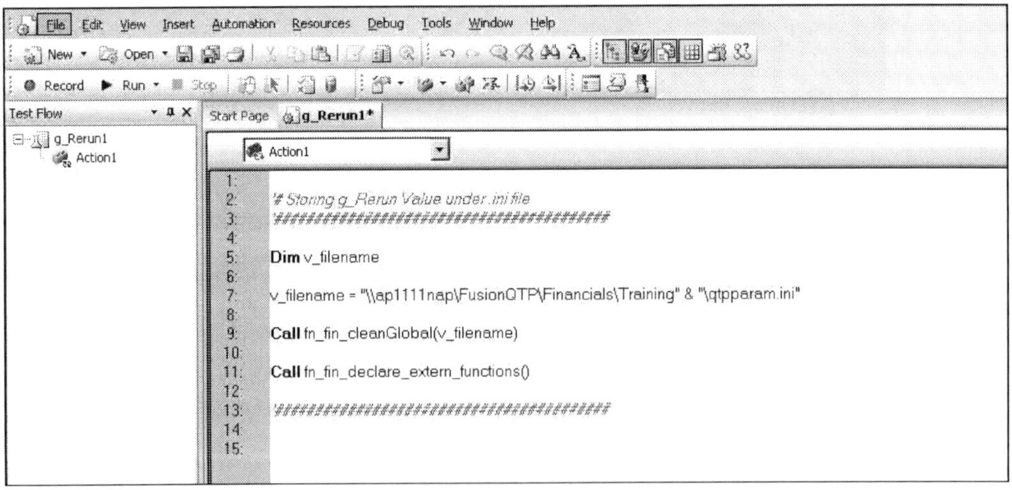

Figure 12.4 *Call Function to Declare .ini Variables.*

5. In the same script, function "*fn_fin_setGlobal()*" needs to be called. This function helps in setting values to the variables in '.ini' file. It also helps in creating ".ini" file, if the same is not existing . If .ini file exists, then function appends variable and variable value under specific block, as specified by the engineer. Definition of "*fn_fin_setGlobal()*", can be found in Chapter 13.

Example:

Call fn_fin_setGlobal (v_filename,"PARAMETERS","g_Re-run",minute(now)&second(now))

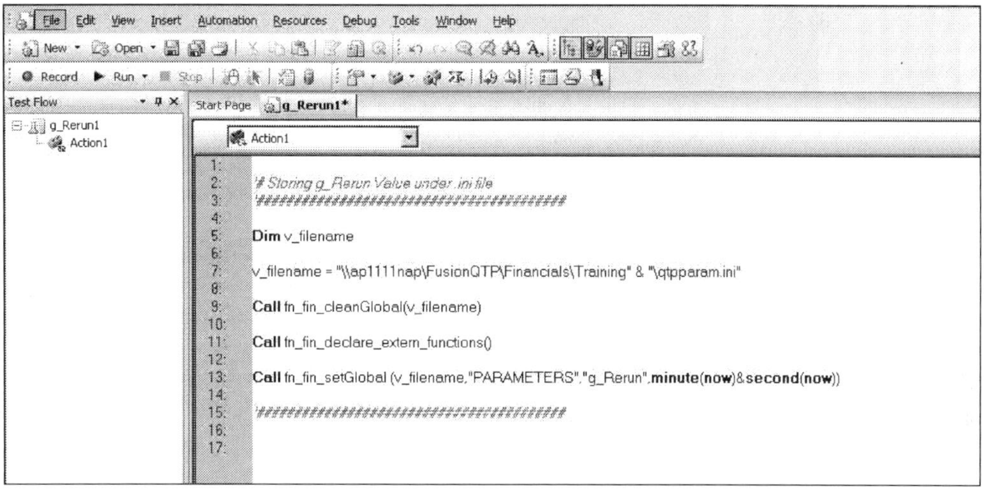

Figure 12.5 *Code Snippet for Function Call fn_fin_setGlobal.*

(Or) –, Alternatively, you can even call the below mentioned functions.

Call fn_fin_setGlobal (v_filename,"PARAMETERS","g_Rerun",minute(now)&second(now))
Call fn_fin_setGlobal (v_filename,"PARAMETERS","g_Partrun",minute(now)&second(now))
Call fn_fin_setGlobal (v_filename,"VARIABLES","v_inv_number",minute(now)&second(now))
Call fn_fin_setGlobal (v_filename,"CONSTANTS","EXIST_SYNC","5")

Note: Definitions of all the discussed functions will be discussed in Chapter 13.

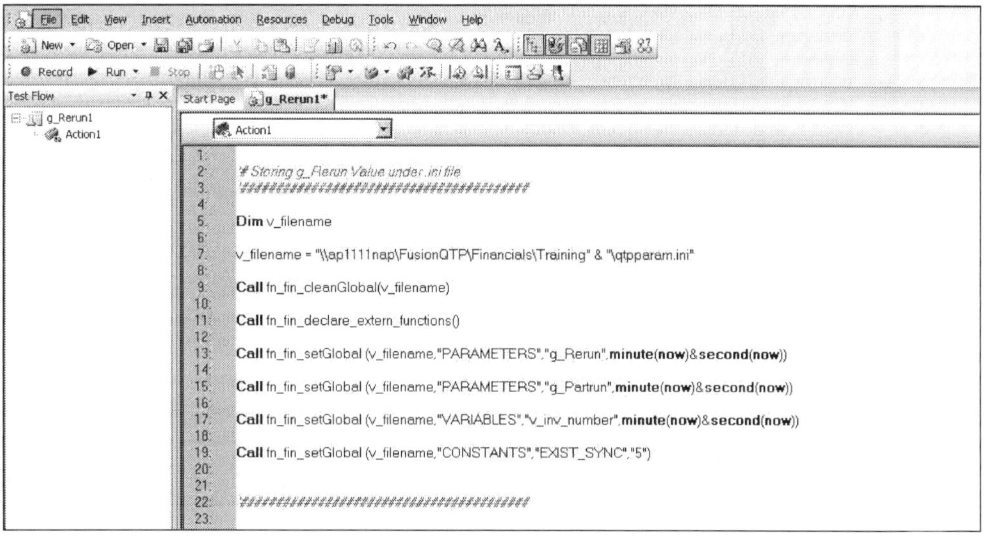

Figure 12.6 *Set Global Functions.*

- In the code snippet, "v_filename" holds the path of the actual .ini file
- *"PARAMETERS" or "VARIABLES" or "CONSTANTS"* are the block names
- *"g_rerun"* is the variable name
- *"minute(now)&second(now)"* is one of the methodologies to generate random number

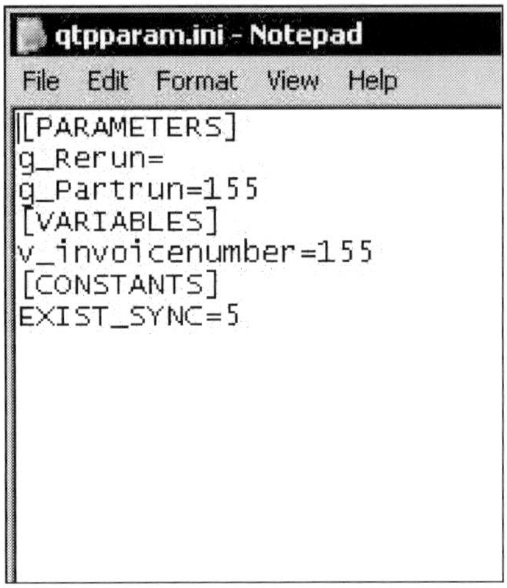

Figure 12.7 *.ini File Snapshot.*

If all the functions as discussed above get executed successfully, all the variables will get populated in the displayed .ini file. Else, if any function isn't executed successfully then that variable value will come as blank.

12.1.2 How Can I Use the Random Number Value Within the Required Area of My Script?

1. You need to first read the variable value from '. ini' file. Use the below displayed code snippet, in order to read the respective value from .ini file.

Example:

'# Getting values of a variable from '.ini' file

g_value=fn_fin_getGlobal (v_filename,"PARAMETERS","g_Rerun")

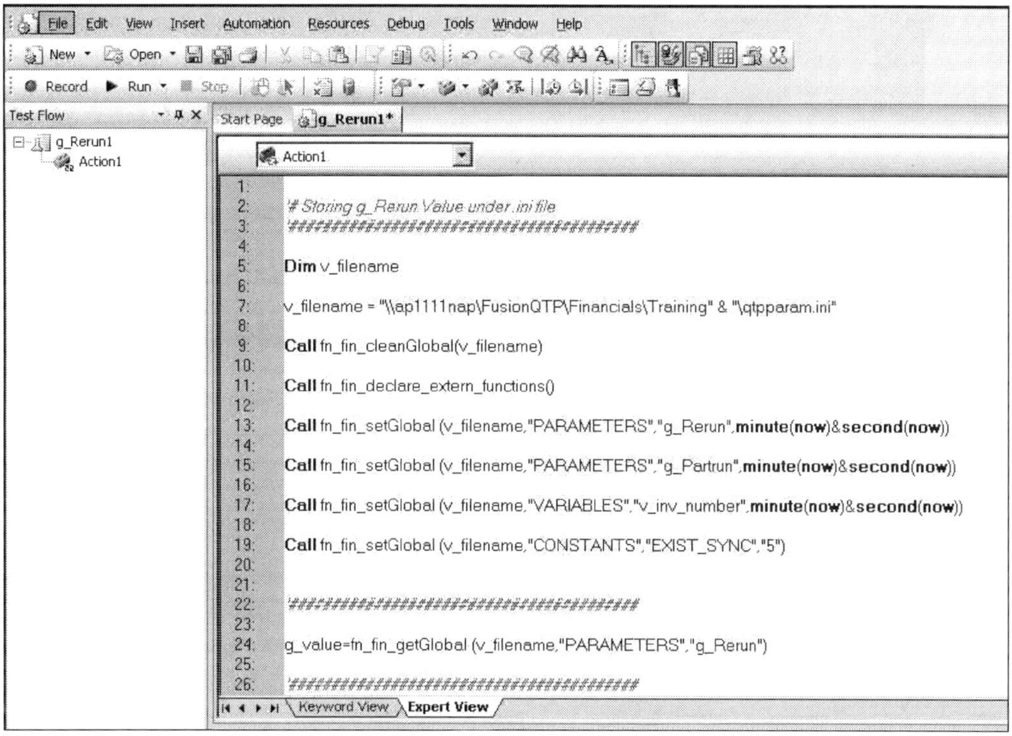

Figure 12.8 *Displaying "g_value" Usage.*

The question that may tickle you here is that whether you can use this across scripts. Answer is "Yes", if scripts are bundled together in a single session run. You can see the below attached snapshot of various scripts, where the same "*g_value*" is being called and used.

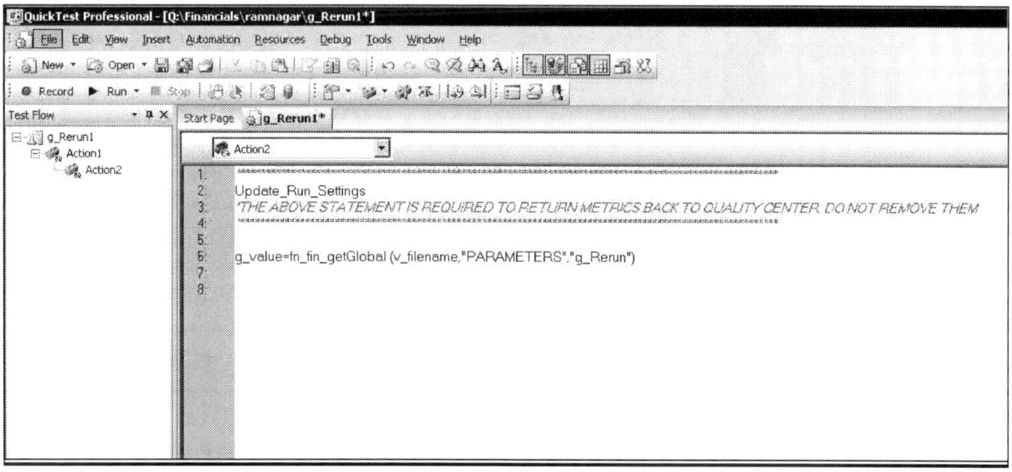

Figure 12.9 *Same "g_value" Used in Script 2.*

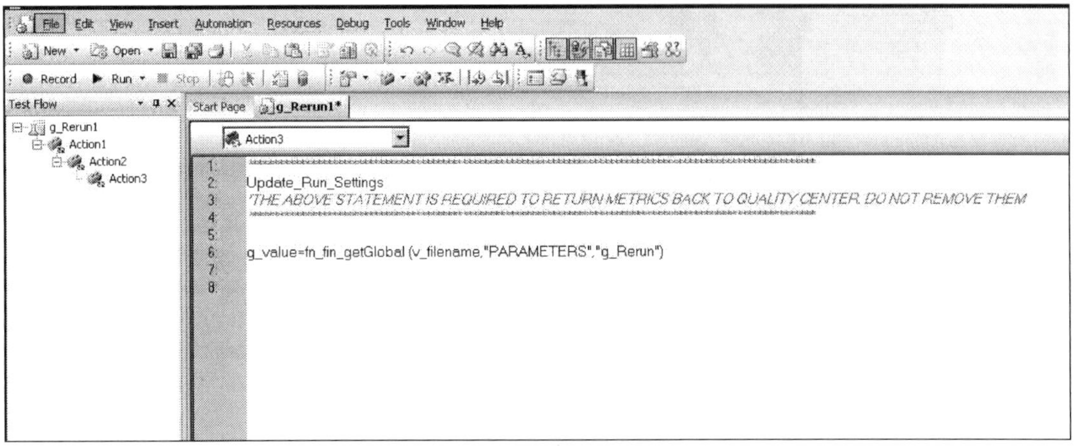

Figure 12.10 *Same "g_value" Used in Script 3.*

12.1.3 Real-Time Issue Faced During Stabilization of Scripts That Use "*g_rerun*" Variable Value

You may be having a question that why we are storing the "*g_rerun*" value in a .ini file. The answer is that as per QTP 9.5/10 behavior, variable value would get lost if test stops in between the execution. Therefore, we are storing these variable values in an external file so that values once generated are stored, and can be deleted only by engineers will but not based on QTP 9.5/10 session management scenario.

However, the other scenario in real time that may arise is that if test fails or stops in between the execution, then the *" File Name path" variable* that stores the path for .ini file will get lost.

How should we tackle this scenario?

The answer is that in order to re-assign the value to the variable, you will have to perform as stated below.

1. When Action aka script has got stopped and after doing required modification, you are good to go with the run then run the script using **"Debug From Step"**, as shown in Fig. 12.11,

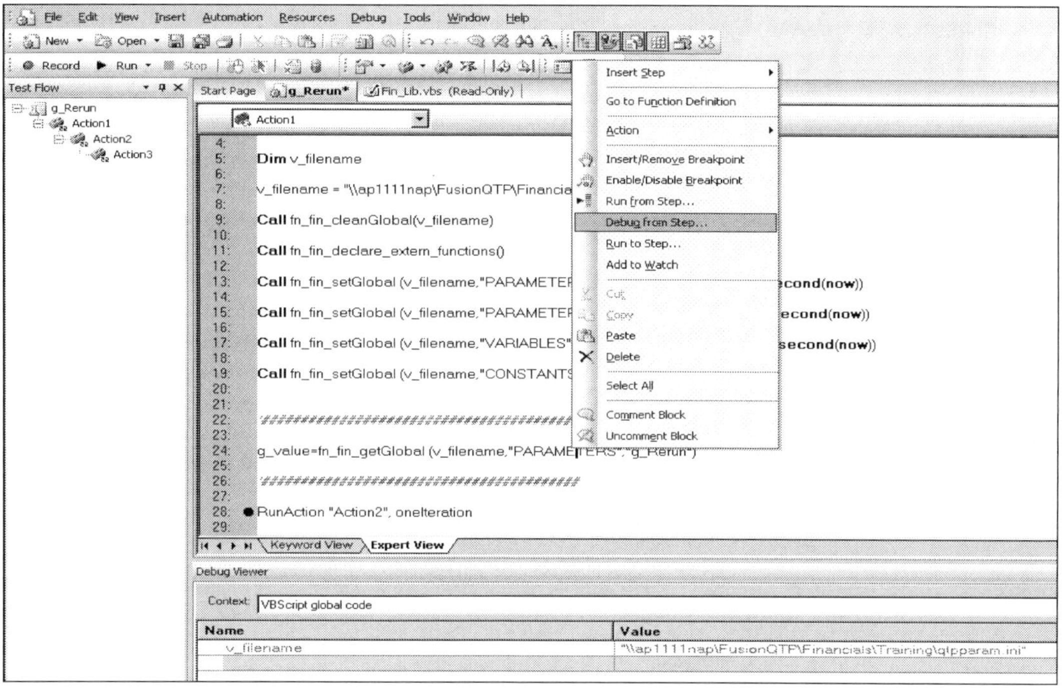

Figure 12.11 *"Debug from step" to Retrieve .ini File Path.*

2. Add variable name to the Debug Viewer. [Select the variable – Debug -> Add to Watch (Ctrl +T)]

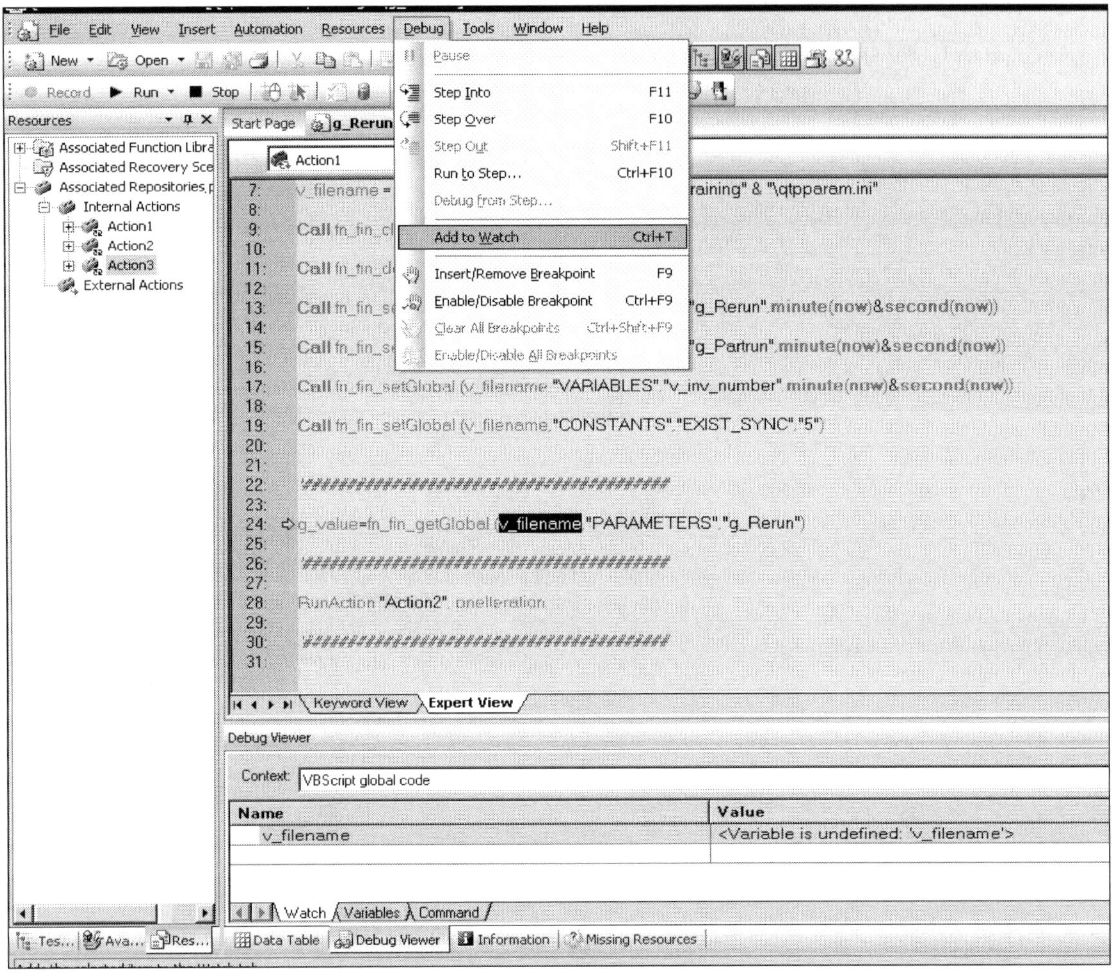

Figure 12.12 *Add Variable Name in "Watch".*

3. Assign the "Path file name" to the variable manually as you know where you have stored the .ini file.

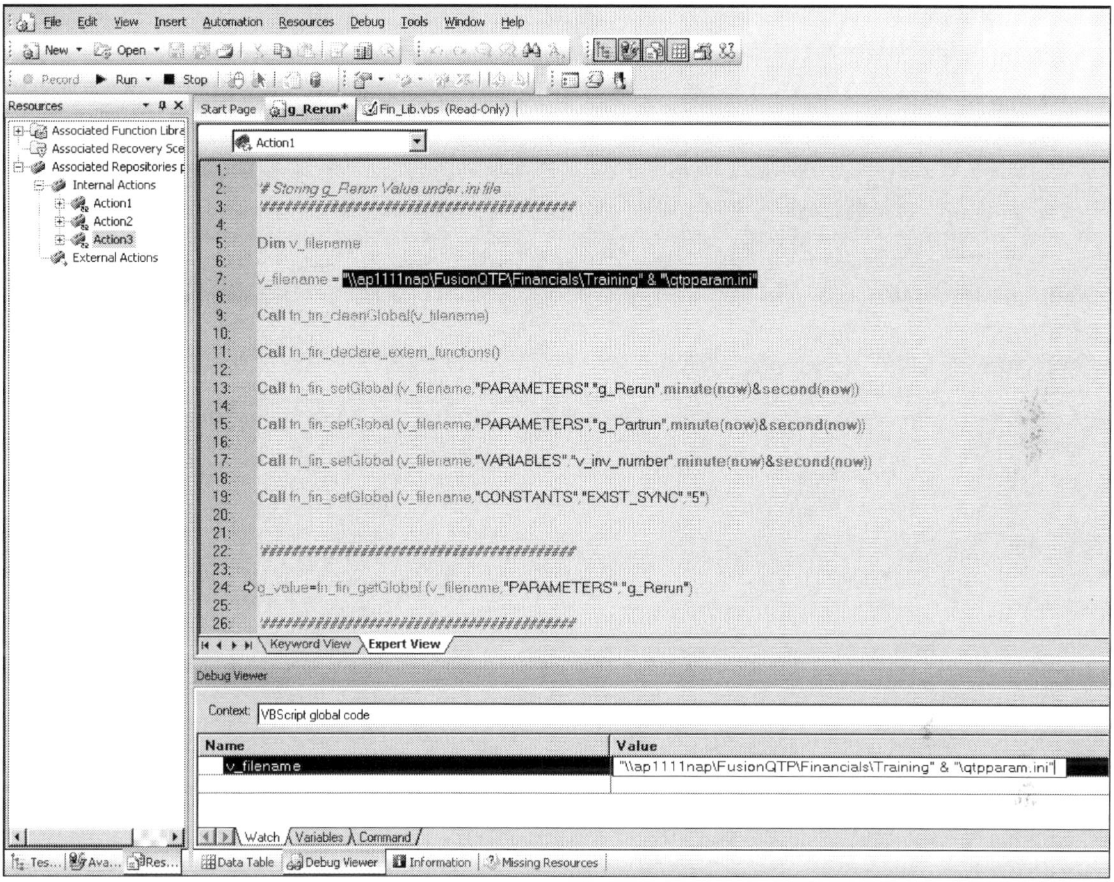

Figure 12.13 *Input .ini File Path Name.*

4. Click on **"QTP -> Run"** for further execution.

Here onwards "Path File Name" variable value gets re-assigned and you are ready to use it across "Actions", wherever this variable is being used.

This brings us to completion of first part of our discussion on automation framework. Next chapter is continuation of this one; therefore, do read this thoroughly before you jump to the next one.

12.2 Automation Development Life Cycle Via QC 9.2/10 + QTP 9.5/10

Until now, you have come to know about basic QC 9.2/10 operation, basic QTP 9.5/10 operation, and finer areas of framework. In real-time scenario, the very first step for any organisation or engineer *per se* would be to start script development. Now, let us see as what is the question that an engineer would like to unfold.

Engineer: I'm starting my script development for the first time via integrating QC9.2/10 and QTP 9.5/10. How should I proceed?

Answer:

Step 1) Launch **QC 9.2/10**

Step 2) Traverse to

"Test Plan->Financials -> <Product>-> UI Test Cases -> <Select Test step to be automated>".

Step 3) Goto **"Details"** tab of that step. Provide the required inputs here:

Automation Designer: *<Select Your Name>*

Automation Status: *"Automation Development"*

As part of process, below mentioned fields should be mandatory for automation engineer to fill up:

"Details" -> Automation Designer name

"Details -> Comments": In comments area, below mentioned areas should be inputted

---

Automation Details:

a. Start Date of Automation:

b. End Date of Automation:

c. Automation Script Dependency: ***Provide script name and complete path to find this script.

Example: "Test Plan->Financials -> <Product>-> UI Test Cases -> GLUI001 - Verify the ASM - Create Primary Ledger page

---

If any bug found, during automation, then:

Automation Status should be set to: "Automation Repair" and below mentioned details should be punched in, under **"Details-> Comments"**

a. Bug No.:

b. Brief Description of the bug:

c. Bug Logging Date:

d. Logged on : ***<Product> or <QTP> or <QC> or <Any other component>***

e. If closed, then bug closing date:

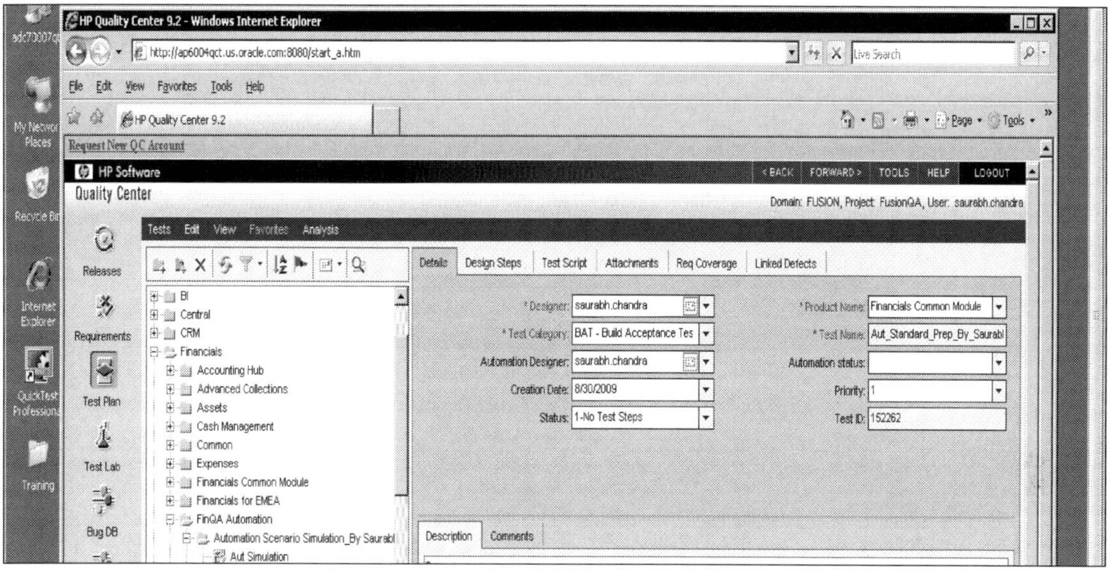

Figure 12.14 *Fields Under "Details" Tab.*

Additionally,

- If bug exists, then under **"Attachments"** tab perform area *"a."* and *"b."* as stated below. Note- This is not a mandatory requirement and needs to be exercised as and when required.
  a. Attach Screen Shot, if there's any. If any Issue found and you have screen shots, related to automation issue, then all such screen shots should contain format as : "aut_bug#".
  b. Under "URL", attach link of the bug.
- If there's any relevant automation related file, and you would like to attach it, then attach all such files having naming convention as ***"aut_<Desc>"***

Step 4) Under **"Design Steps"** tab of that manual step, choose **"Generate Script -> QUICKTEST_TEST".** Manual step icon gets changed to ***"Automation Step"*** icon.

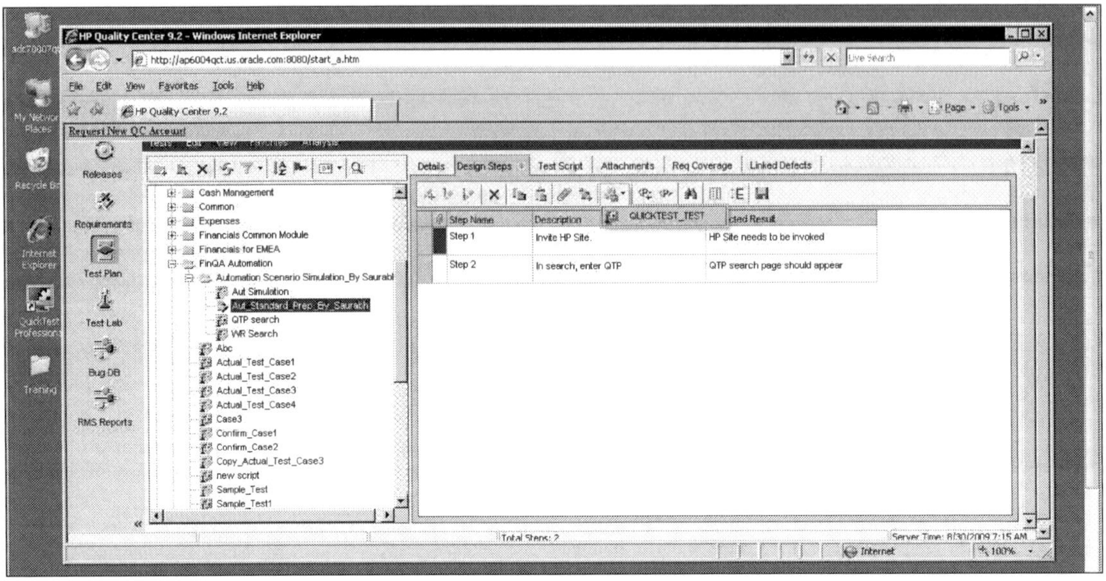

Figure 12.15 *Icon Change When Automation Selected.*

If by any chance, you have scripted wrong and you want to start afresh, you can again choose ***"Design Steps -> QUICKTEST_TEST"***. Your earlier stored script will be overwritten. However, you would lose all earlier data and that can't be retrieved back; therefore, be cautious in doing so.

Step 5) Go to "Test Script" Tab-bar. Click on QTP icon at top left hand side of the pane.

QTP gets launched.

Step 6) Before recording starts:

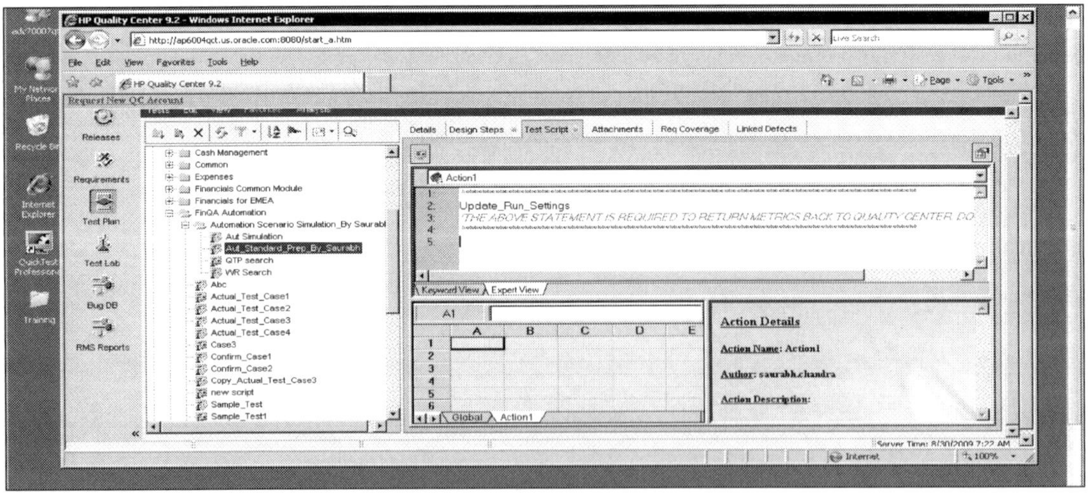

Figure 12.16 *Encircled Area for QTP Launch.*

Associate **"<product family>_Lib.vbs"** from location:

QC->Test Plan -> Automation Assets -> Financials-> Product Family Level–> Common Lib ->Functions

Associate re-usable "Script" for login, from the location:

QC->Test Plan -> Automation Assets -> Financials-> Product Family Level–> Common Lib ->Scripts

After associating all required libraries, record or code your functional scenarios:

Step 7) After recording is done, go to **"File->Save".** Your file will get saved at manual step level itself.

Step 8) Now, before terming your script complete, you will have to stabilize your script.

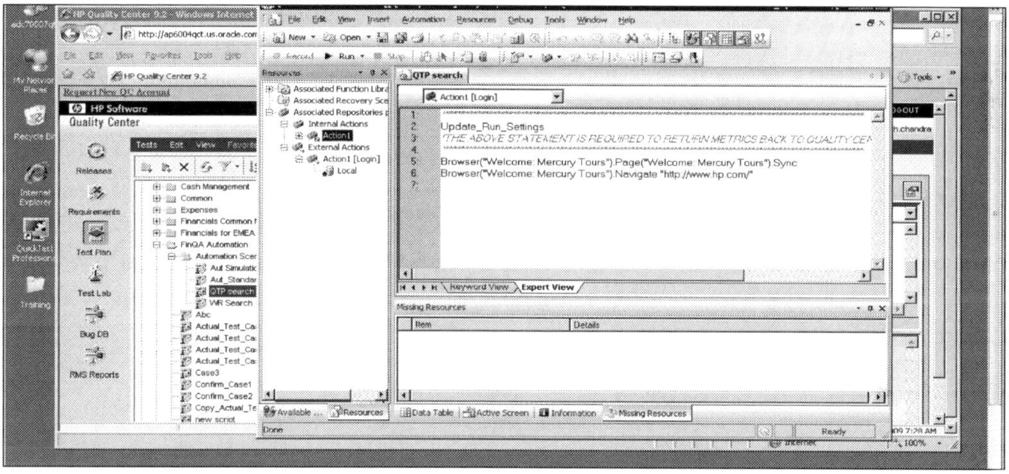

Figure 12.17 *File Association Representation.*

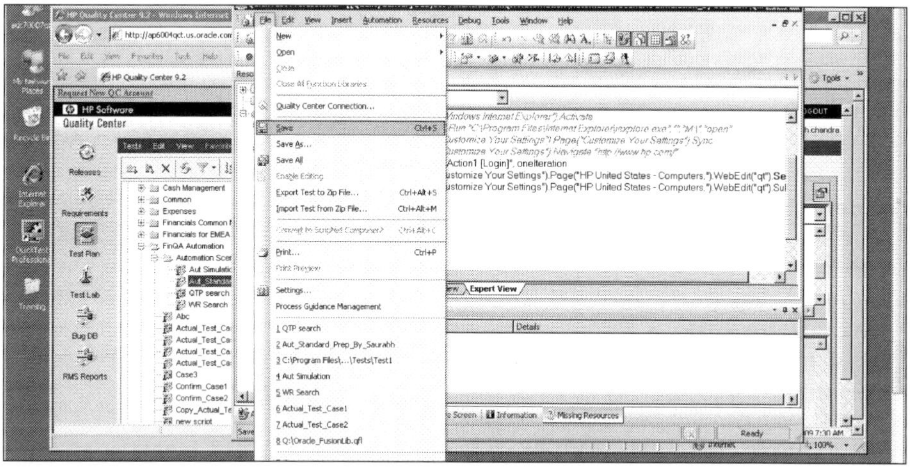

Figure 12.18 *Saving the Test.*

Stabilization Procedure is:

a. Click **"QTP->Run"** (If not launched yet, then you can again come back to that manual step level, click on tab-bar "Test Script" and launch QTP)

b. Go to **"QTP-> Automation -> Record and Run Settings"**. Below displayed window comes up. Select the required URL against which you need to execute this script.

a. Click on **QTP->Run**. Run Result storage window would come up. Choose "Temporary

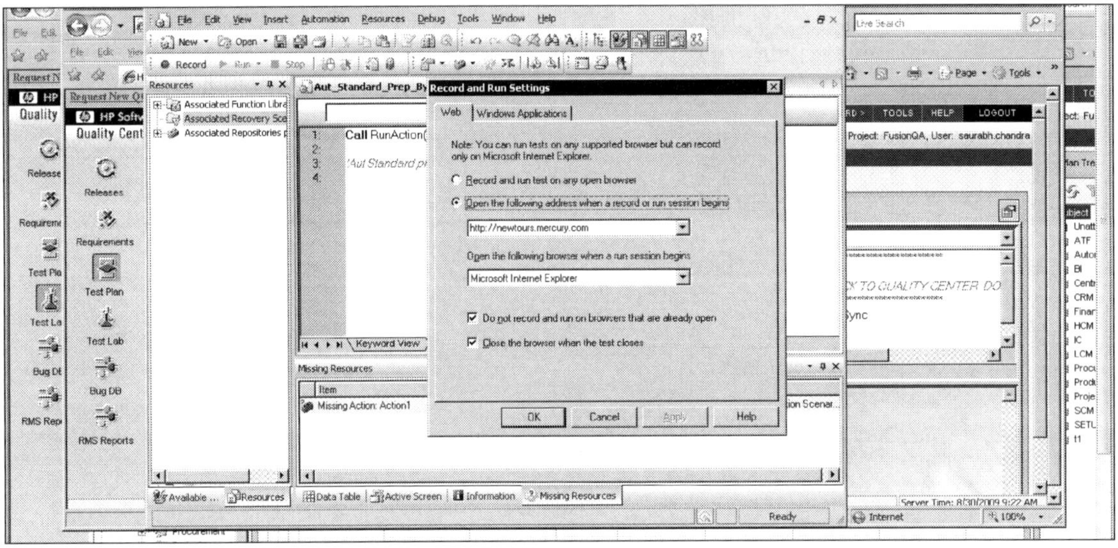

Figure 12.19 *Launching Run.*

Run Results folder" radio button.

b. Till the time you are not fully satisfied, you need to execute your script under "Temporary Run Results folder" itself.

c. After your script is fully stabilized, go to Step 9.

Step 9) Come back to **"QC -> Test Lab"** . Under Test Lab, you would be achieving at least 1 passed status, before terming automation script to be *"successfully completed"*.

Path to execute the script under test lab is:

QC-> Test Lab -> Fusion 1.0 -> Automation Development -> Financials -> UI Test Cases Verification.

Note – You can choose your own path by creating new test set under QC -> Test Lab and need not use the one that has been referred categorically during this discussion.

Kick off your script here and achieve a "P**assed"** status.

Step 10) After you have achieved a pass status, come back to

QC->Test Plan->Financials-> <product>-> UI Test Cases -> "<Select step that was under automation>"

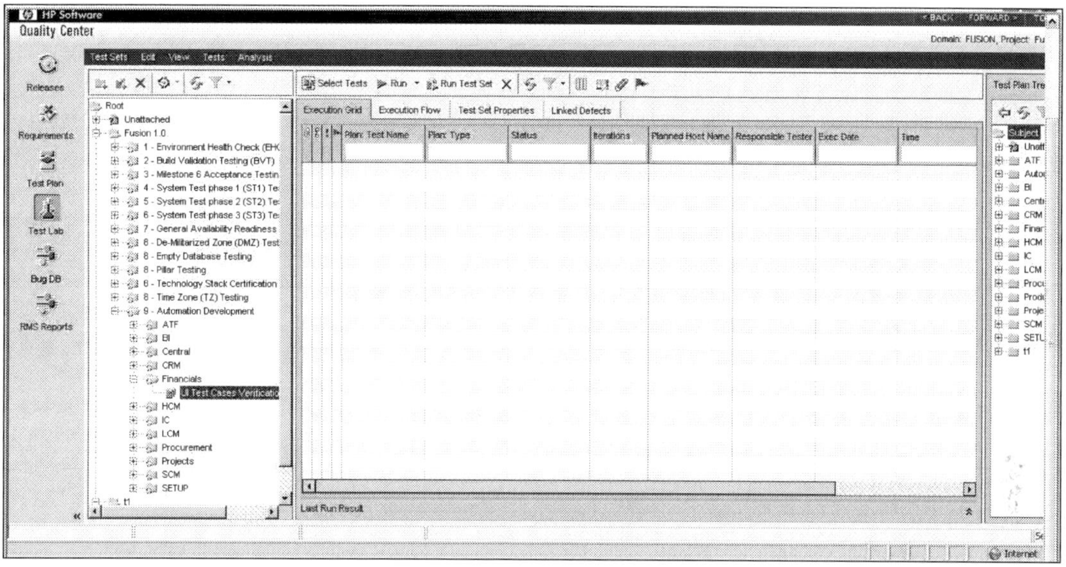

Figure 12.20 *Test Lab Area.*

Under **"Required Step",** goto **"Details"** tab and mark:

Automation Status **as: *"Automation Ready"***

Now you are equipped with all the right knowledge to pick up another test for automation.

With this discussion, the only area left that would conclude the automation framework discussion is: Common Function Library functions and their definitions. Let us unfold the same in next chapter.

HP Quality Center 10: Automation Framework Implementation Using HP QC 9.2/10 + HP QTP 9.5/10 Integration — Part 3

13

Chapter Objectives: This chapter will give an overview of

- *Working Code Snippet for important functions*

Introduction

This is in continuation to Chapters 11 and 12. In this chapter, I will take you through all such important functions that should be part of common product family library, before framework gets rolled out into production.

Note: All the concepts talked here are valid for both HP QTP 9.5, 10 and HP QC 9.2, 10 versions.

13.1 Common Product Family Lib.Vbs Definition

In Part 3 of the automation framework unit, I will take you through the most interesting component i.e. common library for entire product family. In fact, this library can also be termed as common library for entire division.

During framework implementation, one should identify the most basic functions that will come under use by everyone during automation. Now, rather than everyone coding the same function for their independent usage and hence waste man-hours, it is advisable to design them beforehand and hence build a common library for all.

In this chapter, you will be exposed to all such functions and their definition that needs to be available before automation framework is rolled out.

Note: All these functions should be part of single .Vbs file, which will be termed as product family library.

- On QC, as per the folder structure, the location of this file should be:
  QC-> Test Plan -> Automation Assets -> Financials-> Product Family Level-> Common Lib ->Functions:
- **"Product family_Lib.vbs"** should contain at least the below mentioned functions. These are such functions which are the most commonly used ones by each automation engineer in the product family or division *per se*, as well.

1. *fn_fin_declare_extern_functions()* – Function to declare external functions
2. *fn_fin_cleanGlobal()* – Function to clean global variable values
3. *fn_fin_setGlobal()* – Function to set global variable definition
4. *fn_fin_getGlobal()* – Function to get the global variable value
5. *fn_fin_get_current_Mon()* – Function to derive current month
6. *fn_fin_get_current_YY()* – Function to get current year in "YY" format
7. *fn_fin_add_YY()* – Function to add year on exiting year in "YY" format
8. *fn_fin_add_Month()* – Function to add month on existing month
9. *fn_fin_get_current_YYYY()* – Function to get current year in "YYYY" format
10. *fn_fin_add_Period()* – Function to add any period such as 3 months, 6 months etc.
11. *fn_fin_get_current_DD()* – Function to derive current date
12. *fn_fin_get_formatted_date()* – Function to format a date in specified format
13. *fn_fin_justify_str_for_regexp()* – Function to regularize string with regular expression
14. *fn_fin_request_num ( )* – Function to get number from alphanumeric string
15. *fn_fin_pdf_check ( )* – Function to check value in pdf
16. *fn_fin_get_substring ( )* – Function to get string within a statement
17. *Random ( )* – It returns 6 digit random number between 1 and 999999

13.2 Function Definitions

You would be wondering as how to code for above mentioned functions. Therefore, let us see detailed code snippet for each of these.

13.2.1 fn_fin_declare_extern_functions

Description: This function helps in declaration of variables at all such places where the input type for method "WritePrivateProfileString" or "GetPrivateProfileStringA" is being used. For example, the variable related to this method is used in "fn_fin_setGlobal()" function.

Code snippet:

```
Public Function fn_fin_declare_extern_functions()
Extern.Declare micInteger,"GetPrivateProfileStringA","kernel32.dll","GetPrivateProfileStringA",
micString, micString, micString, micString+micByRef, micInteger, micString
Extern.Declare micLong,"WritePrivateProfileString","kernel32.dll","WritePrivateProfileStringA",
micString, micString, micString, micString
End Function
```

13.2.2 fn_fin_cleanGlobal

Description: This function deletes the already created .ini file and the path of the file where .ini existence needs to be verified. It is inputted by user.

Code snippet:

```
Public Function fn_fin_cleanGlobal(file_name)
Dim v_fso
Dim v_my_file
On Error Resume Next
Set v_fso = CreateObject("Scripting.FileSystemObject")
Set v_my_file = v_fso.GetFile(file_name)
v_my_file.Delete
Set v_fso = Nothing
Set v_my_file = Nothing
End Function
```

13.2.3 fn_fin_setGlobal

Description: This function helps in inputting the variable name and variable value in the .ini file, which primarily as per the discussed framework is used for generating "g_rerun" value.

Code snippet:

```
Public Function fn_fin_setGlobal(file_name,block_name,var_name,var_value)
Dim v_rc
v_rc = Extern.WritePrivateProfileString (block_name,var_name,var_value,file_name)
End Function
```

13.2.4 fn_fin_getGlobal

Description: This function helps in getting the variable value from the .ini file, which primarily as per the discussed framework is used for generating "*g_rerun*" value.

Code snippet:

```
Public Function fn_fin_getGlobal(file_name,block_name,var_name)
Dim v_rc
Dim v_var_value
v_rc = Extern.GetPrivateProfileStringA (block_name,var_name,"",v_var_value,256,file_name)
fn_fin_getGlobal = v_var_value
End Function
```

13.2.5 fn_fin_get_current_Mon

Description: This function is used to retrieve the current month.

Code snippet:

```
Public Function fn_fin_get_current_Mon()
fn_fin_get_current_Mon = MonthName(Month(now), True)
End Function
```

13.2.6 fn_fin_get_current_YY

Description: This function is used to get the current year in "YY" format.

Code snippet:

```
Public Function fn_fin_get_current_YY()
Dim v_YY
v_YY = Year(now)
If len(v_YY)=4 Then
v_YY = right(v_YY,2)
End If
fn_fin_get_current_YY = v_YY
End Function
```

13.2.7 fn_fin_add_YY

Description: This function is used to add a year to the current year.

Code snippet:

```
Public Function fn_fin_add_YY(delta)
Dim v_YY
v_YY = Year(now) + delta
If len(v_YY)=4 Then
v_YY = rightv_(YY,2)
End If
fn_fin_add_YY = v_YY
End Function
```

13.2.8 fn_fin_add_Month

Description: This function is used to add a month to the current month.

Code snippet:

```
Public Function fn_fin_add_Month(delta)
Dim v_mm
v_mm = Month(now) + delta
if v_mm > 12 then
v_mm = (v_mm - 12)
end if
fn_fin_add_Month = MonthName(v_mm, True)
End Function
```

13.2.9 fn_fin_get_current_YYYY

Description: This function is used to get current year in four digit format, i.e. in "yyyy".

Code snippet:

```
Public Function fn_fin_get_current_YYYY()
Dim v_YY
v_YY = Year(now)
If len(v_YY)=2 Then
v_YY = "20" & v_YY
End If
fn_fin_get_current_YYYY = v_YY
End Function
```

13.2.10 fn_fin_add_Period

Description: This function helps in adding "x" no. of months more on top of existing period

Code snippet:

```
Public Function fn_fin_add_Period(delta)
Dim v_mm,v_YY
v_YY = fn_fin_get_current_YY()
v_mm = Month(now) + delta
if v_mm > 12 then
v_mm = (v_mm - 12)
v_YY = fn_fin_add_YY(1)
end if
fn_fin_add_Period = MonthName(v_mm, True) & "-" & v_YY
End Function
```

13.2.11 fn_fin_get_current_DD

Description: This function is used to get current date.

Code snippet:

```
Public Function fn_fin_get_current_DD()
Dim v_DD
v_DD = Day(now)
If len(v_DD)=1 Then
    v_DD = "0" & v_DD
End If
fn_fin_get_current_DD = v_DD
End Function
```

13.2.12 fn_fin_get_formatted_date

Description: This function helps in getting date value in specified format.

Code snippet:

```
Public Function fn_fin_get_formatted_date(delta)
Dim v_dt, v_DD
 v_dt = Now + CInt(delta)
 If Day(v_dt) > 9 Then
    v_DD = CStr(Day(v_dt))
 else
  v_DD = "0" & CStr(Day(v_dt))
 End If
 fn_fin_get_formatted_date = v_DD & "-" & MonthName(Month(v_dt),True) & "-" & Year(v_dt)
End Function
```

13.2.13 fn_fin_justify_str_for_regexp

Description: This function helps in regularizing expression to its native description, in case the special symbols are part of string under use.

Code snippet:

```
Public Function fn_fin_justify_str_for_regexp (orgstr)
Dim v_str1
v_str1 = Replace(orgstr,"(","\(")
v_str1 = Replace(v_str1,")","\)")
v_str1 = Replace(v_str1,".","\.")
v_str1 = Replace(v_str1,",","\,")
```

```
v_str1 = Replace(v_str1,"-","\-")
fn_fin_justify_str_for_regexp = v_str1
End Function
```

13.2.14 fn_fin_request_num

Description: This function helps in pulling out numeric value from alphanumeric string.

Code snippet:

```
Public Function fn_fin_request_num(ByVal StringValue)
Dim ReturnStringValue, TempStringValue
ReturnStringValue=""
For i=1 To Len(StringValue)
    TempStringValue=Mid(StringValue,i,1)
    If IsNumeric(TempStringValue) Then
            ReturnStringValue=ReturnStringValue&TempStringValue
    End If
Next
fn_fin_request_num=ReturnStringValue
End Function
```

13.2.15 fn_fin_pdf_check

Description: This function is used to find a particular value in PDF file using "Find" property of PDF.

Return Value: 1 if success, else 0

Code snippet:

```
Public Function fn_fin_pdf_check(ByVal arrayStore,ByVal arrayIndexStore)
  Dim arrayValue,arrayIndexValue,loopIndex,startIndex,flag,countVal
  flag=0
  countVal=0
  Set oBrowser=Description.Create
  oBrowser("CreationTime").Value=".*"
  oBrowser("title").Value=".*outputid.*"
  oBrowser("Class Name").Value="Browser"
  oBrowser("name").Value="FrenchDas2Verification"
  Set oWindow=Description.Create
  oWindow("nativeclass").Value="IEFRAME"
  oWindow("regexpwndclass").Value="IEFRAME"
```

```
oWindow("text").Value=".*outputid.*"
If Browser(oBrowser).exists then
   Set oWinEdit=Description.Create
   oWinEdit("Class Name").Value="WinEdit"
   oWinEdit("nativeclass").Value="Edit"
   oWinEdit("text").Value=".*"
   oWinEdit("width").Value="100"
   oWinEdit("x").Value="491"
   oWinEdit("y").Value="29"
   oWinEdit("index").Value="1"
   Set oWinPage=Description.Create
   oWinPage("Class Name").Value="WinEdit"
   oWinPage("nativeclass").Value="Edit"
   oWinPage("text").Value=".*"
   oWinPage("width").Value="26"
   oWinPage("x").Value="214"
   oWinPage("y").Value="29"
   oWinPage("index").Value="1"
   Set oDialog=Description.Create
   oDialog("Class Name").Value="Dialog"
   oDialog("text").Value="Adobe Reader"
   oDialog("nativeclass").Value="#32770"
   Set oWinButton=Description.Create
   oWinButton("Class Name").Value="WinButton"
   oWinButton("text").Value="OK"
   oWinButton("nativeclass").Value="Button"
   If IsArray(arrayIndexStore), then
      If (UBound(arrayIndexStore)) = -1, then
         For arrayValue = LBound(arrayStore) To UBound(arrayStore)
            flag=0
         'Bring back the page to first page
         Browser(oBrowser).WinEdit(oWinPage).Set "1"
         Browser(oBrowser).WinEdit(oWinPage).Type micReturn
         wait(1)
            Browser(oBrowser).WinEdit(oWinEdit).Set
            Cstr(arrayStore(arrayValue))
```

```
        Browser(oBrowser).WinEdit(oWinEdit).Type micReturn
        wait(1)
        If Browser(oBrowser).Dialog(oDialog)
        WinButton(oWinButton).Exist(3) Then
        Reporter.ReportEvent micFail,"Content Check","
        Content: - "&Cstr(arrayStore(arrayValue))
        &" - Failed To Exist Under Report"
        Browser(oBrowser).Dialog(oDialog)
        WinButton(oWinButton).Click
           Wait(1)
           flag = -1
        End If
        'Bring back the cursor to normal position
        Browser(oBrowser).WinEdit(oWinEdit).Set " "
        Browser(oBrowser).WinEdit(oWinEdit).Type micReturn
        wait(1)
        If Browser(oBrowser).Dialog(oDialog)
        WinButton(oWinButton).Exist(1) Then
           Browser(oBrowser).Dialog(oDialog).
           WinButton(oWinButton).Click
           Wait(1)
        End If
        If flag <> -1 Then
           Reporter.ReportEvent micPass,"Content Check","
           Content: - "&Cstr(arrayStore(arrayValue))&" -
           Successfully Exist Under Report"
           countVal = countVal + 1
        End If
     Next
  Else
     index=0
     For arrayValue = LBound(arrayStore) To UBound(arrayStore)
        flag=0
        'Bring back the page to first page
        Browser(oBrowser).WinEdit(oWinPage).Set "1"
        Browser(oBrowser).WinEdit(oWinPage).Type micReturn
```

```
wait(1)
Browser(oBrowser). WinEdit(oWinEdit).
Set Cstr(arrayStore(arrayValue))
   loopIndex=arrayIndexStore(index)
If loopIndex = 0, then
   Reporter.ReportEvent micFail,"Array Index","
   Array Index Can't Be Zero"
   Exit For
End If
For startIndex=0 To loopIndex-1 Step 1
   Browser(oBrowser). WinEdit(oWinEdit).
   Type micReturn
   wait(1)
   If Browser(oBrowser).Dialog(oDialog).
   WinButton(oWinButton).Exist(1) Then
      Exit For
   End If
Next
If Browser(oBrowser).Dialog(oDialog).
WinButton(oWinButton).Exist(3) Then
   Reporter.ReportEvent micFail,"Content Check","
   Content: - "&Cstr(arrayStore(arrayValue))&"
 - Failed To Exist Under Report for "&startIndex&"
 iteration"
   Browser(oBrowser).Dialog(oDialog).
   WinButton(oWinButton). Click
   Wait(1)
   flag = -1
End If
'Bring back the cursor to normal position
Browser(oBrowser). WinEdit(oWinEdit).Set " "
Browser(oBrowser). WinEdit(oWinEdit). Type micReturn
wait(1)
If Browser(oBrowser).Dialog(oDialog).
WinButton(oWinButton).Exist(1) Then
   Browser(oBrowser).Dialog
```

```
            (oDialog).WinButton(oWinButton).Click
            Wait(1)
         End If
         If flag <> -1 Then
            Reporter.ReportEvent micPass,"Content Check","
            Content: - "&Cstr(arrayStore(arrayValue))&"
            - Successfully Exist Under Report"
            countVal = countVal + 1
         End If
         index = index +1
      Next
   End If
Else
      For arrayValue = LBound(arrayStore) To UBound(arrayStore)
         flag=0
         'Bring back the page to first page
         Browser(oBrowser).WinEdit(oWinPage).Set "1"
         Browser(oBrowser).WinEdit(oWinPage).Type micReturn
         wait(1)
         Browser(oBrowser).WinEdit
         (oWinEdit).Set Cstr(arrayStore(arrayValue))
         Browser(oBrowser).WinEdit(oWinEdit).Type micReturn
         wait(1)
         If Browser(oBrowser).Dialog(oDialog)
         WinButton(oWinButton).Exist(3) Then
            Reporter.ReportEvent micFail,"Content Check","
            Content: - "&Cstr(arrayStore(arrayValue))&"
             - Failed To Exist Under Report"
            Browser(oBrowser).Dialog(oDialog)
            WinButton(oWinButton).Click
            Wait(1)
            flag = -1
         End If
         'Bring back the cursor to normal position
         Browser(oBrowser).WinEdit(oWinEdit).Set " "
         Browser(oBrowser).WinEdit(oWinEdit).Type micReturn
```

```
            wait(1)
            If Browser(oBrowser).Dialog(oDialog).WinButton
            (oWinButton).Exist(1) Then
               Browser(oBrowser).Dialog
               (oDialog).WinButton(oWinButton).Click
               Wait(1)
            End If
            If flag <> -1 Then
               Reporter.ReportEvent micPass,"Content Check","
               Content:- "&Cstr(arrayStore(arrayValue))&"
                - Successfully Exist Under Report"
               countVal = countVal + 1
            End If
         Next
   End If'IndexStore Value Exist
   If countVal = UBound(arrayStore)+1, then
         Reporter.ReportEvent micPass,"Content Check ALL","
         All The Contents Checked Successfully Under Report"
      fn_fin_pdf_check=1
   Else
      Reporter.ReportEvent micFail,"Content Check ALL","
      All The Contents Failed To Check Under Report"
      fn_fin_pdf_check=0
   End If
   Set oBrowser=Nothing
   Set oWinEdit=Nothing
   Set oWinPage=Nothing
   Set oDialog=Nothing
   Set oWinButton=Nothing
Else
      If Window(oWindow).Exist, then
         Set oWinEdit=Description.Create
         oWinEdit("Class Name").Value="WinEdit"
         oWinEdit("nativeclass").Value="Edit"
         oWinEdit("text").Value=".*"
         oWinEdit("location").Value="2"
```

```
Set oWinPage=Description.Create
oWinPage("Class Name").Value="WinEdit"
oWinPage("nativeclass").Value="Edit"
oWinPage("text").Value=".*"
oWinPage("location").Value="0"
Set oDialog=Description.Create
oDialog("Class Name").Value="Dialog"
oDialog("text").Value="Adobe Reader"
oDialog("nativeclass").Value="#32770"
Set oWinButton=Description.Create
oWinButton("Class Name").Value="WinButton"
oWinButton("text").Value="OK"
oWinButton("nativeclass").Value="Button"
If IsArray(arrayIndexStore), then
  If (UBound(arrayIndexStore)) = -1, then
    For arrayValue = LBound(arrayStore)
    To UBound(arrayStore)
      flag=0
      'Bring back the page to first page
      Window(oWindow).WinEdit
      (oWinPage).Set "1"
    Window(oWindow).WinEdit(oWinPage).
    Type micReturn
      wait(1)
      Window(oWindow).WinEdit
      (oWinEdit).Set
      Cstr(arrayStore(arrayValue))
      Window(oWindow).WinEdit(oWinEdit).
      Type micReturn
      wait(1)
      If Window(oWindow).Dialog(oDialog)
      WinButton(oWinButton).Exist(3), then
        Reporter.ReportEvent micFail,"
      Content Check","Content: - "&Cstr
      (arrayStore(arrayValue))&"
      - Failed To Exist Under Report"
```

```
        Window(oWindow).Dialog
      (oDialog).WinButton(oWinButton).Click
        Wait(1)
        flag = -1
      End If
      'Bring back the cursor to normal position
      Window(oWindow).WinEdit
      (oWinEdit).Set " "
    Window(oWindow).WinEdit(oWinEdit).
    Type micReturn
      wait(1)
      If Window(oWindow).Dialog
    (oDialog).WinButton(oWinButton).Exist(1), then
        Window(oWindow).Dialog
      (oDialog).WinButton(oWinButton).Click
        Wait(1)
      End If
      If flag <> -1 Then
        Reporter.ReportEvent micPass,"
      Content Check","Content: - "&Cstr
      (arrayStore(arrayValue))&"
       - Successfully Exist Under Report"
        countVal = countVal + 1
      End If
    Next
  Else
    index=0
    For arrayValue = LBound(arrayStore)
    To UBound(arrayStore)
      flag=0
      'Bring back the page to first page
      Window(oWindow).WinEdit
      (oWinPage).Set "1"
      Window(oWindow).WinEdit(oWinPage).
      Type micReturn
      wait(1)
```

```
            Window(oWindow). WinEdit
          (oWinEdit).Set Cstr(arrayStore(arrayValue))
            loopIndex=arrayIndexStore(index)
            If loopIndex = 0 Then
               Reporter.ReportEvent
               micFail,"Array
Index","Array Index Can't Be Zero"
               Exit For
            End If
            For startIndex=0 To loopIndex-1 Step 1
               Window(oWindow). WinEdit(oWinEdit). Type micReturn
               wait(1)
               If Window(oWindow).Dialog(oDialog). WinButton(oWinButton).Exist(1) Then
                  Exit For
               End If
            Next
            If Window(oWindow).Dialog(oDialog). WinButton(oWinButton).Exist(3) Then
               Reporter.ReportEvent micFail,"Content Check","Content: - "&Cstr(arrayStore(arr
ayValue))&" - Failed To Exist Under Report for "&startIndex&" iteration"
               Window(oWindow).Dialog(oDialog). WinButton(oWinButton). Click
               Wait(1)
               flag = -1
            End If
            'Bring back the cursor to normal position
            Window(oWindow). WinEdit(oWinEdit).Set " "
            Window(oWindow). WinEdit(oWinEdit). Type micReturn
            wait(1)
            If Window(oWindow).Dialog(oDialog). WinButton(oWinButton).Exist(1), then
               Window(oWindow).Dialog(oDialog). WinButton(oWinButton). Click
               Wait(1)
            End If
            If flag <> -1 Then
               Reporter.ReportEvent micPass,"Content Check","Content: - "&Cstr(arrayStore(arr
ayValue))&" - Successfully Exist Under Report"
               countVal = countVal + 1
```

```
            End If
            index = index +1
        Next
    End If
Else
        For arrayValue = LBound(arrayStore) To UBound(arrayStore)
            flag=0
            'Bring back the page to first page
            Window(oWindow).WinEdit(oWinPage).Set "1"
            Window(oWindow).WinEdit(oWinPage).Type micReturn
            wait(1)
            Window(oWindow).WinEdit(oWinEdit).Set Cstr(arrayStore(arrayValue))
            Window(oWindow).WinEdit(oWinEdit).Type micReturn
            wait(1)
            If Window(oWindow).Dialog(oDialog).WinButton(oWinButton).Exist(3), then
                Reporter.ReportEvent micFail,"Content Check","Content: - "&Cstr(arrayStore(arr
ayValue))&" - Failed To Exist Under Report"
                Window(oWindow).Dialog(oDialog).WinButton(oWinButton).Click
                Wait(1)
                flag = -1
            End If
            'Bring back the cursor to normal position
            Window(oWindow).WinEdit(oWinEdit).Set " "
            Window(oWindow).WinEdit(oWinEdit).Type micReturn
            wait(1)
            If Window(oWindow).Dialog(oDialog).WinButton(oWinButton).Exist(1), then
                Window(oWindow).Dialog(oDialog).WinButton(oWinButton).Click
                Wait(1)
            End If
            If flag <> -1, then
                Reporter.ReportEvent micPass,"Content Check","Content:- "&Cstr(arrayStore(arra
yValue))&" - Successfully Exist Under Report"
                countVal = countVal + 1
            End If
        Next
End If'IndexStore Value Exist
```

```
            If countVal = UBound(arrayStore)+1, then
                Reporter.ReportEvent micPass,"Content Check ALL","All The Contents Checked Successfully Under Report"
                fn_fin_pdf_check=1
            Else
                Reporter.ReportEvent micFail,"Content Check ALL","All The Contents Failed To Check Under Report"
                fn_fin_pdf_check=0
            End If
            Set oWindow=Nothing
            Set oWinEdit=Nothing
            Set oWinPage=Nothing
            Set oDialog=Nothing
            Set oWinButton=Nothing
        Else
            'MsgBox "Browser is not opened or Mismatch with Browser title!!!"
            Reporter.ReportEvent micFail,"Browser Check","Browser is not opened or Mismatch with Browser title!!!"
            Set oBrowser=Nothing
            Exit Function
        End If 'Window exist
    End If'Browser exist
End Function
```

13.2.16 fn_fin_get_substring

Description: This function helps in pulling out combination of strings from a statement, depending upon the start string input and end string input by the user passed within the function argument.

Inputs Parameters: actualstring, startstring, endstring

Example for usage:

var=fn_fin_get_substring("Expense report ALLBU:21498266 for 55 USD was submitted for approval. ","report","for")

Output: *ALLBU:21498266*

<u>Code snippet:</u>

```
Public Function fn_fin_get_substring(ByVal actualstring, ByVal startstring, ByVal endstring)
    Dim stpos, endpos
```

```
stpos = instr(actualstring, startstring)
  stpos = stpos+len(startstring)
          endpos = instr(actualstring, endstring)
 fn_fin_get_substring=trim(mid(actualstring, stpos, (endpos-stpos)))
End Function
```

13.2.17 Random

Description: This function returns 6 digit random number value between 1 and 999999

Code snippet:

```
Public Function Random()
    Dim MyValue
    Randomize  'Initialize random-number generator.
  MyValue = Int((999999 * Rnd) + 1)  'Generate random value between 1 and 999999.
    Random = MyValue
End Function
```

This now equips you with all the detailing that is required to lay out a fully operational, effective and efficient automation framework to support functional automation development and execution activity, using QC 9.2/10 and QTP 9.5/10.

14

HP Quality Center 10: Test Automation Infrastructure Layout Strategy

Chapter Objectives: This chapter will give an overview of

- *Introduction*
- *Some Hard Facts*
- *What is TESTING – Quick Byte*
- *Plan Layout For Successful "Test Automation Infrastructure" Implementation*
- *Best Practices: Organizational Level*
- *Project Management and Best Practices: Team level*
- *Real Time Case Study: "Test Automation" Implementation and ROI Analysis*
- *Challenges faced during exercising the case mentioned in "case study"*
- *Conclusion of the "case study"*

14.1 Introduction

The primary purpose of the chapter is to walk the readers through the strategy about laying out automation infrastructure and best practices. The strategy discussed in this chapter can be utilized to roll out automation infrastructure for any tools, be it performance or functional. Noteworthy point here is that, the excerpts shared in this chapter is also a part of "award winning" white paper by the author.

The audience who would be highly benefitted out of this would be Senior staff, Vice-presidents, Directors and Architects, who generally are in dire need to have some strategy to roll out such infrastructure that can ensure test automation success.

Earlier, almost all the companies used to channelize most of their energy towards the development of the product, but could not justify the rigor required for thorough testing of the product. One of the reasons behind this was lack of technological resources in the market to perform the same. However, as and when time passed by and competition within the market started growing, the thorough testing of the product or application was touted as one of the key areas to be focused on before the launch of any product or application. Therefore, many organisations felt the need of efficient and effective way of testing their product. This resulted in the emergence of testing tool into the market and hence the term "Automation testing" came into existence. Many organisations started implementing the test automation infrastructure but realized that there are several challenges that need to be tackled for better testing success rate. There's so much of research it has gone through to leverage the automation success rate. However, achieving the ideal model for "Test automation success" is still a challenge for various organisations around the world.

The chapter will be contributing towards the knowledge pool of "Test automation success" criteria, by sharing my experiences that I believe will help my fellow readers to identify and pick the relevant areas required for the successful implementation of "Test automation infrastructure" within their organisation and hence leverage the test automation success by manyfolds.

My area of study is confined to describing my approach towards implementing functional/performance testing tool infrastructure for testing GUI based applications within IT organisations and IT divisions. However, the concepts discussed within this chapter can also be applied for successful implementation of other automation testing tools for leveraging "Test automation success" rate within an IT division. The examples cited in the chapter will primarily constitute from some of the most famous automation tools i.e. WinRunner, Quick test Professional, Quality Center and few in-house tools.

Based on the subject matter discussed in the below sections, citing a case study, I will also discuss a real time case for implementing test automation techniques within one of the core teams of a leading IT software services company. The success achieved because of successful implemetation, will be mapped to ROI gained by the organisation over the same.

14.2 Some Hard Facts

As per the survey conducted by several Software accredited bodies across the globe it was found that:

- For every 100 IT projects started, 94 are "restarted".
- Average IT project cost overrun is 178% in large companies.
- Average IT project time overrun is 230% in large companies.
- 42% of original features proposed of IT projects in large companies actually get ported in the final product.

A significant section of above mentioned percentage is also due to lack of proper testing infrastructure available or due to lack of appropriate testing methodology being practiced within an organisation.

The tangible and intangible cost involved for the company because of poor testing is immense. Going further, let us see what best is required for setting up a sound automation testing infrastructure for achieving better automation testing success rate in an organisation.

14.3 What is Testing — Quick Byte

Let me first take you through the basics from where "automation testing" was generated. Automation testing is a branch of testing, where "Testing" is a branch of "Quality Assurance". Testing can be defined as "*Exercising the program using data similar to the real data that the program is designed to execute, observing the outputs, and inferring the existence of errors or inadequacies from anomalies in that output.*"

14.3.1 Test Automation Definition

It is the technique of mapping the manual steps into software codes, in the most cost effective and efficient way. The life cycle for automating (Fig. 14.1) any application for testing is:

Figure 14.1 *Life Cycle of Test Automation.*

Does this mean that anybody can create, run and analyze tests? The answer is No. There's a systematic planning that an organisation needs to go through in order to achieve the automation success.

There are several advantages of practicing systematic and planned Automation testing technique. Few of the critical ones are:

- Cost effectiveness
- Bias free testing
- Localizing faults
- Better and faster "Boundary Value Analysis"
- Re-usability
- Time effectiveness
- Better quality product
- Descriptive error reporting
- Easy reproducibility of the issue

Pictorial representation of the few major advantages of automation testing, at organisational level, can be seen as:

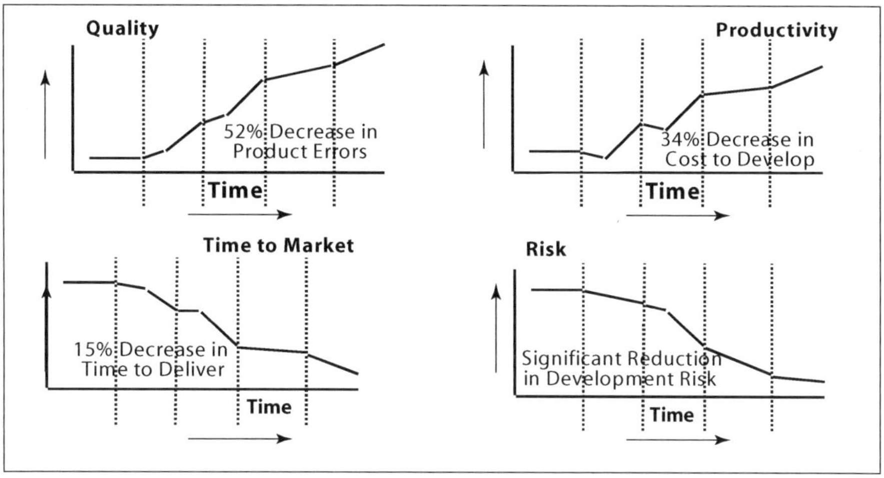

Figure 14.2 *Four Major Benefits of Automation Testing at Organisational Level.*

14.4 Plan Layout for Successful "Test Automation Infrastructure" Implementation

For an organisation to achieve test automation success (Fig. 14.3), it should have a proper planning, processes and testing infrastructure in place. Unless the organisation has effective planning, viable processes and robust testing infrastructure into place, test automation success is not possible. Therefore, to implement a robust testing infrastructure for test automation success, few of the most important areas to be worked upon are:

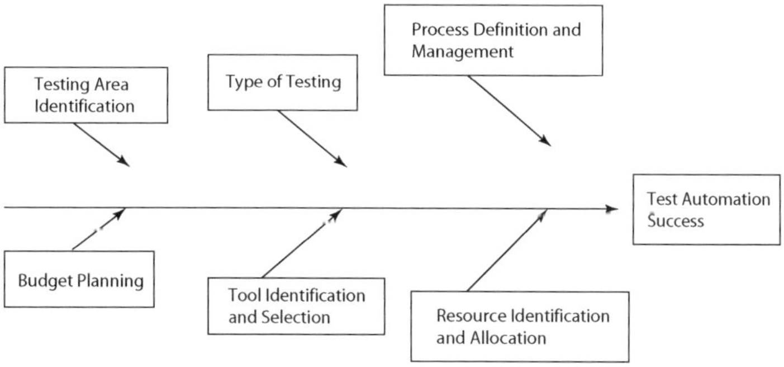

Figure 14.3 *Fish Bone Diagram for Plan Layout of "Test Automation Success".*

1. **Testing Area Identification:** Do we need test automation? This is the basic question that needs to be resolved before going ahead with further planning for automating any tests. In addition, if an organisation plans to go for setting up automation testing infrastructure, it should have a proper business justification, projecting dollar saving prospects for the organisation in addition to assuring better quality products. Therefore, in sum, the need for automating any tests should always be backed by appropriate business requirements and goals. Once the testing need is identified and justified accordingly, then further processing with respect to laying out Test automation infrastructure should be planned.

   How can I identify whether my product requires automation?

   (a) *Depth of the product:* If the product contains numerous functionalities, which give the scope for creeping of some human error while development and if this error can cost the company a lot in terms of tangible and intangible benefits, then company needs automation testing for reducing the error percentage by using effective tool testing.

   (b) *Competition:* If several companies have similar kind of products to be released into the market, then the First Time Right approach counts a lot towards the company's product success. In order to have the bug free product, a robust and reliable bias free testing is required. The same can only be achieved through tool testing.

2. **Type of Testing:** Once the need for testing has been identified, then the organisation should decide upon the type of testing required for the product. There are several types of testing that need to be done before release of a product. However, due to restricted software resources available, every area can't be automated. Therefore, one needs to identify the most critical area, that can be automated and which when automated delivers the best testing results and yield better returns to the company.

In real world, the most critical testing scenario is one that simulates the users experience while using the product. User experiences are based upon either taking into account the functional aspect of the application or taking into account the performance of the application. Most of the available testing automation tools cater to the two most critical domains of testing i.e. "Functional" and "Performance" testing. Therefore, after identifying user experience aspects in addition to several other important aspects, "Type of Testing" and "Automation Aspects" need to be decided upon by the organisation.

Making a mistake at this level can cost a lot to the organisation. Hence, proper identification of appropriate type of testing and automation tool, while building up testing infrastructure, is highly important for the organisation. In addition, decision taken upon these two aspects should not be on perception but should be on metrics gathered from the past experiences of the organisation, which can show the gap and justify the selection of type of testing and automation tool, accordingly.

3. **Tool Identification and Selection:** After the organisation has decided upon testing area and testing type, it should look for appropriate testing tool to be purchased.

   Mostly used and readily available testing tools in the market are:

   For testing functional aspect of the application: WinRunner, Quick test Professional, Silk, etc.

   For testing performance aspect of the application: LoadRunner, etc.

   For appropriate Test Management and tracking: Test Director, Mercury Quality Center, etc.

At times, it has been seen that several large MNC's build their own tool to automate their product. It is because the tool available within the market does not give the comprehensive testing coverage to test their product and hence most of the work still needs to be tackled through manual testing in spite of availability of the testing tool. In this case, if the organisation decides to develop its own automation tool, then it should set up a dedicated team for requirement gathering and identification of the best technology to be used for development of their tool. Furthermore, the organisation, in parallel, should decide upon the number of resources required for development, assistance and further maintenance of the tool.

However, alternatively, if organisation decides upon purchasing the tool from the available software vendors, then after careful analysis of the tool's licensing policy, support mechanism and market feedback, the decision needs to be taken.

In sum, besides the company's allocated budget for purchase of the tool, keeping in mind the automation requirement, licensing policy of the tool vendor, tool services and support mechanism, technical competency and coverage of the tool, testing automation tool needs to be identified. Appropriate tool identification for automation testing is one of the most critical aspects for the success of "Test Automation".

4. **Process Definition and Management:** Well-researched and bias free processes lay the foundation of the organisation. However, setting up of right processes is a big responsibility. Therefore, management should set up a centralized team, which will be responsible for formation and implementation of the best practices at organisational level.

   - *Inception of Centralized team:* "Subject matter expert (SME)" should be given the responsibility to head the team. This team should be responsible for automation tool infrastructure maintenance and support. Few of the critical responsibilities of this team should be:
     1. To define the best practices for the organisation.
     2. To have periodic regular interaction with the application development team to understand future enhancements, which might affect the tool usage while creating tests and hence to work upon resolving the same.
     3. To have a periodic interaction with Tool vendor support team POC either to learn about the latest patches to be released or to request for tool enhancement as per the testing requirements.

4. To Support organisation wide Testers who are using the tool.
5. To design, validate and release the tool level patches.
6. To develop and maintain automation best practices and standards portal.

5. **Resource Identification and Allocation:** This section can be categorized into two parts:
Hardware/Software resources: Subject matter expert and his team along with senior management need to take the decision upon implementing effective hardware/software infrastructure for efficient and maximum utilization of testing tool. For example, WinRunner functional testing tool licenses can be purchased either for single user or for multiple users using it concurrently on a single machine. To get the tool installed with single user license needs specific m/c configuration and to get the tool installed with concurrent users' license, needs different m/c configuration. Now, if there are multiple users who need to use the tool concurrently, then using a single machine having concurrent license of the tool installed over it can solve the purpose in the most cost effective way rather than investing several extra dollars over single desktop installation which would further require additional hardware and software licenses per resource. In addition, the pricing structure over concurrent license purchase is cheaper in rates as compared to single user license. Therefore, for having cost effective infrastructure, hardware and software infrastructure implementation requires lots of quantifiable homework and planning.
Human resources: For any company human assets are the most critical assets. This demands SME along with senior management, team managers and HR, to have some guidelines for getting right candidate on the job. This could be one of the most critical and crucial selection which otherwise, if went wrong, could have huge impact on testing cycles along with quality shipment.
6. **Budget Planning:** No plan can be successful unless it is supported by sound budget. Hence, this is the preliminary phase and the most critical aspect to be worked upon after having identified the need of setting up of test automation infrastructure.

14.5 Best Practices: Organisational Level

For efficient working of test automation infrastructure within budgeted cost, there should be well-researched processes and standards laid out at the organisation level and properly drilled down to the team level. In this section, we will be discussing over implementation of test automation best practices at organisational level and in later section we will be taking upon the implementation of automation standards at team level.

Implementing highly effective standards is a challenging and full time task. This is where the conceptualization of central team comes in. Organisation should set up a central automation team for deriving the best practices (Fig. 14.4) and automation standards to ensure "Test automation success" at organisational level. Automation central team should be responsible for gathering the quantifiable data set and lay out the best practices into several areas for better functioning and usage of test Automation infrastructure. These best practices should be laid out by maximum participation of the real time testers and not on perception and bureaucracy.

Note: In this section, I will be providing an overview of the critical automation best practices by taking examples of WinRunner, Test Director and QTP functional tool, wherever applicable.

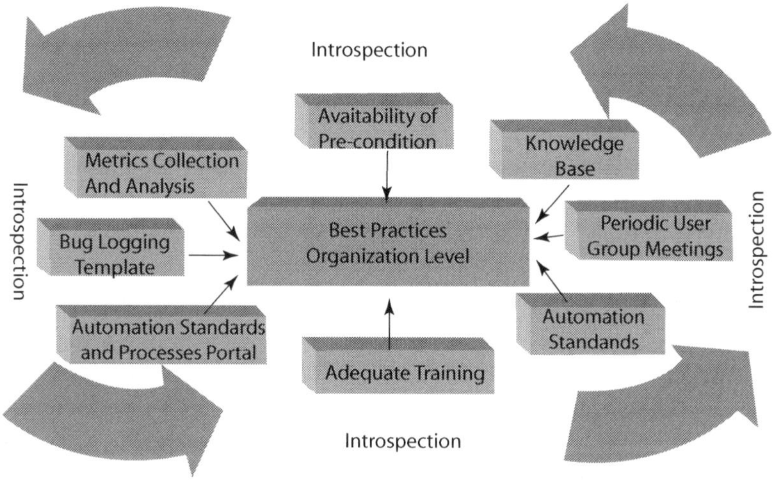

Figure 14.4 *Best Practices: Organisation Level.*

1. **Availability of Pre-condition:** Automation can't be conducted on perception or on *ad hoc* basis. To start with automation of any test, besides availability of resources and tool, there are several other things that are needed. They are:

   - *Development environment simulating the production environment:* Development environment should be available, simulating the production environment, on which automation will be conducted.
   - *Use case documentation:* This documentation talks about the cases which user will experience while traversing through the application or software product
   - *Business case documentation:* This documentation contains the business requirements pertaining to application functionality.
   - *Functional documentation:* This documentation describes the functional flow of the application or software product.

   Without these, automation of tests will not prove to be beneficial.

2. **Adequate Training:** Centralized team should have proper periodic technical training schedules to educate people over better understanding of the tool and benefits of the best practices. In addition, besides in person training facility, training materials should also be hosted on web-enabled "Automation Portal". Having training materials online gives the flexibility to the employees to refer to their pain areas 24x7 and hence, work upon improving the same as per their comfort.
3. **Automation Standards:** Centralize team should work closely with all the product teams to understand and gather the testers need and should chalk out the most efficient workable standards for better tool usage and hence, leverage testing productivity of each resource. This section should completely cater to solving technical intricacies while using the tool for automation.

The most important areas, which certainly need to be catered, are:

- *Standards: On Supported Application By The Tool:* This section should provide the list of supported platforms and applications by the tool.
- *Standards: On Testing Tool Settings:* While using concurrent licenses, multiple users work on a single m/c having the single tool installed on it. Hence, proper guidelines should be provided as not to alter machine level settings of the tool in order to avoid impact on other users working concurrently on the similar machine accessing the same tool.
- *Standards: On Script Creation:* Proper guidelines should be laid out for script creation.

Example: Batch files should be created to club different scenarios of single functionality.

A Appropriate header format should be used within batch script.
B Appropriate header format should be used within each sub script.
C Starting condition and ending condition should be recorded in each script.
D Each script should be re-runnable without having any hard coded values

- *Standards: On Coding Practices:* In order to have better understanding and maintainability of the code, correct coding practices should be designed. Doing this not only saves time during code enhancement but also reduces dependencies on specific resource of that product.
- *Standards: On File Naming Conventions:* Files without proper naming conventions consume lot of time reaching to the correct file. Therefore, proper naming convention should be laid out and communicated throughout the organisation.

Example: <Product Name>_<Version>_<Product Functionality>_<Test case name>_<Test no.>

- *Standards: On Tool Object Repository Management:* Object repository is the centralized repository of the tool, which gives definition to the code for further processing. Every automation tool has different object repository management mechanism. Therefore, if object repository descriptions are not correct then code will not work. Hence, proper management of these repositories is very important. For example: the object repository of WinRunner is known as GUI Map, for QTP it is known as Object Repository and for managing each, proper guidelines should be followed. Refer section 10.6 for details.

- *Standards: On Advanced Recording Techniques:* Advance techniques are the ones which are used to draft intelligent script. Intelligent scripts are those that are coded with a view to handle all the scenarios occurring frequently or intermittently during code execution. Therefore, to handle these scenarios every automation tool has some advanced features such as parameterization techniques, exception handling techniques, recovery manager, etc. The central team should give all the details regarding the correct usage of these advanced features of the tool.
- *Standards: On Code Reusability:* Central teams, at the beginning itself, after interacting with the entire product teams, should host reusable codes and functions on the automation portal. This can save tremendous efforts at each resource level and hence ensures efficient testing.
- *Standards: On Source Control of Scripts:* The most important asset for any company is its data. Therefore, to ensure maximum security of the automated code set, central team should define the processes for source controlling the scripts.

Example: After the script has been termed as "golden script", store it in Visual Safe Source/arcs/clear case, etc.

Note: The "Automation Portal" should host all these details along with explanations on each.

4. **Knowledge Base:** To compile data set, issues and suggestions experienced by internal employees during their daily work tenure and to create a cohesive knowledge sharing pool, central team should create a "Distribution List" where testers within the organisation can discuss issues or can exchange information on various tool usage principles. In addition, a proper threading of all such discussions should be hosted over a portal so that they can be referenced and queried as and when required.
5. **Metrics Collection and Analysis:** Effectiveness of any process depends upon how effectively the metrics data is collected and its completeness, and finally on the metrics analysis. The central team should define a process within the team to study these metrics on periodic basis for root cause analysis and to take effective corrective measures for permanent correction of the most frequently issues. This ensures a robust testing infrastructure and hence contributes towards the test automation success of the organisation.

6. **Periodic User Group Meetings:** The challenge for central team is to re-examine their best practices and keep it bias free. Since the customers of central team are the respective internal teams using the automation tool, for collecting the latest requirements, the central team should have a schedule for periodic user group meeting to take feedbacks over issues on regular basis and hence work over the same.
7. **Bug Logging Template:** Central team will be responsible for handling so many critical areas, such as tool installation, central function library maintenance and enhancements, etc. Therefore, there should be a mechanism by which users can report their issues to central team. Hence, to report the issues in the most effective and understandable manner, a correct bug logging template (Detail 5) should be designed. A proper bug logging template would ensure effective triaging of the issue and immediate resolution of the same.
   Several companies nowadays use bug-tracking tools such as "Test Director", "BugZilla", etc. for better tracking of the bug. However, several companies such as Oracle Corporation and Microsoft use their internal tool, which has been designed keeping in mind the requirements within their company.
   Irrespective of the kind of tool being used, well-defined template is necessary for triaging issues effectively. I'm enclosing a template that I have tried creating after studying the bug logging procedures within Birlasoft Ltd., GE capital – Commercial finance, Tata Consultancy services, Mphasis Ltd., and Oracle Corporation.

Detail 5 Bug Logging Template

- Bug logged by:
- Bug logging date:
- Reviewer:
- Priority:
- Severity:
- Dev Priority:
- O/S:
- Product ID:
- Components:
- Subcomponents:
- Customer(INTERNAL/External):
- Subject:
- Tool Version:
- Tool Add-in's version and name:
- Testing Environment:
- Log in credentials:
- Application Details:
- Additional software details(if any used) :
- Browser and Version:
- Server name (if applicable):
- Problem description:
- Steps to reproduce the issue:
- Expected Behavior:
- Sample Script:
- Script getting Error out at which line:

8. **Automation Standards and Processes Portal:** Central team should have a dedicated portal to list all the above-mentioned details pertaining to best practices. This ensures better knowledge sharing across organisation and in addition, hosting details on web-enabled portal is also independent of boundaries.

9. **Introspections:** Introspections are conducted with an objective to gain structured opportunity to look back at the completed project or at milestones and learn from the same. The team analyses what went wrong, what went right, and how the team performed with respect to the objectives of the team. The learning from this analysis is documented and an appropriate action plan is chalked out.

Central team, in addition to its own team, should encourage all the respective teams to introspect their area of work and provide feedback for improvement of best practices on periodic basis.

Introspections with open door policy ensure smooth and productive functioning of Test Automation infrastructure and are the key for "Test Automation Success".

14.6 Project Management and Best Practices: Team Level

After laying out a concrete automation process to cater to organisational needs, senior management needs to lay out the plans at a more minuscule level, i.e. at respective team level. Project manager of each team should be assigned task of designing complete process definition for automation project for their respective teams.

Note: Team level best practices should not conflict with the organisational level best practices. Team level best practices are laid out for sorting out issues that can crop up at team level.

With respect to my analysis and experience, the most important automation best practices to be laid out at team level are:

1. **Tool Usage and Training:** Using automation tool for recording specific product is totally different from using tool to train yourself over the same. Therefore, project manager should have a proper training schedule in place to train people new on job. The training should consist of tailored courses that can project the real time issues and the solution while automating product with automation tool.
2. **Test Plan and Test Case Creation:** No automation can be successful without having a proper test plan and test case in place. Hence, it is the responsibility of team project manager to draft an appropriate test plan and hence get sound test cases drafted before start of test automation.
3. **Coding Practices:** After abiding with the organisational level coding practices, if team needs to have their own coding standards for better knowledge sharing and maintainability, then proper standards should be designed for creating and maintaining a team level knowledge pool. In addition, every team member should be educated properly over practicing the framed standards.
    a) For example: While automating Oracle Financials Account Payables module, Invoice No should not be hardcoded.
    b) After logging into forms, always use "forms_initial condition ();" function.
4. **Folder Structure:** At respective product level, an appropriate folder structure should be practiced for storing scripts and its subsequent sub-scripts.

Example: Folder structure standards for storing "Invoice" scripts for "AP" product:

- Under "AP" folder, "Invoice" test suite folder should be stored. Invoice test suite folder should contain the below mentioned sub-folders.
  1. Masterdriver folder: Masterdriver will contain the code for calling sub-scripts.
  2. Scripts folder: This folder will contain all the sub scripts of that suite
  3. Data table folder: Data table folder will contain all the .xls files pertaining to each script.
  4. Test case folder: This folder will contain test plan and test cases of the whole suite
  5. Function folder: This folder will contain all the common functions being used within each script.

5. **Test Review Process:** There should be proper process in place for the review of the drafted automated tests before terming them as "golden script".

   Example: Definition of golden script within AR product team:
   A script will be termed as golden script only when all the test cases steps have been properly automated and script passes at least two times consecutively on fresh environment.

6. **Issue Reporting:** In case the team feels to add upon few sections over and above the already defined bug template under organisational level best practices section, then project manger should take initiative to identify the required sections and hence educate the team on using the same. In addition, a proper guideline should be provided to testers to take appropriate action on each status of the bug.

   Example: Bug logging process in QA-COE team:

- When bug is logged, status should be set as "Open".
- When development team changes the status of the bug to "Need some information", then the bug should be the priority task to be worked upon.
- When status of the bug is "Dev to QA", then tester should thoroughly check all the regressions and accordingly update the bug. If bug needs to be opened, then proper justification along with issue reproducible steps should be provided else bug should be closed with status "Fix verified".

7. **Automation Task Reports:** Project manager should design the appropriate reports pertaining to each automation task and should accordingly design processes for filling up those reports. The primary purpose of each report should be to track the efforts of each resource along with capturing issue list while performing the respective task. Accurate reporting gives platform for better planning and delegation of work by project manager. In addition, these reports provide insight about the progress on test automation on regular basis. The most critical automation task reports to be maintained are:

- *Script Creation Report:* This provides the figure for number of flows automated and bugs found.
- *Script Execution Report:* This provides the figure for number of flows executed and bugs found
- *Script Enhancement Report:* This provides the detail about number of flows enhanced and regressions found, if any.

  All these reports, besides automation coverage, also provide complete project snapshot of that specific automation task.

8. **Appraise Tester For The Role:** Retaining good resources is the most critical aspect for the success of Test automation. Every manager, at the team level, should be responsible to appraise the best people on automation job.

14.7 Real-time Case Study: "Test Automation" Implementation and Roi Analysis

Project Overview: The below discussed project synopsis is a real time test automation infrastructure implementation project in one of the teams of a well known IT services company. All the scenarios discussed in the earlier section have been practiced for successful project completion.

Business Case: Team, "QA-Center Of excellence", deals with preparation, modification and manual execution of test cases. In one of the observations, it was found that manual execution of test cases takes "5.166 minutes/resource for executing 10 pages where each page has 10 input fields and 1 action to perform" whereas the same case when executed through automation tool takes 1.466 minutes/resource. Hence, it shows that approx. 252% more time is invested by each resource/day executing the cases manually when compared to doing the same through automation tool. This time needs to be saved to the maximum extent.

Problem Statement: Effort required to execute test cases manually takes approx 252% more time when compared to doing the same through automation tool.

Project Goal: To implement test automation infrastructure which can save approx 250% time/resource/day as compaed to what is being invested in current scenario.

Project Scope: The scope of the project is restricted to QA-COE team. After implemetation of automation tool within the project, the effort and money should be saved by 200%–230% as comepared to effort and money being invested in current scenario.

Project Synopsis: This project was divided into two phases:

- **Phase 1:** Study for tool identification
- **Phase 2:** Migration from manual testing to automated testing with cost benefit analysis

Phase 1: Study for tool identification

In this phase , firstly we sorted out the types of applications to be tested within QA-COE team. The types of applications were oracle applications, siebel applications, and html-based applications. Later on ,we identified our requirements with their priorities and divided them into specific category. For each requirement, if tool meets our requirement we used to assign defined weighted score to each. Therefore, after capturing weighted scores for 90 requirements falling into 13 categories, we arrived at the right tool. The analysis was done for three tools, WinRunner, QTP and SilkTest. (Refer Fig. 1. attached for better understanding of the tool identification procedure). Finally, after detail research, QTP was shortlisted as the right tool.

S.No	Category	Numeric score [weighted Total]		
		QTP	WinRunner	Silktest
1	Tool coverage while executing Oracle apps	4,265	4030	2,785
2	Tool coverage while executing Peoplesoft apps	4,265	4030	2,785
3	Tool coverage while executing Siebel apps	4,265	4030	2,785
4	Tool coverage while executing html based apps	4,265	4030	2,785
5	Tool coverage while recording/playback peoplesoft apps	4,315	4030	2,785
6	Tool coverage while recording Siebel apps	4,315	4030	2,785
7	Tool coverage while recording Oracle apps	4,315	4030	2,785
8	Tool coverage while recording html apps	4,315	4030	2,785
9	Platform Porting / Desktop Configuration / Client Testing Portability by the tool	715	715	340
10	Reporting of Testing Results by the tool	570	520	100
11	Fault Management / Defect Tracking mechanism of the tool	140	70	0
12	Installation / Upgrade and Usage	190	190	50
13	Tool's vendor services and support	430	315	235
14	Total Numeric weight/tool	36,365	34,050	23,005

Evaluation weighted score allocation criteria	Value
Fully supports requirement	100
Partially supports requirements	50
Does not support requirement	0
Unknown or Not Tested	?

Fig. 1 *Data Sheet Depicting Total Numeric Weighted Score for Each Testing Tool.*

In this phase, we did a detailed analysis by synopsis of the analysis done.

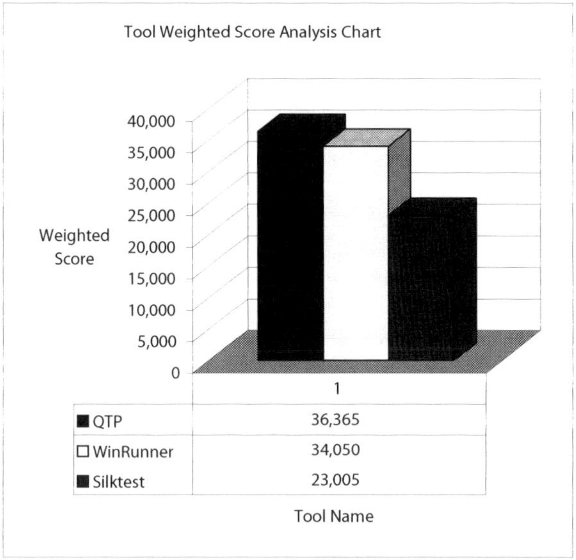

Fig. 2 *This Figure Depicts the Total Numeric Weighted Score Awarded to Each Requirement Under Each Category for Further Short Listing of the Automation Tool Mapping Correctly With QA-COE Project Requirements. QTP was Awarded the Maximum Weighted Score Amongst the Three Tool and Thus Got Selected to be Used Within QA-COE Team.*

Phase 2: Migration from manual testing to automated testing depicting cost benefit analysis

In this phase, we did a detailed analysis by studying the effort per resource and amount per resource that can be saved while using automation tool. 4 resources, automating 16 work packets for approximately about three and a half months were involved in this analysis. Let me share with you the most important synopsis of the analysis done.

Total	Estimation Done by:	Work Packet	Manual Testing Effort(in hrs)	No. Of Days Taken for Manual Testing	Script Development Effort (in hrs) while automating manual flows afresh	No. Of Days Taken for automation Script Development	Script Execution Effort (in hrs)	No. Of Days Taken for automated Script Execution
Total	4 Resources	16	565	71	658	82	176	22

Analysis 1: Complete Effort Analysis Statistics / 4 Resource / 16 Work Packet

Based on Analysis, Effort Benefit and Cost Benefit analysis was derived at, assuming the billing charge for each resource/hr is $80.

Net Cost Benefit Analysis when script is not available = [2*Amount Manual Testing effort] - [Amount Script development + Amount Script Execution] = $1520 (Refer Chart 1)

Task Type	Resource	Work Packet	Days	Amount
Manual Testing	1	1	4.44	**2840**
Script Development	1	1	5.13	**3280**
Script Execution	1	1	1.38	**880**

Analysis 2: Cost Benefit Analysis /Task type/ Resource/Work Packet

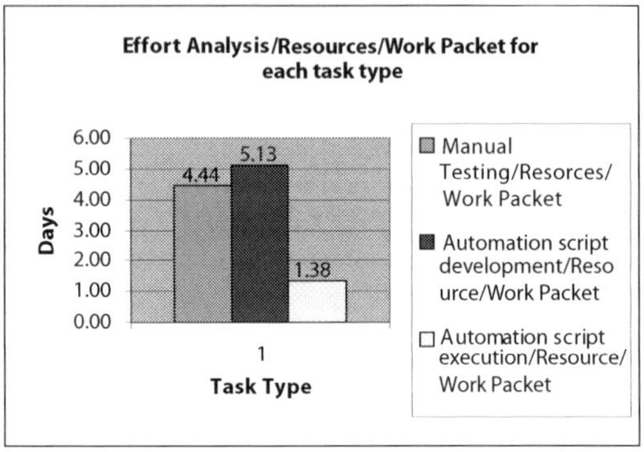

Chart 1: Task Effort Analysis/Resource/Work Packet

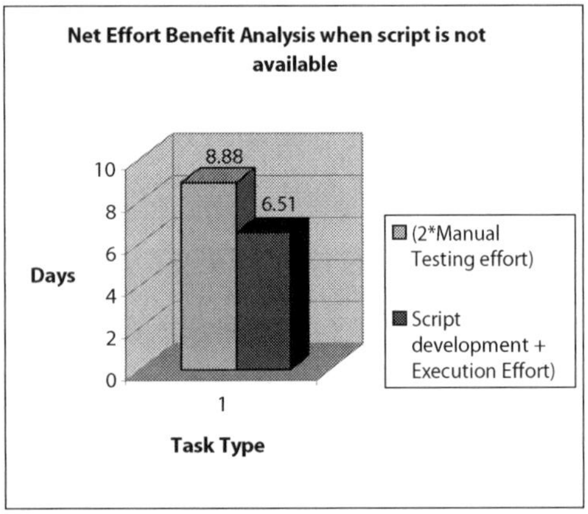

Chart 2: Net Effort Benefit Analysis when script is not available = 2.37 days / resource / word packet

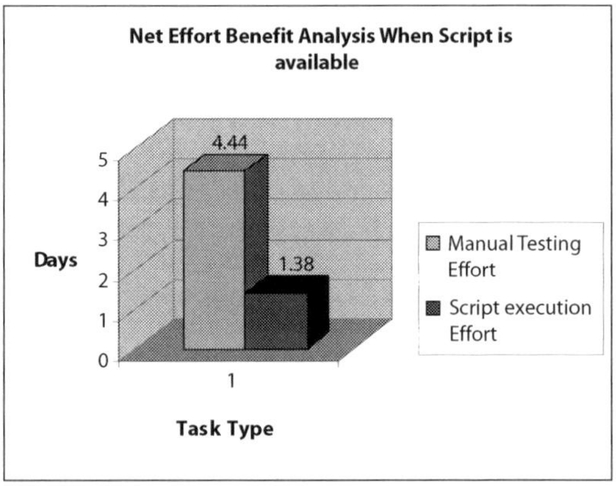

Chart 3: Net Effort Benefit Analysis when script is not available = 3.06 days / resource / work packet

Analysis 3: Net Effort Benefit Analysis when script is not available = [2*Manual Testing Effort] - [Script development Effort + Script Execution Effort] = 2.37 days / resource / work packet (Refer Chart 2)

Analysis 4: Net Effort Benefit Analysis when script is available = [Manual Testing Effort - Script Execution Effort] = 3.06 days (Refer Chart 3)

Analysis 5: Net Cost Benefit Analysis when script is not available = [2*Amount Manual Testing effort] - [Amount Script development + Amount Script Execution] = $1520 (Refer Chart 4)
Analysis 6: Net Cost Benefit Analysis when script is available = [Amount Manual Testing - Amount Script Execution] = $ 1960 (Refer Chart 5)

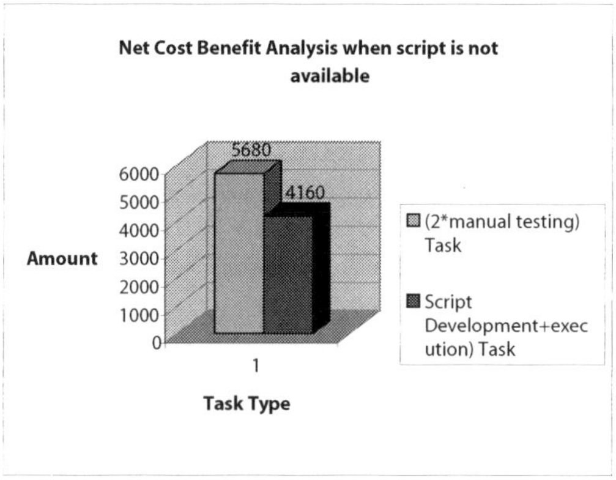

Chart 4: Net Cost Benefit Analysis when script is not available = $1520 / Resource /Work Packet

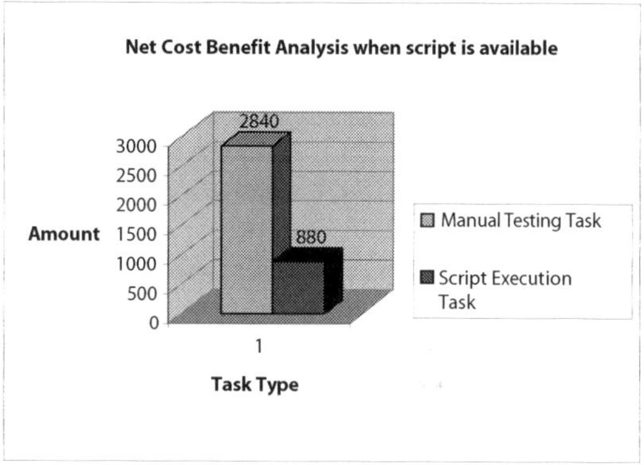

Chart 5: Net Cost Benefit Analysis when script is available = $ 1960/ Resource /Work Packet

Effort

		High	**Low**
Benefit	**High**	Process Definition And Management	Test Area Identification
		BEST PRACTICES FORMULATION AND PRACTICE: Adequate Training, Automation Standards, Metrics collection And Analysis, Introspection	Identification Of Type Of Testing
			Implementing And Using Coding Practices
			Resource Identification And Allocation
	Low		
		Time required for analysis with respect to Types Of documents provided	

Analysis 7: Pay-Off Matrix Analysis

Note: All the above-said areas have been discussed in detail within the respective subject matter section in this white paper.

Project Conclusion: After implementation of test automation tool:

Effort/Resource/Work Packet got reduced by 221% when script is available for execution.

Amount/Resource/Work Packet got reduced by 222.72% when script is available for execution.

14.8 Challenges Faced during Exercising the Case Mentioned in "Case Study"

The challenges that I witnessed during this journey and the probable solutions that I practiced, are listed here for the benefit of my readers. Nonetheless, all the suggested solutions are being practiced by me on regular basis and have shown great results in tackling these challenges effectively.

Challenge: Since there is an estimated time length for the development of automation processes and best practices, there's always a scope of missing out few areas, which can prove to be critical.

Solution: Do take regular or periodic suggestions from testers imbibing these practices in their daily work. Do take suggestions for further improvement of best practices which can further reduce their burden while doing automation task

Challenge: Automation scripts are not something which are generated through any machine. Human drafts scripts and hence there's always a scope of human error involved.

Solution: First, insert message-reporting statements within scripts, after completion of each scenario. In this way seeing the test results, one can identify the gap, if there. Secondly, train reviewers review the script with respect to each test case action and hence map reporting messages with each test case scenario.

Challenge: Since automation testing is an upcoming field, it is pretty difficult to find experts on these tools. Not getting the right people on job can have huge impact on quality of automated tests and hence the purpose of automation is lost.

Solution: Foremost is to try to retain best resources. Alternatively, to hire new people make appropriate checklist such as" good C programming skills, communications, aptitude, etc. and shortlist on the basis of weighted marks. After hiring, train the for almost 6-8 days on tool usage and tackling real time issues found with respect to past experiences.

Challenge: In real day-to-day scenario, even after the final draft of the requirement documentation, requirements do change during the development period and the updated requirements are generally not communicated to the testing team. Hence, in this case, creation of automation tests within stipulated time becomes challenging.

Solution: Test Team point of contact and Development team point of contact, of the product being tested, should felicitate regular discussions.

Challenge: Testers perceive that to adhere to standards and to incorporate them while creation of automation scripts requires approximately 20% of their scripting time. To encourage and motivate them to invest over practicing the same is a challenge in the practical working scenario.

Solution: Educate testers on the importance of standards and maintaining correct report. Encourage them by showing the real time usage of these standards and reports and if the same not followed then impact over the same on each resource and hence team *per se*.

14.9 Conclusion of the "Case Study"

Detailed bias free planning during automation tool selection and implementation along with sound process, both at organisational level and team level, backed by maximum participation of primary automation testers ensures a highly robust testing infrastructure, which in turn helps in achieving "Test Automation success" and a lucrative ROI to the organisation.

- In sum, the success of test automation depends upon:
  1. Detailed planning over implementation of robust "Test Automation" infrastructure
  2. Laying out automation testing best practices both at organisational level and at team level
  3. Effective project management.
  4. Periodic self – examination of the derived best practices.

All these factors, if practiced and implemented religiously, help in deriving higher tangible benefits.

In addition, the intangible benefits, which are gained because of test automation, are also incomparable. Some of them are:

- Good quality product and Good Voice of customer (VOC)
- Repeat Customers
- Employee satisfaction
- Automatic creation of knowledge base

Index

Author's Profile

Saurabh Chandra is currently working with Computer Associates (CA), where he is heading automation development, performance and automation testing of the Clarity R&D unit, India Technology Center. Saurabh has done his graduation from BITS Ranchi and holds an Executive MBA in Senior Management Programme by Indian Institute of Management, Lucknow (IIM-L). He has four internationally acclaimed research papers and two patents to his credit. He is one of the youngest Green Belt Six Sigma certified professionals. He is also the president for Indian Testing Board – Hyderabad. In his professional career span, he has worked with major MNCs including Oracle. He is also a certified *Agile Scrum Master*, one of the very few in the world. Furthermore, he is chairing Indian Testing Board – Hyderabad chapter as President.

His expertise lies in setting up Testing, Automation, Performance and development practices in MNC's. He has set up several core testing and automation competencies in top-most software product companies worldwide. Because of his ability to combine technology with business acumen from a management perspective, he is regarded as one of the finest strategist of IT industry, for getting optimal ROI from automation, performance and testing domain.

As an established author his first book, *Automation Testing*, discusses QTP 9.5 and 10. Saurabh is also a guest lecturer in several top engineering colleges and B-Schools in India. He firmly believes in "what you give is what you get".

The author can be reached at sauchand@gmail.com

Made in United States
Orlando, FL
04 November 2026

90200628R00164